Dear Bill

William Deedes – legendary as a plinth of twentieth-century journalism and public affairs – has written a memoir both startling and, characteristically, modest. And not before time.

Lord Deedes is familiar to many as the 'Bill' recipient of fictional letters from Denis Thatcher in *Private Eye*. Many assume him to be the model for Boot in Evelyn Waugh's classic novel *Scoop*.

What is certain is that he *did* cover that war in Abyssinia in the 1930s, that he was a fearless war correspondent, that he was editor of the *Daily Telegraph* (for which he still writes every week) and that he had a distinguished political career as an MP and Cabinet Minister during the 1950s and 1960s.

Memory as sharp as a diamond, and as cutting, of Suez, the Profumo scandal and of colleagues in Government is expressed here with quiet wit and astonishing perception.

His memories provide unique and idiosyncratic perception on matters political and social, British and global for the greater part of the century.

A measure of good fortune tempered with uncompromising vigour as a journalist have informed his life and career. His book will prove both inspirational to the professional and a sheer, diverting, delight to others.

Dear Bill

A Memoir

W. F. Deedes

PAN BOOKS

First published 1997 by Macmillan

Updated and published 2005 by Macmillan

First published in paperback 2006 by Pan Books
an imprint of Pan Macmillan Ltd
Pan Macmillan, 20 New Wharf Road, London N1 9RR
Basingstoke and Oxford
Associated companies throughout the world
www.panmacmillan.com

ISBN 978-0-330-35410-3

7 9 8 6

A CIP catalogue record for this book is available from
the British Library.

Typeset by SetSystems Ltd, Saffron Walden, Essex
Printed by Mackays of Chatham plc, Chatham, Kent

Visit **www.panmacmillan.com** to read more about all our books and to buy
them. You will also find features, author interviews and news of any author
events, and you can sign up for e-newsletters so that you're always first to hear
about our new releases.

Contents

Acknowledgements

I owe an immeasurable debt of gratitude to Anne Allport for her help and encouragement with this patchwork quilt of memoirs. For a long time, I took the view that to do this job properly a journalist should keep his eye fixed on the present and future. To be delving into the past would be a distraction.

Anne Allport persuaded me otherwise. She has not only done much of the delving into my papers; she has read the copy as it emerged sluggishly from the spare hours in my life, and made sensible suggestions. She carries, I must add, no responsibility at all for the opinions I have expressed.

Material has been quoted from the following titles:

Butler, R. A. *The Art of the Possible.* Hamish Hamilton, 1971

Gilbert, M. *Winston Churchill. The Wilderness Years. 1929–35.* Companion Vol. V. Part 2. William Heinemann, 1981

Gill, R. and Groves, J. *Club Route in Europe. The Story of 30 Corps in the European Campaign.* Hanover

Hastings, S. *Evelyn Waugh: A Biography.* Sinclair Stevenson, 1994

Horne, A. *Macmillan 1957–86.* Vol. 2. Macmillan, 1989

Howard, A. *Rab: The Life of R. A. Butler.* Jonathan Cape, 1987

Roberts, A. *Eminent Churchillians.* Weidenfeld & Nicolson, 1994

The 8th Armoured Brigade. Printed in Germany

1

Saltwood Childhood

There is a photograph of me at the age of about three with my toy horse and cart looking twee in a sun hat, which makes my toes curl with embarrassment. It is the sort of picture young women doing research work for a television programme latch on to. 'Oh my,' they say, 'I think that's cute. We must have that one.' I plead for a let, but in vain.

Yet I could never bring myself to destroy the photograph for it does convey the tranquillity of my early life; and, for my mother and father, a peace of mind which was soon to forsake them. My photograph was taken in the garden of a Queen Anne house named Symnells in the village of Aldington, which lies midway between Ashford and Hythe in Kent. My parents had lived there since their marriage in 1912. They had an income from the estate of some £900 a year, on which they could comfortably afford an indoor staff of five, including my nanny and nanny maid – and two gardeners. My father's health, never robust, had been undermined by military service in the Boer War. That invalided him out of the First World War. He dabbled in radical politics, became friendly with rising figures in the Labour party, wrote letters to prominent people which worried his children and otherwise lived the life of one who could eventually inherit a family estate.

At the height of the virulent flu epidemic of 1919 – which killed almost as many people in Europe as the war itself – the occupant of Saltwood Castle, who was my great-aunt Mrs

Halifax Wyatt, died. My grandmother, who had married in 1870 and been a widow since 1891, determined that my father should occupy the place. It turned out to be a sorry decision. In my early schooldays, some boys thought we must be very grand to be living in a castle. They little knew what it entailed.

In the first place, the early post-war years were proving disastrous for farmers and landowners. Land values had tumbled. On top of that my father soon discovered that he had inherited burdensome feudal responsibilities. There were four maiden Deedes aunts living in the dower house, otherwise Castle Lodge. They were a charge on the estate. I recall the day, years later, when the sole survivor of this quartet fell ill. 'It would do her the power of good,' said her earnest doctor to my unhappy father, 'if you could run to half a bottle of champagne a day.' As well as the aunts there were dependants of those who had worked on the estate and who looked to my father for support.

To cap it all, the castle itself was falling down. It was surrounded by ruins, which could be left alone. But the residential quarter was also in bad shape. The lavatories were primitive but were fitted on the inside with enormous bolts. While staying at the castle, one of my great-aunts, who was mentally unstable and always accompanied by a kindly minder, succeeded in bolting herself in one of these loos. I can see now the gentle minder outside the loo vainly calling instructions through a thick oak door. For us children it was high drama. Eventually the matter was reported to my father, who summoned an ironmonger from the nearest town. He brought ladders and broke in through a heavily mullioned window.

There was of course no electricity and no heating other than from fires, which had to be lit every day. The water tanks in the roof were defective and the chimneys were threatening to fall down. In the early 1920s my father put some of this essential work in hand and received ruinous bills. He sold off land from the estate at regular intervals, but prices were low and his then socialist beliefs inclined him to give away what he was unable to sell. To make ends meet he began to play the Stock Exchange.

One of our neighbours was Lord Wakefield of Hythe, who had amassed a fortune from oil sold to the burgeoning motor trade. He built a fine mansion across the valley from the castle, on a promontory above Hythe looking over the town and the English Channel. Relations between our houses were strained. In his liberal way my father had given away or sold for a song a long stretch of land for new housing in Hythe. It lay directly in line of Lord Wakefield's view of the English Channel. The houses, which stand to this day, were built fairly expansively for a rising lower-middle class, so they took a prominent place on the horizon. They were also colourful, with roofs of red tiles. This benevolent enterprise became known locally as Lobster Row, and helped to established my father's reputation as an eccentric.

At some point in the mid-1920s, Lady Houston, a seriously rich woman, walked into the drawing room at Saltwood Castle where my father and mother were having tea and announced: 'I have come to buy the castle!' I have never fully understood why they refused to accept her offer. Unsurprisingly the dank surroundings began to affect the health of my mother and my eldest sister. This called for spells in a different climate. The family paid regular visits to the South of France and at one point rented a house in Switzerland for a year. Contrary to his socialist principles, my father travelled in style. When crossing Paris to the South of France, he engaged a representative from the travel agent Thomas Cook to travel with us and ease our passage. His tips were lavish to the point of eccentricity. His theory was that capital and income were capitalist inventions and that life was simplified if you avoided making too much distinction between them. It was to prove his undoing.

From the secret point of view one holds as a child, Saltwood Castle was full of delights. The ruins were extensive, mysterious and occupied by countless birds whose nests I raided for eggs –

this was not then a statutory offence. The ancient gardener, Mr Brogdale, seemed constantly engaged in exciting ventures and regularly gave me cigarette cards for my collection. In the middle of the castle keep lawn, I created a cricket pitch; I kept it cut and rolled throughout the summer and marked it out. It was pure fancy. There was no one to play cricket with; but I liked to imagine there might be. Castles are lonely places, and Saltwood, with its moat and portcullis and thick walls, looked fairly unapproachable. Young friends did not feel drawn towards it or me.

Close companions for my three younger sisters and myself therefore were sparse. Two, who grew up with us as children, were Alan and Ruth Hardy, whose family occupied Sandling Park, a mile from the castle. Their grandfather, Lawrence Hardy, had bought the Sandling Park estate from my grandmother in the 1890s when as a relatively young widow she had sought to restore the Deedes family to solvency. The Hardy family fortune had been solidly founded in the iron trade. Lawrence wore a monocle, which made him look formidable to young eyes, was the local Member of Parliament and a Privy Councillor. His son Arthur devoted himself to Sandling's extensive gardens and cultivated some of the finest rhododendrons in the South of England. A tour round his rhododendron woods in early summer was a rich experience and it made a lot of money for charity. Later in life Arthur Hardy exhibited regularly at the Royal Horticultural Society. Among early scenes of my life implanted in my mind were summer days at Sandling where my sisters Frances and Hermione and I would spend the day with a picnic at Sandling Park in company with Ruth and Alan Hardy. As we grew older, we played tennis and held small dances there. I came to see it as a refuge from our own grim castle.

Though he had acquired Saltwood Castle in an exchange of lands with Sir Brook Bridges of Goodnestone near Canterbury at the end of the eighteenth century, my great-great-grandfather, William Deedes, had additionally built Sandling Park in the years 1795–6. One glance at the castle, I have always supposed, convinced him that it was no place in which to bring up a family. Yet Sandling itself was not altogether comfortable. Jane Austen occasionally came over from Godmersham and stayed there. Somewhere in her letters to Cassandra there is a reference to the discomfort she suffered at Sandling. The best to be said about the house was that it was a degree or two cosier than Saltwood Castle. During the Second World War, it was destroyed by a German bomb. A smaller house was built on the site. The gardens remained to delight.

My earliest recollections of Saltwood Castle carry the distant sounds and sights of the First World War. On days the wind blew from France, the distant rumble of big gun barrages on the Western Front could sometimes be heard. During a wartime visit to the Castle before we occupied it, I remembered being carried up to the flat lead roof of one of the towers to watch two German planes flying towards London and flickering in our searchlights. Shorncliffe Camp, a vast place in that war, lay not far away and the lanes round the castle were often full of marching men: 'Soldiers marching . . . all to die'.

Up to the age of eight or nine one has little inkling of the problems of one's elders. There was a certain amount of fuss about my private education, which my father declared to be a waste of money – though whether this attitude sprang from approaching penury or from his socialist principles was never clear to me. My mother fought a winning battle on this issue. At the appropriate time I was dispatched to a preparatory school at Westgate-on-Sea. She hoped I would go on to Winchester, where her two brothers had been pupils. Alas, I disappointed her. My prep school headmaster made it sadly plain that I would be lucky to pass the Common Entrance examination, and would certainly not attain the higher mark required for Winchester.

So it was Harrow, which in those days offered an easier

entry to dull boys. I made some good friends there, but was never particularly happy nor successful at work or games. A year or so before I got there, a scandal had risen over a handful of senior boys who were caught in one of Mrs Merrick's London night clubs. They were spotted by a master with a dame of his own there, which always struck me as off-side. It left a gap at the top of the school and also in the cricket XI, which played Eton at Lords. The headmaster retired and Dr Cyril Norwood replaced him, without making much marked difference to the tone. At the close of my last term at Harrow his speech included a remarkable sentence which I remember only because a contemporary at Harrow whom I met during the war had memorized it and loved to recite it in Cyril Norwood's slightly Cockney accent: 'This has been the worst term I have ever known. I have today had to dismiss six boys. They were found behind the tombstones with women of the serving class.'

The Wall Street crash of 1929 and its repercussions resolved everything, including my future education. Saltwood Castle was sold to a local estate agent for £12,000, in terms of today's money, about £400,000. It seemed a lot less at the time. Stock Exchange losses accounted for much of it. Shortly afterwards, my father ran out of money altogether. I had to leave Harrow in a hurry, after barely three years there. The family became dependent on the support of my uncle, Sir Wyndham Deedes, who had been as good at saving money as my father was bad at it.

My swift departure from Harrow led to a quaint succession of events which ran through my life. My housemaster hastily gave me a form to fill in, so that I would be able to join the Harrow Association. I forget what the subscription was, but my parents were in low financial water at the time, so I put the form in a drawer and forgot about it. After the war, when invited to deliver a talk at the school, I encountered a master who said rather plaintively, 'We could not trace you in the book.' His assumption was, I felt, that I had left Harrow under a cloud. To hell with that, I thought, and perversely decided to keep him guessing. 'I left Harrow a year early,' I said shortly, as if it explained everything and stopped there. He did not pursue the question. Years later I paid another visit, and went through much the same routine. *Mal y soit* . . . I said to myself rather absurdly. If they choose to think I was sacked for an unmentionable offence, so be it.

I kept the game up until the mid-1990s, more than half a century after I had left. Michael Cockerell of the BBC was making a television documentary about me. Filming included a day at Harrow School. On my arrival there, Cockerell told me that the headmaster had been very co-operative. 'He is having his breakfast and would very much like a word with you. Will you pay a call?' After an exchange of greetings, the headmaster remarked lightly on my lost past. I decided instantly to come clean; and rather shamefacedly explained why I had become a small mystery at Harrow. He laughed. Shortly afterwards I received an invitation to be guest of honour at Harrow School's Songs. This is a main event in their calendar, and was regularly attended during and after the war by Winston Churchill. As I sat listening to those matchless songs in company with Churchill's youngest daughter, Mary Soames, I realized that the long shadow which had hung over my name at Harrow – entirely through my own folly – had at last been dissipated.

A consequence of my father's sale of Saltwood Castle was that it came swiftly into the hands of a wealthy couple, Mr and Mrs Lawson, in about 1930. After Lawson's death by his own hand, which occurred almost immediately, the widow decided to devote her life and fortune to restoring the entire castle and its ruins as a memorial to him. Assisted by Lord Conway of Allington, whom she eventually married, she heavily restored the place, but, eccentrically, in the style of a Roman villa. On her death, shortly after the Second World War, Sir Kenneth Clark removed the stone baths and fonts from what passed as bathrooms and made the place habitable. I have looked in there occasionally since, without ever feeling the smallest desire to return.

2

Starting on the *Morning Post*

Early in the spring of 1931 there came a strong intimation from my family that at the age of 17 I should be seeking gainful employment. My eldest sister was outspoken on the subject. I found the prospect unattractive, but reluctantly agreed to consider it. Since leaving Harrow in 1929 a year early, life had been surprisingly congenial. For nine months I had studied at home with a clever and not unattractive woman tutor called Eva Wampach. We worked in the morning and evening. Afternoons were free for golf. She sent me through what was then School Certificate with flying colours. I returned to Harrow for the examination, sleeping in the sanatorium. Old friends entertained me generously.

That hurdle passed, my mother thought a spell at a local secretarial college to learn shorthand, typing and book keeping might be useful. That also left afternoons free for golf. Such shorthand and book keeping as I learned had a short life, but the ability to touch-type – which means using all your fingers and not looking at the keyboard – has proved a valuable friend. To be able to type letters as fast and as professionally as a secretary has saved me hours of time, and more recently has sped work on a word processor. I felt reluctant to break this pleasant routine of learning and golfing. In any case, I had no particular aptitude or skill to offer anyone.

It is surprising, if we think about it, how much our passage through life depends on pure chance. During a week-end visit to us at Hythe, my distinguished uncle Sir Wyndham Deedes caught wind of the family's unease about my future. From his wide range of friends and acquaintances he found three whom he persuaded to grant me an interview. The first was Israel Sieff of Marks and Spencer. To my astonishment and alarm he offered me immediate employment as a storekeeper in Haifa or Jaffa, I forget which, at £300 a year – good money in those years. The family viewed this favourably until a golfing friend, who had spent much of his life with oil in Arab countries, shamefully persuaded my father that promotion might come slowly to a Christian in a Jewish company. My uncle also accompanied me to an interview with Sir John Reith, director-general of the BBC. He received us politely, twirled his thick horn-rimmed spectacles for a while, and pronounced me to be lacking in any useful experience – which was sadly true.

Undismayed, my uncle played a court card by introducing me to Guy Pollock, who was at that time managing editor of the *Morning Post*. He was the only prospective employer in the United Kingdom who could be said to have a small vested interest in me. He was renting a cottage on what was then the considerable estate of Chawton House in Hampshire. It belonged to an uncle by marriage, Lionel Knight, who had married my eldest aunt shortly before the First World War. In addition to its close association with Jane Austen, whose cottage on the estate is now a museum and a place of pilgrimage for her admirers, it offered excellent shooting. Pollock craved a gun in my uncle's shoot. In return for that he asked Lionel Knight whether one of his sons would welcome an opening in journalism. No, said my uncle Lionel, but he had a nephew who was looking around. When Uncle Wyndham and I arrived at Pollock's room at the *Morning Post* therefore, the dice were already to some extent loaded in my favour. Pollock was the sort of man who liked to come into the office around lunch time on Sunday, bearing a brace of pheasants for his secretary.

He summoned the news editor, who obligingly said that he

needed another reporter to work 'on space', but that due to holiday leave and so on the candidate would have to appear in the reporters' room by the following Monday. My uncle thanked them warmly. I nodded my head with what I hoped was a show of eagerness, though I had never reported anything in my life. My number had come up, though in circumstances which many will condemn today as a deplorable example of privilege, nepotism, elitism – there is hardly a word strong enough to condemn it. Adding icing to the cake, my saintly uncle announced, while escorting me to Charing Cross station, that I would be welcome to a room in the ample grace-and-favour residence which he and his mother kept in East London. They occupied University House on Victoria Park Square, which had once been the Bishop of Stepney's palace. It was owned by the Oxford House, where graduates of that University intending to enter the church spent a short time. Since his retirement from public life, my uncle had been engaged in social work in Bethnal Green, hence his occupation of University House.

On the following Sunday night I travelled expectantly to London, to be in good time for my introduction to journalism on Monday morning. By today's conventions, it was an outrageous way to start in journalism. As I know well from talking to so many aspiring journalists, it can be a heartbreaking task to reach even the foothills of the national press. Reporters are expected to have served an apprenticeship outside London. My eldest son was indentured to a county weekly paper for three years. Sometimes graduates of exceptional promise are given a trial run by the national press. Having left Harrow with no sporting or scholastic achievements of any kind, I brought no such bounty to the *Morning Post*.

It is true that the *Morning Post*, conscious of its ageing profile, had been looking out for one or two younger reporters. Thus in its small reporters' room of not more than ten, I found one or two congenial companions who had just come down from university. One of the new arrivals was Hugh Speaight, brother of Robert the actor, and soon to die of tuberculosis. Another was Ian Colvin, son of the *Morning Post*'s distinguished chief leader writer, only a few months older than myself and, like me, without university education. Later, from Berlin, he became one of Churchill's principal informants on pre-war Nazi Germany; and a tribute to him is to be found at the opening of Churchill's war memoirs.

We were fortunate young men, more fortunate than we realized. From the time of my arrival in the summer of 1931, the *Morning Post* became for me the university I had missed. Compared with the *Daily Telegraph, Daily Mail*, or *Daily Express* of those years, it was a small, close, proud family. At some point the *Daily Mail* had boasted what great advantages its circulation offered to advertisers by contrast with that of the lowly *Morning Post*. Ian Colvin senior was set to work on a leading article about this. 'A cigar merchant is not galled', he wrote, 'when he learns that his neighbour has sold more of Woodbines in a year than he will sell of Corona Coronas in a lifetime.' The *Morning Post*'s small senior editorial staff seemed always to have time to advise and encourage us. The newspaper had been founded in 1772, which made it the oldest national daily. It was extremely right wing, it was patriotic, its circulation when I joined it was well under 100,000, its profits, when it was not actually making a loss, were at the lowest end of five figures.

Early in the century control of the newspaper had passed from Lord Glenesk to his daughter Lilias Lady Bathurst, a woman of strong character and opinions. In 1911 she had parted acrimoniously from her editor Fabian Ware. His replacement, H. A. Gwynne, was still in the chair to greet my arrival. He had been a reporter in the Boer War, along with Winston Churchill and Edgar Wallace. He was close to leading political figures of the day, and conducted his newspaper in the confident belief that it still wielded great political influence.

A very old hand at the *Morning Post* once explained to me that its fortunes in the early part of the twentieth century had been to some extent founded on an Upstairs–Downstairs principle. When the great houses advertised for a butler, for footmen, cooks, valets or maids, they chose the *Morning Post* as their medium. We were the sort of paper that butlers ironed before laying us alongside the breakfast dishes. Correspondingly, those seeking employment as butlers, footmen, cooks or maids bought copies of the *Morning Post* to discover the opportunities. Our classified advertising was posh and lucrative.

After the First World War, shutters began to go up on the great town and country houses. Butlers were less in demand. So this profitable classified advertising in the *Morning Post* began to decline. The style of life in this country changed radically. The Labour party was on the horizon. Round a true-blue newspaper of mildly eccentric habits, which declared that it stood foremost for King and Country, shadows gathered. They were gathering fast when I joined the happy band.

There had been one glorious hour in 1926, at the time of the General Strike. Lady Bathurst had reluctantly relinquished the baton in 1924. A group under the Duke of Northumberland bought the newspaper for £500,000, but it continued to occupy the grandest newspaper office in London – Glenesk House in Aldwych, which is still to be seen, with its commanding view of Waterloo Bridge. This was the building the Government commandeered in May 1926 as the national press closed down. In its long history the *Morning Post* missed only nine editions, and eight of them fell while the General Strike was on, and its staff and presses were called on to produce what was in effect a Government newspaper called the *British Gazette*. It was the sort of enterprise in which Churchill, then Chancellor of the Exchequer, revelled, and his enthusiasm outstripped his usefulness. Gwynne, with huge administrative difficulties of his own, sent messages to the Cabinet begging that Churchill be kept away from the offices where the *British Gazette* was being printed, because 'He butts in at the busiest hours and insists on changing commas and full stops until the staff is furious.'

Churchill sought also to rewrite the editorials. Round his part in the *British Gazette* all sorts of myths were spun. One, still running when I joined the newspaper, was that he had ordered machine guns on the roof of the old Gaiety Theatre, opposite the *Morning Post*'s building, to deal with strikers who might try to interfere. Another episode, which a colleague insisted he had witnessed, related to Churchill arriving after dinner to cheer on the workers, stepping backwards and falling head over arse across a news reel.

Two years later, suffering heavy losses, the Duke of Northumberland sold the *Morning Post* building at 346 Strand. The newspaper was moved to humbler premises at 15 (business) and 27 (editorial) Tudor Street, which runs parallel between Fleet Street and the Embankment. There it became a tenant of the Argus Press, which printed the paper, and there it entered its final phase. I arrived there punctually on Monday morning, piloted by my grandmother, who feared I might lose my way. In the afternoon the chief reporter, S. R. Pawley, took me on one of his inquiries. We travelled on a tram towards the Elephant and Castle, where he interviewed a firm of timber merchants about the disgraceful way the Soviet Union was dumping 'red' timber on us. This was one of the *Morning Post*'s favourite topics. On the second or third day, I was a little late leaving the office and was caught by the news editor's deputy. He handed me a scrap of paper reporting that the Indian Rope Trick had just been performed in Cheltenham, of all unlikely places, before the International Brotherhood of Magicians. Would I call up Mr Jasper Maskelyne, the well-known conjuror, and seek his reactions? The request took my breath away. As a boy, I had been taken by London-bound aunts on treats to the capital's great conjurors – Maskelyne, Devant and Cook. Now I was to call up one of these giants and obtain an interview. To my amazement, Jasper Maskelyne responded generously. I was too inexperienced to realize how warmly he welcomed the publicity. He spoke at length. The story appeared. I had arrived.

Hugh Speaight was establishing a fashion for news stories about quaint social trends. I followed eagerly and wrote stories about why freckles were on the wane – because of beauty parlours; why books were getting slimmer; and why 'bilking' on London's buses was increasing. Because the *Morning Post* liked to mix a little frivolity with its intensely serious true-blue views – the term 'right wing' had not then been invented – this proved a profitable vein. I scored a hit with a story which revealed that flats without chimneys were sealing the doom of sweeps. Being 'on space' meant you were paid for what got into print. To earn two or three pounds a week while at the same time being taught how to do the job was bliss. During the 1931 election campaign, when miscellaneous duties fell to me – mainly interviewing prospective Conservative candidates whom nobody else in the office wanted to see – my weekly pay packet rose to £5. With the aim of widening its popular appeal, the *Morning Post* began an unoriginal series called 'Other People's Job'. Its leading stylist in the news room, with whom I was learning to drink beer at lunch time, was put in charge of this. For his opening gambit he chose to be an organ grinder, and invited me to join him. Unshaven and in reeking clothes which he found somewhere, we spent our day wheeling a barrel organ slowly from Holborn to Marble Arch. We collected an astonishing amount of money.

At the start of 1932, with an eye to the *Morning Post*'s sense of humour, I proposed a wheeze of my own. I offered to sleep a night in the Chamber of Horrors at Madame Tussaud's. My application was turned down, but for reasons so bizarre that it made a good news story. Up to 2,000 people a year, they explained, applied to sleep in the Chamber of Horrors. Some were out to impress girl friends. Most were attracted by a rumour that the Exhibition offered £5 to anyone willing to see the night through. At the time of my application this mythical sum had risen to £100. A rat catcher had been sent down there one night, scorning fear. In a short time he was beating on the door for release. All the figures, he declared, seemed to be staring at him. He had discovered the horror of the place. Figures in the Chamber of Horrors had been designed to ensure that in whatever position you stood their eyes stared directly at you.

My story won prominence. I was becoming a reporter. One rainy evening, the *Morning Post* sent me down to Eton. Dr Cyril Alington, headmaster there since 1916, had announced his retirement. 'Get an interview with him,' they said. On the way down I wondered what it had been like there in 1916, when most of the boys who left Eton would quickly join up and, if they went to the Western Front, probably die soon. By the time I got there, it was past eight o'clock. Dr and Mrs Alington were out to dinner, the maid announced unpromisingly.

I decided to await their return in a damp and chilly porch. By the time they got back, I was feeling well below my best. Dr Alington politely shrugged off the idea of an interview. His wife, observing that I was suffering from a heavy cold aggravated by my vigil, invited me into the house. Even the headmaster was moved by my pitiable condition. He pointed towards a door leading to the butler's quarters. 'He will give you something for your cold,' he said shortly. I gratefully followed his directions. He could hardly be expected to know that he was addressing an Old Harrovian.

'They don't touch the stuff upstairs,' explained the butler, and helped me to a whisky as if he were pouring out a bottle of beer. While I sipped it thankfully, we discussed plans for my return to London. The last train from Windsor had gone. The kindly fellow worked on a Green Line bus timetable. He told me where to find the bus. I polished off the whisky and was led back to the hall for my departure. As we entered it, two things happened simultaneously. Dr Alington and his wife left their drawing room, presumably to retire to bed. Tired, wracked with cold and fairly tipsy, I missed my footing and sprawled on the hall floor. It looked bad. As I climbed to my feet, the subconscious disciplines of my own public school, from which I had not long departed, asserted themselves. 'Good night, Dr Norwood,' I said with dignity.

At the start of 1932 the decline of the *Morning Post* entered its penultimate phase. The Great Depression, which had begun with the Wall Street crash three years earlier, had struck. Up on Clydeside Cunard White Star's great liner *Queen Mary*, bleakly known as 534, standing unfinished and frozen, symbolized this deep winter we had entered. We were reminded of it whenever Sir Percy Bates, chairman of Cunard White Star and now also chairman of the *Morning Post*, entered the office, a doomladen figure. Early in 1932 my benefactor Guy Pollock was invited to draw up a list of redundancies. He put his own name at the top and added a dozen others. The Hon. Edward Russell, younger brother of Lord Ampthill – whose wife had featured in a sensational divorce case – took Pollock's place. My insignificance saved me. The following year Gwynne summoned me and invited me to join the staff – I think at seven guineas a week.

There were conditions attached to this. The high point of the *Morning Post* year came in the summer when a cricket XI of the newspaper's staff travelled to Dunmow in Essex and played a match against the village in which H. A. Gwynne dwelt. 'You play a lot of cricket, I expect,' he said when the formal part of our conversation ended. I could not in all honesty bring myself to say yes, but I nodded my head. 'I hope you will be joining the newspaper's cricket side.' I nodded again. Gwynne shook me warmly by the hand.

The Dunmow cricket match was treated with great seriousness by those chosen to represent the *Morning Post*. Alan Fairfax, a former Australian cricketer, had set up a coaching school in the basement of a Thames house. We took nets there. On the day of the match, however, we fell from grace. Three or four of us would travel down together by car in time for the editor's lunch preceding the match. Our route lay through what was then known as Benskins country. The beer from that brewery was delicious and had great authority; to ignore it would have been sinful. So we would arrive at Dunmow just in time for lunch in a convivial state. Then Gwynne would say considerately, 'You must be tired and thirsty after your long journey,' and pour us out enormous drinks. There was wine at lunch followed by an obligatory glass of port. What saved us from disaster in the field more than once was the inclusion in our XI of R. C. 'Crusoe' Robertson-Glasgow, who was our cricket correspondent. He drank as much as any of us, but he had played for Somerset. The Dunmow batsmen were no match for 'Crusoe' no matter what he had drunk for lunch. It could be said that we owed him our jobs. Gwynne seemed always content with the outcome of the match, and would solemnly thank us for taking part in it.

Having got through that and won a place on the staff, I was expected to take life more seriously. The news editor warned some of us against staying in Fleet Street's pubs too long, and urged us to 'stay clean on the teapot', a phrase we found hilarious. 'Clean on the teapot,' we would exclaim solemnly when ordering a fresh round of drinks. With hindsight, I ought to have spent evenings at somewhere like the London School of Economics filling the gaps in my education. I should at least have sought a grounding in economics, on which tuition is essential. There were too many distractions. At least two nights a week there was a party somewhere. There was a night club in Upper Regent Street, the Milray, where we could drink and dance with girl friends until all hours. There was a good supper to be had at the Café Royal for a few shillings. On relatively high pay and with no domestic responsibilities whatever, we could afford to enjoy ourselves. Leaving a night club just before dawn one summer's morning a friend and I discovered that we had our golf clubs in the boot of his car. We drove to a Surrey golf course (which I have never since been able to identify) and played eighteen holes in white tie, wing collar, tails and patent-leather shoes.

I think back with shame of Mrs Trampleasure. She was listed in the London telephone directory and lived somewhere in South London. There came a point at every party when we would decide to give her a call. The conversation went something like this: 'Mrs Trampleasure? How extraordinarily kind of you to answer the telephone at this hour. May I say how deeply I appreciate it. But, Mrs Trampleasure, there is a question that I have urgently to put to you. Mrs Trampleasure, how are all your little trolley buses?' The test was seeing how long you could keep Mrs Trampleasure on the line before she slammed the receiver down. Naturally, as the game took hold among our circle of friends, this became progressively more difficult. There was no excuse for it. It causes me a pang whenever I hear Streisand singing 'The Way We Were . . .'

Not all the hours were misspent. Journalists who are learning the job tend to become useful towards the end of their second year. By 1933 I could find my way about, and was being entrusted with more difficult stories. Late one evening, I was told to go down to the House of Commons – the first time I had set eyes on the place – where there had been a bitter debate on the plight of the Lancashire cotton industry. My instructions were to hear what the Lancashire Members had to say, then take the sleeper to Manchester and describe what was happening in the mill towns of Lancashire. Our political correspondent had rounded up one or two members. They were lachrymose and slightly sozzled, realizing full well that their constituents would take the outcome of the debate even more bitterly than they did. We drank more whisky until I left for the sleeper.

The assignment proved to be the beginning of my true education. During the next three or four days I started to learn about the condition of England. In the shipyards, in the steel works, in these smokeless, silent cotton mills Britain's supremacy had come to an end. In 1913 we had had 805,000 looms working in Lancashire; by 1933 there were fewer than half that number and they were dwindling fast. Not only had our export trade gone to Japan, the unemployed cotton workers were themselves driven to buy Japanese goods because they were cheapest. In Manchester men's shirts were being bought wholesale from Japan at 15s 6d a dozen. In Coventry, Japanese hats were being sold at 17s 6d a dozen. It made a sensational story, which until the House of Commons debate had somehow escaped public notice. I scrambled a thousand words or more together on the first day which were splashed under the headline: 'Japanese "Invasion" of Lancashire'. On the second day I travelled to Macclesfield, where the silk trade had also collapsed. That made a second splash. Then I looked into Japanese tricks of the trade and Japan's gathering threat to the wool industry. It was an instructive week.

But I had glimpsed only a small part of what was happening to us. The state of all our old staple industries was grave. Germany was recovering. America was growing fast. Japan was reaching out. We were falling rapidly behind. Ten years earlier the Conservative leader, Stanley Baldwin, had foreseen this. His family ran an iron and steel business. He knew what was happening. As the main plank of his Conservative platform in the General Election of 1923, he offered the country the safeguard of protection. The Opposition's retort to that was 'Your food will cost you more.' It prevailed. Baldwin lost the election. Later he wrote to his private secretary, Tom Jones: 'I wanted it because I saw no other weapon to use in the fight against unemployment.' It was almost ten years before tariffs were back on the political agenda again.

At this point in the early 1930s, Baldwin had another fight on his hands, within his own party. The theme was Indian Home Rule. For years the tide of Indian nationalism had been rising. In 1927, Lord Birkenhead, Baldwin's Secretary of State for India, had appointed a Royal Commission under Sir John Simon to examine the workings of the Government of India Act of 1919. It was ill received, indeed boycotted, in India. Perceiving that something more positive was needed, in 1929, the Viceroy of India, Lord Irwin – later to become the Earl of Halifax – suggested to the new Labour Government that there should be two announcements. The first proposed that, after the Simon Commission had reported, a round-table conference should be convened. It would represent all sections in British India, the Indian princes and British political parties. The second announcement was more controversial. Since it was to create the most serious division in the Tory party until the issue of Europe arose, it is worth giving in full:

> In view of the doubts which have been expressed in both Great Britain and India regarding the interpretation to be placed on the intentions of the British Government in enacting the statute of 1919, I am authorized on behalf of His Majesty's Government to state clearly that, in their judgement, it is implicit in the Declaration of 1917 that the natural issue of India's constitutional progress as there contemplated is the attainment of Dominion status.

Loosely translated that meant that the Viceroy of India, one day to be a Conservative Foreign Secretary, and Wedgwood Benn, Labour's Secretary of State for India, later Lord Stansgate and proud father of Tony Wedgwood Benn, had resolved to speed the pace at which India would become a self-governing republic. The implosion the words caused in the Tory party were to give me many hours of gainful employment and further education. Baldwin was an admirer of Lord Irwin, the former Edward Wood. Partly on this account, he determined that self-government for India should be his next great mission. On this he broke with Winston Churchill; and from that breach much history flowed, none of it to our advantage. More than Europe has done, the future of India became a subject which separated not only Tory Members of Parliament from their party leadership, but also constituency associations from their Members of Parliament. Some of those who supported Baldwin's progressive policies for India found themselves out of favour with their local officers. In other constituencies, Tory MPs in support of the so-called 'diehards' led by Winston Churchill were in trouble for the opposite reason.

My task on behalf of the *Morning Post* was to search for trouble and report every battleground where it could be found. Faithful to its traditions, the newspaper backed Churchill and the diehards. We reported every episode we could find which made Baldwin's policy for India look wrong-headed. In the latter part of 1934, a by-election occurred in the Wavertree division of Liverpool. Winston Churchill's son Randolph decided to stand as an independent Conservative candidate there primarily on the issue of India. I was sent to report this epic. In the landslide of 1931 the Tory candidate, R. Nall-Cain, had won the seat by something like 33,000 to 9,500 votes. This time the Conservatives were represented by a dull man called James Platt. At one point in the campaign he was reported to have sold scrap from derelict cotton mills to the Japanese. It was that sort of campaign.

I set about reporting the campaign more or less objectively. Randolph became enraged. We were both staying at Liverpool's Adelphi Hotel, which had become the nearest thing Britain had to the Ritz Hotel in Paris. Designed to cater for wealthy Americans crossing the Atlantic and disembarking at the Port of Liverpool, it afforded every comfort. Never subsequently have I eaten better than I did in the Adelphi's French restaurant, where the *table d'hôte* dinner of six courses cost 8s 6d. One morning soon after I arrived I was awoken by a telephone call from Randolph. He had just read that day's issue of the *Morning Post*. My account, he declared, was wretched. It wholly lacked the support which he had been led to believe the

Morning Post would be providing. He was reporting the matter to his father.

The sequel is on record. Churchill's papers, edited by Martin Gilbert, include this item: 'Randolph Churchill to Winston S. Churchill: telegram, 29th January 1935. Morning Post almost our worst Press. Can you do anything?' Gilbert adds a footnote: 'On 29 January 1935 the *Morning Post* gave a full-column account of the Wavertree campaign, stressing the support building up for James Platt. Some 3,000 young Conservatives, it reported, had joined together in a Conservative Youth Drive, opposed to what they called Randolph Churchill's "interloping return". The *Morning Post* also reported a speech by Anthony Eden, the Lord Privy Seal, speaking for Platt on the previous night . . .' Randolph assured me that his father was approaching my editor, H. R. Gwynne, with a view to having me replaced. I heard nothing. The storm passed.

As the campaign entered its closing stages, the Churchill family joined us at the Adelphi. Two of Randolph's sisters, Diana and Sarah, entered the fray. Brendan Bracken, Churchill's closest companion, turned up. On Saturday afternoon of the final week-end we attended a fête which Randolph was to address. I was returning home for the week-end. So were the Churchill girls. The recent past forgotten, Randolph asked if I would escort his sisters to London. Our taxi, arriving late, had to race to the station. This being the Churchill family, it then drove on to the platform from which the train was about to leave. Diana carried an armful of flowers presented to her at the fête. 'They're married!' someone shouted. We scrambled on to the Pullman car amid cheers. On the way down over dinner, the girls discussed their family with me. Such a pity, they thought, that their father was so much less relaxed than their brother, who could get up and speak readily without a note in his hand. By contrast, days on which father was preparing a speech were agony. The household was still and tense. I have often thought back to that conversation.

Dear Bill

On the eve of poll Winston Churchill arrived to address Randolph's closing meeting in Liverpool's Sun Hall. He greeted me warmly, expressing gratitude for my support of Randolph. It seemed to me that silence was the right policy. They had made the mistake of inviting the Duke of Westminster (Bendor) from nearby Eaton Hall to take the chair. His notes for this task had been written on several small sheets of heavily embossed Eaton Hall writing paper. From the press table under the platform I observed him shuffling these sheets nervously. In consequence his introduction of Winston Churchill came out in a curious sequence which was difficult to follow. No matter, he received a tremendous cheer. Winston followed with a phrase, not quite original, about this being an occasion 'dear and refreshing to a father's heart'. The outcome of the election was a disaster for the Tories. Randolph split the vote. Labour's horse cantered home. No more was heard of Mr Platt.

3

Abyssinia

In his book *The Cruise of the Nona*, Hilaire Belloc describes his vision at dawn, as this country stood on the brink of the First World War:

> Like ghosts, like things themselves made out of mist, there passed between me and the newly risen sun, a procession of great forms, all in line, hastening northward. It was the Fleet recalled. The slight haze along the distant water had thickened imperceptibly; or perhaps the great speed of the men-of-war buried them too quickly in the distance. But, for whatever cause, this marvel was of short duration. It was seen for a moment, and in a moment it was gone. Then I knew that war would come, and my mind was changed.

I experienced no such vision, but somewhere in the course of 1935 I sensed that war was more likely than not. In June I had written a story under the headline: 'Nation's Defence Against Gas'. Elaborate plans for defence of the entire civilian population of the country, I reported, had been prepared by the Air Raid Precautions department of the Home Office, and were about to be published. The scheme, I added, had been under consideration for three years. 'It was to have been made public next April, but diplomatic visits between this country and Germany caused a postponement.' The *Morning Post* began its editorial: 'We do not suppose that our Pacifists would deny the right of the oyster to wear his shell or the right of the rabbit to go to ground. It would be as foolish on their part to raise any objection to the programme of Air Raid Precautions of which we give an intelligent anticipation today.'

It was the year in which the outline of the war to come began to take shape. In January, Mussolini of Italy and Laval of France had made a pact. What it amounted to was that Italy would support France in stopping Hitler from intervening in Austria. In return, France would give Italy a free hand to annex parts of Abyssinia. A month later, Italian troops in tropical uniforms sailed for Africa. At the beginning of March, Hitler repossessed the Saar, a state of West Germany administered by France since 1919. He introduced conscription, at the same time demanding air force parity with Britain and France, a navy not far short of our own at 400,000 tons, and an army roughly five times larger than that permitted by the Treaty of Versailles. Jews were banned from German public life.

Baldwin succeeded Ramsay MacDonald as Prime Minister in June. Eden was dispatched to Rome, vainly to warn Mussolini against invading Abyssinia. At this point, Lord Robert Cecil of the League of Nations Union announced the result of the Peace Ballot, for which polling had been taking place for eight months. The questions were held to be tendentious and the results misleading. The fact remains that some 11,559,165 had voted in a way which confirmed what Baldwin was already thinking. Since the East Fulham by-election in the autumn of 1933, when the Conservative candidate had been humiliated mainly on the pacifist issue, Baldwin had doubted whether the country would give him a mandate for outright rearmament. The Peace Ballot result fatally tipped the balance in his mind.

I was not paying much attention to this. I had been sent back to Liverpool, where in the West Toxteth by-election the National Government established in 1931 had suffered another heavy reverse. A Tory majority of 5,635 had become a Labour majority of 5,343. Conservative Central Office decided there was something fundamentally wrong in Liverpool, and persuaded the *Morning Post* to send me up there to investigate. It was a complicated tale. Like certain American cities, Liverpool had a weakness for political bosses. The most famous had been Sir Archibald Salvidge (1863–1928) of Bent's Brewery, who had been Conservative leader in the city. In 1935 it was Sir Thomas White, also a brewer and leader of the Conservative party in Liverpool. He treated the city as his fiefdom. As I began to unravel some of this, my presence became unwelcome; but it made a good story.

On my return to London in July, the *Morning Post* asked me if I were willing to become their war correspondent in what promised to be an unavoidable conflict between Mussolini and Abyssinia's Emperor Haile Selassie. Already in evidence were all the signs along the road to the Second World War with which we later became so familiar; 'border incidents', 'intolerable provocation', 'unprovoked aggression'. Nobody could establish the truth in what was then a primitive and highly inaccessible country. Everyone could see, however, that Mussolini intended business.

I put in a telephone call to my benevolent uncle, Sir Wyndham Deedes, a reliable counsellor. He knew nothing about the country, but saw no objection. It was difficult to find anyone who did know anything about the country. The journey was long and uncomfortable, and nobody had any reason for going there. Being independent, it lay outside everyone's colonial empire. There was only one route by which to reach Abyssinia's capital. It lay along a single-track railway line which the French had built earlier in the century and which ran from the port of Djibouti on the East African coast to Addis Ababa. In the rainy season the trains ran only in daylight hours, so that with two night stops the journey took the best part of three days. At the coastal end, the early part of the line was vulnerable to unfriendly tribesmen. Anticipating that in these circumstances its correspondent inside Ethiopia might be trapped indefinitely by the war, the *Morning Post* took elaborate precautions on my behalf;. My luggage was designed to withstand a long siege. Most of it came from Austin Reed.

Khaki shirts, riding breeches for winter and summer, solar topees, mosquito boots, a camp bed and roll and much else besides were bought regardless of the *Morning Post*'s precarious bank balance. For iron rations and a medicine chest we went to the Army and Navy Stores. A cedarwood trunk lined with zinc to repel ants and two uniform cases added considerably to the weight, which finally came to about 600lb, or a quarter of a ton.

With this I travelled from Victoria to Paris, thence to Marseilles. A Messageries Maritime steamer took me through the Mediterranean, the Suez Canal and the Red Sea to Djibouti, which in those days was the sort of place where an Englishman who had broken the rules might hope to die soon. There one waited, in strenuous heat and surrounded by flies which fell idly into every drink, until the next train was ready to leave for Addis Ababa. I had been lucky on the journey out. The Chief of Police at Port Said had been a wartime friend of Wyndham Deedes. He sent an impressive launch to meet me, and gave me details of what Italy had already sent through the Canal. These included shipments of mustard gas.

He also drew my attention to what was going back to Italy. Mussolini had sent a huge labour force to build roads and establish camps. With hats but without spinal pads to protect the spinal column many were struck down by the strength of the sun. Some were temporarily blinded. They lay in rows on the decks of ships returning to Italy. According to the newspapers, our own Anthony Eden and Pierre Laval of France were designing oil sanctions against Italy. In the Canal I observed a household name supplying Italy with all the oil it wanted – on French credit. Since then I have never put much confidence in international sanctions.

I bore with me a splendid letter of credentials from my

editor, H. A. Gwynne: 'To all whom it may concern. The bearer of this is Mr William Francis Deedes, a member of the staff of the MORNING POST. He has been appointed Special Correspondent for this paper in Abyssinia, The Sudan, Somaliland and British East Africa. I would be obliged for all permissible facilities which may be granted him.' The letter bore an impressive blue seal. There was also a long personal letter of advice from Gwynne, clearly founded more on his own experiences in the Boer War than on the realities of Abyssinia. Sixty years on, it is hard to read while keeping a straight face:

As an old war correspondent myself, I realize that the difficulties that await a correspondent in Abyssinia are enormous. In the first place, there are two fronts – in the north, Eritrea, and in the south, Italian Somaliland. Presumably, so far as one can make out, the attack in force will come from the north, but I have no doubt that the Italians will try to make a diversion from the south. One man can only be in one place at a time, and, therefore, it would be ridiculous to expect you to cover all the fighting – if fighting takes place – in Abyssinia. All I suggest to you is that you should keep as near headquarters as you can, for there news of every engagement will ultimately arrive. By keeping in touch with general headquarters you will be sure to get all the big news as soon as anybody does.

I am not laying this down as a positive instruction for, obviously, you must be allowed a large amount of discretion, but, from my own experience of this kind of open warfare, I have found it myself to be of great advantage to keep in general touch with the GHQ. This does not, of course, preclude you from going wherever you think you can get the best copy.

I do not know Abyssinia, though I have been very close to its borders, but I do know something about its climate. It is very hot in the plains and at Djibouti and you will, therefore, have to provide yourself with clothing for a tropical climate. At the same time, on the heights the weather is cold and the wind keen and, therefore, you will have to make provisions also for these tremendous drops of temperature which occur in Abyssinian highlands.

Gwynne could not have anticipated that we would be confined to Addis Ababa, which at 8,500 feet up is often well below English spring temperatures. One or two people thought it unlikely they would see me again, including a godmother who sent me to Harrods with a fiver, now worth about £140. The chief reporter touchingly gave me his compass. Having never previously travelled further than the Swiss Alps, I felt troubled by the prospect of a complicated journey ahead with nine pieces of luggage. There was no room for any other kind of anxiety.

In reality, the *Morning Post*'s precautions on my behalf were not as superfluous as they now appear. Sir Sidney Barton, the British minister in Addis Ababa, foresaw serious trouble, if and when the Italians, with modern weapons, scored victories on the northern and southern fronts. He reckoned there might be anti-white rioting in the city which the Italians, with miles of mountainous and hostile country still to cross, could do nothing about. He therefore commissioned a military survey of his legation's extensive compound – it was then about one square mile in extent – with a view to offering sanctuary to the small white population, if the worst came to the worst.

In great secrecy, Barton arranged for an Indian contingent to be dispatched to Addis Ababa. An elaborate plan was hatched whereby it arrived via the French railway in the dead of night and was transferred in unidentifiable vehicles to the British compound, which lay some seven miles from the centre of the capital. The Emperor was persuaded, not without difficulty, to accept this import of foreign troops and to order a curfew on the night in question.

Abyssinia

One of several strokes of luck I have had in my life lay in the date I sailed from Marseilles, towards the end of August. One boat ahead, another small group of correspondents had sailed. They included Evelyn Waugh and a friend of mine from the *News Chronicle*, Stuart Emeny. With them travelled a mysterious Englishman named F. W. Rickett, reputed to be a master of foxhounds. The journalists were intrigued by him and speculated about his business, but received no enlightenment. Once in Addis Ababa, Rickett went to ground. Waugh, representing the *Daily Mail*, and Patrick Balfour (later Lord Kinross), of the *Evening Standard*, left Addis Ababa to explore the ancient city of Harar.

Unobserved, Rickett, acting on behalf of American financiers, negotiated with the Emperor Haile Selassie and his advisers a concession for mineral rights which covered a large part of the country. On his side of the deal the Emperor calculated that by involving American interests he might yet win that country's support. What Rickett hoped to gain is less clear. The deal signed, he passed on the news to only two reporters, Jim Mills of the Associated Press of America and Sir Percival Philips of the *Daily Telegraph*. They filed something like 3,000 words to their respective offices. The story created an international sensation, for it was widely seen (as the Emperor intended) as bringing America closer to conflict with Italy. It turned out to be by far the best story of the war, but it was short-lived. The dangers perceived, America's Secretary of State, Cordell Hull, and other political leaders moved swiftly. The deal was called off.

Caught in Harar, where nobody knew anything about Rickett, Evelyn Waugh was ill placed to answer the *Daily Mail*'s frantic and persistent inquiries. It was the start of increasingly strained relations between him and the newspaper. Their acrid exchanges inspired the comic telegrams which William Boot received in *Scoop*, Waugh's novel about the war. Still at sea, on a boat of the *Morning Post*'s choosing, I was blameless. I arrived in time to see the *Daily Mail*'s angry messages homing in on Waugh at the breakfast table which half a dozen of us shared at a pension called the Deutsches Haus. It was run by two efficient German citizens, Mr and Mrs Heft, and was a refuge from the town's main hotel, which was packed three to a room by the world's special correspondents.

In retrospect, the Abyssinian War was a romantic episode, but thin copy for reporters. I travelled on the railway with two distinguished Hearst correspondents, H. R. Knickerbocker, who boasted a salary of $10,000 in gold, and a much older man, Karl von Weigand. The American newspapers and agencies were for some reason more drawn to the war than the British. They also sent a flamboyant character in Lance Stallings, author of two popular wartime plays, *What Price Glory?* and *The Big Parade*. He had been given charge of the swaggering Fox Movietone expedition. There were other Americans, whose appearance was rendered startling by the extraordinary clothes they wore – laced riding boots, breeches and weird hats. I joined Knickerbocker's nightly poker schools, where we played for that magnificent coin, the Abyssinian thaler, the only silver coin I have ever handled with a higher intrinsic value than its exchange rate. As Selena Hastings has since reminded us in her admirable biography, Evelyn Waugh found it impossible to take Americans seriously, and enjoyed mimicking and offending them. It led to estrangements. He also suffered strained relations with the British legation, where Sir Sidney Barton had remained minister since Waugh's visit as the *Times* correspondent for the Emperor's Coronation in 1930. Waugh's thinly disguised portrait of him and his daughter Esme in his novel *Black Mischief*, written after that trip, had left scars. I was with him, drinking his foul mixture of brandy and *crème de menthe* in one of Addis Ababa's two night clubs, when he re-encountered Esme. She threw a glass of wine in his face. At some point, however, relations between Waugh and the legation must have improved, for I vividly recall both of us being invited there for a Sunday picnic on horseback. I had only just learned to ride with early-morning practice under Waugh's eye. Egged on by Waugh, the military attaché poured gin into the fruit salad. The gallop home was wild.

There was plenty of colour in that wild and beautiful country to fill early cables; but after Italy had declared war and we were kept holed up in Addis Ababa, without sight of the action, our offices became fretful. The Abyssinian communiqués were useless. We all employed boys, or spies, who fed us with improbable gossip, but after a while this ran thin with foreign editors in London hungry for news of battle. The cost of cabling was prohibitive, and must have gone some way to defraying the cost of the war. At ordinary rates it cost 1s 3d a word to cable London. But everyone filed at urgent rates which cost half a crown a word – about £3.50 in today's money. The office devised a code list for me. 'AAland' meant 'Going . . . expect delay before next message.' 'Elba' meant 'Please cable more money.' 'Skeleton' warned 'Following message is much abbreviated; please elaborate.' Eventually 'Skeleton' proved our salvation. Our most talented reporter, J. C. Trewin, later a renowned theatre critic, was set the task of expanding, rewriting and polishing my cables.

Not long ago, his son Ion Trewin, the publisher, came across a letter I had sent his father to cheer him in his task. It reminded me of the enormous debt I owe to the memory of J. C. Trewin. He was a fine writer, and swatted up enough about Abyssinia to be able to describe the country, its ways and its people sensitively. My 'skeletons' became *belles lettres*. All of them appeared under my name, unfairly but unavoidably. To have added Trewin's name to mine would have given the game away. So my dispatches appeared in peacock's feathers, and were made to look entirely my own work; a deceit for which one day I may be held to account.

As well as journalists a number of odd characters arrived in Addis Ababa with an eye to the main chance. Having missed

Rickett, the journalists watched arrivals at the station as cats watch holes down which mice have escaped. One of the more colourful adventurers to appear was Colonel Julian, who declared himself to be a famous air ace. For a short spell he got his hands on the Emperor's minute air force. At some point H. R. Knickerbocker persuaded Julian to take him up in the air – something nobody else managed to do. He was not thought to have seen very much, but it produced a sensational piece for the Hearst Press in America.

In mid-November, officials in Addis Ababa intimated that permission to go north to Dessie was at hand. Waugh and Emeny rented a lorry, recruited staff and bought rations. I decided to join them and share expenses. On the appointed day, confusion took charge. The expedition was neither sanctioned nor postponed. We decided to take a chance, and in the early morning, concealed under the lorry's tarpaulin, we left the capital, and for several hours made astonishingly good progress towards the north. Then we were stopped at a telephone station and questioned. We showed our press card, which created a favourable impression. But there had been an urgent message from the capital to stop us, which created a less favourable impression. We gave the chief a lot of whisky and were allowed to move on. We made camp and spent a cold night under the stars.

Next day we moved on again. At Debre Birhan our luck ran out. The mayor, declining our offer of whisky, declared that he had orders to stop us. During negotiations the Abyssinian equivalent of Dad's Army surrounded us, clicking the bolts of their ancient rifles. Then they hauled rocks round our lorry. It was an uncomfortable night. Too cold to sleep, we began a game of three-handed bridge. I had never played bridge, which rendered the game fraught. Waugh's reproaches were humiliating, banishing all fear of what was happening outside our little compound. Next morning they told us we must go back to Addis Ababa. We returned in mild disgrace. Lacking any other news, some journalists had sent cables to their offices about our misadventure. Sir Sidney Barton's rather stuffy interpretation was that we had let our country down. 'Old booby,' said Waugh.

Two days later, permission to go north was finally granted. By then I thought the southern front looked more promising, and with George Steer of *The Times*, Dick Sheepshanks of Reuter and two girls representing Spanish newspapers I set off for Harar. The most striking episode turned out to be the Italians' use of mustard gas on the southern front. The hospital in Harar became crowded with very nasty casualties. The Spanish girls folded their notebooks, put their newspapers on hold and went in to help. They were an attractive pair, and one of them subsequently married George Steer. By December, the *Morning Post* felt it had had enough and proposed that I returned home for Christmas.

Despairing of Waugh, the *Daily Mail* had dispatched a second correspondent, W. F. ('Binks') Hartin, whom I had met a year or so earlier when we were both working on the Brighton trunk crime, a stirring murder story of that decade. But the Abyssinians, reckoning that one *Daily Mail* representative at a time was enough, refused to allow Hartin entry until Waugh had left. Waugh, with two books in the making, was unwilling to leave. Hartin, languishing in Djibouti, unsurprisingly succumbed to dysentery. On learning of this, Waugh aggravatingly declared that he wished to hear the bells of Bethlehem at Christmas, and departed, leaving the *Daily Mail* without cover.

Years later, when preparing the introduction for a new edition of Waugh's *Black Mischief*, I persuaded *The Times* library to trace Waugh's dispatches from Addis Ababa during the Emperor's Coronation of 1930, which represented his first writing from Africa. He had boasted to me that he had posted rather than wired his principal dispatch on the Coronation itself, thus furnishing *The Times* with late and useless copy. This turned out to be quite untrue. Though anonymous, the pieces I traced from *The Times* files were unmistakable and distinguished. Waugh's failure with the *Daily Mail*, which turned on the Rickett affair, gave no fair impression of his talents. He was incomparably the best writer among us. His novel based on our adventures, *Scoop*, is rightly hailed as a classic. He was simply unwilling to submit to the disciplines of a reporter. He affected to think that our dogged responses to the demands of our foreign desks were comical and he mocked them. In reality, I sensed, his failure to give the *Daily Mail* satisfaction, starting with the Rickett story, rankled. This, I have always thought, is reflected in the plot of *Scoop*. After suffering humiliating cables from his newspaper, the *Beast*, as Waugh did, William Boot improbably triumphs in the end.

Some weeks after our return to England one of the wilder American correspondents came to look me up at the *Morning Post* office. He appeared not to have changed his clothes since leaving Abyssinia, and still wore laced riding boots, a bizarre habit and a sombrero hat. After I had entertained him in a discreet quarter of Fleet Street, he asked me where he might find Evelyn Waugh. I instructed the cab driver to drop him off at White's in St James's, and this must have scored a direct hit, for in due course I received a card from Waugh: 'That was not kind. E. W.' Some years later, when his eldest son Auberon suffered an almost fatal accident during his National Service, I sent Waugh a note of sympathy, and received a card, 'Thanks awfully. E. W.' Our paths did not cross again.

4

Children's Fund

I came back from Abyssinia to find that the march to war was quickening. Defying the Treaty of Versailles and Locarno, Hitler had entered the Rhineland. A bloody Civil War broke out in Spain. 'Italy at last has her empire,' Mussolini proclaimed from the Palazzo Venezia, as his one-sided war against the Emperor Haile Selassie ended.

I was sent to interview the Emperor on his arrival at 6 Prince's Gate. The sub-editors indulgently allowed me to open my news story with lines from *Paradise Lost*, almost certainly suggested to me by the invaluable J. C. Trewin:

> With grave
> Aspect he rose, and in his rising seem'd
> A pillar of state; deep on his front engraven
> Deliberation sat; and public care;
> And princely counsel in his face yet shone,
> Majestic though in ruin . . .

Haile Selassie sat silent and still while an official read his testimony. 'We have never desired war. It was imposed upon us. Devastated fields and ruined villages . . . the bodies of the aged and of the women and children . . .' As the statement ended with the words, 'rule of force over right', the Emperor bowed stiffly to intimate that the interview was over. On subsequent visits to Africa, I have often called his words to mind.

The *Morning Post*, increasingly alarmed by the state of our defences, asked me to make a thorough inspection of the Territorial Army in London. It was a convivial experience, because I was welcomed with much hospitality; but also a depressing one, in respect of both the anti-aircraft units and the field army. The first, on which the defence of London depended, had recruited 6,450 of the 16,892 men it needed. The London Infantry Division was below two-thirds of its establishment. Finance was stringent, equipment deficient, morale low. One of the searchlight units had two trucks, both of them made in 1917.

About this time Oswald Mosley began his London marches, the worst of which occurred in October 1936 when the British Union of Fascists attempted to march through the East End of London. By chance, I stood close to Sir Philip Game, Commissioner of Police for London, as he confronted Mosley in Aldgate ten minutes before the march was due to begin. There were 2,500 marchers on the scene. To the east, a human barrier barred their way. The Commissioner, who had the support of some 3,000 policemen, summoned Mosley and pointed the situation out to him. The interview took place on a street corner opposite the Royal Mint. It was like some bizarre scene on a battlefield. Mosley, who had arrived in an open car, accompanied by Blackshirt motorcycle patrols, declared he must have direct orders to cancel the march, and retired to consult his officers. It was at this point that rioting in Cable Street reached its height. On Mosley's return, Game repeated his order. Mosley consented and the march was turned west. Later the British Union of Fascists issued a mendacious statement, declaring: 'The decision was immediately obeyed because the British Union obeys the law and does not fight the police . . .'

A week or so later, I reported the sequel. The Communists organized a march of 10,000 anti-Fascist demonstrators from Tower Hill to Victoria Park. Windows were smashed, shops belonging to Jews in the Mile End Road were looted, there was a razor-slashing. 'The events of Sunday afternoon in White-chapel, Stepney and Bethnal Green,' I reported, 'offered a disturbing glimpse of the bitterness and hatred which six months of active political and race strife have generated in the East End of London ... East London today is threatened by open social warfare. Political passions have reached a pitch when ordinary, apparently decent citizens are ready to vilify, spit upon and injure their neighbours.' I was living in Bethnal Green and had gathered ample supporting evidence. We were witnessing a mild version of what was happening in Spain between the extremes of right and left.

In the 1970s, while I was editor of the *Daily Telegraph*, Mosley invited me twice to lunch privately at the flat he kept in West London. He was an excellent host, still physically fit and mentally alert. Though living abroad, he took such a close interest in our political scene that I found myself wondering whether he had altogether given up hope that a call might come. He was a phenomenon, rich, handsome, eloquent and to my eyes slightly dotty. He had broken away from the Labour party largely because of its failure to deal with rising unemployment. He was an apostle of direct action, and this carried a certain appeal, for his rise in the 1930s coincided with a great deal of industrial despair. Insofar as he is remembered at all, Mosley is regarded by my own generation as a nut; but he represented more than that. His underlying message was that democracy could not do the job and that something more autocratic was needed to resolve the difficulties of those times. Stalin's Russia, Mussolini's Italy, Hitler's Germany were – at that point – giving people the impression that he might be right.

The Commissioner for what were euphemistically called the Special Areas – later known as the Distressed Areas – had resigned his post with forthright criticisms of the Government's failure to attract industrialists to these regions. Alarmed by the drift of industry to the South and into London, the Commissioner, P. Malcolm Stewart, wanted state-aided inducements to counter the movement and to draw industry back to the North. Faint-hearted measures, he declared, were ineffective.

Around this time in 1936, the Jarrow marchers had set off, aiming to draw public attention to the level of unemployment there, which was the hideous figure of 68 per cent. Baldwin, Prime Minister, refused to see them on the ground that the march had been organized by the Communist party. 'This is the way civil strife begins,' he said, 'and civil strife may not end until it is civil war.' Right or wrong, his words conveyed fears which lurked in many minds at the time. Sent to witness the end of the march in Hyde Park, I described the marchers as 'exploited'. 'In ludicrous contrast to the unemployed marchers,' I wrote, 'young men and women, many of them still students at the Universities, union officials, and healthy-looking sympathizers waving red banners, shouting slogans and singing the *Internationale* made up the greater part of the procession.' In retrospect, I am not sure I would use the same words were I reporting the event today. But then I was reflecting the sympathies of the *Morning Post*, for which all left-wing activity bore sinister implications.

The climax to all these misgivings came when in November 1936, and close to the end of his reign, King Edward VIII visited the Welsh valleys and saw the stricken Dowlais steel works outside Merthyr Tydfil. There he delivered a judgement which reverberated round the country like a thunderclap, and has echoed down the years. His actual words were: 'These steel works brought the men here. Something must be done to see that they stay here working.' 'Something must be done' made the headline. I was not on the tour, but I heard a lot about it from other journalists who were, and from my uncle Sir Wyndham Deedes, with whom I resided in Bethnal Green. He worked closely with Lionel Ellis of the National Council of Social Services, who had accompanied the King and who witnessed at first hand the strain he was under.

But to set this in its proper context, I have to jog back to the early summer of 1936, when it became clear that the press of America (where Mrs Simpson was a citizen) was being far less restrained in commenting on her affair with the King than we British journalists were. My editor, H. A. Gwynne, took it into his head to convey this to the Prime Minister, and I was called on to gather the evidence with which Gwynne hoped to convince him. This was not particularly easy because the wholesale distributors of overseas publications were understandably apprehensive of libel. Mrs Simpson, in the eyes of the law at that time, was still the wife of Ernest Simpson. They therefore cut or blacked out passages in overseas publications which could give offence. Working through Hachette, the international publishers and distributors, I garnered a bundle of cuttings and passed them to Gwynne.

Gwynne showed them to the Prime Minister, who we now know was already acquainted with most of the facts. He said he must have more time. There was an interval. It seemed to me the situation was becoming untenable. A flood of information from overseas was building up which sooner rather than later would breach the dam we had created. The *Morning Post* possessed some fine writers. I felt we were the right newspaper to bridge the gap between established facts and public knowledge of them. Looking back, I recognize that I was motivated barely at all by the public interest, much more by the prospect of securing for the *Morning Post* a vulgar scoop. Baldwin then repeated his plea to Gwynne for more time.

I have often been asked to explain why the newspapers in 1936 showed such restraint by contrast, say, with the way in which the Royal Family's private affairs are reported today. Until 1 December, when Dr A. W. F. Blunt, Bishop of Bradford delivered his fateful homily to the King, virtually nothing about King Edward's association with Mrs Simpson had appeared in our own national press. Indeed, Dr Blunt had not intended his remarks, delivered to his Diocesan Conference, to be much more than a rebuff to Bishop Barnes, the somewhat outspoken

Bishop of Birmingham, who had suggested that the Coronation should be secularized. But after such a long period of strained silence, Blunt's mildly reproachful words, given prominence in the *Yorkshire Post*, acted as a sort of starting pistol.

On 27 October of that year Mrs Wallis Simpson was granted at the Ipswich Assizes a decree nisi by Mr Justice Hawke on grounds of adultery by her husband, Ernest Simpson. *The Times* carried twelve lines about this, the *Morning Post* a ten-point paragraph, the *Daily Telegraph* twenty-two lines – but on an away page, sandwiched between 'Colonel accused in private' and 'Boy with a mania for silk stockings'. The co-respondent in the case was a professional lady named Marigold. I have often visualized her sitting fully clothed in Mr Simpson's bedroom, virtuously knitting or sewing, but providing just sufficiently compromising evidence for the waiter who brought in early-morning tea. Imagine what the tabloids of today would have made of her!

Some historians have attributed the unnatural silence of the newspapers to a conspiracy among the press lords. I have never accepted this. Lord Beaverbrook, who owned the Express Group, and Lord Rothermere of the *Daily Mail*, *Sunday Dispatch*, and *Evening News* sometimes hunted together. Neither Lord Camrose of the *Daily Telegraph* nor his editor H. A. Gwynne of the *Morning Post* was likely to enter any pact with him. Nor was Geoffrey Dawson of *The Times*. The plain truth is that newspapers showed more deference to the Royal Family in those days than they do now. There was also a far greater distance kept between Royalty's close circle of friends and the rest of us. Gossip was harder to obtain. And of course there was this risk of a writ for libel from the Simpson *ménage*.

After the abdication, most of the arrows were directed at Baldwin and the Archbishop of Canterbury, who for a while were accused by a minority of conspiring to rid the country of a politically dangerous king. I did not hear Baldwin's final speech to the House of Commons; but years later Tommy

Dugdale, then his parliamentary private secretary, told me a remarkable story about its delivery which is not in the history books. He and Baldwin had gone to the House of Commons together. Suddenly Baldwin began to feel in his pockets for the notes of his speech, which had been hastily put together on scraps of paper. He drew a blank. Dugdale hastened back to 10 Downing Street, picked up a clue on the staircase and followed a trail of paper back to the loo. It was like a paperchase, he said.

On the day of the King's departure from the country, what we now call a 'reliable source' told me he expected the King to leave from Lympne airport in east Kent. It sounded a likely tale, for Lympne was barely twenty-five miles from the coast of France and was close to Port Lympne, then the home of Sir Philip Sassoon, a long-standing friend of the King's. I had a hard decision to make. My eldest sister was having her coming-of-age dance in a Folkestone hotel. I reached a compromise with our news editor. I would attend the dance in my white tie and tails. The *Morning Post* would provide a car and driver so that I could keep an eye on the airport during the night – a journey of about fifteen miles. I did this two or three times and around midnight, for some inexplicable reason, I found the place lit up and bustling. It must have been a mirage. The King, as we learned next morning, had left the country by destroyer. During the course of the evening we stopped the dancing to hear his valedictory speech. I stood beside a girl of whom I was fond. When we went back on the floor, we danced in silence. Neither of us could think of anything to say.

What echoed on for me – for three years as it turned out – were the King's words, 'Something must be done.' The *Morning Post* chose to see this as a challenge. It would send by post, anonymously, to arrive on Christmas morning, a present to every child of unemployed parents in the Distressed Areas – South Wales, West Cumberland and Tyneside. I was invited to take charge of this enterprise. I think the stars chose to shine on our endeavours for they met with a remarkable response.

What happened provides a true portrait of England in those days, which is worth giving in some detail.

Plainly I had to obtain the name, age, sex and address of every child whose father was unemployed. The presents were to be addressed to children between the ages of three and thirteen. With the blessing and help of the Board of Education, as it then was, we wrote to all the school teachers in the Distressed Areas and asked for their help. The request, mark you, came from a strongly Conservative, true-blue newspaper. To the best of my recollection, no teacher declined. The lists rolled in. I had approached five of London's biggest stores, the Army and Navy, Harrods, Civil Service Supply Association, Marshal and Snelgrove, and Selfridges. All agreed to help. Indeed, most of them did more than that. We had determined that each gift must be worth at least half a crown. The shops generously threw in toys worth considerably more than that. Their staffs volunteered to work overtime on the packing and addressing for nothing. After a day's work in the office, one or two of us would tour the packing centres and cheer them on.

In that first year the total of children involved was about 120,000, so that each store had about 25,000 parcels to prepare. The Post Office and the railways perceived that extra resources would be needed on Christmas Eve and Day, and set about providing them. Meanwhile, my colleague J. C. Trewin was touring the Distressed Areas and writing about them in a style which greatly assisted my appeal to *Morning Post* readers for the necessary funds. The King himself sent us a cheque – it must have been one of the last to go out in his name. His mother, Queen Mary, not only sent a donation but took a close personal interest in our efforts. We raised the money.

On Christmas Eve, the news editor of the *Morning Post*, Mervyn Ellis, and I travelled to South Wales, indulging ourselves in a bottle of champagne for dinner on the Cardiff express. On Christmas Day we toured the valleys. The weather was fine, and what we saw fulfilled all our hopes. Nor was that quite the end. When schools resumed after Christmas, some of the teachers (who of course knew the source) asked children to send us letters of thanks. In recent years I have had more than one letter from those who had received a present and remembered it.

When, towards the end of 1937, the *Morning Post* died and some of us moved over to the *Daily Telegraph*, Lord Camrose asked if I would take it on again. In return for more professional help than had been available on the *Morning Post*, I agreed. In this second year, 42,000 readers responded to the appeal and 214,000 children received presents. The much higher figure, I have always supposed, came about because teachers included deserving children as well as those with unemployed fathers. In 1938, the last year before war overtook us, Lancashire had been added to the Distressed Areas and presents went out to 261,000 children.

In these two final years my task was enriched by the close association I had to keep with H. J. C. Stevens, the talented but irascible chief accountant and secretary of the Daily Telegraph Ltd. He had been appointed by Viscount Camrose some years earlier at the age of twenty-eight, and had become in every sense chief steward of his lordship's interests. As he worked on the open mezzanine floor of our old office at 135 Fleet Street, and was often in the corridor berating someone about money, he also conveyed the impression of being the newspaper's chief custodian.

He was a demon on reporters' expenses. One morning I strolled into the office to find Leonard Crawley, then our golf correspondent, fuming in the hall. Dressed in battered plus-fours, pale-blue stockings and a torn shooting jacket, he had just returned from the Masters of Augusta in America, and was making a rare visit to the office to collect his expenses. 'I envy you,' I said. He turned a bloodshot eye towards me. 'Bill,' he said in a voice on the brink of rage, 'I have just flown the Atlantic in a cheap seat – because apparently this office cannot afford anything better – sitting next to a negress breast-feeding twins. My old friend – and, Bill, he is an old friend – Sam Snead gave me a new set of woods. They have been impounded by the Customs. And now, that old b—' – he waved a hand distastefully in the direction of H. J. C. Stevens's office – 'has queried my expenses!'

Stevens and I got on well, but nobody would have thought it after hearing our daily exchanges while the Children's Fund was in progress. He had convinced himself that the Fund would bankrupt Lord Camrose. 'His Lordship must be off his head,' he would snort, 'and *you* in charge!' Every morning after the post had been opened and the money counted, he rejoiced to tell me how far behind target we had fallen. 'I tell you, his Lordship faces ruin over this!' He also objected to the secretary I had appointed for the duration of the appeal. She was an excellent girl, willing to work all hours and at week-ends, which is why I had chosen her; but she aspired to be a film actress and turned herself out on those lines. 'You and your Miss Scarlet Lips,' Stevens would snarl. 'In the office at all hours . . . hanky panky . . . I know.' After we closed the Fund, I took her out for a sumptuous lunch in West London – and that was all there was to it. Stevens, who was among other things vicar's warden at St Bride's Church in Fleet Street, chose to see it otherwise. 'Why does she have to dress like that? Tell me . . . Has his Lordship seen her?' To torment him further, I would respond by giving him a sly smile and closing one eye.

The climax to our relations, however, came about for other reasons. In 1938, the Fund's final year, the gift side had been turned over to other, more experienced hands. I wrote the daily appeal and progress report for our readers, while travelling in the Distressed Areas at week-ends to find suitable material. For one week-end I chose Merthyr Tydfil and the desolate steel plant at Dowlais which had so moved the King. Arthur Watson, then editor, heard of my plans and asked if I thought it was really a wise choice. Our owners, the Berry family, he pointed out, had at one time owned the Dowlais steel plant before the Great Depression. They might not welcome a tear-jerking piece from me about it. I held Arthur Watson in respect, but on this occasion I felt he was doing our owners too little justice. As it turned out, I found a better tear-wringer than the Dowlais plant.

Late one misty winter evening on the hill between Merthyr and Dowlais, I came across a girl of about nine peering longingly into the window of a toyshop. She had her arm round a much younger brother. Clad in a boy's worn jacket far too big for her, she was a child of her times, with a thin white face and faint blue circles under her eyes. To a reporter seeking copy to move the hearts of *Daily Telegraph* readers, she was a dream. On the train back to London that Saturday night I scribbled away and gave her the imaginary name of Elizabeth. This had unforeseen consequences. Some readers instantly switched from the main appeal to 'Elizabeth'. They offered to adopt her, pay for her education, send her food and clothing. Cheques arrived marked 'for Elizabeth'. Stevens was beside himself with rage. 'You and your blasted little Rosie,' he cried, 'you'll be the ruin of his Lordship. False pretences ... that's what they'll get us on. How are you going to get out of it?' I forget what we did, but the crisis passed. Thereafter, Stevens never let me forget little Rosie, as he persisted in calling her. Years later, after I had become editor and he was happily still with us, if we had the smallest difference of opinion, he would invoke her: 'Remember your little Rosie!' She is etched in my memory. If she lived, she would now be drawing her old-age pension.

5

Prelude to War

At the close of 1936, the *Morning Post* appointed me its political or lobby correspondent, with what at that time was the generous salary of £15 a week, plus an expense allowance of £5 for which no accounting was required. In those days the Inland Revenue was easier about such matters than it is now. Much later in life I compared notes with a former chairman of ICI, who had been earning roughly the same amount in the 1930s. We came to the conclusion that we had never felt quite so rich since. I succeeded in the lobby H. J. Wilson, one of a famous Fleet Street family, who only a year or so earlier had succeeded the veteran R. G. Emery. After fifty years as *Morning Post* political correspondent, Emery had retired, with a silver coffee service from the Cabinet. He was reputed to take a pint of ale and a steak for his breakfast. The fact that he had been in the lobby with Mr Gladstone gave the position considerable lustre at the *Morning Post*, and I felt called upon to dress the part. I went to my tailor in Sackville Street to discuss clothes. By a stroke of luck, one of his clients was the Government's Chief Whip, Captain Margesson, a handsome, well-dressed former cavalryman. My tailor, a Mr Keogh, declared that I must be no less well dressed and turned out one or two superbly cut black jackets to go with striped trousers. To these, whimsically, I added a fresh clove carnation every day. It helped Ministers and Members to identify the *Morning Post* man.

At that time, the corps of lobby correspondents was less than a tenth the size it has become today. There were, I think, about twenty-four of us. Only the *Daily Express* had two men in the lobby. The rest of us flew solo. I reached an amicable arrangement with Harry Boardman of the *Manchester Guardian* and Arthur Holdsworth of the *Yorkshire Post* whereby we pooled all but genuine scoops. The lobby itself, like a secret society, had some odd conventions which it took time to discover.

Soon after I arrived, for example, I encountered the Tory Member for Rye, Sir George Courthope, who had been my father's fag at Eton, or the other way round. It offered a pretext for approaching him. Sir George proved unexpectedly forthcoming. A Select Committee of the House of Commons was sitting at the time, early 1937, to discuss the King's Civil List. There was talk of transferring the revenues of the Duchy of Cornwall to the Treasury. King George VI was involved in financial arrangements being made for his elder brother, the former King Edward VIII, now Duke of Windsor. Sir George was a member of this Select Committee. He seemed eager to discuss these confidential matters with me. I was astounded, but listened to all he had to say. It led the paper next day.

A day or two later I was approached by an officer of the lobby journalists. We understand, he said heavily, that you have been seen talking to Sir George Courthope. Indeed, I said. 'Were you not aware that the lobby does not speak with Sir George Courthope?' No, I said, and explained that I had conversed with him because he had been at school with my father. It transpired that donkey's years earlier Sir George (it was alleged) had been rude to a lobby journalist. As a punishment, they elected to ostracize him. He became a 'non-person'. Ignorant of his fate, he simply forgot what it was like to be approached by a political correspondent. I must have made his day when I introduced myself. The *Morning Post* had been well pleased by the outcome. So I took the rebuke for breaking the embargo on Sir George Courthope in a good spirit, while reflecting on what a rum circle I had joined.

It was a good time to be close to politics. In the first story I wrote early in the New Year of 1937, I listed some of the issues which would be before the Cabinet. The Spanish Civil War was raging, and so was controversy about whether or not we should intervene. There was a tussle going on between defence departments – wakening from a long sleep – and the Treasury. There would be legislation to give more help to the Distressed Areas. The Coronation of King George VI and Queen Elizabeth lay just ahead.

One afternoon a friendly source warned me that all work on a huge redevelopment scheme in Whitehall (which now houses the Ministry of Defence) was about to stop. At 550 feet long and 330 feet broad, with accommodation for 5,400 Civil Servants, it had been deemed too big a target for air attack. The story rang alarm bells in Whitehall and was energetically denied, but it was true. So the shadow from Europe grew longer. British volunteers were flocking to Spain to fight Franco. In horrors like the air raid on Guernica, the dictators Mussolini and Hitler were said to be showing their hand.

Our National Government at this time presented an unreassuring appearance. It had swept into total power in 1931 on the tailwind of a financial panic. In 1935, while I was in Abyssinia, it had been returned at a General Election with a reduced but still ample majority. Ramsay MacDonald who had been more or less ordered by King George V to take command in 1931, had handed over the reins to Stanley Baldwin in 1935, as we have noted. Baldwin, who suffered frequently from nervous exhaustion, planned to go after the Coronation in May 1937. Neville Chamberlain was in line to succeed him.

Early in 1937, lobby correspondents were summoned to take farewell of Ramsay MacDonald. We sat in a small room awaiting his return from Buckingham Palace, where he had been taking his leave from the King. He eventually arrived with a parcel under his arm which he set down carefully. Then, because of his rapidly failing sight, he asked us all to turn our chairs round so that light from the window fell on us. More in sorrow than in anger, he proceeded gently to reproach one of our number, Ernest Hunter, political correspondent of the *Daily Herald*. The *Herald*, a Labour paper, had been pretty brutal to MacDonald after he had sunk the Labour Government of 1929–31, taken command of a national administration and acquired the reputation of a traitor from all loyal Labour supporters. Hunter wept.

That scene accomplished, Ramsay MacDonald turned to his parcel, which he slowly unwrapped. This, he told us, was the only gift that he had sought from their Majesties. He had declined the high honour to which a Prime Minister was then entitled. Instead, he had asked for a signed portrait of the King and Queen. This gesture must have been arranged some time earlier, because the portrait had been duly signed and was neatly framed. Worn out by his extraordinary career – at one point MacDonald had been his own Foreign Secretary as well as Prime Minister – he died later the same year.

In the early 1990s, while golfing in Scotland, I visited his birthplace and his grave. Born illegitimately, and mistrusted for his opposition to the First World War, he became Labour's first Prime Minister in 1924. Until overwork drove him almost dotty in the mid-1930s, he was a considerable figure. History will treat him in kindlier fashion than the Labour party of the 1930s did.

In May of that year, 1937, Baldwin went, but more memorably. On the eve of the Coronation an ugly dispute in the coalfields threatened at Haworth colliery in Yorkshire. Clement Attlee, then Leader of the Labour Opposition, called for a debate on a motion for the adjournment of the House. I shall speak, Baldwin told an intimate overnight, but we will not inform our colleagues. On the afternoon of 5 May 1937 he rose to follow Attlee and made what was suddenly perceived to be his last speech to the Commons. After touching on the coal dispute, he rehearsed the industrial philosophy of his life, an echo of a famous speech he had made in March 1925 on the Trades Disputes Bill.

Then he came to peroration:

The whole world has its eye today on London. The whole world is represented in London, and they are coming here to be with us in what, to the vast majority of our people, will be a period of rejoicing for many days, culminating in that age-long Service in the Abbey a week today. In the Abbey on this day week our young King and Queen, who were called suddenly and unexpectedly to the most tremendous position on earth, will kneel and dedicate themselves to the service of their people, a service which can only be ended by death. I appeal to that handful of men with whom rests peace or war to give the best present to the country that could be given at that moment, to do the one thing which would rejoice the hearts of all the people who love this country, that is to rend and dissipate this dark cloud which has gathered over us, and show the people of the world that this democracy can still at least practise the arts of peace in a world of strife.

As Baldwin sat down, there was a moment of absolute stillness. Then I saw Emmanuel Shinwell, who was due to follow him, deliberately tear up the notes of his speech. The debate was virtually over. The House soon adjourned. Baldwin had his faults, but he had a gift for such occasions. Observe how many words in that unpolished peroration are of one syllable. In making such speeches, Baldwin drained himself emotionally. One of his last speeches outside the House of Commons was delivered in Westminster Hall to a gathering of ex-servicemen from all parts of the Empire. Baldwin spoke of having to brush aside ghosts of the dead as he entered the Hall. When the speech was finished, he retired to the Smoke Room with his parliamentary private secretary, Tommy Dugdale, later Lord Crathorne. There he asked for several measures of sherry in a tumbler and drank it down. 'There was no question of tippling,' Dugdale told me years later. 'It was as if he had suffered a haemorrhage, as if something vital had drained out of him and had to be replaced.'

On the night of the Coronation, Baldwin had made a short broadcast, which closed with the words: 'Let us dedicate ourselves – let us dedicate ourselves afresh, if need be – to the service of our fellows, a service in widening circles, service to the home, service to our neighbourhood, to our county, our province, to our country, to the Empire, and to the world.' Then with an unconscious echo of the General Thanksgiving, he concluded: 'No mere service of our lips, service of our lives, as we know will be the service of our King and Queen, God bless them.' Young men and women in politics, who aspire to move audiences, as not many can today, would do well to study Baldwin's style. He aimed at classical simplicity. Churchill, who had been influenced by Macaulay, had a more rotund style.

Many, who saw Baldwin as the man who had neglected our defences, in 'years the locusts have stolen', as he put it, came to despise him and saw no virtue in him. I have never concealed my admiration not merely for his speeches, but for the way in which at times like the General Strike of 1926 and in the industrial turmoil of the 1930s he contrived to hold his party and the country together. The two decades between the world wars were industrially bitter. The Great Depression destabilized much of Europe and severely tested us. Yet we contrived to enter the Second World War more or less a united nation. Baldwin's contribution to that has been underrated. I have always been thankful that I was there to witness his final days. David Lloyd George, perhaps the best debating speaker in this century, was also there in 1937. I heard him only on a couple of occasions when he was past his best and increasingly mischievous, but he still had the knack of making opponents look remarkably foolish with spontaneous banter.

Though in the lobby only a short time, I made many

political friends there, several of them, such as Arthur Jenkins, father of Roy, on the Labour side. Arthur Jenkins, a miner most of his life, still bore the marks of a coal explosion on his face. One day Sir Philip Sassoon, then First Commissioner of Works, approached me and proposed a game of golf. He was Member for Hythe and Folkestone, our local seat. He suggested that we play on the Hythe golf course, of which we were both members. It was a singular experience. Sir Philip had chartered four caddies, all of whom he paid for. Two carried our clubs, two went forward to observe where our drives finished. Thus we were able to canter round this hilly course without ever pausing to look for a ball. We finished in not much over two hours. Turning our backs on any form of refreshment, we jumped into a waiting car and were driven fast to the sea, where Sir Philip kept an extensive beach hut. After five minutes in the water, we raced back to the hut and changed rapidly. I had cut my foot slightly. Waving a hand towards a well-stocked first-aid cabinet, Sir Philip tore off to Port Lympne a mile or so away, with promise of a second car to bring me to lunch.

As I limped into Port Lympne, Sassoon's cousin Mrs Gubbay greeted me. 'What have you been doing to Philip?' she asked. 'He has retired to bed, exhausted.' My host recovered in time for our lunch, and then proposed a game of tennis. His cousin, a woman in her late forties, beat him soundly. 'He cheats so dreadfully,' she said, as if dealing with a small child. He then proposed a quick flip from Lympne aerodrome across the way, where he kept a light plane. I pleaded another engagement. This was his style of life, and it did him no good at all, for he died a relatively young man of a sudden infection a year or two later.

I had been in the lobby about six months when Lord Camrose of the *Daily Telegraph* bought the *Morning Post*. There followed an interval, while we speculated on his likely intentions. My friends in the House of Commons were solicitous. Brendan Bracken, whom I had come to know while campaigning with the Churchills, invited me to keep in touch. Harold Nicolson proved a good friend. By September, Camrose had made his decision. The *Morning Post*, the oldest daily newspaper in England, closed its doors. In its final issue on 30 September 1937, six years after I had entered the office, I had the doubtful satisfaction of leading the newspaper with the Cabinet's decision to address a note to Mussolini on the withdrawal of foreign troops in Spain. A long leader headed 'Farewell, and Hail!' was written by the editor, H. A. Gwynne. He was retired on a pension rumoured to be £5,000 a year.

For most of the rest of our small staff, the outcome was less happy. A few of us accepted fresh appointments at the *Daily Telegraph*. Older members of the *Morning Post* staff were retired. Most other newspapers behaved generously with offers, particularly the *Daily Mail* and the *Daily Express*. What is *The Times* doing? someone asked, as we sat over a gloomy beer in Fleet Street soon after the fall. As one whose future seemed secure, I was deputed to explore this. I rang a shipowner, Sir Philip Haldin, with whose daughter I was friendly, and who had promised any support I might need with *The Times*. Then I went round to Printing House Square, and sent in my card to Barrington Ward, who was deputy editor to Geoffrey Dawson. He received me graciously, heard my request for a job, and called for a form which I had to fill in. An early entry was not 'Which university?' but 'Which college?', the assumption being presumably that one could only have been at Oxford. That side of my education having been cut off by the Wall Street crash of 1929, I fell at the first fence and so reported to my colleagues.

On arrival at the *Daily Telegraph*, I was told that the post of political correspondent was already occupied, but not entirely to the newspaper's satisfaction. The occupant was a former Member of Parliament, who had to his own astonishment won some Labour stronghold in the North after the landslide of 1931, had then lost the seat in 1935 and, though possessed of little professional experience, had been awarded the job as political correspondent. It was proposed that I filled some of the gaps he left. I saw small joy in that, only a series of muddles. So I became a general reporter again, but with increasing responsibility for civil defence and air-raid precautions, the deficiencies of which were becoming a live political issue. I also joined forces with Victor Gordon Lennox, then the newspaper's diplomatic correspondent, whom I occasionally assisted.

This last association proved a fortunate arrangement, for it afforded me a front seat at Neville Chamberlain's Munich a year later. By then I knew a good deal about the state of the country's defences and so had a fair idea of the cards Chamberlain held. News of Hitler's invasion of Austria in March 1938, for example, reached me at breakfast in Wiltshire, after I had flown most of the night on an RAF exercise in a Vickers Virginia bomber stationed at Boscombe Down. The plane had a cruising speed of 90 m.p.h. It had a small cockpit on the tail for a rear gunner. From this I observed an experimental blackout over part of England. Many were surprised by Hitler's audacity at the time of Munich. After this flight with the RAF and other similar experiences, I was less surprised. 'The prime factor of uncertainty in the world today is the menace from the air,' Winston Churchill had written at the time. That was true. As I investigated our chronic state of unreadiness to meet this uncertainty, the future began to take shape in my mind.

In the spring of 1938, so I recorded at the time, London had recruited less than one-fifth of the 120,000 air-raid precautions volunteers it needed. Outer London had 7,700 volunteers out of 40,000. The same state of affairs prevailed in most of our big cities – Liverpool, Manchester, Sheffield and so on. A month after Hitler had invaded Austria, I wrote an article about air-raid precautions for the *Daily Telegraph* which carried this sentence: 'If peace could be guaranteed until the end of 1939 – some 20 months ahead – we could afford to view the rate of progress with equanimity; but for any emergency which might arise, say, before the end of this year, the whole of the civilian population and London in particular is still highly vulnerable.'

It was not until June 1938 that Geoffrey Lloyd, then parliamentary under-secretary in the Home Office, was called on to give all his time to air-raid precautions. We became closely acquainted. Only weeks before Chamberlain flew to Germany, plans for evacuating people from our threatened cities were incomplete. 'The bomber will always get through,' Baldwin had said. That was the factor that weighed on everybody's mind. The more I saw of experiments with modern bombs, and with mustard and phosgene gas, which everyone expected to be used against them, the clearer it became to me that we could not yet go to war. To do so would expose our urban population to a war from the air for which we were grievously unprepared. That was the consideration uppermost in the Cabinet's mind as Neville Chamberlain shuttled back and forth between London and Germany. I went to Paris to report on the French preparations. They were no better than our own. Eventually I secured permission to do the same in Germany. At the last minute some hitch arose, and the visit was cancelled.

Why were we so woefully unprepared? The answer which has been handed down to us by most historians of that time is that Ministers in the mid-1930s, after the advent of Hitler, lacked the courage to tell the country we had urgently to rearm. That belief was enormously strengthened by an entry in the index of Churchill's first volume of war memoirs, *The Gathering Storm*: 'Baldwin: confesses putting party before country'. In a speech of what he called 'appalling frankness' to the House of Commons in November in 1936, Baldwin had put a noose round his neck by saying this: 'Supposing I had gone to the country and said that Germany was rearming and we must rearm, does anybody think that this pacific democracy would have rallied to that cry at that moment? I cannot think of anything that would have made the loss of the election [1935] from my point of view more certain.'

Baldwin hanged himself politically with that admission, yet he was right. As a reporter of those times I knew what a 'pacific democracy' we were. I was also just old enough in the early 1920s to sense how deeply the slaughter of 1914–18 had implanted in hearts and minds the resolution 'Never again'. When I began work as a journalist in 1931, we were only a little over twelve years away from that slaughter. Hearts were still bleeding. Some of my mother's women friends, who had lost lovers on the Western Front, would remain spinsters for the rest of their lives. In his novel *Tender Is the Night*, Scott Fitzgerald caught the authentic note. Dick Diver and his friends are going over the old trenches near the hill of Thiepval:

> 'See that little stream – we could walk to it in two minutes. It took the British a month to walk to it – a whole empire walking very slowly, dying in front and pushing forward behind. And another empire walked very slowly backward a few inches a day, leaving the dead like a million bloody rugs. No European will ever do that again in this generation . . .
>
> Dick Diver added: 'This western-front business couldn't be done again, not for a long time. The young men think they could do it, but they couldn't. They could fight the first Marne again, but not this. This took religion and years of plenty and tremendous sureties and the exact relations that existed between the classes. The Russians and the Italians weren't any good on this front. You had to have a whole-souled sentimental equipment going back further than you could remember. You had to remember Christmas, and the postcards of the Crown Prince and his fiancée, and the little cafés in Valence and beer gardens in Unter den Linden and weddings at the mairie, and going to the Derby, and your grandfather's whiskers . . .

'Why this was a love battle – there was a century of middle-class love spent here. This was the last love battle . . .'

That well conveys the mood that I remember. Books were still appearing and being serialized in the Sunday newspapers which revealed appalling truths about battles on the Somme, at Passchendaele, Ypres and Verdun. There was Blunden, Sassoon and Wilfred Owen. Then we had, first as a book, then as film, *All Quiet on the Western Front*. Never again. Never again.

Of course, Churchill was right from the mid-1930s onwards constantly to parade before the House of Commons the German order of march and our own deficiencies. But in a democracy like ours the question is whether the programme of rearmament he sought would have won the support of electors in 1935. My judgement is that it would not. R. A. ('Rab') Butler, then a slowly rising star, has recorded how he was reviled in the 1935 General Election campaign as a warmonger and a militarist on the issue of more arms. And if Labour had won, do we really suppose that a stronger programme of rearmament would have been set in hand? Labour put its faith in the League of Nations and 'collective security'. The League, which America had never joined, was without Japan, Germany and Italy; and, as I had learned from the Abyssinian War of 1935, was virtually toothless. 'Collective security' was founded on the misconception that the more nations alarmed by Hitler banded together, the less rearming each one had to do. In any case, the National Government was engaged in an expanding rearmament programme, though it was always behind Germany's. And Churchill, who had fought against independence for India, and had supported the Duke of Windsor, carried nothing like the weight we attribute to him today.

Neville Chamberlain, who succeeded Baldwin while I was in the lobby, had built his reputation on two offices, as Minister of Health 1924–9 and as Chancellor of the Exchequer 1931–7, an exceptionally difficult period. It has been often said that this political experience in home departments rendered him unreliable in foreign affairs. I am not sure about that. Anthony Eden was pre-eminently a Foreign Office man, yet when he finally succeeded Churchill at No. 10, it was his misjudgement over Suez that brought him down. There was, however, an ominous streak of obstinacy in Chamberlain, which none of his colleagues could overcome. The only man who might have done it was Lord Swinton, who as Air Minister got the Spitfire and radar on to our drawing board and who, in my view, emerges untarnished from those times. But after the 1935 election Swinton mistakenly chose to go the Lords and in May 1938 Chamberlain unaccountably sacked him.

Ian Colvin, whom I mentioned earlier as a close colleague of mine on the *Morning Post* and (many years later) the *Daily Telegraph*, and one of Churchill's pre-war sources of intelligence in Berlin, wrote a book about Chamberlain's Cabinet. Swinton described to Colvin his final interview with Chamberlain: 'He gave me no reason: but the row over air strength was going on in Parliament. He wanted a quiet political life and he didn't believe war was coming. He offered me other jobs in the Cabinet . . .' In 1971, not long before he died, I had lunch with Swinton at his home in Yorkshire. He had given me good advice at one point of my life in politics, and I had grown fond of him. I opened conventionally. 'How are you, sir?' 'Well,' he replied, 'my sight is bad, my hearing unreliable, my legs have given up. Pretty well everything has gone, except what my friends are kind enough to call my mind.' Chamberlain got rid of that mind too soon.

So we were not ready. But why does Munich carry such an ineradicable stigma of disgrace? It was because, in order to save our bacon, we forced Czechoslovakia to make humiliating concessions to Hitler – all of which proved wholly in vain. As I expressed it many years later in a piece I wrote for the *Spectator*: 'This proud Empire sacrificed a small power to slavery. That is what turned stomachs. There is the blot we shall never quite be able to sponge away.'

Historians of *The Times*, which likes to record its own history, have to their credit never tried to conceal or brush over the part it played in this. On 7 September 1938 Geoffrey Dawson and his deputy Barrington Ward produced an editorial suggesting that Czechoslovakia might become a homogeneous state by 'the secession of that fringe of alien populations which are contiguous to the nation with which they are united by race'. This of course was a reference to the Sudeten Germans, on whose behalf Hitler was ostensibly barking.

The Foreign Office immediately issued a statement dissociating the Government from *The Times*' proposal. The world read it otherwise. In any case, on the previous day Rab Butler, then parliamentary under-secretary at the Foreign Office, had seen (or thought he had seen) Geoffrey Dawson leaving after a long interview with the Foreign Secretary, Lord Halifax. It was, as I later explain, no end of a lesson for editors to keep a hygienic distance between rulers and themselves. During my time as editor of the *Daily Telegraph*, I tried to bear it in mind.

It was not the only episode in which *The Times* revealed its true colours at that time. My closest friend there was Anthony Winn, who had joined the paper in 1938 as a lobby correspondent. He wrote a story about Duff Cooper's resignation as First Lord of the Admiralty (in protest against appeasement) on 3 October. Dawson spiked it, and wrote a version more critical of Duff Cooper. Winn resigned. 'My distaste for what I frankly regard as a silly and dangerous policy has been hardening for weeks,' he wrote to Dawson. He joined us at the *Daily Telegraph*, but our friendship had not long to run. He was killed in action in Egypt late in 1942. When I think back to Munich, I think of friends like Tony Winn and Ronald Cartland, who saw more clearly than I did where appeasement was taking us, who hated it, and eventually had to die for it.

When the crisis finally came upon us, Chamberlain made three separate expeditions to Germany. I watched him climb into his little plane at Heston for the second of these at 8.30 one autumn morning, Tuesday, 22 September 1938. 'Unknown to Mr Chamberlain,' I wrote, 'almost the entire Cabinet had arranged late on Monday night to be present at Heston to wish him Godspeed on his fateful journey.' My mother had a snapshot of the Heston take-off, in which I featured, but she did not approve of the shape of the hat I was wearing – a porkpie homburg – and the picture was spirited away.

Chamberlain, I reported for the *Daily Telegraph*, walked through a line of cheering friends, then stepped up to the microphone and delivered these homilies: 'When I was a little boy, I used to repeat, if at first you don't succeed, try, try, try again. When I get back, I hope I may be able to say as Hotspur in *Henry IV*, "Out of this nettle, danger, we pluck the flower safety."' Alas, when he got to Bad Godesberg, the nettles had grown thicker. He returned empty-handed, to find that his Cabinet's mood had stiffened. No more concessions to Hitler. In Cabinet, Duff Cooper on the brink of resignation proposed general mobilization as the only way to deter Germany from war. This intervention led to a lively discussion, with Chamberlain opposing the idea.

But on the night of 27 September there came the announcement that the British Fleet was being mobilized. Against that solemn background, Chamberlain rose on the 28th to give some account of events to the House of Commons. He had almost concluded his forlorn survey when a note was hurriedly passed to him. Harold Nicolson has described the scene:

He adjusted his pince-nez and read the document that had been handed to him. His whole face, his whole body seemed to change. He raised his face so that the light from the ceiling fell full upon it. All the lines of anxiety and weariness seemed suddenly to have been smoothed out: he appeared years younger and triumphant. 'Herr Hitler', he said, 'has just agreed to postpone his mobilization for 24 hours and to meet me in conference with Signor Mussolini and M. Daladier at Munich.'

So it came about. On his final return at Heston and from the windows of 10 Downing Street, Chamberlain flourished the agreement he and Hitler had signed at Munich, saying: 'This is the second time in our history that there has come back from Germany to Downing Street peace with honour. I believe it is peace in our time.' Immediately he had said this, he regretted it. Alec Home, then his parliamentary private secretary, declared that the mistake haunted him for the few remaining years of his life.

I returned from these scenes, confused in my mind, to a sceptical office. Our acerbic night editor, Bob Skelton, met me in the corridor, shouted for early copy (as they always do) and aimed a mock blow at my midriff, declaring, 'You young fellows are for it!' Victor Gordon Lennox, our diplomatic correspondent, was even grimmer. He worked closely in those days with Helen Kirkpatrick, a young American journalist who had been reporting in Europe. She and Victor ran the *Whitehall Newsletter*, designed to warn Western leaders of Hitler's intentions. It enjoyed a distinguished readership in London, and when Victor asked if I were prepared to join it, I was tempted. I was deeply attracted by Helen Kirkpatrick. But it was not the moment to leave mainstream journalism. Of the Munich pact Kirkpatrick wrote at the time: 'This truce may well induce rather than prevent war.' Early in 1939 she produced a book for British readers, entitled *This Terrible Peace*. With her good looks, brilliant academic record in America and Geneva, and sleepy drawl, Kirkpatrick was impressive.

In the summer of 1938, Victor and his wife, Kirkpatrick and I spent an evening watching the Tidworth Military Tattoo. The massed bands played 'Fair Rose of England'. Lights came up on the surrounding hills. For some reason at that moment I became convinced that war was inevitable. William Stoneman, chief of the *Chicago Daily News* bureau in London, whom I had come to know well during the Abyssinian War, recognized Helen Kirkpatrick's talents and hired her. Then she set about persuading Colonel Frank Knox, publisher of the *Chicago Daily News* – which refused to have women on its staff overseas – to change its policy. He refused, but decided to make an exception of her. She joined the front rank of influential American war correspondents. It was over forty years before we met in London again.

Chamberlain genuinely thought he had brought back peace. At fearful cost, he had bought a year's respite. I returned to the subject of civil defence and, at Lord Camrose's request, started work on a short book advising our readers how to stay alive in air raids. In 1990, during a visit to Prague, I went to the vast neo-Renaissance National Museum which looms over Wenceslas Square. There in a small corner I found relics of that shameful September. There was a scrap of cotton, the size of a handkerchief, woven in coloured thread, a tiny memorial to 'the end of our country 1918–1938'. 'In the face of overwhelming political and military pressure from France, England, Italy and Germany,' the text ran, 'Czechoslovakia had no option but to yield 44,000 square kilometres of Sudetenland to Hitler.' This final message ends: 'We have not been frightened for a thousand years, and we are not afraid now.' I looked at this, and thought of Chamberlain's words in September 1939 – 'a quarrel in a faraway country between people of whom we know nothing'. In the cold dusk outside of the museum, they were lighting candles around the Wenceslas statue in gratitude for their deliverance from the yoke first of Germany, then of the Soviet Union. I found myself in tears.

6

War

When nations move to war, the volunteer enters a lottery of his
own. I drew a lucky ticket. At some point in the spring of 1939,
I ran into Lord Killanin, an acquaintance who was working on
the *Daily Mail*. The Territorial Army was to be doubled. His
interest lay in the Queen's Westminsters, formerly Civil Service
Rifles, with headquarters at Buckingham Gate. The new battalion, he explained, would have one company composed of his
friends and acquaintances who were actors or journalists, or
who worked late hours. To suit their working practices, drills
would be held in mid-morning instead of the evening. I thought
the idea had strong appeal and enlisted on the spot. Around
Easter 1939, Mussolini had invaded Albania. King Zog and his
beautiful Queen, Geraldine, fled to Greece. She must be
avenged, I said to my friends. Many years later, I met her for
tea at Claridge's. 'You were the reason I joined up,' I told her.
She smiled, and invited me to play some golf in Spain where
she lived.

C Company, 2 QW became an unusual unit. I made the
opportunity known to colleagues on the *Daily Telegraph*. They
responded well, so well that I was summoned by our then
managing director, Lord Burnham, descendant of the family
which had owned the newspaper until Lord Camrose bought it
in 1928. He was fretful about the number of *Telegraph* staff
who seemed committed to joining the 2nd Battalion Queen's
Westminsters if war broke out. Burnham himself was then a

senior officer in the Territorial Army, and was later to be one of the few to distinguish themselves on the beaches of Dunkirk. I thought pot was calling kettle black, and recruited one or two more. We drilled around noon at Wellington Barracks, which is a good address for budding soldiers.

We had just time to join a sodden camp in Hampshire. Then in the last days of August 1939 we were called up. In a matter of hours we ceased to be actors or journalists and became subject to the disciplines of the Army Act and the *Manual of Military Law*. Arthur Watson, then editor of the *Daily Telegraph*, called me anxiously from his desk. At a stroke, he complained, a score of his staff had left the premises – including a number of sub-editors who should have been putting the newspaper 'to bed' that night. Would I have a word with our Colonel and send some of them back? I mentioned it casually to my commanding officer, and for a moment or two feared he would suffer apoplexy. At that moment I realized we had crossed the great divide.

The Colonel, his second-in-command and the adjutant were former regulars with experience of the First World War. The rest of us were raw recruits. This left a gap after war had been declared, and we had serious duties to fulfil. At some point in the summer, I had been offered a commission, and assumed the duties of second lieutenant and platoon commander, while remaining totally ignorant of the duties involved. The first of them, early in September, was to take my platoon to guard the railway bridge at Staines. This was labelled a vulnerable point (VP) because trains carrying naval stores and munitions between Portsmouth and Scapa Flow had to cross it. The nights were growing chilly. For want of anything better, the riflemen were issued with blue overcoats worn by London Transport drivers.

I sought to impress on my small command the serious nature of our duties. The more sophisticated of them thought it a tremendous lark. One evening soon after we arrived, while doing the rounds I came across Guy Middleton, a popular West End actor, whose sentry post was on the sidewalk under the bridge. A short queue of young women were seeking his autograph. Middleton, rifle tucked between his knees, was chatting them up and signing. I remonstrated. He responded with a broad wink. The girls giggled. Another well-known actor who had fallen under my command was Tam Williams, who had been appearing in a new version of *The Barretts of Wimpole Street*. Careless in money matters, he owed a large sum to the Inland Revenue. While we were at Staines bridge the riflemen had their first pay day. For some reason, there were considerable deductions. I handed Williams about 9s 8d. He glanced at it with an expressionless face. Later in the day, when I walked down the railway track to inspect his post, he invited me to look at what he described as an interesting experiment. He had put his pay on the line. The coins, crushed by heavy trains, were twice their normal size and useless. We smiled together. It was still all very matey. We were all sharing a new and extraordinary experience that transcended rank.

We moved around the London area on duties of this kind until the end of the year. During this time I learned the psychological drawback of having small groups out on detachment and separated from battalion headquarters for too long. Loyalty becomes fragmented. 'It's them again,' my platoon sergeant would exclaim, after some tiresome missive reached us from battalion. It became 'us' against 'them'. The wisest commanders, I found, sought to bring their regiment together, even if only temporarily, before this mood could develop.

At Greenford in October the actors sprang on me the idea that we should stage a celebrity concert. I was doubtful. They took it over. Gilbert Miller's stage carpenter from Moss Empire Theatres set up the local dance hall. We invited the whole battalion from their various posts together with brigade and divisional headquarters, and laid out 500 chairs. My actors recruited Renée Houston, who brought the house down,

Dear Bill

Stanley Holloway, Turner Layton of Layton and Johnstone, Oliver Wakefield, Donald Stewart, Jack Strachey and Max Miller. Enid Stamp-Taylor compered the show. These names ring few bells today, but they were top of the bill then. My hardest task was collecting petrol coupons for the stars. The local greengrocer produced sixteen gallons, but Max Miller, who turned up from Brighton in a straight-eight Packard, declared that his journey had cost him all of that. The battalion's motor transport officer siphoned it out of battalion trucks.

This was the twilight period, later known as the Phoney War. We seemed to have wound ourselves up for no particular purpose. The winter of 1939/40 turned out to be a hard one for men who, for the first time in their lives, had to stand out all night in harsh weather. 'They really are a fine lot,' I wrote home at the time, 'with no grumbles, and it is quite difficult to find out when a man is really ill.' I look back with gratitude to the actors in my platoon, far removed from their own world, who yet tried to give us a taste of it, and so cheer everybody up. Their wives and girl friends, who occasionally visited us, were extremely pretty and a welcome distraction from what seemed to be a dull war.

After the arrival of Churchill in May 1940, Dunkirk in June and the fall of France we began to enter a totally different world. Two battalions of the King's Royal Rifle Corps to which we belonged, the 2nd (Regular) Battalion and the 1st (TA) Battalion Queen Victoria's Rifles, had defied the German Army in Calais, adding, as Churchill put it in his speech to the House of Commons on 4 June, 'another page to the glories of the Light Divisions'. One or two riflemen who had been in my platoon at the start of the war, and had been pulled out for commissions, were captured in Calais. War became real. After Dunkirk, the War Office offered to send us senior officers who had taken part in the Dunkirk affair to recount their experiences. Our Colonel rebuffed the offer. 'I do not need riflemen taught how to retreat,' he said crossly.

War

While a German invasion seemed likely in 1940, we were moved rapidly – it seemed to some of us mindlessly – to different parts of the country. But a new mood was taking shape. If we were going to get back into Europe, it would be by attacking, not defending. I was sent to one of the new 'battle schools' in the North of England, designed to teach us realism. We had to swim across rivers in full equipment, climb cliffs and crawl on our stomachs under live fire. The battle school instructors delighted in telling us how many casualties this had caused. After such a false start to the war, I found the realism consoling. The instructors awarded me a 'D' which stood for 'distinguished'. My Colonel, woundingly, expressed astonishment at this award.

At about this time I was summoned to the War Office by Major-General Harry Willans, director-general of welfare and education. He asked if I would be willing to become editor of the pamphlets which were supposed to keep the soldier in touch with current affairs. This struck me as an unattractive idea, and I said that I preferred to remain with my battalion. 'You have determined to be a fighting soldier,' said the General, with a faint whiff of sarcasm. 'Of course, I must not deter you.' He misread the position. I had just met my future wife Hilary Branfoot whose family came from Northumberland and was then living in the North Riding where our battalion was stationed, so I felt no urge to transfer my war effort into education. After the war, some declared that the material provided on this front carried a strong left-wing slant, and so had contributed to Labour's success at the 1945 General Election. I have always thought that doubtful. In any case, I made the right choice.

In the summer of 1941, our future took shape. We moved to the North Yorkshire moors for training as an armoured division. We occupied quarters along the main road from Scarborough to Helmsley. The armoured brigade settled in Duncombe Park, home of the Earl of Faversham. Our battalion headquarters was at Ampleforth, and we became familiar with the high qualities of that school. Father Paul, then the head, arranged for his senior boys and our senior sergeants occasionally to meet in his study on Sunday evenings for discussion. He knew what he was about. The discussion invariably ended with the sergeants declaring that they were fighting the war so that places like Ampleforth could survive. The boys, critical of Ampleforth's exclusiveness, thought the war was about making it possible for the sergeants' sons to enter the school.

There was one less happy event. Ampleforth challenged our battalion to a modified form of Olympic Games. It turned out to be a disastrous afternoon, with the boys in, say, a quarter-mile race leaving the leading riflemen a hundred yards behind. Our only winner was a bald, squat and heavily tattooed soldier from the Pioneer Corps, who had been seconded to us. Amid ringing cheers, he putt the weight twice as far as any boy. In a way, this performance made it worse. Towards the end of the afternoon, the Colonel summoned his company commanders, of which I was one. 'This has been a dreadful performance,' he exclaimed, hoarse with anger and distress. 'The riflemen are simply not fit. I look to company commanders—' and so on. It seemed to me that prowess on the running track had little bearing on a soldier's fitness for war. During the battle in Europe, for example, young officers, almost straight from school and fit as fleas, would join us to replace casualties. When it got rough and sleep was lost for more than twenty-four hours, they found it desperately hard to stay awake. The old sweats with long charge sheets and officers who had trained in pre-war night clubs were more dependable. But it was not a moment to put that to the Colonel. We agreed to extend early morning PT by fifteen minutes.

Gradually, we took shape as soldiers. Some were posted to the Desert war in Africa or to the Far East. A few were promoted to the staff. I stayed in my groove, and when the war ended was found to be the only officer who had been with 12th

KRRC from start to finish. By contrast with an air-raid warden or a Red Cross nurse in London, a merchant seaman on the high seas, a Battle of Britain pilot or the crew of a bomber raiding Germany, we enjoyed a pretty cushy life between midsummer 1941, when we settled down in the North Riding of Yorkshire, and the call to action in June 1944.

After various permutations, we finished up as a motor battalion in an armoured brigade, composed finally of three tank regiments, the 4th/7th Dragoon Guards, 13th/18th Hussars and the Notts (Sherwood Rangers) Yeomanry. Our gunners were the 147th Field Regiment RA (Essex Yeomanry). In command of the 8th Armoured Brigade for most of the battle in Europe was Brigadier Errol Prior-Palmer, father of the well-known rider, Lucinda.

One evening in the spring of 1944 our Colonel returned from a long day at the War Office. He had, he confessed to his officers over dinner, head in hands, failed to get us a place on a D-Day landing craft. We all wore suitably despondent looks. Privately, I felt it was a blow from which I could readily recover. The three tank regiments were going in with a secret weapon, the Duplex Drive. Fitted with a rigid canvas screen to keep the tank afloat they could propel themselves towards the shore, though almost submerged. On reaching the shore, the screen collapsed and the tank reverted to its normal role. Dropped off two miles out to sea, these tanks had a crucial role to play. They were to swim to shore and destroy the German guns in heavily fortified emplacements at both ends of the beach. The tank crews had been trained to fire directly into the slits of the gun emplacements. Despite rough seas, which drowned several tanks, the operation, known in the brigade as 'posting a letter', was brilliantly successful and saved countless lives. The Germans had not expected tanks to land for five days.

Meanwhile our motor battalion, which was designed to support the tank regiments, sat disconsolately near London docks at West Ham awaiting its turn. On the night before we sailed, the first V1 or pilotless plane fell on London. 'The police are baffled,' Major Fred Coleridge confided in me. He was our battalion second-in-command, and later a legendary figure at Eton. Well they might have been. Later in the morning, he called me from the docks. 'We have a problem,' he said. 'Join me.' The scene at our berth in the docks was confused. Our vehicles, which were semi-armoured cars made in America, stood on the quayside. Our ship was empty. 'The dockers,' said Coleridge, 'declare they cannot handle us. They haven't got the "rate".'

'The rate?' I said, puzzled.

'Trouble is, mate,' said a friendly docker, 'we don't have the rate.'

'The rate?' I repeated foolishly.

'That's right,' he said, 'the rate for loading these 'ere vehicles. Never seen 'em before.'

Coleridge invited me to address them on the lines of 'Friends, Romans, countrymen . . .'

'Look,' I cried, 'some of you have sons, relations out there, clinging on to that bridgehead. We've got to get there fast.'

The dockers gave these sentiments enthusiastic support.

'That's right! You've got to get there fast,' they echoed. 'But, you see, we haven't got the rate.' After more on these lines, we struck a bad compromise. Our riflemen would load the cars under the supervision of a retired docker.

Loading on these lines took two days, but that was not the worst of it. All our vehicles had been waterproofed, so that they could move through up to three feet of seawater without drowning. As unskilled hands dropped our vehicles into the holds like spillikins, some of the waterproofing was damaged; and it was further damaged when the ill-stacked vehicles were hauled out on the shores of Normandy early in the morning of 15 June. Thus it came about that about a quarter of my company's cars sank shortly after entering the sea. Nobody drowned, but it took time to clear the cars' systems of seawater.

My company joined a testing phase of the war with a broken wing. To make it worse, a party of senior military figures were on the shore to witness our humiliation. They included General Montgomery.

I had often wondered how I would feel on entering battle for the first time. As it turned out, my mind was wholly occupied by the loss of my vehicles and the likely reactions of my commanding officer. 'Why were your vehicles not properly waterproofed?' 'Colonel, can I tell you about the dockers?' It would not have been well received. They warned us that there were German snipers on the road to Bayeux. Alongside my worries, they seemed insignificant.

Half a century later, just before the fiftieth anniversary of VE-Day, I wrote a piece for the *Daily Telegraph*, pointing out that mixed up with all the valour shown during the war there was also some extraordinarily bad behaviour. Several correspondents, angered by my treading on their dreams, accused me of fabrication. I replied gently, while reflecting, 'Would that you had been with me at the docks!'

As everyone discovers on entering battle, a lot of boredom is mixed up with the danger. It must be said on behalf of 8th Armoured Brigade under Brigadier Errol Prior-Palmer, that the boredom was kept at a low level. Our battalion's duties were mixed. At times we abandoned our vehicles and fought with the infantry. Later, when the advance from the Normandy bridgehead got going, we were attached to the armoured regiments and called on to 'winkle out' – in the blithe language of our commanders – German opposition to the tanks. It lay with me as the company commander to agree with the commander of the tank regiment whether any proposed 'winkle' was feasible or suicide.

As Churchill wrote to Sir Edward Bridges, Secretary to the Cabinet in 1946, when seeking permission to use certain official memoranda and correspondence for his memoirs: 'in telling a tale the words written in the circumstances of the moment are of far greater significance than any paraphrase of them or subsequent composition'.

That is certainly true of experience in war. My mother kept all the letters I wrote home from Europe. So did my two sisters, Frances and Hermione. At the end of June, after a fortnight in Normandy, I wrote to my mother: 'The whole thing is slightly unreal. A few, very few, soldiers derive great pleasure from shooting Germans, most of them feel it is a job to be done, and so try to do it methodically. Maybe that's because as a nation we haven't suffered yet. Perhaps this war has been too light on us to generate enough hate.'

On 9 August, just before we broke out of the Normandy bridgehead, I wrote to my eldest sister Frances:

Yes, shades of Bifrons [a country house where we had sometimes stayed for Canterbury Cricket Week at the beginning of August] and the Canterbury tents this week! I thought about it a lot on Monday, at least in fleeting moments between an action which started at 5 a.m. and finished at 3 a.m. next day. About midnight, I was standing outside a shattered barn listening to stuff crumping around, and seeing the wounded coming in. Out of the darkness, a Lieut.-Colonel whom I did not know at all said reflectively, 'Well, there are a lot of things I'd rather be doing than this.' I said at once, 'Canterbury, for instance.' He caught the note. 'Yes, it would have been a good day there today, good hard wicket and 14,000, I dare say.' We reflected like this in the darkness, and he went off without my even having met him, and I shall never meet him I suppose – and that's the nearest I got to Canterbury . . .

August 1944 was exhausting. 'I dare say we are winning,' I wrote to my sister Hermione on 17 August,

but it seems slow where I am and rather expensive, and tiring into the bargain . . . The CO [Commanding Officer] has gone and all the company commanders except me, [have been] wounded or found other employment – now I remain the last chap in the battalion of 1939. One gets very tired, I find, even though we do not get all the blood and slaughter reserved for the infantry divisions. I find the endless destruction and slaughter wearing. Never, I would say, has such complete and utter destruction been wrought on human property. It's a wonderful performance and a colossal tribute to the gunners and airmen.

I had encountered a number of Germans accidentally.

I met the last pair at dusk, face to face, luckily when I was brandishing a revolver, feeling a little lonely and not liking the atmosphere. They were happily unarmed, about 17 years old, and said Kamerad and whipped their hands up all in one ... We are going to finish this war, if and when we do, so exhausted as to be like a man turned into the street in mid-November after three weeks in bed with 'flu. This seems to me the main danger. Some chaps don't even know what month of the year it is; and many can't give the date or day within two or three!

When modern authors pick over the bones of those days and point to all the mistakes we made, I marvel that we did not make many more. By 18 August, the outlook was a degree sunnier. American armour was in full swing. We had broken out of Caen, and the German Army was in retreat. 'I am too disillusioned,' I wrote to my sister Frances, 'to be very hopeful about this new break, but at least we are no longer going field by field, and Paris is nearer. God bless the USA. As far as I'm concerned, as some wag said to me the other day, they can have all the whisky and virgins south of the Tweed if it helps them to get a move on ... The destruction is horrible. I find endless villages and hamlets smashed and destroyed, scores of dying and rotting cattle, almost the worst feature of all . . .'

We were in fact heading for the Falaise gap, where a great part of the German Army was destroyed. In a letter to my mother on 26 August, I described the scene:

I hope I never have again to set eyes on the sight of the German Army as we saw it a few days ago. It was a triumph but a messy triumph. And most of us felt fairly sick, three of my crew have been sick the last 48 hours, due mainly to shock and stink. However, as I view it, it brings the day when B Company is sitting on the damnable bomb sites which worry you a good deal closer, and to that end I am prepared to see a lot more slaughter and carnage . . . Many of our new chaps have never seen death before, and I am afraid they had a bad day. On the advice of the Padre – we have an ace padre now – we all try to take death very seriously and not get used to it. Even so, it was difficult not to get numb. I suppose it will make history, and I am glad to be here. These are men who have terrorized Europe, and made your lives unhappy for five years. I feel no sense of pity at all. Never, I imagine, has an Army been visited by more terrible retribution. It must rank with Napoleon's retreat from Moscow and Foch's 1918 advance. Our modern machinery has been at work with terrible and ruthless efficiency. The Americans are wonderful, and I am completely won over and prepared to withdraw all unkind remarks . . . in truth they are fresher and brilliantly equipped. But their organization is lovely and their speed is of no world our Army knows. They'll say they won this war, and this time they are entitled to, in my view.

It's all too near and recent to realize how great this moment is. One hardly realizes that the last ten days have [granted] all we toiled and strove and sweated for from 1940 to 1944. That, after Dunkirk, when our hopes seemed so slim – and you and I saw those German bombers sailing west – we should live on to smash to dust the German Army which has caused these awful five years! Just to treat it all as inhuman and horrible and unnecessary I feel isn't fair to the millions who have toiled towards this moment.

It's thrilling here now to hear our tanks roaring east and the guns pouring up behind, and to see the RAF following up, wave upon wave. I'm as peace-loving a chap as the next, but the Germans have bought this, and they deserve every stick of it. In the farm where we now are is a French widow – of 4 days. This week a young SS Nazi, seventeen years old, walked into her kitchen and said, 'The so-and-so English are coming . . .' and as he spoke, he shot her husband, a harmless fellow, dead on his own hearth, and ran out laughing.

General Horrocks's 30 Corps, of which we were part, was now racing towards the Seine. A brief history of 8th Armoured Corps, published after the war, described the scene: 'For miles on either side of Chambois the roads and fields were littered with dead soldiers, dead horses and smashed equipment; the scenes of chaos belie description, as also does the stench.'

By the last days of August we were moving so fast that no feat of liberation seemed beyond our grasp; but it was a grisly experience. On 28 August, I painted the scene for my sister Frances:

I wish I could describe to you our moves, the dust, the end-less swirling columns of tanks, half-tracks, guns and echelon vehicles, pouring along all roads eastwards. It is very impres-sive and the French standing in crowds to cheer us past, and give us cider and calvados and apples, seem impressed too.

We have come through the first graveyard of the German Army. Never have I imagined such chaos and such fearful destruction. Here as you know the German 7th Army caught a packet. Mile upon mile of wrecked vehicles burned, twisted, blown up, shattered; or with many tanks just out of petrol and destroyed by the Germans themselves. Not just hundreds but thousands, and with them the fearful wreckage and litter and carnage of a great military disaster. Hundreds of dead pack horses, and booty in quantities, which will take months to clear up. Horrible really. I find death in large quantities still shocking and tragic.

Looking back on these letters, I perceive that I was torn – as I think many others were at the time – between horror and triumphalism. We had waited a long time, and many had suffered so much for this hour.

'We have all got a great kick from this breakthrough,' I told my mother, 'but no one has rested since D-Day and the men are tiring. So it's pretty encouraging to know these Yanks in vast hordes are packing the roads and roaring eastwards with us. This I feel is history and I am indeed glad I've been spared to see it, and have a front seat.'

By 29 August we were close to the Seine. Beauvais, which I associated with the crash of our airship R101 in 1930, fell to one of our companies. Early in September my own company occupied Doullens and slept in the historic town hall, where Marshal Foch of France had assumed supreme command in the final stages of the First World War. On 1 September I was able to report to my mother:

Having just captured a German truck with a brand new typewriter, 2 crates of Martell and 600,000 francs, I can at last write legibly to you. The French are wonderful. They stand in crowds as we go by, cheering and hurling fruit, flowers and presents into our half-tracks. If we stop for half a minute, they rush up with drink and food. The old folk look so tired and so incredibly happy it makes one's heart feel quite lumpy to go through and see them salute and bow and so on. They seem to have been through hell, and to them, as we arrive, it is like the end of a prison sentence . . .

A day later, I reported to my sister Frances:

The French have had the pleasure of watching an utterly broken and weary-to-death German Army stagger through with farm carts, bikes without tyres, even perambulators – that proud and wonderful Wehrmacht, with rags round their feet and no food, no orders and slam all idea of what is going on ... The only big trouble is disposing of prisoners. When you are moving at 40 miles a day, getting rid of hundreds of prisoners is a game. They are terrified of being handed over to the Maquis, who mutter 'caput' delightedly with throaty chuckles, and lead them off on a course of their own.

On Sunday, 3 September, there fell to my company and a squadron of tanks the prize of Lille, then with a population of about 200,000. On the way in, I recall, we questioned the local population closely. A few said Lille was filled with Germans. Most were non-committal. By noon we were on the city's outskirts. Half an hour later, fruit, flowers and wine over-whelmed us. The squadron leader and I agreed that complete occupation of Lille was impossible. But we split our forces between La Gare and a major road junction, and reckoned we had the best of it. In the great square and its surroundings there had assembled a crowd I put at about 10,000. Ladies of all ages strove to embrace us. 'This is revolting!' cried the squadron leader, as he watched from his turret his crews trying not very hard to resist these attentions. Nobody had eaten much since dawn, so the wine was going down on empty stomachs. Suddenly a German medical officer in uniform appeared, clutched my sleeve and sought safety for fifty badly wounded Germans near by.

Amid the tumult, my mind drifted back to years when our prospects had seemed so forlorn and victory so far away. Like the ancient Greeks, I began to get a sudden sense of proportion, to suspect that it is not granted to mortals to enjoy triumphs of this kind. It is too good to last, I thought distantly, and so it was. At the other end of the city, German guns began to announce a heavy presence. Urgent messages came in to our wireless operators from Brigade. In gathering dusk we assembled our tanks and half-track cars round another great square outside Le Préfecture. My mind was wholly occupied with getting the company and the squadron safely home in the dark.

Not until long after that day did awareness of what we had done begin to trouble me. Liberation in the Europe of those days was indescribably precious. For an hour or two those citizens of Lille had been led to believe by us that their deliverance was at hand. And in return for that, we received all the emotions of which they were capable. Then we failed them. We had to pull out. So little did I feel it at the time that I wrote a comic piece about the drinking and the kissing for our regimental history. I suppose total war had hardened us. It hardly crossed my mind what agony some of these people must have endured as we retreated, and the Germans returned. After our adventure, it took some time to recapture Lille. Around the fiftieth anniversary of this event, Lille offered a generous celebration to those who had taken part in its liberation. I could not bring myself to go.

Casting Lille aside, we rolled on. By 10 September we were moving on to Bourg Léopold outside Brussels. The *Daily Telegraph* carried a sentence: 'The great barracks of Bourg Léopold, converted into a strong point by the Germans, were stormed by the Belgian Army.' I have not subsequently raised the matter with the newspaper, but it rankles. A squadron of 13th/18th Hussars and my company liberated Bourg Léopold and handed it over to the Belgian Army.

Of course, D-Day in June 1944 was critical for our return to Europe. It is less well recognized that September 1944 was no less critical for the ending of the war in that year, with all the consequences for the world which might have flowed from that. As we paused at Bourg Léopold for a few days' rest, it hung in the balance. From there we saw the start of the great airborne invasion, designed to carry us into the heart of Germany. According to the Duke of Wellington, Waterloo had been 'a damned nice thing – the nearest run thing you ever saw in your life . . .' The Arnhem operation, forever to be known as 'a bridge too far', turned just the other way. My main interest in the battle came on 22 September. We had reached a climax in the crucial battle to relieve Major-General R. E. Urquhart's Airborne on Arnhem Bridge. Our ground forces in 30 Corps led by the Guards Armoured Division and 43rd (Wessex) Division were meeting stiff opposition. In those last desperate hours a fresh idea was conceived.

Around 11 a.m. on this grey chilly day, 22 September, Brigadier Errol Prior-Palmer, commanding 8th Armoured Brigade, breezed into our battalion headquarters with the plan. A squadron of 13th/18th Hussars tanks, to which my company was then attached, would charge down the road and seize Arnhem Bridge. To deal with matters when we got there, my company of riflemen would ride on the outside of the tanks. According to the operation order, it would be a piece of cake.

While I was studying this uninviting proposition, Company Sergeant-Major Hooper sidled towards my half-track armoured car. I had acquired CSM Hooper without much opposition from other company commanders when my own CSM became a casualty in Normandy. Hooper was considered to be a bad disciplinarian, but his insolent sang-froid strongly appealed to me. In all conditions, his morose calm was reassuring. Now he approached me with the air of a man who had got wind of Brigadier Prior-Palmer's slice of cake. 'Bit of a rum do?' he said. It was the nearest he ever came to expressing alarm. We examined the order, which had features in common with the Charge of the Light Brigade, though this time no one had blundered. It was deliberate.

I have kept a copy of the operation order. We were to be supported by Typhoon and Medium bombers. We would form up at Elst station. Our speed would be flat out from the 'off'. Household Cavalry armoured cars would secure us this flying start; no 'off' till they did. For the rest of that long day we remained under starter's orders. The riflemen wrote letters home. Then: 'No move before first light.' Had we known the true state of the battle, we could have put on pyjamas and overslept. Well into the next day, word reached us that, in the jargon of those days, 'It simply isn't on.' Such are the perverse workings of the human mind that the riflemen took this happy news badly. 'We've been buggered about,' they said crossly. It occurred to me that some would have written home: 'Darling, if we never meet again, I want you to know...' In my experience, such letters are invariably best sent by first post in the morning rather than by last post at night.

Many times since then I have thought about that day and the imponderables of war. Had we pulled it off, the casualties would have been enormous – but the rewards incalculable. Capturing that last bridge in September 1944 would not have won the war overnight, but it would have shortened it. It might even have ended the war by Christmas. Instead, like Caesar, we effectively entered winter quarters. With astonishing tenacity, the German Army recovered and reformed. We began by occupying a German village called Birgden, which was uncomfortable because it was in full view of the enemy. There lay between us a pond, full of duck. I had been given a new automatic pistol from Canada to test. One morning at first light, I tested it on the duck. It was a pleasure later in the day, as our Colonel made his rounds, to present him with a couple of brace. But whether on duty in Germany or resting in Holland, it was a dreary winter, with a slow but steady drain of casualties.

Early in March 1945, we came to life again and for perfectly respectable reasons – got on to the front page of the *News of the World*. In unforeseen circumstances, my rifle company achieved an unexpected meeting between the British and the

American armies. Early on the morning of 3 March, we were leading 30 Corps on the road to Geldern. A muffled voice came up on my wireless: 'Lots of "Yerman" tanks 500 yards to our right.' 'Did he say "German" or "Sherman"?' I asked the wireless operator. Mercifully, they were Sherman and they belonged to American 9th Army. Andrew Burnaby-Atkins, my carrier platoon commander, acted with speed and audacity. He made a banner out of our fluorescent aircraft-recognition panel. Then, accompanied by one rifleman and as if leading a procession of invisible hunger marchers, he set off across the fields. At that point the fog came down. We could see nothing. After a while the tank squadron leader and I decided we must follow in the footsteps of Burnaby-Atkins.

His meeting with the Americans had been eventful. Black American troops, manning about fifty Sherman tanks, had followed his advance suspiciously. 'Boy,' they chortled when he arrived, 'we'sa certainly had you covered.' There were other risks entailed. A German observation post in Geldern church tower, surprised to see an aircraft cerise panel moving across a field, had loosed a salvo of *Nebelwerfer*, which flung Andrew to the ground and made his nose bleed. His accompanying rifleman, never dressy by nature and soiled by three days and nights in action, said a few appropriate words to mark the occasion. 'So you ain't washed neither,' he observed in sour Virginian to the negro commanding the leading tank.

An American staff officer arrived to discuss with me a plan of action. We were under orders to capture Geldern, I explained. No, he said, the Americans were doing that. Under each American tank lay piles of 75mm Browning empties. All the shells had been pumped into Geldern. I hesitated to press the claim of a tank squadron and a rifle company against America's 9th Army. I handed it over to them. We had then to discuss a revised boundary between our two armies. The staff officer obligingly allotted me a minor road for our brigade, well off to the left. I suggested to Burnaby-Atkins that he used the high-power US radio to report these arrangements to our own army commander – in case he differed from me. Only later did we discover that British and American radio nets failed to meet. To seal arrangements, we ate some raw eggs together and shook hands. As we trudged back, two war correspondents caught up with us, taking names and addresses. Nearing home, we were heavily shelled. 'All good colourful stuff,' said the war correspondents, brushing mud off their tunics. Andrew Burnaby-Atkins featured in the Sunday newspapers as an 'absolutely mad Eton boy'. His sister gave an interview saying she had 'known it all along'.

My next and last main venture with Burnaby-Atkins, a month later, was less happy. On 2 April, the orders came to secure a crossing over the Twenthe Canal, south or south-west of Hengelo. Most of the bridges had been blown. We found one, combined with a lock, that was not. It ran between high, wooded banks, making observation of the other side difficult. The high canal bank on our side rendered support by our tanks' guns impossible. All seemed quiet as my company was brought up to do the assault. But when the leading riflemen stepped on to the bridge, dreadfully accurate crossfire from German Spandaus began to sweep it. The bridge was in two halves, linking an island between the locks with either bank. We got two platoons halfway across. The Germans then directed mortar fire on to the third reserve platoon, just as it was forming up to join the assault. The casualties became such that we ceased to be an effective force. Two officers, who had served with me throughout Europe, were killed, another was wounded, leaving only Burnaby-Atkins and myself. Brigade ordered us back. The withdrawal was slow, because we had to bring the wounded with us. So there were more casualties. This barely a month before the war ended. For this luckless encounter, Andrew Burnaby-Atkins and I were both awarded the Military Cross. Survivor's medal, I said rather bitterly at the time. Receiving a military decoration is always an honour to be worn proudly –

but none too joyfully if you have been called on to lead men into a shambles like the battle for the Twenthe Canal. Nor was that all. A week later, in the advance on Bremen, the last subaltern who had left England with me (excepting Andrew Burnaby-Atkins) was killed clearing houses at dusk in Cloppenburg. The death of these young friends while under my command bore certain consequences for me. I have felt ever since that they left a gap which those of us who survived must try, however inadequately, to fill.

I confess that in these circumstances I ended the war indignant at the demand for 'unconditional surrender' being made by Churchill, Roosevelt and Stalin. There seemed to me an unquenchable thirst for the total destruction of Germany, the innocent as well as the guilty. My feelings, which no doubt will seem to most people unreasonable, were compounded by the losses we had suffered so late in the day. Partly on this account, partly because most of us were thoroughly overtired, I greeted news of the ceasefire on 4 May 1945 sourly. It came to us while we were finishing dinner with the 13th/18th Hussars, the armoured regiment to which my company had for most of the time been attached. The message from Commander 30 Corps (General Sir Brian Horrocks) reached us in this form: 'Germans surrendered unconditionally at 18.20 hours[.] Hostilities on all Second Army front will cease 0800 hours tomorrow 5 May 45[.] NO repeat NO advance beyond present front line without orders from me.'

I held copy No. 14 of orders from 129 Infantry Brigade for the next day's task, named Operation Curling. It bore an unhealthy look. Well, I reflected, at least the buggers won't be able to kill any more of us with operations like that. With more alcohol inside me than usual, I wandered out into the darkness alone to indulge my gloomy thoughts. It was not a singular condition. A short history of 8th Armoured Brigade, which had fought from D-Day 1944 until the night of 4 May 1945, carried this sentence. 'Rejoicing there was, but this sudden break in the tension reacting upon men far more tired than they were prepared to admit, had a quietening effect.'

It certainly had on me. There were other considerations. I thought of my company's losses so close to the finishing line. I was also dimly aware, with recollections of keeping a rifle company in some sort of order in England, how much the perils of battle impose their own disciplines. These were now removed. I reflected on the likely state of my men's billets next morning. I heard an echo of my Colonel's voice from distant days in England: 'Bill, I have to tell you that I am not altogether happy about the way things are going in your company.' Oh God, we would be back to all that again.

Worse, discipline would have to be restored amid a colossal shambles. Germany was in tatters. We had been warned to expect mob violence. Instead, a great many Germans, on starvation rations, stayed in bed to conserve their energies. Countless displaced persons roamed the streets begging and stealing. Fraternization with the Germans was forbidden; but German girls foraging for part of our ample rations for their hungry families offered temptations to the riflemen. It is hard to convey at this distance what much of Germany looked like in that early summer. A whole country, as I expressed it later, had been battered to a stop.

I thought we had made a mess until I entered Hanover a day or two later, and saw what 84th US Infantry Division, with Allied air forces, had achieved. Brigadier Errol Prior-Palmer, commander of 8th Armoured Brigade, who had led us through the battle, was sanguine as ever. He thought it would be a good idea to open the opera house in Hanover in order to take the German mind off things. We set to work and in a surprisingly short space of time paved the way for an excruciating perform-ance of *La Bohème*. Still, it was a start.

My more immediate duties were to take charge of some thousands of German prisoners-of-war and guard a local depôt which stored the powerful fluid which had fuelled the flying bombs. The German prisoners, among them 400 officers and 1,600 NCOs, were a pain in the arse. Quite properly, they demanded their rights and entered constant complaints about their treatment. None of them escaped, but some of the displaced persons raided the fuel dump, with fatal consequences. We had conflicting orders about the treatment of German property. Our most senior commander, Field Marshal Montgomery, held distinctly old-fashioned views about the entitlement of victorious soldiers to booty. Our corps commander, General Horrocks, held stricter views. Throughout the campaign in Germany I had followed rules of my own. If you entered a German home, you were at liberty to make whatever use you liked of it in the prosecution of war, but you did not wantonly defile or loot it. If you found wine in the cellar or geese in the orchard, you did not consult higher command on the right thing to do.

I recall one strange experience with a magnificent German cellar. About a dozen of us were dining in a large house. For the dessert we opened a bottle, crusted with age. It went round the table. The first officer to receive it was enraptured. The last spat it out. It had turned a murky colour in his glass. Somebody who thought they understood wine declared that it was such an old wine that exposure to the air had killed it.

Then there was the future. Though I had enjoyed eight years in journalism before the war, after five years in uniform I felt unqualified for anything except soldiering. Our battalion was asked to submit names of suitable officers to pursue the war against Japan. In my perverse mood, I volunteered my services, mercifully made superfluous by the atom bomb on Hiroshima. Looking back on those times, I find my attitude difficult to explain. I had a wife and young son, Jeremy, whom I longed to rejoin. The long-suffering editor of the *Daily Telegraph*, Arthur Watson, was complaining of staff shortages and (vague about demobilization arrangements) kept begging me to return.

For obvious reasons, none of us could take what we needed most, which was a holiday. When you are very tired, self-confidence dwindles. I seriously doubted my ability to succeed in journalism. I dreaded the effort of returning to total responsibility for myself – let alone a wife and child. The Army is wonderfully supportive. It may sometimes command you to take on unreasonable tasks, but it cares for you, body and soul. The quartermaster and the medical officer cater for the first; the padre for the second. My mother wrote during the summer of 1945, faintly regretting that a local parliamentary seat had fallen vacant and that I had not been on hand to enter my name. I ought to have felt gratified by this expression of maternal confidence. Instead, I was unreasonably irritated by my mother's expectations, which seemed so far out of my range.

Labour had won the General Election, but my riflemen had led me to anticipate that. With the peace had come training hours marked 'Education', during which I had to discuss current affairs with my company. They made their political feelings clear to me. As a political journalist since the early 1930s, I was familiar with the shortcomings of the National Government, which, under an astonishing variety of leaders – starting with Ramsay MacDonald in 1931 and ending with Winston Churchill in 1945 – had been in charge of our affairs for fourteen years. General Elections nearly always hang on public expectations for the future, not gratitude for the past. Churchill's contribution to victory shone from the skies, but for those about to return to civilian life it was heavily over-clouded by recollections of vast unemployment between the wars. I had seen some of it. I had come to know the Distressed Areas. What happened in the 1945 General Election seemed to me a perfectly reasonable process.

Dragging my feet, endowed with stout shoes and a thick demob suit, I returned in November to greet my family joyfully, my future doubtfully. Arthur Watson readily granted me a fortnight to visit families of the bereaved. Some of them

Above: Early days at Symnells, Aldington. 1915.

Right: First Eton collar.

Leaving for Abyssinia, July 1935. My uncle, Sir Wyndham Deedes can be seen in the background.

12th Battalion King's Royal Rifle Corps, companion unknown, c. 1941.

Friends in the 12th Battalion King's Royal Rifle Corps.

Above: Voting. William Francis Deedes and Evelyn Hilary Deedes. 1950.
(*Douglas Weaver*)

Opposite page: After the count. WFD and Evelyn Hilary Deedes. 1950. (*Douglas Weaver*)

At New Hayters, Aldington. *Left to right*: WFD, Juliet, Evelyn Hilary Deedes, Jill, Julius, Jeremy. April 1951. (*The Field*)

With the family at New Hayters. April 1955. (*Douglas Weaver*)

Tea with the Tory ladies. (*Folkestone Herald and Gazette*)

Listening to the debate at the Conservative Party Conference, October 1962.

had lost an only son. All the future they had dreamed for him was gone for ever. Most of my future still lay before me, to make what I could of it. Chastened, and to some extent rested, I gratefully accepted Arthur Watson's offer to reinforce the sole occupant of the Peterborough column. With a couple of short breaks, I was to be there for almost thirty years.

7

Candidate

Travelling from Kent to London one morning late in 1946 for a Sunday stint on the *Daily Telegraph*'s Peterborough column, I read a paragraph in the Crossbencher column of the *Sunday Express* which took me by surprise. E. P. Smith, the Conservative MP for Ashford, had told his Conservative Association that he would not be standing at the next General Election. It was an unexpected decision for several reasons. Smith had entered Parliament after a wartime by-election only three years earlier to fill a vacancy left by Patrick Spens QC, who had gone off in 1943 to be Chief Justice of India. The Labour Government had been elected only sixteen months before with a large majority, so a General Election was some way off. A miller by trade but also an author and playwright, Edward Percy Smith had become a minor celebrity during the war as the author of two popular plays, *The Shop at Sly Corner* and *Ladies in Retirement*. He was, one supposed, enjoying the lustre which that sort of achievement adds to public life. So this sudden decision was puzzling. One was not to know that the Member for Ashford had found a fresh partner and judged that parting from his wife after twenty-eight years of marriage would go down badly with some of his constituents. There was a chapel in almost every village in those days. Nonconformists gave the Ashford division a Liberal tinge, and in 1929 a Nonconformist preacher had captured the seat, mainly on the issue of tithe.

I then reflected on the personal implications of this decision.

Candidate

The Ashford Division was home territory, so to speak. My great-grandfather, William Deedes, had first entered Parliament in 1845 as Member for East Kent – of which the Ashford constituency was now part. Since the seventeenth century several of my forebears had represented the region in Parliament. My spell as lobby correspondent from the *Morning Post* in 1937 had given me an interest in politics. While working at Westminster, I became a friend of Ronald Cartland, brother of Barbara and a Birmingham MP. 'Some of us are going to fight, and some of us are going to die,' he had declared in the House of Commons during the debate in 1940 which brought down Neville Chamberlain. He was killed early in the war. After Sir Austen Chamberlain's death in 1937, Cartland had urged me to put in for his seat in West Birmingham. It was out of the question, but it was a flattering proposal and put ideas in my head. I reflected on all this as my train travelled towards London – in about three-quarters of the time it takes today.

Looking back on my circumstances at the time, I was barmy to give the matter a second thought. After five years of war, I had been back with the *Daily Telegraph* barely a year – on my pre-war salary of £18 a week. My wife and I had just spent what capital she possessed on buying a large Victorian farmhouse in East Kent. Workmen were inside it, restoring the ravages of war. During the working week, I occupied lodgings run by a retired butler in Eaton Terrace. My wife had sold our wartime home in the North Riding, and was lodging in the village of Aldington to keep an eye on the workmen. We met at week-ends.

I had also to weigh the feelings of my immediate boss. H. E. Wortham, who unconsciously had done more than anyone else to help my transition from war to peace. Hugo Wortham was a character. He had taken on the Peterborough column in the 1930s and run it single-handed throughout the war. After I joined him in the last days of 1945, he became the tutor I had missed at University. He was an accomplished art and music critic and had countless friends in both spheres. On summer days he would sometimes appear in a grey bowler hat. Lunches at his club, long and mainly liquid, often led him to appear late in the afternoon with virtually nothing ready for the column. This imposed responsibility on me, but also opportunity. I warmed to this tetchy and sometimes tipsy Edwardian, who was both wise and humorous. He was a tremendous wine buff and apt to be critical of other people's wine. One day in the late 1940s we were both invited to an office lunch with our owner, the first Viscount Camrose. There were faint beads of moisture round the decanters of claret on the table. 'My God!' exclaimed Wortham, in one of those silences that fall when someone is about to put their foot in it, 'they've boiled the claret again!' His remark passed without comment at the time. Months later, we were both at the same table again. 'I trust,' said Lord Camrose turning towards Wortham, 'that the claret is entirely to your taste!' Wortham was fun to work with, and we came to like each other. I rang him up to inform him of my selection. 'Oh, God!' he said angrily and slammed the telephone down. Next day he appeared in mid-afternoon slightly sozzled and benign. 'I wish you luck,' he said.

The truth was I saw no likelihood of securing the Ashford vacancy, but thought that to enter my name would be rather a lark. I took an important precaution. On writing formally to the agent at Ashford from London to say that my hat was in the ring, I first sent the letter with a stamped addressed envelope to my wife in Kent. Nothing will come of this, I wrote to her, but if it did then I would like to feel that you took the decision. I told her to post the letter only if she supported the idea. It was a course of action I commend to all married men applying for parliamentary seats. Later on, it eases domestic tension. 'It's time we left for the Executive meeting.' 'But I'm in my bath!' 'Well, five minutes more then.' 'Damn the Executive!' 'Yes, I know; but it was you who told me to go ahead.'

Nothing happened for a while after my application, which

was as well. It took time to make our new home remotely fit for habitation. My wife camped in a corner of it. Towards the end of the year, family furniture arrived from my uncle's house in Bethnal Green which ill-health had compelled him to abandon. It was stacked in another corner. Then suddenly a summons came from the agent to meet Ashford's selection committee. I missed the appointment because my wife's car refused to start. She telephoned to tell them I was indisposed. A second appointment was made, for which I mistook the time and arrived slightly late in country clothes. Years later this choice of dress was turned into an embarrassing legend by Humphry Berkeley, a great prankster, who became the unpredictable Conservative Member for Lancaster. My corduroy trousers and tweed jacket, he advertised, had been preferred by the selectors to the blue suit and stiff white collar worn by Ted Heath, who was also applying for the seat.

We met in a stately home on the outskirts of Ashford. Presiding over the small committee was Sir Edward Hardy, a man of vast experience and an old family friend. He had been chairman of Kent County Council from 1936 until 1949, thus bearing heavy responsibility for a county which was more in the front line than any other. He had been president or chairman of Ashford's Conservative Association for thirty years, and in the 1931 General Election had masterminded a handsome victory for Michael Knatchbull, 14th Baronet, father of the present Lord Brabourne, over the Rev. Roderick Kedward, the Liberal Nonconformist.

Sir Edward knew the state of my mind better than I knew it myself. Was my application a serious one, he asked, looking me in the eye. I hedged, saying I had not expected to get very far in the selection process because of my father's well-known socialist leanings. He had, indeed, playfully sought one or two seats in the Labour cause. I left the examination oddly reassured that the risk of selection was small.

Ten days before Christmas, I received a call to meet the

chairman of the constituency, Hugh Thoburn, at the Goring Hotel near Victoria station. He was the chairman of a building society and lived comfortably in a house at Benenden, oddly named Pympe Manor. Thoburn explained over a gin and martini and in confidence that I had been selected, hastening to add that I was no doubt anxious about the financial consequences. Until then, these had not even entered my head, though they should have done, because up to that point Conservative candidates had been expected to pay all their election expenses and often to add an annual donation to their Association. I had £350 in the bank at the time.

Over our dinner, Thoburn spoke earnestly of reforms afoot in the post-war Conservative organization which would change all that. By the time the next election came along, he declared, Conservative candidates would not only be relieved of all election expenses, they would be forbidden to contribute to them. The Association would raise the money. All this was news to me. It crossed my mind that Thoburn feared that financial considerations might cause me to run out. There was something in this. Unknown to me, Sir Edward Hardy had warned the selectors that owing to the Wall Street crash of 1929, which, coupled with the burden of a dilapidated castle, had ruined my father, they had an impecunious candidate. Plied with reassurances about these unforeseen difficulties from the homely Hugh Thoburn, I left the Goring Hotel in alternating moods, triumph predominating. Human vanity is such that success can subdue any number of anxieties. During the night it occurred to me that my employers, the *Daily Telegraph*, would have to be informed.

On that score, fears were groundless. Arthur Watson, who had been editor since 1924 and had appointed me in 1937 after the *Morning Post* was absorbed by the *Daily Telegraph*, conveyed reassurances from Viscount Camrose, our proprietor. His own son and heir, Seymour Berry, had been Conservative MP for Hitchin in 1941–5. Camrose himself had become during the war a close crony of Winston Churchill, and was instrumental after the war in raising a large sum from wealthy friends with which to buy Chartwell in Kent for the nation, and so endow Churchill with welcome funds. He had also arranged the purchase of Churchill's war memoirs for serialization in the *Daily Telegraph* and other leading world publications. All this may have helped. The fact remains that, by contrast with so many employers in modern times, the *Daily Telegraph* was wonderfully supportive; and, in a position as shaky as mine, this was welcome. Until his death in 1954, I received warm messages of encouragement from Camrose. I remained with the Peterborough column, which fitted well into parliamentary life. I reflect on all this gratefully whenever some Member of Parliament is accused of supplementing his parliamentary pay in unsuitable ways. The *Daily Telegraph* kept me out of temptation.

As the day approached for my adoption by the Conservative Association as Ashford's prospective parliamentary candidate, I sniffed an air of uneasiness at Conservative headquarters in Ashford. Living locally at Chilham Castle was Somerset de Chair, who had been Conservative MP for South West Norfolk since 1935, but had narrowly lost his seat in the 1945 election. A day or two before my adoption meeting he delivered a speech to the Ashford Young Conservatives, declaring himself dissatisfied by the arrangements which had led to my selection.

My adoption had been arranged for 2.30 p.m. on 22 March in what was then Ashford's theatre. During the morning, I sauntered into the Association offices. Chairman Thoburn and the agent had their heads together. There might, they thought, be a spot of trouble ahead, but nothing to worry about. I was to concentrate on my acceptance speech.

The theatre was packed. Subsequently I was to learn that most political meetings are only well attended when the audience anticipates trouble. My wife and I were lodged in one of the theatre's dressing rooms, there to await unveiling after the necessary preliminaries. We could hear but not observe the proceedings. They began, ominously, with points of order directed at the unhappy chairman. Thoburn had sound qualities, but life in the sheltered chair of a building society had not trained him to navigate through stormy political waters. The point deployed by Somerset de Chair and his allies was a simple one, and not easily countered. The meeting, they declared, was being presented with a *fait accompli*. My selection had taken place behind closed doors, and was contrary to established democratic practice. Through the theatre's dressing-room door there reached us sounds with which people in politics become distressingly familiar – a chairman under fire and losing his grip on the proceedings. There was reason for Somerset de Chair's resentment. Sharing many cultural interests with the retiring Member, Edward Percy Smith, he had reckoned the Ashford seat would come his way. After losing his Norfolk seat, he had taken Chilham Castle with the support of the first of his four wives, Thelma.

It lay conveniently between the Canterbury and Ashford seats. It would be too much to say that de Chair and the Member reckoned to have it sewn up, but Edward Percy Smith would plainly have preferred him to me as his successor. But for the political instincts of Sir Edward Hardy, this might well have come to pass.

In the changing room of the Ashford theatre, time passed slowly. My acceptance speech began to seem a sadly inadequate contribution to the drama that was taking place. Two of Somerset de Chair's allies in the meeting were a Mr and Mrs Robert Tritton, who lived at Godmersham Park close to Chilham, near by. He was an Old Etonian who had become an antique-furniture dealer. She was heir to Carreras. At some decisive moment, I was told, she had sold all her holdings in tobacco, short of those needed to retain control, and had reinvested the money in Marks and Spencer. This had made her hugely rich. From the dressing room she and her husband, in support of de Chair, sounded formidable. Subsequently, Elsie Tritton became a close friend and a generous supporter.

It was roughly two hours before we received the summons. Much of the audience looked exhausted. A minority was curious to inspect the subject of the row. With a dry mouth and a slight headache I delivered my speech. At the close of proceedings, Somerset de Chair leaped to the platform, shook my wife and me warmly by the hand, wished us all the best, and went out of our lives. The time for tea had long passed. We went straight from the theatre to a drinks party.

When I reflect on the number of young political friends who over the years have had to fight at least one election in a Labour stronghold as an apprenticeship to politics, I had nothing to complain about. At the high tide for Labour in 1945, Ashford had returned Smith with a majority of 5,000. Coming in behind him at that point presented me with a relatively safe seat for life.

But difficulties arose. I was not the son Smith had hoped would be his heir. His attitude towards me was correct but not warm. While he continued in Parliament, I thought it best to play my small part as prospective candidate modestly. This was interpreted in some quarters as indolence. The elders of Ashford town – who had been irreverently known as the 'Forty Thieves', but who later regrouped as the 'Straight Eight' – complained they never saw me. Thoburn had been succeeded as Conservative Association chairman by the Viscount Allenby.

He summoned me to lunch and told me I must pull my socks up. There had been a week-end conference for Kent's Conservative candidates. An unknown young woman, Margaret Roberts, then Tory candidate in the Labour stronghold of Dartford, had asked intelligent questions and shone. My chairman observed that I had turned up in the wrong clothes – corduroy trousers again – asked no questions and looked bored. I was bored.

On top of that, we had acquired a new agent, Sam McCall,

who fuelled his enthusiasm with enormous quantities of alcohol. He and the lady we all supposed to be his wife were living under our roof. We had ample space. They could not find a home. It was not a satisfactory arrangement. As we charged round the constituency in a car which he occasionally overturned, my wife grew anxious. But the sitting Member made no complaint. While working on his behalf, McCall remained relatively sober. It seemed to be the candidate who drove him to drink. We went through a phase when well-intentioned people assured me that between us we would lose the seat. A useful portion of it, the Romney Marsh, was being transferred to our neighbours in Folkestone and Hythe. 'That will cook your goose,' they said confidently. I began to wish I had never taken the thing on.

It turned out to be all right on the night. Through the dreariest and coldest election campaign I have ever experienced, in February 1950, McCall exceeded expectations. In political tactics, drunk or sober, he outclassed the other two party agents. My Labour opponent, a young barrister called Neville Sandelson, displayed even more naivety than I did. There was a hideous scene in the Ashford market after he explained to local farmers that the Romney Marsh – where they could fatten fifteen sheep to the acre – was 'marginal land'. My majority was 6,000. Undeterred, Sandelson later fought the 1951 and 1955 elections against me before seeking greener pastures. I came to admire him as someone more adventurous than myself. He eventually won a Labour seat at Hayes and Harlington, took on Labour's left wing, and became a founder member of the Social Democratic party.

During our count in 1950, while nerves jangled, E. P. Smith, warmed by the prospect of leaving Ashford and his wife for ever, took my arm and advised me confidently on how to set about making my maiden speech in the Commons. Then, looking wonderfully cheerful, he disappeared.

8

New Member

I had heard so many gloomy forecasts about the future of the Ashford seat during my three years as Conservative candidate that I entered the House of Commons early in 1950 with a strong sense of self-satisfaction. In reality, we all entered the House of Lords. The new chamber of the House of Commons, replacing the one destroyed by war in May 1941, was not ready until the end of that year. Years later, when I had joined the House of Lords, I picked the same spot from which to make my second maiden speech, reflecting that not a great number could have done that.

In 1950 my smugness did not last long. There was a touch of the ring-master about my agent, the dynamic Sam McCall. Having secured the election of a novice – against all the odds, as he saw it – he displayed a heavy sense of responsibility for my performance. A lot of people, he advised me, only days after I had entered the House, are wondering when you will make your maiden speech and what it will be about. I bided my time. The 1950 intake of new Conservative MPs was unusually large – something over eighty – and all of them wanted to make maiden speeches.

Then there was the constituency. By present-day standards, Ashford was not demanding, but constituents expected to see the new Member and I detected a subtle change in our relations. Under the new rules, they had financed my election and bore the cost of my agent and his office. Those who pay the piper call the tune.

In every constituency there are folk obsessed by some long-standing grievance about an injustice that cannot be remedied. Often it is over a petty quarrel within their own family. Even more often it is about some nuisance committed by a neighbour. Disputed boundaries between houses can become tribal. Sometimes it relates to a pension entitlement. To all this the legacy of the wartime years added a pack of complications. Many could not get a licence for the raw materials they needed for their businesses, or to repair or improve their homes. Pretty well all those with personal long-standing grievances had tried it on the preceding Member of Parliament and probably the one before that. A new MP presented a fresh target. My agent thought that if I proved successful where others had failed, it would help to build up my slender credentials.

'As Member for a constituency largely agricultural, and with many farms producing fruit, I dare say you are familiar with the plight of apple growers,' wrote a prominent land agent, A. J. Burrows, within weeks of my election. He complained that in the preceding year he had received exactly £304 for 35½ tons of apples. I addressed the problem to Tom Williams, Labour's Minister of Agriculture. The answer was a lemon. Burrows expressed dissatisfaction with my efforts. Others wrote in the same vein. In self-defence I joined the Conservative party's Standing Committee on Agriculture, whose chairman was Anthony Hurd, father of Douglas, later to be appointed Foreign Secretary by Margaret Thatcher. He persuaded me to stand for election as secretary to the Committee. Thereafter we worked amicably together, ran the weekly meetings, and became close friends.

Anthony Hurd, who was also agricultural correspondent for *The Times*, represented an invaluable element in the Conservative party of those days. In common with many other senior Tory back-benchers, he had no desire for ministerial office. His roots were in the business of farming. On behalf of this business, he occasionally visited sheep farmers in the Falkland Islands. Yet his judgement on all political matters, particularly in political crises, was shrewd and reliable. He was one of perhaps a score of senior Tory back-benchers to whom Ministers in trouble deferred, and whom whips consulted. I was with him during the row over Crichel Down in 1954 which eventually led to the resignation of Sir Thomas Dugdale, the Minister of Agriculture (who had been Baldwin's parliamentary private secretary).

Crichel Down was a typical post-war episode, originating from the labyrinth of wartime regulations which Labour had done little to refine in the years 1945–51. The Air Ministry had taken land in Dorset for use as a bombing range, and had later passed it on to the Ministry of Agriculture. The original owners sought to repurchase the land, but the Crown Land commissioners, absurdly, found another tenant, without informing the owners. As this muddle unfolded, there was public uproar, led by farmers and landowners. One of Tommy Dugdale's handicaps was that he was a slow reader. He failed to spot this one in the red box. So did his parliamentary under-secretaries, who were Lord Carrington and Dick Nugent (later Lord Nugent).

There were then many more landowners and farmers in the House of Commons than there are today. As the crisis broke over the head of the Minister, Hurd realized that the attitude of the party's Agricultural Committee would probably be decisive. He consulted widely, and came to the conclusion that events must take their course.

We were assisted in those days by the level-headed and attractive Elizabeth Briggs (later Mrs William Buchanan), who represented agriculture in the Conservative Research Department. On the evening of Dugdale's resignation, Elizabeth Briggs, Anthony Hurd and I were taking a consoling drink in the Harcourt Room, where there entered Mr Marten, owner of the land which had led to Dugdale's downfall. Determined in passionate loyalty to vent her wrath on Marten, Elizabeth rose to her feet. Hurd's restraining hand was timely. At a later point in his career Hurd was offered a knighthood. He consulted his editor at *The Times*, where he still worked. Nobody on this staff, he was told, receives a knighthood except the editor.

Crichel Down threw light on the thicket of wartime controls which chronic shortages forced even Conservative Ministers to keep. As I soon discovered in my constituency, a high proportion of complaints had to be addressed to Government departments. There a huge bureaucracy prepared bland and unsatisfactory answers. This extract from a letter I received about an application from Ashford High School is a sample:

> I find that the licence could not be granted because of the limitation on capital investment. The sum available for all such licences is limited, and the allocation for 1950 was exhausted by other jobs more urgent even than the work at this school before this application was made. [This letter was written in mid-July.] The School Authorities have been advised to renew their application in time for it to be considered when the amount of money available in 1951 for work of this kind becomes known.

Such responses were not conducive to winning the sort of reputation my agent desired for me. There was a strong call in the county for a late-night train service to serve Ashford, Folkestone, Dover and Deal after 9.15 p.m. – the absence of which effectively imposed a curfew on anyone seeking an evening's entertainment in London. Sheaves of paper were spent on failing to get satisfaction.

I had more luck with a local squire, George Brodrick, who was farming a thousand acres at Eastwell Park, where many years earlier King Edward VII had sometimes carried a gun. Early in 1952 one of his ploughs turned up a couple of antitank mines. Local sappers disposed of them. Brodrick then, reasonably, asked General Officer Commanding Eastern Command for a 'sweep' of the area. He got no response, and three months later referred the matter to me. I wrote to the War Office and a month letter got a reply from a Conservative Minister, declaring that there were few men available to do such work and that such men as there were had their hands full in Scotland. Nonetheless, he added, part of a Battle Area Clearance Team would be detached from Scotland and sent to Eastwell. They found, as we had suspected all along, that some of the land had formed the military defence line when invasion threatened in 1940. By May the BACT team had gathered up sixteen mines, some of them fully armed, and a variety of other dangerous ordnance.

An MP's personal vote is nearly always much smaller than he likes to think. On the other hand, one small service to a constituent – particularly if he belongs to another party – gets talked about and does good. A few months after my election I received a letter from Harold Nicolson:

> I am really very much obliged to you for your intervention on behalf of Mrs Hoemberg. Would you convey to Bottomley [Arthur Bottomley, then Labour's Overseas Trade Minister], when you see him, my sincere thanks for what he has done? How I wish that our Ministers had been equally considerate and prepared to make exceptions in hard cases when they bagged the savings of wretched German governesses in 1919. All my battles on that occasion ended in failure, but you have been far more successful with Mr Bottomley.

It was an astounding case. Mrs Hoemberg was a Canadian woman who had married a German. She had written a successful book called *Thy People, My People* about wartime experiences. Her profits from it (after the deduction of 45 per cent income tax) were impounded by the Administrator of Enemy

Property. I have no doubt the favourable answer owed more to Harold Nicolson's standing than my own; but his home at Sissinghurst Castle lay within my constituency. Thereafter, I treasured his personal vote.

On many counts, I was an extremely fortunate Member of Parliament. My home, a large Victorian farmhouse overlooking Romney Marsh, which we had bought cheaply in 1946, lay within the constituency and was ample for my growing family. In London I was offered free use of a bedroom in Eaton Terrace, where my mother's two spinster sisters and unmarried brother lived. The Chenevix-Trench family were Irish Protestants. Robert, the brother, had been born in the wrong year. He was just old enough on leaving Winchester to qualify for the trenches in the 1914–18 war; and just young enough to rejoin the London Rifle Brigade in 1939. He joined the Royal Military Police and became part of Lieutenant-General Percival's ill-starred division which surrendered to Japan early in 1942. He spent the rest of the war as a prisoner. On his return in 1945, though handicapped by poor sight and bad hearing as a result of his ordeal, he joined the London Stock Exchange and accumulated a substantial fortune.

His sisters had inherited more of the Irish temperament. On certain subjects, such as the Royal Family, they came out with unexpected remarks – though usually through a third party. 'My hairdresser boy', Oonah Chenevix-Trench would remark at breakfast, apropos of nothing in particular, 'tells me the Queen is not at all popular, you know.' Then she would add, as a saving grace, 'Well, not in his circle, anyway.' On hearing that I would be attending a Buckingham Palace garden party, both sisters would observe silence. Because of their brother's experiences, not only Japan but the whole of the Far East became unmentionable. But they were thoroughly kind, and put up with me for the best part of twenty-five rent-free years.

As well as these benefits, I enjoyed support from the *Daily*

Telegraph, from the Berry family itself and from its editor, Sir Colin Coote who had succeeded Arthur Watson. In return for contributions to the newspaper's Peterborough column and occasional signed articles, they kept me on the staff at full salary throughout my time in Parliament, excepting only the few years in which I held office.

In May 1954, MPs voted themselves a pay rise from £1,000 a year to £1,500. I took a close interest in this. As a lobby correspondent in 1937 I had been urged by Ministers to support a proposal to raise the parliamentary salary from its starting point of £400 to £600 a year. They were genuinely concerned by the plight of some of the Labour MPs, to whom Baldwin always tried to give a fair deal. At that time, I was earning the best part of £1,000 a year. The Labour MPs, many of whose contituencies lay far from London, had in effect to maintain two homes on £400 a year. I did myself well every evening in the press dining room. I was urged to go over the road to the two tea rooms, Lyons and ABC, to observe what some Labour MPs gave themselves for supper. They ordered tea and two pieces of toast which were made into a step. By perching the egg on the top step, they could enjoy two slices of toast impregnated with egg. For this they paid a few pence. I urged the *Morning Post* not to oppose the pay rise.

After the early sensation of having to be in six places at once, which all new Members of Parliament suffer, I began to enjoy the parliamentary career. My constituency was rich in thoroughly nice people who loved to work for the Conservative party. In those days it spread over most of the Weald of Kent, which made all summer outings a treat. My speaking improved and led to more requests from the party's Speakers' Office to visit other people's constituencies. The Minister of Agriculture asked me to join a working party on farm policy. In September 1952, the Chief Whip, Patrick Buchan-Hepburn, wrote to tell me that the party was about to press for party political broadcasts on television. I was instructed to undergo coaching in television technique, so as to be ready to interview Ministers. As it turned out, I interviewed Harold Macmillan, then Housing Minister, in the first party political broadcast ever on television – 'a vintage piece of television comedy', as Michael Cockerell of the BBC was later to describe it.

One of the things that made it comic was the necessity of learning our lines by heart. There was no way of recording the performance. Professional actors can repeat a line fifty times and still sound as if they mean it. We were not in that class. At one point, for instance, I was required to put a question to Harold Macmillan: 'What about Scotland?' At which he was supposed to look mildly taken by surprise and say: 'Ah, Scotland! I am glad you asked about Scotland.' After we had repeated this exchange like idiots a dozen times through the day's rehearsals, it lost all spontaneity and assumed a surreal quality. Naturally, Cockerell finds it funny. 'What fun it was!' Macmillan scribbled at the foot of a thank-you letter to me. We did not think so at the time. After sundry rehearsals earlier in the week, we spent the whole of a Saturday under the iron hand of Grace Wyndham Goldie of the BBC. An hour before the broadcast, which in the then primitive state of television had to go out live, she ordered us to rest on bunk beds in the basement of Lime Grove. 'Awfully like the trenches,' Macmillan murmured to me, as we dozed off.

Winston Churchill, now Prime Minister, wrote asking me to play a part in the Consultative Assembly of the Council of Europe. I decided the job was not for me, and declined. I was offered a modest brief with the United Nations for three months and took the same decision. In the autumn, the Foreign Office dispatched me on an exhausting eight-week speaking tour of the United States. Under our arrangements the British Information Service, New York, paid all my travel and hotel expenses and gave me an allowance of $25 a day. I returned to them all fees received. 'Remember, always look under your plate after the meal,' they advised, 'often the cheque is there.' I looked under every plate, and considering I was totally unknown received generous fees, but BIS finished up in the red. My tour began in New York, moved through Pittsburgh, Philadelphia and Washington, then plunged south through the Georgias and Florida, crossed the southern states – I was granted a three-day break in New Orleans which I spent in bed – and then turned northwards through St Louis, and homewards via Cincinnati and Detroit.

One of the subjects I was required to speak on was the new National Health Service. 'You need to be careful on that one,' they said. 'Americans call it socialist medicine.' On the contrary, I found American audiences eager for information about it. The cost of their own medical arrangements could financially cripple families of modest incomes in a sudden emergency. Travelling through the southern states, I was embarrassed by the fact that the prominent English figure who had taken the same lecture route and met much the same people only a few weeks earlier had since been charged in Britain with homosexual offences. This, of course, was before a change in the law. My hosts could hardly bring themselves to mention the subject. They were profoundly shocked, in a way that is inconceivable today, which illustrates how swiftly social attitudes can change within half a century.

Within the confines of this country's post-war world therefore, I felt myself for a while to be moderately successful. I was on the tail end of an old order, which was about to change rapidly into something for which I was less well equipped. The post-war Tory party under Winston Churchill was not dramatically different from the party which I had come to know in the 1930s. Gentlemen from the landowning class, with moderately good war records, were well regarded and, irrespective of their academic record, were seen to be ideal parliamentarians. Tory MPs of working-class origin were rare. There was a tendency to treat them as mascots. From the mid-1950s onwards, as we slowly recovered from post-war trials, the English revolution began to take shape, leading on to the 1960s. Much that we attribute to the 1960s had began in the 1950s and continued long afterwards, indeed still continues.

It has always been my belief that the British ruling class lost its authority on the Somme in 1916. 'Lions led by donkeys,' as Max Hoffman observed to General Ludendorff. After 1 July, 1916, when the British Army suffered 60,000 casualties in a single day, men would never again trust their leaders in the same way. That war cost us a generation of leaders at every social level. Glance at any village war memorial. You will find the names of families which are part of the history of that village. Those losses, though discounted as the years went by, have had profound consequences for the history of this country during the past seventy-five years. They thinned the ranks of leaders in every walk of life. The dissolution of Empire, which began with India soon after the First World War, and which continued more rapidly after the Second, also played a part in thinning the ranks of those ready to answer for heavy responsibilities. Some would have us look back on those days with a sense of shame. I have always felt profound respect for men and women who were ready to devote the best years of their lives to overseas service. That is why in recent years I have come to admire their successors, who in the difficult and often distraught post-colonial era have chosen to give a life of service to aid and development organizations.

The English have long been half in love with the amateur – in all games, particularly cricket, in the City of London, and at Westminster. Someone like Prince Ranjitsinhji, with his silk cricket shirts and habit of putting gold sovereigns on stumps in the nets to encourage professional bowlers, became a legendary figure in the cricketing world of my youth. It took a long time to wean this nation off this preference for amateur status, its faint mistrust of the professional. In my early days at Westminster the first figure to emerge from this process was Iain Macleod. 'Too clever by half,' was Lord Salisbury's verdict – a brilliant illustration of the point I am making. *Bridge Is an Easy Game* was the title of one of Macleod's books on bridge – at which he excelled. After three or four years at Westminster it struck me that politics was an easy game as well. But in politics, as in cricket, the amateur was on his way out.

9

Junior Minister

One Saturday morning in October 1954, my first week-end at home for three weeks, I was called to the telephone by one of Winston Churchill's private secretaries. Would I come to No. 10 and see the Prime Minister at 4.45 p.m.? To be on the safe side, I arrived in London early and went to my club in Pall Mall to fortify myself with tea. A further message from No. 10 arrived: could I make it a little earlier, say 4.30 p.m.? Tealess, I walked from Pall Mall to Downing Street. At No. 10 they seemed surprised to see me, and experienced some difficulty over the name. They led me to a waiting room which had some good pictures, a well-stocked bookcase and three comfortable chairs. I felt the best posture to strike would be that of an intelligent critic of the pictures. While I was doing this, a secretary looked in. 'The Prime Minister will not keep you long. He's on the telephone.' Then the Chief Whip, Patrick Buchan-Hepburn, sidled round the door with a conspiratorial eye. 'Don't tell him I've seen you. It's a job. I hope you'll accept.' I think the corners of my mouth went down. 'The finance might be difficult,' he said. 'For any young man with children,' I replied. Quite, but he hoped I would really try to accept. 'To get on the bandwagon.' That was important. He departed. Another ten minutes passed. Then a male private secretary. 'Can we persuade you to come along?' My goodness, the ritual! In these days junior posts are usually arranged on the telephone.

I was shown into the Cabinet room. Sitting at one end of the long table was Winston Churchill. He rose, not without an effort, and shook me by the hand, then pointed to the vacant chair on his right. A spotlight from above and behind his head shone on me. A weak whisky and soda in a wine glass stood before him. It had a white card on top, I supposed to keep the flies out. 'We are undertaking a reshuffle of the Government,' said Winston. He hoped I would be able to join. 'Duncan Sandys would like to have you at the Ministry of Housing.' Macmillan was leaving Housing for Defence. I said this was a great honour, and of course I must accept. Of course, he said. I added I thought it best to be frank about these things; it was not an easy decision for a married man with young children. My salary as parliamentary secretary at Housing and Local Government would be £1,500, to which £500 of my parliamentary salary only could be added: £2,000 in all. I enjoyed no private income. He took the point. 'I know, I know. I can assure you the Chancellor has it at the very forefront of his mind.' At this point I felt I had lowered the tone of our conversation and hastened to add, 'It's not really important; it's just that I have more than number one to consider.' 'It matters like hell,' said Winston. 'I know. I've been through all the same difficulties.'

The softening-up process continued. Duncan would like to have me, he explained. He wanted someone with parliamentary ability – a highly musical note. 'I'd better have a talk with Duncan,' he said suddenly and pushed a button. A private secretary entered. 'Get Duncan,' said Winston. I made to go, but he detained me. Would I have a whisky and soda? No. 'You're not teetotal?' he exclaimed. Then he fingered a piece of paper lying face down on the table. 'Twenty moves,' he murmured. Twenty moves had been going round his head. He was a month off his eightieth birthday. Government was a very complex business, he said, now more than ever. Then he got up, took a large lighter and lit his cigar. He rang another bell and had the spotlight extinguished. A few personal questions. I had a feeling it was an effort. He wore an evening soft shirt and bow tie. His waistcoat was crumpled and ashy. Had I been in here before? No. He'd had it changed. A few bookshelves removed. The walls looked white and clean. He rang again. Any sign of Duncan? Apparently not. I felt I must slip out. Again he rose and shook hands, smiled and thanked me. At the door, 'Nothing until Monday!'

I encountered the Chief Whip and Christopher Soames, then parliamentary private secretary to his father-in-law the Prime Minister. 'Another happy officer,' murmured Soames. I was helped into my coat and escorted out, this time by the back way. 'Did you accept?' said the Chief Whip. Yes. 'Well done.' He thumped my back. I felt a rather taut hero.

Next day I travelled to London again to lunch with Duncan Sandys in Vincent Square. I began to feel that I had surrendered all control over my personal life – as indeed I had. He warned me that we would, as usual, return to the fag end of the old session that week, after the long recess, and would be expected to deal with a mass of Lords amendments to some Town and Country Planning Bill, about which I knew nothing. We spent Monday at the Ministry, which was then in Whitehall, dividing responsibility for this forlorn task between our two selves and the Solicitor-General; and then swotting up the amendments. The Labour party's spokesmen, who were of course thoroughly familiar with the Bill and the amendments, were merciful. Duncan Sandys had feared they might, on plumbing the depths of our ignorance, call for the adjournment of the House. I think they rather enjoyed the sensation of having us totally at their mercy. We scrambled through. The day haunted me for a long time, like one of those recurring nightmares where you find yourself chasing trains which departed a day earlier.

There was quite a bit of that. Sandys and I had replaced a famous team, Harold Macmillan, an accomplished politician, and Ernest Marples, who was a practising engineer. Marples had been moved from Housing to Pensions on grounds that his partnership in an engineering company called Marples Ridgeway rendered him vulnerable at the Ministry of Housing and Local Government. It had in fact enabled him to be of great technical assistance to Harold Macmillan, when he was called on by the party to speed up the housing drive – and to deliver 300,000 new houses in a single year. It was a hard act to follow. In the first ten days of my new career I had to deliver a learned address to one of the main local government organizations at Blackpool – and then to answer their questions. My advisers saw me through. A certain Mr Pilgrim, after conflict with authority over the building of a bungalow, had committed suicide. It made a meal for the popular newspapers. Churchill's orders to Sandys were: 'No more Mr Pilgrims.' Against the united scepticism of our permanent officials, we set about drafting legislation on those lines.

Outstanding among the department's officials was Evelyn Sharp, then deputy permanent secretary, a woman of charm, determination and formidable intellect. Educated at St Paul's Girls School, where she had won athletic distinctions, and Somerville College, she had entered the Home Civil Service in 1926. By the time I reached the Ministry she had acquired a big reputation in Whitehall. Her qualities included a directness in all her dealings which occasionally left one breathless. In the following year she was to become the first woman ever to be appointed a permanent secretary. Her recreation at the time was tennis. I found that any encounter with her on a matter about which she felt strongly ended 6–1, 6–0 in her favour. A fair-minded woman, she allotted me a handicap. At the end of any argument in which she felt that I had played well, she would gracefully concede a point or two. Most of the arguments related to local authorities, who saw her as their champion. One of her achievements was to bring central and local government more closely together. She was a driving force behind the New Towns and the town development schemes designed to take the pressure off London. More than anyone I had yet met she brought home to me in the most charming fashion that my intellectual equipment for high office was inadequate.

On my other flank was Duncan Sandys, another of Churchill's sons-in-law and an experienced politician. He had won a reputation for being the most thorough Minister in the Government. What he lacked in brilliance, he made up for in doggedness. I came to suppose that Winston Churchill had trained him to test every proposition from Civil Servants to breaking point. It involved long hours. On Monday evenings, supposedly refreshed by the week-end break, we would embark on what Duncan called a 'session'. We would meet the officials around 7 p.m. at the Ministry and then work with them until the small hours. Any draft of a Bill or White Paper attracted this process. We would go through it not simply clause by clause but word for word. 'I don't follow the meaning of this word,' Duncan would say. Half an hour later, with Big Ben chiming 2 a.m. he would grudgingly concede the point, and we would move to the next line. He found it difficult to persuade his personal staff to submit to this system. 'I have good news,' he confided to me one day. 'My new stenographer is a widow, anxious to educate her children well. The overtime is most welcome to her. It means that we can count on her services however late we sit.'

On personal grounds, I could not have wished to have a more generous master. Early in his career as a junior minister, Duncan declared, he had suffered from Ministers who kept all the main business to themselves and treated him as a bottle washer. Our relations, he promised, would be otherwise. I was given full responsibility for certain functions in this ramshackle department. Duncan would generally approve whatever recommendations I chose to make. Innumerable planning appeals piled on to our desks. He apportioned a share of them to me. They were usually accompanied by a note of advice from

Evelyn Sharp. Occasionally I disagreed with her simply on wider political grounds. That would take anything up to an hour of friendly wrangling. There were frequent adjournment debates, usually late at night, and conferences and dinners which had to be addressed. On top of all this, I found the late Monday sessions increasingly trying. Early in 1955 I began to feel thoroughly ill, and took an enforced rest. My doctor declared me to be fit but exhausted. In truth I did not have the intellectual ability to meet the demands of the department, which called for mastery of fine detail over a wide range of subjects. Nowadays the Department of Environment has half a dozen Ministers of various ranks. In those days there was only Duncan Sandys and me. There was, however, one major test to come.

In the autumn of 1955, the Conservative party conference took place at Bournemouth. I dutifully attended and, because junior ministers had to pay all their own expenses, gratefully accepted hospitality from a cousin in the district, Rachel Grylls. We had occasionally gone out together in London before the war. I counted on a few days of jolly relaxation. Early on the second morning of my stay, I received a telephone call from Lord Woolton, then chairman of the Conservative party. No doubt, he said, I had heard that due to urgent personal reasons Duncan Sandys would be unable to speak in that afternoon's debate on Housing. I would replace him. I was aware that Duncan's relations with his wife were under increasing strain, and felt every desire to help. I had just four hours to prepare an adequate speech. Civil Servants are not supposed to assist in party political speeches. There was therefore no brief. My symptoms of nervous apprehension returned. Rachel Grylls, who had recently been involved in a bad car accident, offered some pills which her doctor had prescribed to take her mind off it. In those days they went by the name of 'purple hearts' – a judicious mixture of amphetamine and barbiturate. I swallowed one and composed what seemed to me a brilliant speech. Just before the debate I swallowed a second. The speech was well received.

On the following Monday officials in the department gave me encouraging smiles. They were a thoroughly nice lot, who made every allowance for my inadequacies. My private office was perpetually watchful for encounters which might land me in trouble. On one occasion they accepted on my behalf an invitation to lunch with a prominent builder at the Connaught Hotel. I was drinking a champagne cocktail with him when I was suddenly summoned to the telephone. 'Minister, we owe you an apology. Your host has a long-standing appeal pending and he will raise it with you. We should have spotted this. We know you will be careful.' By the time I had returned, my host had set up a second champagne cocktail. I swilled it confidently. 'I have your measure,' I said to myself.

They were wonderfully supportive in the private office. There was an occasion when I had suddenly to take the place of Duncan Sandys and open a large housing estate in the Potteries. The lady mayoress approached me. 'You are', she murmured, 'about to be offered the choice of patterns for a complete dinner service. May I offer a word of advice? The Queen was up here the other day and received this pattern.' She pointed to a sample plate. 'I think it is lovely. If I were you, I would choose it. After all, you and the Queen are unlikely to be dining much in each other's houses!' It was rather like accepting a well-bred stallion from a prince in Saudi Arabia. You do not lightly brush it aside.

When eventually the entire dinner service fetched up in my private office, they moved to panic stations. 'Minister, you realize that this is totally unacceptable.' Truthfully, I said, 'I have not given it much thought.' 'Minister, it must be returned at once.' That was okay by me, I said, but the courtesies must be observed. 'We can hardly shunt the whole dinner service back into their laps without a word of explanation.' 'Minister, we could suggest a small token to mark this occasion.' So be it, I said. They took it all in good grace in the Potteries, and came back with an exquisitely designed plate of bone china made by Minton. It passed by a whisker in my private office. Some years later when Tony Crosland, a Labour Minister in the same department, became involved in a bizarre row about acceptance of a silver coffee pot, it struck me how well they had looked after me.

My personal relations with Duncan Sandys, notwithstanding his workaholic approach to everything, remained good throughout. But towards the end of 1955 I was physically relieved to receive a telephone call from Anthony Eden, who had replaced Churchill earlier in the year, inviting me to be junior minister at the Home Office. Sir Colin Coote, still editor of the *Daily Telegraph*, wrote to congratulate me on what he interpreted as promotion. To me, it was simply a blessed relief. I had by then begun to suspect that office in Government was not my world. Journalists are vagrants. Their world and the Minister's world are poles apart. I found the disciplines of life in Whitehall irksome. It was a benevolent yoke, but it was still a yoke. Experience at the Ministry of Housing, I have since concluded, was a voyage of self-discovery. I was simply not equipped to be a good Minister. I hankered after one of those long winter nights when half a dozen of us had been chasing the same story and, copy filed, met up in the same pub to hoist a beer or two and compare notes.

Gwilym Lloyd George, son of a famous father, and Home Secretary 1954–7, was an altogether more relaxed figure than Duncan Sandys. He had been a Minister throughout the war, and had no thought of further advancement. He was a rare bird in Government in that he was thoroughly considerate about other people. Early in our year together, he told me that shooting was his recreation. To make the lives of the Special Branch men who had constantly to be with him more interesting, he had paid for them to shoot on a clay-pigeon range. They could then have the pleasure of judging whether he was shooting well or badly. Gil Lloyd George came closer than any other Minister I worked with to fulfilling Arthur Balfour's aphorism, 'Nothing matters very much; and very little matters at all.'

His phlegmatic attitude was seen at its best when the two leaders of the Soviet Union, Marshal Bulganin and Nikita Khrushchev, came on an official visit to this country, which included a call at the Home Office. For some reason we were totally unprepared for this event. When the pair arrived at the Home Office they were shunted into a small, unattractive waiting room reserved for unwelcome visitors, aliens and so forth and told to cool their heels while inquiries were made. There was a tremendous bustle in our private offices. The Home Secretary, Lord Mancroft (who was joint parliamentary under-secretary of state with me) and I arrived breathless and more or less simultaneously at the main entrance. That was not the worst of it.

While the pair were in the Home Office a certain amount of booing went on from the crowd outside. 'Quite right too,' one of the policemen inside the building murmured, 'but I mustn't say so.' Lord Mancroft thought this droll and passed it on, attributably, to the press. It appeared in the evening newspapers. The Prime Minister, Anthony Eden, was enraged. He summoned Stormant Mancroft to No. 10. Stormant came hastily to consult me. Unfeelingly, with beatings at school in mind, I advised him to put a silk handkerchief in the seat of his pants, but on no account to resign. He kept his job.

The most stimulating figure among us at the Home Office was the permanent secretary, Sir Frank Newsam, a West Indian, who after a good war with the Royal Irish Regiment had arrived at the Home Office in 1920. He had been permanent secretary since 1948 and was held in awe, not simply in our department but by Cabinet Ministers who had made the mistake of crossing him. Newsam had the virtue of being far ruder to his superiors than to his inferiors. I came off well. We never had a cross word. It was custom and practice in the Home Office for a parliamentary under-secretary to visit the permanent secretary's room if he wished to consult him, not the other way round. Newsam brushed this aside. 'If I can help, ask me round,' he said.

The only person who did not hold Newsam in awe was Stella Reading, formidable founder and chairman of the Women's Royal Voluntary Service and widow of a former Viceroy of India, the Marquess of Reading. When she visited the Home Office, as she sometimes did to discuss civil defence, senior figures hid under their desks. I had only one light brush with Newsam. There was an adjournment debate in the House of Commons seeking to move the remains of Sir Roger Casement, who had been hanged as a traitor in 1916, from the grounds of Pentonville prison to another grave. [His remains were returned by the British Government to Dublin in 1965 and are now in Glasnevin cemetery.] Called on to answer the debate, I felt I had a right to see the Home Office files about him. 'Nobody ever sees the Casement files,' said Newsam firmly. 'I am not taking on this debate without seeing it,' I retorted. We agreed, more or less amicably, that the Home Secretary should arbitrate on the matter. Lloyd George obligingly said he personally wished to see the Casement files, which were then fetched up from the basement. He handed them over to me. It was a disappointing exercise. I found nothing sensational, but enjoyed the feeling that I had scored over Newsam, and that no one could spring a surprise on me during the debate.

From the autumn of 1956 onwards, the Suez crisis called senior Ministers constantly to Cabinet. In such crises junior ministers have the worst of all worlds. They are not consulted by those taking decisions, nor can they plot in corridors with back-bench MPs. We were neutralized. My only share in the drama was attending increasingly disorderly scenes in the

House of Commons. One consequence of the crisis was that a larger share of Home Office business came my way. It included the short-lived Homicide Bill, a last-minute attempt to retain capital punishment for murder by gangsters. Lloyd George had consulted me about this. He had visited prisons occupied by men serving exceptionally long sentences. He formed the view that this constituted a living death, and was reluctant to abandon capital punishment altogether. I was moved by his attitude, because I knew what torment the death penalty was to him. In those days the final appeal on behalf of a man about to be hanged came to the Home Secretary, who was required to read through all the relevant papers and a transcript of the trial. This could take the best part of two days. On the Home Secretary's desk stood a grisly message in Latin to the effect that it is impossible to take too much trouble when a man's life is at stake.

Frank Newsam, who had no illusions about my capacities, determined that the Suez crisis and Lloyd George's enforced absence should not imperil the Homicide Bill. He put me though stiff rehearsals. One of my last sights of Newsam was of him sitting at his desk in shirtsleeves, handling three telephones simultaneously and barking instructions for our reception of a sudden influx of Hungarian refugees. His portrait hangs in the Police College at Bramshill, for which he was the inspiration, and there is a memorial lecture in his name. I was lucky to enter his orbit.

On 9 January 1957 I returned from inspecting something at Harwich to be told by an old friend among the lobby correspondents that big political moves were afoot. The Queen was returning from Sandringham. I took the next day off and spent it in glorious weather watching the President's Putter at Rye while deliberations took place in London on who should be the next Prime Minister. That being resolved in favour of Macmillan, there were two or three days to wait while he made appointments. On these occasions the bush telegraph among the Civil Servants is efficient, and sometimes right. They were confident I would remain in the Home Office, and were nice enough to express the hope that I would. I thought otherwise. I intimated as much to Rab Butler, one of whose several consolation prizes for not being Prime Minister was the Home Office (he had been Chancellor of the Exchequer under Eden). It seemed to me that two years on £2,000 a year was sufficient duty – and penalty for my family – for the time being. I put this as tactfully as I could to the new Prime Minister. He expressed regret, and a hope that I would return at some point. 'I will write you a little letter,' he murmured, and was as good as his word. It put on record that I had retired from office at my own wish. My father was happy to receive it to show his friends.

Sir Colin Coote wrote quickly to say that he would be delighted to have me back on the *Daily Telegraph*, and proposed a lunch to discuss matters. In consequence I would be £1,000 – or 50 per cent – a year better off. It made a difference.

At the same time Rab Butler asked me to lunch with him privately in his house in Smith Square. I noted down at the time 'sherry, claret, a good hash, but comfortless'. A housekeeper was in charge. We commiserated over the lunch table – though Rab had more to be sorry about than I had. Our lunch produced many 'Rabisms', which I found difficult to interpret. 'Anthony was loyal to me at the end. I knew that we did not always agree. But he was loyal.' I took this to mean that Eden had recommended Rab as his successor. He reported for my benefit that Lord Salisbury had said to him, 'It matters less what position you hold than being *in* politics.' He approved of this, and commended it to me. He badly wanted reassurances that he had done the right things. He had telephoned Winston – 'I went for the older man ...' – and left that sentence hanging in the air, repeating, 'I went for the older man ...' We turned to Rab's new appointment as Home Secretary. Gwilym Lloyd George had said to me, 'Harold Macmillan told me how embarrassed he was ... Rab had insisted on being Home Secretary, would accept no alternative.' So Lloyd George, not disposed to make difficulties, went. Rab's report to me was different. 'He [Macmillan] wanted me to do it. Otherwise one is out in a boat...' I was left to weigh whether Butler or Macmillan was guilty of slight deception.

We talked of the departed Prime Minister. 'Eden has not been well for a long time. The operation had done in his liver. The liver affected his nerves. This led to day drugs and night drugs. Clearly a fearful struggle.' John Morrison, MP for Salisbury, Chairman of the Conservative Party back-bench 1922 committee 1955–64, had lunched at No. 10 soon after Eden returned from Jamaica, where he had gone to recuperate shortly before deciding to resign. Eden had arrived from the Cabinet at 1.20, plainly done in, and had taken half a bottle of champagne, but then made no sense at all. It emerged that Rab's life at the Treasury under Eden had been a considerable trial. Perpetual telephoning was often complicated by the fact that Eden would never leave time for the scrambler to warm up. At the height of the Suez crisis he had telephoned Anthony Head, then Minister of Defence. All Head could hear were the concluding sentences. He asked Eden for a rerun, which went down badly.

One of my few regrets on leaving office, and the Home Office in particular, was the loss of an opportunity to work alongside Rab Butler. I felt his influence and I learned more from him than any other figure I encountered in politics.

Always excited more by failure than by success among politicians, journalists have dwelt exhaustively on why Rab Butler failed to become Prime Minister in 1957 and again in 1963. This does less than justice to one of the considerable political figures of this century. Rab was a heavyweight. I first came to know him while I was the *Morning Post*'s political correspondent in 1937. He had made his mark as a junior minister during the passage of the Government of India Bill. In the teeth of opposition from Winston Churchill and his diehard friends, Rab and his chief, Sir Samuel Hoare, had pushed this enormous Bill through the House. It was Butler's mastery of it that attracted admiration.

He was rewarded in a somewhat back-handed fashion by a move to the same ministerial rank at the Ministry of Labour. When I congratulated him in the lobby on this, he gave me one of his sideways looks, and said there seemed to be a lot to learn quickly. He then drew a copy of the Ministry's standing orders from his pocket and observed: 'I have to study these in the lavatory.' A year later he received serious promotion and went to the Foreign Office as parliamentary under secretary to Lord Halifax. Thus he became spokesman for the Foreign Office in the House of Commons. I came to admire his stonewalling against the call for intervention in the Spanish Civil War.

He was at the Foreign Office through Munich, with all that that implied, until 1941 when Churchill, who respected his brains but never treated him as a crony, put him in charge of Education. The fruit of that was the monumental Education Act of 1944.

Years later, I came to know well James Chuter Ede, Labour Home Secretary 1945–51, who had been Rab's parliamentary secretary at Education in the wartime Coalition. He thought the delicate negotiations which Rab had conducted with the teaching profession and the Churches represented an historic achievement. Accordingly, he told me, he had kept all his papers from those times and proposed to put them into safe custody.

Rab Butler was not only an intellectual heavyweight; he was also part of an older order in the Tory party. He came from a family which had rendered long public service to this country, much of it in India; and that tradition, I came to see, counted for more with him than personal advancement. He once baffled his colleagues by trotting out a trite ditty: 'Nations earn their right to rise by service and by sacrifice.' Rab had ambitions, as every politician should have, but they were subordinate to this innermost devotion to public service for its own sake. Some have said that Butler's reluctance to press his claims more forcibly in 1957, and still more in 1963 – when he could have killed Alec Home's chances of forming an administration – betrayed a weakness of character. I differ. There was a strong element of service before self in Butler.

Many, including Churchill himself, were surprised by Labour's overwhelming victory in the General Election of 1945. As we began to settle down after the war, I became less and less surprised; for I perceived what a tremendous gap had lain between Tory thinking in the 1930s and public expectations in the mid-1940s. Rab Butler saw that more clearly than anyone else, and so became a principal architect to the post-war Tory party. At Churchill's direction, he took charge of the Conservative party's Research Department and revived it, while drawing to its ranks some extremely able young men. For the next eighteen years, as Anthony Howard declares in his biography of Rab, it 'was to provide the essential power base on which Rab's influence over the Party rested'. He persuaded Churchill to accept the Industrial Charter, a restatement of Tory philosophy in the new industrial world. He established himself among the younger element of the Tory party as the man with a mind for the future.

He had a difficult time at the Treasury, which coincided with the death of his first wife, Sydney. At the Home Office he produced *Penal Policy in a Changing Society*, which I have always ranked high among state papers of this century. Naturally, journalists – and some members of his own party – dwelt heavily on what came to be known as 'Rabisms'. Asked at one point if he thought Anthony Eden was the best Prime Minister we had, Rab replied, 'Yes,' and so went on record as declaring, 'Eden is the best Prime Minister we have.' Rabisms were not all due to inadvertence; a sense of mischief lurked. But it was petty stuff compared to the contribution Rab Butler made to the politics of his time and to the fortunes of his own party.

So why did the Tory party choose Harold Macmillan? I remember very well the critical 1922 Committee of Tory back-benchers meeting after Suez, at which both Butler and Macmillan spoke. Macmillan talked in self-deprecating style about taking a back seat in the Lords as if he was happy to leave high office. They rather liked that. There was uncertainty within the party as to how senior figures in the Cabinet had behaved in the last critical days of the Suez crisis. Macmillan won the benefit of the doubt; Rab Butler did not. Macmillan looked the more publicly reassuring figure – and at that point the Tory party was aware that a great deal of public reassurance was needed. As constituency correspondence I have kept since those days reminds me, Suez had shocked a lot of people. Macmillan looked the better therapist.

Because I chose this moment to leave office, I had no close experience of working with Macmillan until five years later. In some ways he was more suitable than Butler for the public of the late 1950s. His style had more popular appeal, and with the advent of television that was beginning to count for more and more. I recall a by-election at which I reported Macmillan's eve-of-poll speech. His peroration ran on these lines: 'There are two kinds of progress – the Rake's Progress and the Pilgrim's Progress. My friends, let us be pilgrims!' It went down a treat. In public, Macmillan appeared to be the extrovert, Rab Butler the introvert. In private, it was the other way round. Rab would talk with bewildering candour about his colleagues and his innermost feelings. I never heard much of that from Macmillan – possibly because I never came to know him well enough. He had a rich fund of political recollections, but most of them related to past events. Rab spoke more pointedly – and often naively – about his contemporaries.

Back in the 1950s, Macmillan was a wonderful friend to

many of the Tory party's new intake to the House of Commons. In our eyes, much of Churchill's front bench was composed of Olympian figures. They were men who had served him during the war. Macmillan was among them but, unlike most of them, he was an experienced parliamentarian. He would hear of small enterprises which some of us were concocting to embarrass the Labour Government of 1950–51. He would seek us out. 'If you will allow me,' he would say, 'I think we can have a lot of fun with this one.' Then he would adroitly add a sting to our proposed amendment.

Early in my parliamentary career, I was called upon to contribute a talk to a Saturday conference being held in Harold Macmillan's constituency of Bromley. His wife Lady Dorothy greeted me apologetically. 'Harold has to be elsewhere today. He will look in to greet you, but then has to be off!' Mine was the first address. Harold, as the local Member, rose to apologize for his impending departure. It was no great loss, he told his audience. They were going to hear about the future, not the past. His own political days were numbered. They would get better value from me, someone who represented the days ahead . . . But, before he went, he would just like to impart in a few sentences his own view of the future. Harold Macmillan then proceeded neatly to encapsulate in about three minutes all that I had intended to say. Amid tumultuous applause, he then left me to it.

Soon after my release from office early in 1957, a letter came from Grace Wyndham Goldie at the BBC television studios in Lime Grove, whom I had not met since the first televised party political broadcast of 1953 with Harold Macmillan, which I have described. She asked me to lunch with her to discuss ideas. As television developed, she pointed out, politics increasingly demanded attention. It was difficult to find enough people on the right to match the increasingly professional left. As a Conservative MP, might I be willing to help? She wanted to know the best way of presenting Westminster. I sent a long letter expressing my views on that question, but reserved my own position. Television was opening up, and plainly there might lie a fresh career there. I was an admirer of Mrs Wyndham Goldie, whose ideas were ahead of the pack. I liked the idea of working for her. On the other hand, the *Daily Telegraph* had just welcomed me home, like the prodigal son. I felt I must match its loyalty. I gratefully returned to the Peterborough column room at 135 Fleet Street. They had kept my name on the door!

10

Back-bencher

They talk of the 'fruits of office'. On leaving the Government as a junior minister, I found there were also fruits of being out of office. Toby Low, later Lord Aldington, and friend and neighbour, had retired from Government for the same reasons. Both of us were generously invited to join the One Nation group, the first ex-ministers to receive such an invitation. Founded in 1950 by a group of Conservative MPs disappointed by the performance of their own front bench, One Nation came to represent a certain philosophy. It was partly inspired by Disraeli's novel *Sybil, or the Two Nations*, in which he condemns a society divided by unbridled laissez-faire capitalism. Among the founders of the One Nation group in 1950 were Iain Macleod, Angus Maude, Cub Alport, Gilbert Longden and Enoch Powell. Macleod and Maude were joint editors of the first and seminal booklet the group produced just before the Tory party conference of 1950. Rab Butler wrote a foreword and called it a 'healthy piece of constructive work'. The group held a weekly dinner at the House of Commons, usually attended by ten or a dozen members. I found the political discussions of high value and sometimes a useful political lever. For after the Tories took office in 1951, the group would occasionally fire a shot across the Government's bows. It carried more weight than any single Member of Parliament. During my final years in the House of Commons I became the informal chairman of One Nation. Though unable to match the qualities of its founder members, I was happy to hold the baton for a while.

Out of office, other opportunities arose. Rab Butler invited me to join the Council of the Institute of Criminology at Cambridge University, then directed by that eccentric genius, Professor Leon Radzinowicz. Experience at the Home Office had given me a taste for penology. Crime and punishment in the modern world is an inexhaustible subject. I began to write articles about crime for the *Daily Telegraph*. Because I had also worked at Housing and Local Government, the Town and Country Planning Association asked me to join them, and I came to know that master of town planning and inspiration of the garden-city, Sir Frederic Osborn. That also was a good topic for journalism. I have always thought that Labour's promotion of the New Towns in its first post-war term of office was a distinguished achievement. Something had to be done to check London's sprawling boundaries. The New Towns helped to do this and to a great extent became self-contained. The New Town corporations, appointed to set these towns up, became in effect unchallenged directors of their enterprise. Local government, indeed local democracy, was temporarily suspended. It helped the corporations to get a move on. During my time at Housing and Local Government, I had occasionally to ask the House of Commons to vote large sums of money for these corporations. It was readily granted. Years later, I was invited to deliver a lecture in America on our New Towns, because they have never succeeded over there. My lecture was not a success. The audience at Miami University applauded politely but found the proposition outside their range of thinking.

There came also an invitation to join the Historic Building Council for England, which in many ways was the jolliest appointment of all. My knowledge of architecture was negligible, but the Council found space for two Members of Parliament, presumably as stewards for the taxpayer. My opposite number was the formidable but friendly James Chuter Ede, the former Home Secretary. He had also been junior partner to Rab Butler at the Ministry of Education throughout the war, and so co-architect of the Education Act of 1944. Our chairman was Sir Alan Lascelles, who had been assistant private secretary to the Prince of Wales (later King Edward VIII) and King George V, and private secretary to King George VI and, for the first year of her reign, to Queen Elizabeth. He had also had a wide range of good stories which enlivened our frugal lunches of Ministry of Works sandwiches. He once outlined to us the supper preferred by King George VI, when he returned to the Palace too weary to eat dinner after a long day out. It began with a cup of Bovril, laced with a tablespoonful of sherry. The main course was half a tin of sardines. To fill the chinks, there followed a little guava jelly on toast. I have tried it more than once, after a tiring day. It tastes better than it sounds.

Members of the Council included Christopher Hussey, who had been architectural contributor to *Country Life* for half a century, Sir James Mann, director of the Wallace Collection, Sir William (later Lord) Holford, a leading architect, Sir John Summerson and Lady Radnor. To hear them discussing the merits of historic buildings great and small was equivalent to taking a postgraduate course at a university. An added joy was our summer tour, when we spent a week in a chosen region of England visiting our clients and their properties. My recollection of those tours is that we ran into more grievances than gratitude. But I learned some facts of life about restoring ancient buildings, the most important of which was that, if dry rot is involved, then when estimating the cost, take the number you first thought of and quadruple it.

Rab Butler remained a friend and a political mentor. My wife and I occasionally spent a week-end with him at his home in Essex. On arrival before lunch on Saturdays, Rab would usually be found dialling local numbers on his telephone. He kept a long list of people from all walks of life who lived in his constituency. On Saturday mornings, he would call up a selection of them and ask them individually how they felt about things. Such a custom offers double value. The Member of Parliament gets to know where the shoe is pinching. At the same time, the constituent is pleased to be consulted by his distinguished Member. One can hear him at a well-appointed dinner party: 'As a matter of fact – and this, of course, must go no further – the Member of Parliament sought my advice on that very point . . .' Never feeling over-secure in his Essex seat, Rab knew very well how to win hearts and minds.

While he was Foreign Secretary under Alec Home in 1963–4, he invited me to go down and address a large meeting in his constituency. Some tremendous political row was going on over Cyprus, as there often was in those days. Since 1955 there had been a guerrilla campaign for *enosis* or union with Greece, started by Archbishop Makarios and General Grivas. In 1956, Makarios and some of the *enosis* leaders were deported. In 1959 a compromise was reached and Makarios returned to be elected president of an independent Greek–Turkish Cyprus. A year later, full independence was achieved, with Britain retaining its military bases. That was the start of further trouble. Cyprus must occupy a lot of shelf space in the Foreign Office and was still plaguing Butler in 1963.

Nobody therefore felt sure whether the Foreign Secretary would be able to get to the meeting. Just as I finished, he arrived. I expected him to talk about the urgent international topic which had detained him. Not a bit of it. He opened by declaring that he had been following closely in the county press some parish-pump dispute in the neighbourhood. Having demonstrated his knowledge of its detail, he then outlined his own solution to the problem. He had the meeting rapt with attention.

During his years in that grim department, the Home Office (1957–62), Rab won a reputation for displaying a sense of humour. Tom Critchley, who worked there for many years, once gave me a sample of it. A demonstration outside 10

Downing Street became noisy and the police were called in. Suddenly a police dog, standing with its handler under the Foreign Office arch, barked threateningly. This apparent act of intimidation aroused furious indignation among the demonstrators. Parliamentary questions were tabled, files flew round the Home Office. Eventually, they arrived on Rab's desk. The officials' line was that the dog had been taken by its handler in case of need; and that it was most unfortunate it had had the temerity to bark, and so unsettle the nerves of the demonstrators. Rab's minute on the file read: 'Who advised the dog?'

In the course of 1957, free from the tyranny of having always to speak in the Government's name, I inflicted thirty-seven speeches on different audiences, half of them at conferences or occasions outside my constituency. I began to find that, if the wind was in the right quarter, the audience in the right mood, and I had prepared the speech sensibly, what I had to say was well received. I became interested in the art of making speeches which held the audience. By far the hardest place to do this is the House of Commons – not simply because of its political divisions, but because the audience there will instantly spot the difference between a good and a bad political speech.

On 8 July 1958 I was unexpectedly asked to wind up from the back benches a major debate on a report from the Committee of Privileges. The issue, which cut across party boundaries, was complex. A Labour Member and Privy Councillor, G. R. Strauss, had been threatened with a writ for libel by the chairman of the London Electricity Board, in respect of a letter he had written to the (Conservative) Paymaster-General about the LEB's disposal of scrap. In accordance with the conventions then relating to nationalized industries, the Paymaster-General declared the matter to be one of day-to-day administration and so outside his responsibility. But he sent a copy of Strauss's letter to the LEB chairman, who foolishly took offence and told Strauss that he must withdraw his allegations and apologize, or face a writ for libel. Strauss reported this threat to the House, and it was solemnly referred to the Committee of Privileges.

I was opposed to invoking parliamentary privilege in this matter and spoke accordingly. 'The risks we run today', I argued, 'are incomparably lighter than some of the risks which have been borne in past centuries by our predecessors. Men who sat on these benches in pursuit of public duty, according to their lights, have met with more violent ends than the issue of a writ. We are rightly proud to be their heirs and successors and we ought not to take too timorous a view of the consequences. Public duty cannot be made altogether safe for anybody.'

I went on: 'That brings me, in conclusion, to some wider reflections which I venture to put before the House. In whatever way we may regard parliamentary democracy, it does impose upon us, the elected, certain obligations of leadership. By and large, democratic leadership is not doing too well in the world outside at this moment. It is getting badly knocked about – mercifully much less here than elsewhere. It is always difficult to define the ingredients which go to make it up, though countless speeches have been made on the subject. One can say it rests, this leadership – certainly as we represent it here – on certain tacit, unwritten but accepted terms between the people and Parliament, between leaders and the led. I do not think parliamentary privilege or rights play a very large part in those terms. The main element, I think, can be expressed in one word, "trust".

'We are trustees. I prefer that word to "servants" or "leaders". To some, that trust between those whose govern and those who are governed has never been quite the same since the events of the First World War, and in particular since that fearful battle on the Somme that was going on just forty-two years ago. After that, no one was going to feel quite the same towards the Government or towards their leaders. After that, the trust was never again going to be quite so implicit . . . It follows that there is a need today to foster and to cherish that trust by all means. It is the cement of our parliamentary democracy . . .'

Quoting speeches from the past is nearly always a mistake, but I enter these passages because this question of trust between those who govern and those who are governed went to the root of my own philosophy and has become so much more doubtful than it was in 1958. The House, though full and excitable, was kind enough to hear me through fifteen minutes of this without interruption. For a short while I felt I had command of the House, and that, once in a lifetime, is enough.

The House of Commons is susceptible to tone. David Lloyd George, perhaps the best debater there this century, liked to begin provocatively. He would create uproar on the benches opposite in the first minute or two and so give the chamber time to fill before making his main points. A witty speech will always be heard appreciatively. Aneurin Bevan, who at his best was in the Lloyd George class, occasionally contrived to have the Tory benches wincing and laughing at the same time. Members will also listen joyfully to someone who is attacking his own side. Short of that, I often found it helpful to concede at least one point to a Member who has spoken on the other side and to express doubt about something that has been said on your own side. It creates an impression of fairmindedness, which the House likes. There are many tricks attached to the game, of which few are master. One of them is to secure the ear of the House by pointing to some Member on the opposite side and saying in effect: 'the Honourable Member is quite right! I agree with every word he said . . .' You then go on to turn his words round so that they appear to support your own arguments. It calls for a quick ear and even quicker thinking.

Harold Macmillan once showed me a good way to prepare for any debate. He took a sheet of paper and ruled off the left-hand third of it. The substance of his own speech was then written or typed on the remaining two-thirds. During the course of the debate he jotted down in the left-hand margin in the appropriate places anything said relevant to his own remarks, and the speaker's name. Thus, when he came to reply, he could hold to the frame of his own speech, yet constantly refer to what other people had said. I have found the method particularly helpful for debates in places like the Oxford or Cambridge Union, which sometimes become pretty knock-about and it is well to have something solid on which to base a winding-up speech.

These debates are usually opened by undergraduates, who are speaking from the front bench for the first time. In all probability their parents will have attended the dinner beforehand and will be sitting anxiously in the gallery. As a visiting speaker, I have found it politic to open by saying nice things about their performances – particularly the performance of the undergraduate speaking against you. It gives pleasure to the parents and pleases both sides of the House. The object of these debates, after all, is not wholly to win, but also to suggest to the generation ahead that courtesy never comes amiss in our style of debating.

In the past, great political figures have been able to address large audiences for an hour or more off a single sheet of paper with half a dozen ideas on it. Perhaps they had more time than we have these days to prepare and memorize what they wanted to say. Stanley Baldwin could do it. His speech to the Commons on the Abdication of King Edward VIII was delivered, as I have shown, off scraps of paper. Clem Attlee could do it in that clipped manner of his. Churchill liked a full note in front of him; so did Macmillan, and so usually did Margaret Thatcher. But there is more than one way of preparing the note. I have always used Churchill's method, which is to set down the speech like poetry on quarto sheets of papers. If it is properly done, the eye can pick up two, three or more lines at a glance, and so convey the impression of speaking almost extempore. Underlining key words helps. Having learned early in life to be a touch typist, I could set out my speech exactly as I wanted it.

Speaking and writing call for different styles. A good piece of prose is often hard to deliver and will not sound well. A speech which holds the audience will not always read well on paper. I admired the style of the speechwriters who worked for Jack and Edward Kennedy, and Peggy Noonan, the Irish housewife, who drafted speeches for Presidents Reagan and Bush. The simplest sentences almost always sound best, viz.: 'I do not think that we can go on as we are now . . .' The Kennedy speechwriters were good at what I call the cascade method, such as: 'Let every nation know, whether it wishes us well or ill, that we shall pay any price, bear any burden, meet any hardship, support any friend or oppose any foe to assure the survival and success of liberty . . .' Rhythm is important. I once spent a long time constructing a single sentence in a speech for CARE, the international aid and development organization. It ran something like this: 'The work goes on, the risks are faced, the challenges met, the losses endured' – pause – 'for there is a spirit behind this movement that will never die.' Cadences are also important. Jesse Jackson, who has twice sought the Democrats' Presidential nomination in the United States, is good on cadences. At half a dozen points in one of his convention speeches, he intoned the words, 'Keep hope alive.' It was effective.

The modern school of thought is that only the substance of what you say counts, and that the delivery is unimportant. Some university lecturers exemplify this with unstructured sentences and careless enunciation. When I attend seminars and hear this, I am struck by what a waste it is of our fine language.

After almost a decade in the House of Commons, I was conscious of a shift in my priorities. I no longer felt I had publicly and perpetually to convince my constituents that I was a hard-working MP by bouncing up and down in the House of

Commons or by calling in the local press to advertise my local accomplishments. Having voluntarily left Government office. I felt no desire to persuade the whips by public performances that I had the making of a Minister. There is a lot of useful work to be done by a Member of Parliament which attracts little or no public attention. I began to devote more time to it.

Late in the 1950s, Harold Macmillan came to the conclusion that his Government was badly out of step with the Church of England. He and Charles Hill, who was then Chancellor of the Duchy of Lancaster conceived the idea of giving a private dinner party at the House of Commons to half a dozen bishops, whenever Church Assembly was being held in London. Sir Hubert Ashton, who was Church Commissioner as well as a Member of Parliament at the time, was asked to be convenor. I was called upon to act as host and chairman. For the next two or three years, we held a number of these private dinners for bishops of widely different political views. I always invited one senior Cabinet Minister to join us, not to speak, but to discuss frankly with the bishops political issues on which they felt strongly. I appointed the best food and wine the House of Commons could offer, reckoning that for the most part our bishops no longer lived in the style of Anthony Trollope's Barchester. Good wine eased the faint tension and loosened tongues. The bills were paid by Conservative Central Office, and on the whole I think the party got value for its money. The aim was not of course to change the politics of any bishop but to clear up misunderstandings – and there were lots of them. Life for senior public figures has become more compartmentalized than it was. Bishops cannot be expected to follow more than a fraction of what goes on at Westminster; and few politicians are abreast of what goes on in Synod.

In politics, things are never quite as good nor quite as bad as they may seem at the time. But in the autumn of 1959, after the General Election had been won by Macmillan, they seemed pretty good to me. In the Ashford constituency we ran up a five-figure majority for the first time. I found this gratifying because since the late 1940s the town council had been engaged in converting the market town of Ashford into a growth centre. It had entered into an agreement with the then London County Council to accept what was elegantly termed 'overspill'. Expanding towns were in some ways the poor cousins of the New Towns. In return for relieving London of some of its surplus population, they received substantial help towards housing and industry, but precious little for fresh amenities. In the early days of this scheme, I was left in no doubt that the town council, then Labour, perceived an influx of Londoners as one way of wresting the seat from Conservatives. To everyone's surprise, it went the other way. Families who emigrated from still war-battered parts of London and found themselves decently housed, locally employed and only a few miles from the sea saw life in a brighter light. It tended to change their politics. As the population rose, so did the Tory majority. I found this satisfactory.

My agent, Sam McCall, had been replaced by Leslie Whickman – a delightfully laid-back character, but shrewd. When it came to the 1959 campaign, I persuaded him that if I played a round of golf in the mornings I would be at my best for the evening meetings. He raised no objection. Electors are not impressed by a candidate who appears to be in the last stages of exhaustion. In this campaign, I got an unexpected boost from Jane Austen. In the election of 1813, she had written to her sister, Cassandra: 'I will put Mr Deedes first because I like him a great deal the best.' This related to my great-great-grandfather, William Deedes, who had been elected Member for Hythe in 1807. Pleased by this discovery, the Vicar of Godmersham – a village in my constituency closely associated with Jane – conveyed it to the press. The full text of Jane's letter written from Godmersham Park on 26 October 1813 revealed her preliminary words to have been – 'Mr Deedes and Sir Brook

[Bridges] – I do not care for Sir Brook's being a Baronet...'
Unfortunately, Sir Brook won the election.

On return to Westminster after the election, Rab Butler
(who was chairman of the Conservative party as well as Home
Secretary) asked me to become chairman of the party's National
Advisory Committee on Local Government. I thought this
would require more time than I could afford to give, and
declined. But I was content to be elected chairman of the
Conservative party's Home Affairs Committee in the House of
Commons.

Soon after we got back, I drew first place in the ballot for
Private Members' motions, which were then debated on certain
Fridays in the year, and I tabled a motion about the countryside
and its preservation. It afforded me a chance to outline my own
philosophy on the balance which has to be struck in a small
island like ours between beauty and the beast; between our
matchless countryside and the unrelenting claims of housing
and industry and motorways and new technology. At the back
of my mind there had long lain Stanley Baldwin's description
of the countryside in a speech he made to the Royal Society of
St George in 1924. The passage, which created a stir of
admiration at the time, is worth quoting in full:

To me, England is the country, and the country is England.
And when I ask myself what I mean by England, when I
think of England when I am abroad, England comes to me
through my various senses, through the ear, through the eye,
and through certain imperishable scents. I will tell you what
they are, and there may be those among you who feel as I do.

The sounds of England, the tinkle of the hammer on the
anvil in the country smithy, the corncrake on a dewy morning, the sound of the scythe against the whetstone, and the
sight of a plough team coming over the brow of the hill, the
sight that has been seen in England since England was a land,

and may be seen in England long after the Empire has perished and every works in England has ceased to function, for centuries the one eternal sight of England. The wild anemones in the woods in April, the last load at night of hay being drawn down a lane as the twilight comes on, when you can scarcely distinguish the figures of the horses as they take it home to the farm, and above all, most subtle, most penetrating and most moving, the smell of wood smoke coming up in an autumn evening, or the smell of scutch fires: that wood smoke that our ancestors, tens of thousands of years ago, must have caught on the air when they were coming home with the result of the day's forage, when they were still nomads, and when they were still roaming the forests and the plains of the continent of Europe. These things strike down into the very depths of our nature, and touch chords that go back to the beginning of time and the human race, but they are chords that with every year of our life sound a deeper note in our innermost being.

Baldwin's words convey a state of mind shared by millions and perhaps inspired John Major's more prosaic 'warm beer and cricket' speech. It is a love affair, this feeling towards the English countryside, and it runs deep. It is a mental vision made up of snapshots, mainly from the past, which become important to us when for any length of time we are in other lands. As Keats wrote in his 'Ode to a Nightingale':

> The voice I hear this passing night was heard
> In ancient days by emperor and clown:
> Perhaps the self-same song that found a path
> Through the sad heart of Ruth, when, sick for home,
> She stood in tears amid the alien corn . . .

Many years ago I stood one night on the roof of Salisbury (now Harare) airport. We were seeing someone off on the

London-bound Comet coming up from Johannesburg. Standing next to me was a man I faintly knew. He had gone out to make his life in Rhodesia many years earlier and would never return to Britain. As the Comet took off into the night, I watched his well-tanned face. By morning that plane would be in England, a country he would never see again. So near, yet so far. Rarely have I seen such a moving conflict of emotions cross a human face. This business of our past roots in the English countryside that Baldwin talked about goes, as he said, to the depths of our being.

So much so that when the slouching beast of modern industry, pylons or power-lines, supermarkets and motorways threaten invasion of the countryside, passions are roused. As we began to modernize ourselves after the Second World War, the demands on virgin countryside began to soar. As Member of Parliament in a constituency which included the Weald of Kent, I found the volume of protests coming in from country lovers oppressive. There came to my rescue a number of intelligent residents in the Weald who decided to form a Weald of Kent Society. I took a close interest in this and spoke at its launch in the village of Biddenden.

We felt that simply opposing outright every threat of development brought little joy in the long run. The big battalions nearly always won; and if it came to a public inquiry, their purse was longer. So we began to develop a new strategy, which took the form of plea bargaining. If the Central Electricity Generating Board wanted a new power-line, we would try to persuade them that in an area of outstanding beauty a mile or two of it should go underground – a very expensive undertaking. If the Home Office wanted to build an open prison, we sought to discuss ways of softening its impact by its design or with a screen of trees. The developer was faced with a choice. He could spend some money on sugaring the pill, or face opposition and delay, which would also cost him money. I am over-simplifying what often became an awkward wrangle.

But the central issue in my mind was whether we could find some compromise between beauty and the beast. Many of the proposed developments were socially desirable. My heart lay with the country folk who wanted simply to fend them off. My head told me that we could not forever defeat the beast, that some form of compromise had to be found. Furthermore, I saw a danger in turning the English village into a mausoleum. The villages of my boyhood had been busy, mainly with the business of farming. Adrian Bell's novels give a fine portrait of that life, almost entirely based on farming.

When I began as a parliamentary candidate in the 1940s the agricultural worker was still a political force to reckon with. Before they left the land their votes for the Labour party were a worrying factor. As time went on, and farming became mechanized, their numbers dwindled. Their cottages were converted into second homes for urban dwellers who came down for week-ends. To many of them, the old village trades became objectionable. The smithy was noisy and smelly. The mill's grinding kept people awake. The smell of pigs, the sound of cocks crowing at dawn – these became nuisances and something to go to court about. Worst of all, they devalued the property.

Yet there are today all sorts of human activities which can be run from the village and offer openings to the young. If these openings are denied by those who want simply to sustain the value of their homes by keeping its surroundings unchanged, then a crucial balance will be lost, and generations to come will suffer. In the House of Commons debate on rural England I entered some thoughts on these lines. 'I am not seeking', I stressed, 'to turn the country into a park or museum. It is part of the tragedy of post-war change in this country that so much effort and so many protests have been misdirected into seeking to halt all scientific, industrial and public development which touches the countryside. I believe that that is vain . . . A war between advance and amenity can achieve very little. They must somehow get to terms . . . we must strive, a little late but certainly not too late, for a remarriage between modern development and the landscape.' The debate attracted a wonderful diversity of Members, including Jo Grimond, Tom Driberg, Fred Willey of the Labour party and Keith Joseph, who wound it up for the Government. A year later, I delivered the same message to a parish councils' conference in London. My local press reported it generously. Their second headline read: 'Accept changes, but insist on conditions.' As a journalist, I could not have improved on that.

Early in 1959, for no good reason I can think of, I set my heart on re-establishing a direct rail link between London and Moscow. It struck me that, with this significant exception, all Europe was linked to Paris by fast and famous trains. The Sud Express ran from Paris to Lisbon. There was the Blue Train to San Remo, and the Rome Express to Naples. To the east, the gloriously named Arlberg-Orient ran through Bucharest and the Simplon-Orient ran from Paris to Istamboul. I asked the railway authorities what obstacles lay in the way of a Paris–Moscow service which would start at Victoria station in London. The answer came back that there were few obstacles. Just before the war there had been talk of running a train from a European channel port to Vladivostok via Moscow. The journey on the trans-Siberian railway from Moscow to Vladivostok was 5,800 miles, the longest railway journey in the world.

An international timetable conference got down to it, and discovered that the Russians were working on similar lines. Inevitably, difficulties arose, but I wrote an article about the idea for the *Daily Telegraph*, and public interest was aroused. A reader sent me a 1931 timetable, offering a service from Victoria to Vladivostok in thirteen days, from Victoria to Tokyo in fifteen days and from Victoria to Shanghai in thirteen days. I kept matters rolling along and finally, in May 1960, received a letter from a long-standing friend at the British

Transport Commission, Jock Henderson, to say that the service would open at the end of the month. There would be four services each way each week. Return fare from London to Moscow would be £47 18s. The train would run from Liverpool Street via Harwich, Hook of Holland, Hanover, Berlin, Warsaw, Brest and Minsk. The journey would take three days and two nights. Henderson hoped the *Daily Telegraph* would buy me a ticket, but I was content to provide this extremely tiring journey for other people.

All this was fun, but being in the chair of the party's Home Affairs Committee became an alarmingly responsible commitment. In September 1961 Rab Butler wrote to me about the crime debate at the forthcoming party conference at Brighton. There were sixty-five resolutions down on the subject, most of them in hanging and flogging terms. 'Quite apart from the Government policy and my own position,' Rab wrote, 'we do not want to emerge with a bloodthirsty image.' He concluded: 'I should be most grateful for your advice on who both inside and outside the House might be encouraged to speak in support of the Government line. Would you be prepared to take a hand if necessary?' I had not given my own position much thought. I was in fact at that time strongly in favour of capital punishment. It dawned on me that I was perceived by the Home Secretary to be a moderate. It came as a great shock to the system.

Early in 1962 Iain Macleod wrote and asked if I would join a committee to study 'the effect of Government policies and their presentation on by-election results ...' Hugh Carleton Greene, director-general of the BBC, invited me to take an interest in the financing and independence of the BBC. I had ideas about this. It seemed to me there ought to be an intermediary body between the Government and the Corporation which advised publicly on how much money the BBC needed from year to year and so what the level of the licence fee should be. We met over two or three dinners to talk about it. Among other requests came an invitation from the Home Office to become a member of the advisory committee on the treatment of offenders.

This is the proper life for a back-bench MP, I thought. I had acquired just sufficient political experience to be useful, but I retained my independence. Life was full of interest. I found ample time to earn my wages at the *Daily Telegraph*. My political duties improved the range of what I could write for them, without betraying any secrets. Life seemed good; but, so often it is when you are feeling on top of the world, somebody loves you and the sun is shining that something awkward comes along.

11

Minister of Information

Towards the middle of July 1962 even a dull political ear could pick up thunder in the air. It had been rumbling round since the Orpington by-election in March when a Tory majority of 14,760 in the 1959 General Election was converted astonishingly into a Liberal majority of 7,855. I had spoken on the Tory candidate's platform during that by-election and detected restiveness. I put it down largely to the fact that the former Conservative Member had retired from the seat in order to join the Bench. Electors are almost invariably disgruntled by by-elections made necessary because the sitting Member of Parliament has gone off to take a better post. Tory party workers who give of their best during a General Election get shirty about it, understandably. The wartime appointment of Patrick Spens QC to Chief Justice of India and a subsequent by-election in Ashford in 1943 was an exception that proved the rule.

But the trouble ran deeper. My friends in the House of Commons were complaining that the Government seemed to be becalmed, and that Macmillan, who had been riding high since taking over from Eden in 1957, was losing his grip. Earlier in the year, after an attack on Macmillan by a senior and respected Tory back-bencher, Sir Harry Legge-Bourke, the *Sunday Telegraph* had observed: 'Those who wish him to remain, and they are the majority, believe that he should revitalize the Administration by carrying out a bold and ruthless reconstruction.'

At the centre of Macmillan's difficulties was an economic impasse. He came to see, as Alistair Horne points out in his biography, that the British economy had, as the human body can, developed a certain resistance to most medicines.

Despairing of any fresh ideas from the Treasury, he set down his own ideas in a long paper which came before the Cabinet in June. On the 21st of that month he lunched with Rab Butler, and found him thinking on the same lines. Thus Macmillan was drawn inexorably towards the conclusion that the Chancellor of the Exchequer, Selwyn Lloyd, must go. At the same time, other voices (including that of Iain Macleod, then chairman of the party) were urging him to rejuvenate his administration. Macmillan was further encouraged to think of radical changes because a number of Ministers had expressed a wish to leave office at the Prime Minister's convenience.

On Wednesday, 11 July, Rab Butler lunched with the *Daily Mail* and, it later emerged, spoke indiscreetly about forthcoming changes. Thus the following morning the *Mail*'s political correspondent, Walter Terry, was able to scoop the fact that the Chancellor of the Exchequer was about to go. This had the effect of holing the ship. What Macmillan had intended to be a leisurely game of shuffle-board on deck became a race for lifeboats. At least, that was the impression conveyed to me. I had read the *Daily Mail* story, and thanked my stars that ministerial office was no longer part of my life. On the ill-starred Friday, I lunched at the House of Commons, then returned to the *Daily Telegraph* office to put the Peterborough column together. The man in charge of the column, Fred Salfeld, was away. So was Auberon Waugh, son of my Abyssinian companion, who was then on the Peterborough staff. In mid-afternoon the Chief Whip's secretary called up and asked me to be at Admiralty House (then the Prime Minister's headquarters while No. 10 underwent extensive refurbishing) by 3.45. I finished the paragraph I was working on, left my colleague

Richard Berens in solitary charge and, as instructed, approached Admiralty House via Horse Guards.

It took some time to get in. Still mystified, I was eventually shown into the Cabinet room where Macmillan sat, a strong whisky and soda before him. Later in the day I jotted down, as journalists instinctively do, an outline of the scene and our exchanges. Macmillan was sucking a pipe, looking weary and watery of eye. 'No idea how you are placed,' he said, 'but wondering if you can help me. Want a Minister, in Cabinet of course, who will not only take over the Information Services, but without department and can do some of the many jobs that fall to Cabinet Ministers.' My heart sank, but I managed a sympathetic smile. 'Political situation very serious. Considered my own position. Discussed with the Queen. Wishes me to stay. But willing enough to go.' I began to feel like Alice in Wonderland.

Macmillan then outlined the dimensions of the shake-up. He was clearly distressed by the departure of Selwyn Lloyd. 'Had to go.' Then, 'Hill gone. Maclay gone . . . admirable young men coming in . . . Joseph, Noble. Will you help? Will you return to the sinking ship?' What on earth is one left to say to that? A sinking ship is my spiritual home. I nodded. Then, in a pleading voice, Macmillan asked if I might find time to help him with his speeches. 'But you make so many, Prime Minister,' I said. Yes, but just help with the drafts. My heart sank even further, but I agreed. 'You must see Harold Evans,' he concluded. He went to the Cabinet room door and called, 'Find Harold Evans.' The secretaries scurried. Harold Evans was a senior Civil Servant appointed to be the Prime Minister's spokesman and press officer at No. 10. Thereafter we worked closely and amicably together.

I heard an anonymous voice call out, 'Are you in or out?' 'In,' I said in a voice of doom. 'Thank God!' said the Chief Whip, Martin Redmayne, from a chair. 'The list's in type!' I returned to the office. My editor, Sir Colin Coote, received the news unenthusiastically. Michael Berry, my proprietor, was more reassuring and set my mind at rest. But in his generous way, Coote, who wrote the *Daily Telegraph* leader, found space to comment on my appointment thus:

> What may seem to the public the most surprising appointment, that of William Deedes to the Cabinet as Minister without Portfolio, will be no surprise to his colleagues in journalism. That he should have chosen to interrupt a brilliant journalistic career, though a sad loss to Fleet Street, is typically to his credit; for it shows how much more than a fair-weather friend he is as a politician.

Considering that I woke up the following morning shocked by the decision I had taken, that was a sensitive comment. Not until I saw the newspapers did I appreciate the scale of the shipwreck. In what became known as the 'Night of the Long Knives', seven Ministers had been dropped from the Cabinet. In truth, as I have said, most of them had expressed a wish to go at some time. But the speed of the operation forced on Macmillan gave it a singularly graceless appearance. I suffered a double embarrassment. I was, in effect, replacing Dr Charles Hill (who had made his name as the 'radio doctor'), because he had had charge of the Information Services. At the same time I took over the office of Lord Mills, former adviser to Macmillan on Housing, and then Minister without Portfolio in the Cabinet. Both were distressed by their treatment. A few days later we had all to attend with our spouses one of the Queen's garden parties at Buckingham Palace. I found it a nightmare to be patrolling round that garden, alternately exchanging stiff little bows with the departed and their sad wives and receiving the felicitations of friends.

Lord Beaverbrook's Crossbencher in the *Daily Express* delivered a characteristic comment, which I quote in full because it is quite funny:

I turn to the most unknown Minister of all time. Mr William Deedes, MP for Ashford, Minister without Portfolio. Hardly one person in ten thousand could pick out his thin, thoughtful face from an identity parade. Yet he has been whisked from the back benches straight into the Cabinet. And he has a vital job. He is 'in charge of Government information services at home'. Which means that he is charge of selling the Common Market to the British people.

Now why on earth should Mr Deedes be shouldering this task? True, he is one of the few genuine working journalists in the Tory party. But, heavens, do not imagine that he is therefore a slick or pushful chappie. His cosy unsigned newspaper column chronicling the daily doings of clubmen and canons was about as slick as a Victorian railway carriage.

Any other qualifications? Mr Deedes is remarkably popular among Tory MPs. He is just the sort of man they like. For 450 years his family has farmed in the Romney Marsh district of Kent. The Men of Kent sent four of his ancestors to represent them in Parliament. But the real reason his colleagues love him is that he is incredibly unambitious. Why, he even told his friends that he was staying in the Commons just to keep the seat warm for his son.

How does it come about, then, that such a retiring fellow is supposed to be selling the Common Market to the country? After all, Mr Iain Macleod once talked of selling it 'with trumpets'. But Mr Deedes is not hotlips. Can it be that the Government has now thought it wiser to play down British entry into Europe instead of playing it up? If so, there is no one more suited to do so than the quiet, unassuming Mr Deedes.

Not for the first time in his life, Crossbencher got the wrong end of the stick. Among the first of my duties was the job of presenting Europe more vigorously to the British public. But a number of other hurdles had to be cleared first. On the following Monday, first day of duty, I had to encounter Percy Mills, bitter at the appearance of having been 'sacked'. He said farewell to his old staff, who then greeted me. In the evening, Keith Joseph, Michael Noble, Edward Boyle and myself went off to kiss hands with the Queen. Proceedings took some time. A lot of seals were being handed in and out. The 'thundering herd', I murmured to myself, and found the whisky and soda which unexpectedly turned up extremely welcome. On Tuesday we had a short Cabinet, on Thursday a much longer one. Ministers began to approach me with their presentational problems, first among them Ted Heath, who was having a hard time at Brussels negotiating with the European Economic Community. Then, accompanied by Iain Macleod and the Chief Whip, I met the lobby correspondents.

The week seemed interminable. I shared a wretched dinner in the House of Commons with Selwyn Lloyd and Martin Redmayne, the Chief Whip. Redmayne was seeking to persuade Selwyn Lloyd much against his will to accept one of the Companions of Honour with which the Prime Minister was consoling some of the fallen. My week ended with a request that I spend Saturday at Chequers working on a speech for the Prime Minister. The task fell mainly to Philip Woodfield, one of his private secretaries, Michael (later Lord) Fraser, head of the Conservative Research Department and myself. After such a week, Macmillan unsurprisingly was tired and confused. We worked for a couple of hours on the draft with pins and scissors, then took a leisurely lunch of soup and ham with the Prime Minister. He had just been to see Winston Churchill and reported his close interest in his own funeral at St Paul's. There were to be lively tunes. We took coffee on the terrace looking over some marvellous roses. But I had my own roses at home and it was Saturday and I was missing them.

We got down to work again at 2.45, when Macmillan retired to the gallery to read a book about the Whigs. Two of the attendant young ladies took our dictation in relays. By 5 p.m.

we had the whole speech ready for typing. I began to think hopefully of home. Not a bit of it. We presented our draft to Macmillan. It received a favourable reception. He liked some of my phrases. Woodfield expertly recorded the changes he wanted. 'You should go,' said Macmillan to me, 'it's not fair to keep you.' But clearly he did not want any of us to go. 'Stay to dinner,' he said, 'and we'll go over it once again.' We took a whisky and soda, then a walk over the lawn to the top of a hill. The landscape round Chequers is spectacular. Sherry before dinner, then soup, fish, chicken, raspberries and cheese. It all took time, but the talk lightened. Then back to the gallery to study a new draft from the apparently tireless girls. More cuts, more inserts. Fortified by a whisky and soda, the Prime Minister contributed a burst of inspiration. By 10.30 he was content and I was released with touching gratitude. My driver, thank God, was awake and alert.

A redeeming feature of this ill-starred reshuffle was that it came close to the parliamentary recess. The House rose on 3 August. Certain duties continued but at a less breathless pace. I used part of the break to visit press and information offices in different Government departments in search of a new strategy. We duly took our fortnight's family holiday in Thorpeness, interrupted by only two meetings of Ministers in London. I became acclimatized but not reconciled to my new life, which struck me as alarmingly full of sudden summonses to Cabinet or to meetings of Ministers. Tony Benn found time to keep diaries. I kept few notes, one exception being a Privy Council at Balmoral in early October. To keep my hand in as a reporter, I took a note at the time:

2 October 1962. Privy Council at Balmoral. London airport by 8 a.m. Quintin Hailsham in bowler hat, blue suit and boots. Rippon in brown tweeds. Very smart pilot officer. Comfortable Heron with four seats and a steward. Substantial elevenses. Arrive Aberdeen 11 a.m. Two cars. Fifty-three

miles to Balmoral. Straight fast road. Not very Highland. Dee in full water. Met by private secretary and aides. Welcome visit to the loo. With half an hour before 12.30, walk across some very springy turf to kitchen gardens, greenhouse, then John Brown's statue. A fine statue with a couplet of appalling banality. Back to Balmoral. Wait in the drawing room. Quintin summoned to the library. Corgi sniffs at the door. We follow. Corgi in with us. [One stood very still when the corgis were sniffing round the trouser legs.] Quintin reads Orders as we stand on his right. HM calls 'approved'. Clerk of the Privy Council, Geoffrey Agnew, handles the paper. All over in three minutes. Back to the drawing room. One bar electric. Fires not lit. Sherry in the drawing room.

The drawing room had some splendid Landseers. Queen Victoria on a pony. Also some excellent heads by Landseer of Balmoral gillies. Plain rooms with natural wood doors, shiny chintzes. Tray of drinks. Lunch at 1 p.m. HM with Margaret and Anne plus two staff, three women, ourselves and three girls. Roast potatoes with poached egg. Chicken *à la king*. Very rich. Wine or beer. Profiteroles. Cheese board. More than enough. Princess Anne on the Loch Ness monster. Then an hour's slightly difficulty conversation. Discuss public buildings. New Hilton Hotel in London overlooks Buckingham Palace. 'No privacy,' says the Queen. Rippon looks suitably contrite. Queens sits on a footstool. Princess Anne looks as if she would like to be elsewhere. Disappears.

Leave at 3. p.m. I travelled back with Agnew.

Extraordinary story of Rab at Privy Council of 16 July – first after the changes. Demanded as First Secretary of State (a new appointment) to be head of the queue. Agnew said, law says Lord President first. 'PM intended otherwise,' says Rab. 'If he changes the law,' says Agnew and sticks to his point. Rab angry in front of others. I must have missed it. Then he says, 'I shall not attend.' Agnew says he must explain that to the Queen. Rab then has to apologize for being late for the Privy Council. Explains to the Queen. Queen very understanding and says, 'I won't put you in the Tower.' A very strange story indeed, indicating Rab's sensitiveness about position.

My immediate task, they told me, when we got down to business, was to give the British public abundant information about life in the European Economic Community. After long – some would say, much too long – and thoughtful deliberations, Macmillan's Government had taken the plunge on Europe one year earlier. On the last day of July 1961, just before Parliament rose for the long recess, Macmillan had told the House of Commons that the Government intended to open negotiations for United Kingdom membership of the European Economic Community.

When it came to a vote on the issue, 313 Members in the Commons voted in support and 5 voted against. It was approved in the Lords without a division. At both the 1961 and 1962 Conservative party conferences, resolutions supporting the policy of negotiating our entry were passed by overwhelming majorities. Ted Heath, then Lord Privy Seal, took charge of the highly complex negotiations in Brussels which opened on 10 October 1961. Oddly, no hint of unfriendliness from the French Government or from President de Gaulle was heard in that year, or indeed in 1962. At this stage in the ongoing negotiations, in July 1962, with a view to keeping Government on side with the British electors, my task was to launch an information campaign, designed to tell them in some detail what life within the European Economic Community would be like.

Under the rules of the game, the director of the Central Office of Information advised me, I must not positively advocate our entry into Europe, but I could present limitless facts about Europe. This, he explained, was because any form of propaganda was forbidden (quite properly); the COI was permitted to spend the taxpayers' money only on information. Two committees were set to work on my behalf. One was a loose group of my friends in the House of Commons, who thought up ideas. The other was composed of officials in the Foreign Office and Treasury who ferreted out the information and drafted the leaflets. I presided over both committees and kept them well apart. We aimed to inform every profession, trade and business in Britain just where they would stand once we found ourselves inside the Common Market. How, for instance, would a British midwife fare in Europe? Would her qualifications here meet requirements there? The COI machines ran off millions of these leaflets, and circulated them through scores of different bodies for distribution among their members. I sensed that the strongest reason for opposition to Europe in many minds was fear of the unknown.

I also conceived the idea of forming a Women's Advisory Committee on Europe, on which every main women's organization would be represented. The National Council of Women worked on this with me, and their chairwoman became co-chairman with me of the Committee. We met once a month in the Treasury. The forty or so members were allowed to name alternates. All three political parties were represented. The object was to discuss aspects of Europe which were of particular concern to women. Officials from the relevant department attended the gathering and either gave immediate answers or undertook to find answers before the next meeting. My main anxiety was to make the meetings of value to women prominent in public life who already had a lot to do. It turned out better than I expected, so much so that when Europe ceased to be an immediate issue the gatherings continued to discuss other national and international issues. Indeed, they went on for a while under Harold Wilson's Labour Government. The key to success was bringing the women as close as possible to the processes of government, and enabling them to call for any witness they wanted. It was not a one-sided process. Whitehall officials benefited from hearing some of the things the women had to say.

I invited Alec Home, then Foreign Secretary, to one of the gatherings. He mistook it for the Tory party's Women's Advisory Council – and produced a mild frisson by speaking to that tune. It said much for the innate good humour of the women present that they accepted this gaffe with a smile. 'I do hope not too much damage was done,' Alec wrote to me later, 'and I don't doubt that you have restored calm.' On the contrary, it was the women who restored my calm.

At Nassau in December 1962, Macmillan negotiated with President Kennedy for Britain to buy Polaris missiles. Happy Christmas. On 14 January 1963 President de Gaulle delivered an ominous speech on our prospects at Brussels. Conclusively, on the 28th, to the mortification of the Government and the particular chagrin of our principal negotiator, Ted Heath, Couve de Murville, de Gaulle's Foreign Minister, told Brussels that negotiations must cease. We were out of Europe. Tuesday, 29 January was one of the worst days I remember, in or out of politics. At 2.15 p.m. lunchless, I met the lobby correspondents. 'I think', Harold Evans told me afterwards, 'they feel confused.' 'Who does not?' I retorted crossly. The rest of the afternoon was spent at No. 10, where different hands worked on the Prime Minister's forthcoming broadcast. In the middle of this, John Diefenbaker, Canada's Prime Minister, came on the line, aggravatingly inaudible. The Prime Minister shouted back at him with effect and not without impatience. We were all edgy. At 10 p.m. we returned for more drafting on the Prime Minister's statement next day. At 11.30 p.m. he hit on a new plan for farming!

It has always seemed to me that de Gaulle's 'Non' at that point did more damage to the Government than anything else. A bridge to the future was demolished. A main objective was lost. To switch to a more relevant metaphor, the Government lost the wind in its sails and was becalmed. In that condition, governments as well as ships become vulnerable to storms.

It brought sharply home to me my own limitations. It would have taken someone abler than myself to present an appearance of business as usual. A Minister of Information, which I was supposed to be, is required in times of national crisis and dismay to be a sort of 'medicine man'. I could only offer placebos. I retain the draft of a speech which kind hands in Whitehall prepared for me at this point. It was designed to prove that, notwithstanding this European setback, we would rise like a phoenix from the ashes. British electors are not that stupid. In any case, as I was learning, a Minister of Information is alien to this country's political culture except in times of war. The longer I worked in the job, the more clearly I came to see that I was superfluous.

All the departments had developed public relations systems. If they had a difficult policy to sell, it was essentially for them to market it. It was up to the Minister privately to call newspaper editors and leader writers, and for their press officers to brief reporters. The existence of someone like myself in the Cabinet was a positive obstruction to this process. It led overworked Ministers to suppose that that side of things would be handled by me. Occasionally I did offer them quasi-professional advice, based solely on my knowledge of how a reporter's mind works. But the only role left for me was to ensure that, if Ministers had good news to tell, the day was kept clear for them. We had a weekly conference of chief press officers to co-ordinate that. If their news was bad, we tried to tie that in with some juicy distraction.

Later in this experience, it occurred to me that the Foreign Office had the right system. Its News Department, which dealt with the diplomatic correspondents and other reporters, was drawn from members of the Foreign Service, who served the department in rotation. Working in the News Department was part of the career structure. Thus a future minister or ambassador at some point acquired experience in handling the press. In nearly all the other Whitehall departments, the press section was a separate enclave, served in large part by former journalists, who were outside the career structure. This had a subtle effect on their relations with, say, the permanent under secretary, and thus on their inner knowledge of what was going on in the department. I considered changing the system towards that of the Foreign Office, and swiftly found myself in the role of Sisyphus.

There was another factor which underlined my redundancy. In every Cabinet, Ministers establish their own private channels to certain journalists; and they take good care to keep them in good repair. If the Cabinet reaches an unpopular decision, it helps to let your friends in the press know that it did not have your full approval. Thus I would find myself giving the Government line to lobby correspondents, who were already fully aware of who in Cabinet had supported or opposed it. I thought it best to take all this in good humour, but came gradually to know not only which of my Cabinet colleagues were spilling the beans but to whom the beans were being spilled.

There were certain points at which one could be useful. I set up a regular meeting with foreign correspondents in London. What appeared in newspapers abroad, after all, had some bearing on the Government's standing. The American correspondents remained aloof from this, but I occasionally saw them separately. It occurred to me that there were hundreds of foreign correspondents in London, some of them living in very humble circumstances, with no main source of information. I started discussions on the possibility of a press centre, where some of them could rent a room, have access to main news sources, and so keep the world informed about us. It proved hard going, and by the time the press centre was established, the original objective had faded. I also arranged briefs for Ministers with week-end speeches.

Possibly my most useful function was to reorganize the Government's attitude to broadcasting. The existing arrangements in 1962 were extraordinary. Broadly speaking, no Minister was allowed to appear on a national network without the consent of No. 10. People like Paul Fox, who was then running BBC's *Panorama*, and Grace Wyndham Goldie persuaded me that this was daft. I sent a long memorandum to the Prime Minister suggesting that we should loosen up a bit, seek to reduce the innate mistrust which politicians and their departments had for broadcasting, and try to turn the broadcasters' desire to do more business with us to our own advantage. Very slowly, we moved in that direction.

Macmillan was a great one for quips, and never more quippish than when we had trouble on our hands. He liked to end a gloomy session in the Cabinet room, when I felt that we had failed him and left him twisting in the wind, with something apt from Horace. I came to appreciate that this was not a reproach, nor designed to impress us with his learning, but showed a desire to demonstrate that behind the politician there lay also the philosopher. Goodness knows, his philosophy was to be tested.

One of the worst of our troubles came in September 1962 when John Vassall, a cipher clerk in the British embassy in Moscow, was arrested for spying. In October he was sentenced to eighteen years' imprisonment. Worse, a whispering campaign began linking Vassall with Thomas ('Tam') Galbraith, who had been a junior minister at the Admiralty in 1957. By 1962, he was an under secretary of state for Scotland. At the Admiralty, Vassall had worked in his private office. Unusually, letters had passed between them. These were the subject of much speculation. When published in a White Paper, they revealed, in the words of the *Annual Gazette*, 'nothing more damaging than the former Civil Lord's interest in his office carpets, crockery, and paper clips. The most that could be said against Mr Galbraith was that he suffered a socially pressing and plausible junior a trifle too gladly.' Vassall had an acute inferiority complex and sought to ingratiate himself with his superiors. But as well as being a spy he was a blatant homosexual. The press smelt blood. I give a full account of what followed because the truth of this matter, on which much subsequently turned, has not been told. In his biography of Macmillan, Alistair Horne writes:

> By his own account Macmillan accepted Galbraith's 'insistent' offer of resignation only reluctantly; but the then Chief Whip, Martin Redmayne differs somewhat in claiming that he [Redmayne] actually had to go, at Macmillan's behest, and ask him to resign ... Macmillan readily admitted later that allowing Galbraith to resign had been a serious mistake, particularly in view of what was to follow over Profumo.

According to a note made at the time, I entered the scene on the evening of 7 November 1962 with a call from the Chief Whip at Admiralty House. 'We have these letters; come and have a look at them.' I found Redmayne and two of the Prime Minister's private secretaries, Tim Bligh and Philip Woodfield, in conference. We broke in on Harold Evans, who was slightly overwrought and preparing a brief for the lobby correspondents. The question under discussion was should Galbraith resign? I murmured no, because it implied panic. The Chief Whip agreed. Bligh and Woodfield demurred. At this point I had to go off and chair the Chancellor of the Exchequer through a press panel. When I returned to Admiralty House at 7 p.m., all four were with the Prime Minister in the Cabinet room. The letters, round which the press had been swooping, had been published in a White Paper in the belief that this would ease matters. Having glanced through them, I doubted it. They were indeed innocent but they were also open to misinterpretation.

'Narcissistic' was the word I used; and, shifting from my earlier position, I laid stress on the gravity of the position. There was then a long discussion on the best course to pursue. Whiskies and sodas were produced and served by Macmillan's parliamentary private secretary, Knox Cunningham. The Prime Minister thought that letters should be written. I amended this by saying that Galbraith should write first, with the Prime Minister responding in these terms: 'I would have preferred to wait until after the inquiry, but in the circumstances I accept your resignation.'

This course was agreed. Lord Carrington, then First Lord of the Admiralty, was called in. All things considered, he was in remarkably good humour. I was asked to forecast the press reaction, and predicted more trouble. But I stressed the need for balance between gravity and panic. We eventually broke up at 9 p.m. The Chief Whip arranged to visit Galbraith in Cowley Street at 10 p.m. I forgot to warn him that the house would be watched. The two private secretaries, Redmayne and myself then adjourned for a grisly supper at Overtons in St James's, and once again went over the letter which Galbraith was to send the Prime Minister, making minor amendments.

Next day, 8 November, Galbraith's resignation was announced. I was summoned to the Cabinet room half an hour before Cabinet to find Carrington furious about a *Daily Express* story on security at the Admiralty. We looked at parliamentary questions and at what the Prime Minister might say to the House at 3.15 p.m. The view seemed to be that the press was better than might have been feared, but it was still bad enough. Discussions on what to do rambled on. On Remembrance Sunday, 11 November, after we had all paraded at the Cenotaph, a further meeting was called at Admiralty House for 2.30 p.m. Iain Macleod and I found the Prime Minister and the Chief Whip in the drawing room. Macmillan then read to us the speech he had prepared strongly attacking the campaign of slander. We discussed it, superfluously I felt, because Macmillan had plainly got the bit between his teeth. This line of attack enabled him on 14 November to yield to the Opposition's call for a full inquiry, but to do so on grounds that it was the only way to stop the rumours and innuendoes that were circulating between Westminster and Fleet Street. There was to be a judicial tribunal under Lord Radcliffe, an acknowledged authority on security. For the time being silence fell.

The tribunal reported on 25 April 1963. It exonerated Lord Carrington personally and the former Civil Lord, Thomas Galbraith, whom Macmillan restored to office at the Ministry of Transport on 3 May. But it censured the Admiralty security system, and then pointed a finger of scorn at the behaviour of some newspapers five months earlier when rumours had been rife. The word 'fiction' appeared at several points in the report, to the delight of my Cabinet colleagues. Unfortunately, in the course of their duties, Lord Radcliffe's tribunal summoned two reporters, Reginald Foster of the *Daily Sketch* and Brendan Mulholland of the *Daily Mail*, who then declined to reveal their sources. For this, the High Court sent them to prison. Fleet Street was enraged. From then on my task of winning hearts and minds in the newspaper world became immeasurably harder. In the trials which lay ahead of us, this was to have profound consequences.

12

'Scandal'

<table>
<tr><td>CAESAR:</td><td>Who is it in the press that calls on me?
I hear a tongue, shriller than all the music,
Cry 'Caesar'. Speak; Caesar is turn'd to hear.</td></tr>
<tr><td>SOOTHSAYER:</td><td>Beware the Ides of March.</td></tr>
</table>

On the night of 21 March 1963 I had a long dinner with Martin Redmayne, the Chief Whip. The 'picture', he thought, was 'okay'. We talked about the programme for a forthcoming Sunday gathering at Chequers in April, to be attended by all senior Ministers and to be devoted to long-term policy. Redmayne was also thinking about the Conservative party's future chairman and favoured someone like Oliver Poole. I held no useful view about this, but said I thought Ministers needed more time to talk about medium-term strategy. We discussed the possibility of occasional 'pink' papers for Tuesday's Cabinets, though accepting that they would be anathema to the Cabinet secretariat, which holds that Cabinets exist to take decisions on current issues, and that since it rarely has enough time to dispose of these the fewer distractions the better.

Redmayne was worried by the silence of certain Ministers, and mentioned Rab Butler and Ted Heath. Were senior Ministers holding back ideas deliberately? I said I thought that we had too many rivals for the top place, adding that if they held back long enough, there might be nothing left for them anyway.

It was a question of getting the Prime Minister the right amount of support in the right way. We agreed that the next few months in relation to the succession were going to be exceedingly difficult.

On this same night, the House was discussing the Consolidated Fund Bill – which meant open-ended debates on a variety of subjects. The second item was about the reporters sent to prison after the Vassall case. Henry Brooke, Home Secretary, and Sir John Hobson, Attorney-General, were replying for the Government. I joined them on the Front Bench. All went calmly until about 11 p.m. when Colonel Wigg from the Labour benches let loose an ominous passage about the press being willing to wound but fearing to strike. 'There is not', he said, 'an Honourable Member in the House, nor a journalist in the Press Gallery, nor do I believe there is a person in the public gallery who, in the last few days, has not heard rumour upon rumour involving a Member of the Government Front Bench . . .' He went on rather grandiloquently to say: 'I myself use the Privilege of the House of Commons – that is what it is given me for – to ask the Home Secretary to go to the Despatch Box' and so on. He was referring to the Secretary of State for War, Jack Profumo, who had become the centre of damaging rumours. The gist of them was that he had had sexual relations with a girl named Christine Keeler, who was herself closely connected with some unsavoury characters. I had known about the rumours for about a week, because certain newspaper correspondents came to discuss them with me.

This affair, with its far-reaching political consequences, took place more than thirty years ago, and it occurs to me that if the reader is going to follow my version of its complex course, I must first summarize the background.

Keeler, twenty-one years old in 1963, had been a show-girl at a London cabaret club. There she was picked up by one Stephen Ward, an osteopath, an artist and a libertine. He collected young girls for his own pleasure and provided them for his well-connected friends. Keeler became one of these girls. He also catered for those with perverted tastes. Ward had a flat in Wimpole Mews, W1, and a cottage on the Cliveden Estate which belonged to Lord Astor. He admired the Soviet Union and one of his close friends was Captain Eugene Ivanov, an assistant naval attaché at the Russian embassy in London.

One week-end in July 1961 the Astors had a party for distinguished guests at Cliveden and these included Mr and Mrs Jack Profumo. Stephen Ward at his cottage near by also had a party, mainly for young girls, including Keeler. It also included Captain Ivanov. Both parties met at the swimming pool. This was how Jack Profumo became acquainted with Christine Keeler. They began an association. Since Keeler was also, through Ward, closely acquainted with Ivanov, two obvious questions added an explosive charge to the rumour. Did Keeler sleep with Profumo and Ivanov at the same time? Did Ivanov ask Keeler to obtain information on defence matters from Profumo? In his report on the affair two years later, I must here interject, Lord Denning gave emphatic answers to both questions. Captain Ivanov, he asserted, never became the lover of Keeler. He also accepted the testimony of Stephen Ward on this particular point: 'Quite honestly, nobody in their right senses would have asked somebody like Christine Keeler to obtain information of that sort from Mr Profumo – he would have jumped out of his skin.' But, naturally, when rumour was running high at this point in March 1963, there was speculation about this, and it was the security angle that gave the Labour party the political pretext to raise the matter on the floor of the House of Commons.

After listening to Wigg's speech on this night of 21 March, I had a word with John Hobson and then went over to the Chief Whip's office to warn him of what had been said. Several Labour MPs, including Dick Crossman, Reggie Paget and

Barbara Castle, followed Wigg's trail. The Home Secretary was given five lines of reply and delivered them calmly: 'I do not propose to comment on rumours which have been raised under the cloak of Privilege and safe from any action at law. The Hon. Member for Dudley [Mr Wigg] and the Hon. Member for Blackburn [Mrs Castle] should seek other means of making these insinuations if they are prepared to substantiate them.' The Press Gallery was full. The debate ended about 1.30 a.m. (it was now Friday the 22nd) and I went home to bed. I had been asleep ten minutes when the telephone rang. 'We are having a conference,' said the Chief Whip, Martin Redmayne. 'Can you come?'

I returned to the House of Commons in a taxi at about 2.30 a.m. to join John Hobson, the Attorney-General, Iain Macleod, Leader of the House of Commons, and Peter Rawlinson, the Solicitor-General, gathered with the Chief Whip. The Law Officers in one room with Derek Clogg, Jack Profumo's solicitor, set about drafting a statement. Macleod, the Chief Whip and I sat next door. The Chief Whip's messenger brought us whiskies. Jack Profumo, who had been summoned from his home, eventually joined us but took no part in the drafting. As many were subsequently to observe, it was not a set-up conducive to discovering the truth, but that was not what we were there to do. Profumo had been extensively interviewed about the rumours earlier in the year, at great length by the Attorney-General in January, and later by the Attorney-General and Solicitor-General together. They had satisfied themselves as far as was humanly possible that Profumo was telling the truth when he denied that he had had sexual relations with Christine Keeler.

Nor was that all. In February 1963 it became known at 10 Downing Street that the Daily Mirror Group had bought Keeler's story. This included passages stating that she was involved with Profumo and Ivanov. The Prime Minister was out of the country at the time, so the private secretary saw

Profumo and warned him of the article that might appear. The outcome was a meeting between Profumo and the Chief Whip, with the private secretary present, on 4 February. They went over the ground and Profumo – while admitting sending Keeler a letter which started 'My Darling' – insisted that the affair had been harmless. He added that he made a full report on the position to the head of the Security Service.

As Lord Denning in his report observed: 'It has sometimes been assumed that this meeting of the five Ministers was an investigation by them of the truth of the rumours. . . . I am satisfied it was nothing of the kind. The Ministers all accepted the assurances of Mr Profumo (previously given) that the rumours were untrue and were concerned to see that they were refuted in the most emphatic way possible, namely by his making a personal statement in the House.' The Chief Whip saw a personal statement by Profumo, in response to what Labour MPs had just been saying in the House, as the best way of setting all rumours at rest.

That was the purpose of our meeting. I have to emphasize this because it was widely assumed at the time, and has been often repeated since, that the five Ministers involved that night culpably failed to discover the truth and thus bore some responsibility for the catastrophic outcome. Richard Lamb, for example, in his book *The Macmillan Years* declared that the Ministers 'blithely accepted Profumo's improbable denial [of his affair with Keeler] as gospel truth'. That is rubbish. Lord Denning's version is correct. Because the House then met at 11 a.m. on Fridays there was very little time to prepare a statement. Hence this meeting in the small hours of Friday morning. As Lord Denning observes:

The reason for the long session (three hours from 1.30 a.m. to 4.30 a.m.) was not because the five ministers were conducting a detailed investigation, but because of the long time it took to get hold of Mr Clogg and Mr Profumo at that hour of night. The actual drafting of the personal statement and discussion of it only took about one and a half hours. The reason for it being done at that hour was the desirability in the interest of good government that these very damaging rumours should be scotched at once without being given further prominence over the week-end. The thought in all their minds was *not*, 'Is Mr Profumo's story true?' – for they accepted it as true coming from a colleague – but *rather* 'He ought to make a personal statement in the House in the morning so as to refute these rumours.'

A draft was hammered out. At first Jack Profumo objected to the sentence, 'Miss Keeler and I were on friendly terms', but eventually accepted it. Peter Rawlinson and I retired to my room – where for old time's sake I kept a typewriter – and I typed out the agreed statement. After that I returned home to Eaton Terrace and tried to get back to sleep again.

The statement appeared to go well. For the time being, the cloud receded. But, unknown to us, the story was about to take on another and more sinister twist, and this reporters were busily unravelling. Ward had introduced Keeler to what Denning describes as Indian hemp but I assume was cannabis. She formed a habit of smoking it and associated with black men who trafficked in it. In October 1962 Keeler was with one of them, a man named Edgecombe, when a second black man, 'Lucky' Gordon, turned up. There was an affray in which Gordon's face was slashed. Edgecombe then disappeared. He took refuge in Brentford, where Keeler went to live with him. A few weeks later she left him and returned to Wimpole Mews to visit Mandy Rice-Davies, who was by then living with Ward. Edgecombe pursued her and tried to enter Ward's flat. Failing in that attempt, he pulled out an automatic and began to blast the lock on the door. He was arrested and charged with both the shooting and the slashing of Gordon.

Keeler was a key witness for the prosecution. She attended

the magistrates' hearings and gave evidence. Edgecombe was committed for trial at the Old Bailey early in February 1963. The trial was adjourned until March. By that time Keeler had disappeared. Later it emerged she had fled to a remote fishing village in Spain with a man called Paul Mann. Not unnaturally, press interest became feverish. It was assumed that she had been spirited away by political interests. In fact, by agreement of both prosecution and defence, the trial of Edgecombe went ahead and was completed without her. He received a sentence of seven years.

Meanwhile, alarm bells were ringing in another quarter. Keeler was thought to have sold her story to the Daily Mirror Group. Ward became seriously alarmed and set about stopping publication. For reasons of their own – presumably the likelihood of an action for defamation – the newspaper group told Keeler they would not be using her story. But what finally put the cat among the pigeons was the *Daily Express* front page on 15 March, the second day of the Edgecombe trial. The main headline was 'WAR MINISTER SHOCK'. The story, accompanied by a picture of Jack and Valerie Profumo, was to the effect that Profumo had tendered his resignation to the Prime Minister, who had refused to accept it. Accompanying this on the front page was a headline 'VANISHED OLD BAILEY WITNESS', with a picture of Keeler. On inside pages were more pictures of Keeler from which, as Lord Denning observed, 'most people could readily infer her calling'. Small wonder the Labour party took an early opportunity to raise the matter on the floor of the House.

Once the Edgecombe trial was over, the *Sunday Pictorial* published the Stephen Ward story. Their fee of £575 went directly to Ward's solicitors, who were owed £475 for stopping the Christine Keeler story. Meanwhile, the *Sunday Pictorial* kept in their safe Profumo's 'My darling' letter to Keeler (which she had sold to them for £200).

All this led to an uneasy couple of months. One night in

May, Jack Profumo approached me in the division lobby and asked for an urgent talk. We went down to my room and it flashed across my mind that I might be about to hear a confession. Jack Profumo and I had been at both prep and public schools together. We had always been friendly. He was in a state of great agitation. News had reached the War Office, he told me, that men in a Gurkha regiment had shot two or three of their officers. How was this episode to be handled with the press? Drawing a deep breath, I gave the best advice I could on the matter and put it out of my mind.

Eventually, on 6 June, the storm which had been brooding over us, and which friendly newspapermen assured me must come soon, broke. We were in the Whitsun recess. The Prime Minister was taking a holiday in Scotland. Profumo and his wife, Valerie Hobson, a fine actress and a highly intelligent woman, were in Italy. My wife and I were taking a brief holiday in Devon. I awoke to read in the *Daily Telegraph* that Jack Profumo, on being summoned back to London by Lord Dilhorne, the Lord Chancellor, who had continued to pursue enquiries, had admitted sleeping with Keeler, having first confessed to his wife.

Harold Evans was soon on the line with a request from Independent Television for a Minister that same evening. We agreed it would not be a good idea. The Prime Minister intended to remain in Scotland. The affair built up over Friday and Saturday and by Sunday we had a thoroughly bad press. I hastened back to London by car and took some press interviews. A fairly grim Cabinet was called for Wednesday. Lord Dilhorne's report was before us. Iain Macleod had just returned from America, exhausted and furious. Macleod made the point that not only did the five of us at the March meeting have reason to accept Jack Profumo's word, but we knew he was prepared to deliver his denial publicly. Enoch Powell then questioned whether this could be made credible. Edward Boyle, whose conscience often tormented him, supported him. There were no other utterances of note, but when the Cabinet broke up there was a certain amount of tension.

I did some press briefing and returned home to prepare speeches for the week-end. Late in the evening my telephone rang, and it went on ringing until the early hours. The main story in the first edition of *The Times* ran under the uncomfortable headline, 'Mr Powell Considers His Position'. The gist of their political correspondent's story was that several Ministers in the Cabinet were considering their position in the light of the way the Profumo business had been handled. Four Ministers were named as having serious doubts – Enoch Powell, Edward Boyle, Keith Joseph and Henry Brooke, the Home Secretary.

I held a three-corner conversation with Harold Evans and the Chief Whip on the telephone and said I would try to talk with Enoch Powell. He was in Wolverhampton. I spoke to Pam Powell, his eminently sensible wife, and agreed to ring at 8 a.m. next morning. 'Not explicit but fairly reassuring,' I noted after speaking to him. During that day's Cabinet he remained silent. From 2.30 until 6.30 a procession of newspaper correspondents came for talks. They cannot have found me particularly enlightening. Later that evening Lady Pamela Berry, wife of the *Daily Telegraph*'s proprietor, Michael Berry, gave a dinner party. With her usual outspokenness, she called for my return to the *Daily Telegraph*. 'I like journalists more than politicians,' she kept repeating. It was a good example of Pamela's well-concealed qualities. She did in truth prefer journalists to politicians. She perceived my position clearly, up to my waist in an Irish bog and likely to sink further, if not out of sight. Come back to us, she said quietly. If only it had been as simple as that.

By now yet another fresh disclosure was entering the headlines. A Labour MP, Maurice Edelman, it was alleged, had sent a letter warning the Prime Minister about the truth of Jack Profumo's affair. I returned to London and took a sleeper to Dunbartonshire for a garden fête. Fêtes are bad places for serious speeches; but I attempted to put matters in proportion.

The reporters present, national and local, were interested only in the Edelman letter.

On 20 June, the crisis took a turn which almost sank the Government. Soon after Cabinet started, a senior member of it began to make a statement. One of the innumerable rumours circulating at the time was that a certain Minister featured in an improper photograph which had appeared at the time of the Argyll divorce, and that Stephen Ward had a copy of it. According to one version of this bizarre tale, the Minister had paid the Duke of Argyll to have his head removed from the photograph. Another had it that he had paid money to avoid being cited in the Argyll divorce. It was on this matter that a senior member of the Cabinet now addressed his astonished colleagues. Victims of rumours, he said, were always the last to know. He was not the 'headless man' and had never paid to be kept out of the Argyll divorce. He proposed to make a statement to the House later that day and, in view of the rumours, to resign. The Cabinet was stunned. No one made a comment. Macmillan, who had been listening to this with a white face, expressed some aspirations about justice. The Cabinet dissolved. The Minister in question remained behind.

I went in search of Harold Evans. 'That is the end of the Government,' he said in a firm voice. I argued for a bit, then left him and found Macleod, Christopher Soames and Ernest Marples, who had not yet left No. 10. I repeated to them what Harold Evans had just said. 'This announcement will be the end of the Government.' As Leader of the House and senior among us Macleod went straight into the Cabinet room. Christopher Soames and I returned to his office in the Ministry of Agriculture to recover our nerves with a drink.

A call reached us from Iain Macleod. 'The announcement has been stopped.' He asked me to call six Cabinet ministers, whom he named, and give them the word, 'Off!' I returned to my office to do this and called Harold Evans again. 'Things move fast,' he said drily. I told him he could have a corner in history. At next day's Cabinet, 21 June, we approved a statement to Parliament on setting up an investigation on the whole affair by Lord Denning. The Minister in question then made a fresh statement. He had, he said, spoken rashly the day before. He had done so in the belief that Oliver Poole (then joint chairman of the Conservative party) and others had met on the night of 19 June, and agreed that he must go. Now he proposed not to resign but to write a letter to the Prime Minister requesting that Lord Denning should include him in his inquiry. He handed the relevant papers over to the Prime Minister, who passed them to his private secretary, Tim Bligh. Amid nervous laughter in Cabinet, he then raised a matter relating to his own department. He got what he wanted. In the penultimate chapter of his report, Lord Denning gave two and a half pages to examination of the allegations and refuting them.

This perilous episode well conveys the atmosphere of those days. I became familiar with it because I was the Minister closest to the journalists; but our national press was not the only source of rumour. Foreign newspapers revelled in the affair. On 18 June a French newspaper printed a long account from London which was headed: 'All the frequenters of Dr Ward's swimming pool have not yet been ducked in the water.' It went on to accuse the Prime Minister of seeking to stifle the Keeler affair, which was a monstrous lie. During his inquiry Lord Denning wrote to the newspaper and asked for the source of all this. He received no reply. This virus of poisonous tittle-tattle has assailed other governments since then, but less severely. In 1963 none of us was exempt. Whenever I went to a function or made a speech, someone would take me aside, recite some nonsensical tale and tell me they devoutly hoped it was not true.

The police began investigations into Stephen Ward's activities in April. In June it was reported that he was about to leave the country. He was then arrested and refused bail. But he was allowed bail from the start of his trial on 22 July until the 30th.

As the judge began his summing up on the 31st, it was reported that Ward had been found unconscious after an overdose of drugs. In his absence he was found guilty of living off immoral earnings (of Keeler and Rice-Davies). Before sentence could be passed, Ward had died.

The air was not cleared until the end of December when Lord Denning produced his report, which struck me as a model of clarity. Some members of the Labour party insisted that it was a 'whitewash', and to this day believe that to be so; but that is the nature of politics.

The principal victim of this wretched tale was John Hobson, the Attorney-General. He was, as a close colleague was to put it later, 'an honourable man, holding what some may think old-fashioned views on the proper conduct between colleagues and friends'. He had known Profumo since boyhood. They had been at Harrow together, at university and in the Yeomanry in the war. Given Profumo's word of honour after close inquiry, he accepted. The outcome struck him a grievous blow, from which I think he never recovered, and which led to his early death. Peter Rawlinson, who worked closely with him as Solicitor-General, was also deeply affected. A year later, when the Conservatives entered opposition, he virtually abandoned his work at the Bar and sacrificed his time to the Shadow Cabinet. According to Denning, Macleod and I had much less to do with the matter. 'They had heard the rumours but had taken no part until this night' the night of 21–22 March.

I have never fully accepted that version of my part in the affair. I was closer to the press than any other Minister; it was my job to be. During my years in journalism I had formed countless friendships with newspapermen, and this weird job in the Cabinet had brought in a lot more. Throughout this affair, the journalists were always a move or two ahead of the politicians. If I had been doing my job properly, I would have made it my business to acquire as well as to impart sensitive intelligence. Instead, I tended to regard the unquenchable thirst of newspapermen for this particular story as a bloody nuisance. So there was failure there. To some extent we were all affected by the outcome of the Vassall affair earlier in the year. Rumours spread about the Minister involved, Galbraith, were so damaging that he had been required to resign. Lord Radcliffe's inquiry showed the evidence against him to be totally false. He was then reinstated as a Minister. At the time, that injustice had coloured our opinion of journalists' reliability. And, after two of their number had been imprisoned for refusing to reveal their source of information, that had coloured the journalists' view of us. We were therefore experiencing a mood of mutual mistrust, which made arrival at the truth more difficult than it might have been.

There are those who still find it impossible to forgive Jack Profumo, notwithstanding the way in which he sought redemption by selfless work in East London. I understand their thinking. For my part, I would find a world in which men and women cannot expiate their sins, as Jack has done, intolerable. I rejoice to think that others share that position. At the dinner party Margaret Thatcher gave at No. 10 on my retirement as editor of the *Daily Telegraph*, Jack Profumo was a welcome guest. At the dinner party held at Claridge's in 1995 to mark Margaret Thatcher's 70th birthday, Jack Profumo sat at the Queen's right hand. Beyond that, it is not for us to judge. If the Christian faith means anything at all, final judgement on Jack lies outside our realm. I believe it will be charitable.

13

Tory Succession

Some dark spirit hovered over my dinners with the Chief Whip. On the last effective night of the 1962–3 session, he entered the House of Commons smoke room while I was finishing a drink there with Harold Macmillan. The three of us dined together in the Members' dining room at what turned out to be the Prime Minister's last meal there. 'Calm after the storm,' I noted at the time. Behaving like boys do on the last day of term, Macmillan looked and sounded in better heart than I felt. He was in philosophical mood. 'If only one could have the seven years back again,' he mused, 'how many things might be done in the light of experience.' He expressed distaste for what he called the bloodless approach of the BBC to current issues and expressed a desire – goodness knows why, after our recent experiences – for something more combative. He was in search of a slogan, he said, and having heard this more than once before I drew myself mentally to attention. Winston's slogans, he thought, had been so good. 'Work, Food, Homes'. 'Set the People Free'. We groped around unsuccessfully, for phrases which caught the present mood. 'One can only do one's best,' said Macmillan suddenly, 'let the people judge.'

Then he turned to his memories of Tunis, and the marking of victory there in March 1943. As Churchill's Resident Minister in North-West Africa, he had stood at the saluting base. 'First the French marched past, ragged. Then came the Americans – horrid helmets and rubber boots. Then a pause, long enough to make one wonder what had gone wrong. Then the distant sound of pipes. Every piper in the Army raised for this occasion. March and counter-march. Another worrying pause. Then the British Army. Shirtsleeve order, no packs. A great spectacle. Reminiscent of the best Army we had before the first Battle of the Somme. How moving it was.'

Later – so he told us – he had flown back with Ike Eisenhower in his Flying Fortress. As they moved over the Mediterranean, they saw the first convoy since the Desert Battle come through – 130 ships. Macmillan turned to congratulate Eisenhower. Ike, with tears in his eyes, exclaimed: 'What a generous people you are.' Then Macmillan went on to speak of Field Marshal Alexander, 'and his wonderful control over other people's armies'. He had persuaded the 'ineffably stupid' US General Omar Bradley to do what he wanted. Alex, said Macmillan, had the gift of command. Finally he turned reluctantly to the temptations of this July – 'to do something, to send a minute, to act, to get on with it ... Usually wrong. I read a great deal. When the urge comes to send a minute, get a book. Cabinets are fun, but tiring in the chair. As a member of the Cabinet I used to write letters. Churchill would say, "What are you doing? I do not think you are attending to our affairs."'

Over our coffee, Redmayne remarked ruefully, 'I've given a lot of advice – and it mostly seems to have been wrong.' They agreed, however, that they had never lost faith in each other. We broke up just before 11 p.m.

My stars were off course that summer. I had set my heart on at least two days at Canterbury Cricket Week in August. Almost everyone has an event in their year which so well retains its character over the years that it becomes a haven in a stormy world. Mine was Canterbury Cricket Week, watching drowsily from a hospitable tent all day, then perhaps visiting that fine amateur dramatic society, the Old Stagers, at the Marlowe Theatre, followed by a county ball, where over the years one had danced with dear friends.

It turned out otherwise. Bank Holiday Monday found me entering the back door of Admiralty House for a meeting with the Prime Minister, Lord Privy Seal (Ted Heath) and six others about Europe. As a concession to the day, one of Macmillan's private secretaries had laid on a special lunch including smoked salmon, fruit salad and cream and hock. After two or three glasses of wine the Prime Minister became talkative. Looking ahead, he observed, 'Either Mr Gaitskell [Attlee's successor as Labour leader who was to die unexpectedly later that year] will be Prime Minister, in which case we shall be somewhat right of where we are now. Or Mr Butler [who was present at the lunch] will be Prime Minister, in which case we shall be somewhat left!' As often happened when Harold Macmillan became talkative, we soon got back to the First World War.

'Extraordinary to think', he said, 'that on 1 August 1914 [three days before the declaration of war] Edward Grey, the Foreign Secretary, was fishing.' With my mind at Canterbury, I reflected that Grey might well have been acting more sensibly than we were, holed up at Admiralty House on a public holiday.

BBC's *Panorama* had been banging about all day, seeking an interview with Ted Heath. In search of me, they had the nerve to ring up Canterbury Cricket Ground and request a tannoy call summoning me to the telephone. I viewed this as a final twist of the knife.

But it took one more twist next day, when I attended a meeting in the Home Office with the Commissioner for the Metropolitan Police and others. They wanted to discuss difficulties with newspapers. The Commissioner was anxious to persuade us that the system whereby newspapers bought information off detectives had ended. He admitted, however, that detectives who 'co-operated' with newspapers got publicity, which they felt was essential to their careers. 'So it works for the police as well as politicians,' I noted at the time. Having just stopped a senior detective from selling his memoirs to the *Sunday Mirror* for £16,000, the Commissioner made his disenchantment with the national press painfully clear. Newspapers wanted scandal. They were not unduly worried about whether the story was true or false as long as it boosted circulation. He illustrated this with a story about a Nigerian diplomat who had been nicked for parking his car in the wrong place. He tried the diplomatic pass, in vain, and then made a dash for it. The police jumped on his bonnet and he crashed into another car, injuring a woman. The story had appeared in the newspapers as police beating up a Nigerian. The editor had admitted the story looked wrong, but was not unduly troubled. It made a story. There was nothing further to be done, the Commissioner assured me, by way of co-operation with the press. 'Always someone among the mass-circulation newspapers will break confidence.' Throughout this dispiriting conversation I tried hard to imagine myself in a deckchair outside a tent on the Canterbury Cricket Ground, panama tipped over nose, sipping something cold.

The final convulsion of this ill-starred year occurred on Tuesday 8 October. It was the week of the Conservative party conference at Blackpool. I had decided to drive to London for an early Cabinet, then on to conference. I think the flavour of this unusual day is best conveyed by the notes I made at the time.

Up at 6 a.m. with heavy cold; motored to London (2¼ hours) for Cabinet 10 a.m. Prime Minister not looking well. Routine business until noon. Air of expectation. At item 4, Macmillan says, 'suspend business'. Cary, Nunn (Cabinet Secretaries) go. Burke Trend, Cabinet Secretary stays. Just before this Prime Minister has left the room twice, looking very shaky. Returned at second turn with a glass of medicine produced by Bligh.

Then there opened unexpectedly a glimpse of our future.

Clearly taking a Cabinet view about himself. Agrees DECISION essential. Mentions doctors. Strain. Hints of bad turns. Check-up. But stresses that if to go to General Election, must be to go on for two years. Cannot fight, and then retire. To do the two years, clean bill of health essential. Then leaves the room.

Rab then took charge.

Before he [Macmillan] went Quintin Hailsham only – burst out in great emotion – 'Well, Prime Minister, those of us who have been with you since 1957 ... Behind you in whatever you do ...' Then wept. Discussion. Alec Home dominant. 'Need to make clear to Prime Minister obstacles before him. Odds against him. Someone must do this ...' Duncan Sandys in favour of a swift, early change. Chief Whip takes note. Majority view clearly a decision is urgent, and seems to be in favour of a change. Alec Home stresses prerogative of the Crown, and the need to protect. Peter Thorneycroft clearly impressed by this. Discussion resolved itself into how to reach a decision by Saturday.

How quickly could it be done? Eden to Macmillan forty-eight hours. Should we send notes to the Prime Minister? Left inconclusive. At end Quintin Hailsham made a statement on his own future. Rather ill done. Loyalty to father, love of Lords, but – he would seek to surrender title. No comment. [We could not have known at the time that (a) Macmillan had seen Hailsham on the Monday night and promised to support his candidature as successor, or (b) Oliver Poole, joint chairman of the Tory party and a powerful influence in all this, was a strong backer of Hailsham.] Our meeting broke up at 1 p.m.

I set off for a weary drive to Blackpool cold and lunchless, Joseph arriving in time for dinner. Meet Knox Cunningham, who says there will be a bulletin at 9.30 p.m. Operation on the Prime Minister. Press overhear. Promise to seek counsel of Iain Macleod and Oliver Poole who are attending Conservative agents' conference dinner. Get John Groves [Harold Evans's deputy] at No. 10. Gist of statement going out. I write down, 'His illness will not however have any effect on the plan for immediate future. Decisions about the future must now depend on outcome of operation.' Back to hall of Imperial Hotel. Press are gathering in bar and ballroom. Convey gist of statement to Michael Fraser and George Christ who had become a sort of intelligence officer and C.C.O. Then take Gerald O'Brien, Conservative Central Office press officer, in search of Iain Macleod at another hotel. Send in card. Wait at wrong end. Special Branch find. Explain to Macleod where we seem to be. He fetches Poole. Short discussion. Then all back in car to Imperial Hotel. Macleod has another press conference. By now 11 p.m. As Macleod goes in to talk to the press, Poole gets me to one side and says very privately that Alec [Home] has a piece of paper signed by Prime Minister giving up, and is bringing it with him.

On Wednesday 9 October, I had a talk on the telephone with Harold Evans at No. 10. He was worried about timing and knowledge of the Cabinet.

Major question of the conference rally on Saturday. Who shall address? Press frantic to get guidance. I find Soames, who agrees it [the rally] should take place. Meeting of Ministers present at Blackpool divided. Brooke, Errol, Marples, Soames, self in favour of rally. Boyle, Joseph, Hare, Powell, Macleod against. Chief Whip comes in and we take a decision. Butler says 12 noon. Chief Whip says 2 p.m. It takes eighty minutes to resolve it at 2 p.m. This then has to be conveyed to Chelmer and Shepherd, chairman and president of the National Union of Conservative and Unionist Associations.

Oliver Poole in the corridor, aching to unburden. He takes me into room 137. Calls Alec Home on the telephone. Then explains to me what happened on Monday night in London. Seems that Poole and Lord Chancellor were with Prime Minister, Poole from 3 p.m. After dinner, Macmillan had collapsed. Drunk too much. Breakdown. Doubted if would get to Cabinet Tuesday. Later I had talk with Amery & Co. [Julian Amery, Minister of Aviation, was the Prime

Minister's son-in-law.] It is quite clear family here think that Macmillan decided to fight, but Oliver Poole dished it. In reality, decision was left with the Cabinet.

Thereafter, much of the conferencing took place in our respective bedrooms, greatly to the distress of wives. A wife would emerge unclad from the bathroom to find her husband, still in pyjamas, talking to three totally strange men in grey suits, who would go on talking. Around the hour women like to dress up for cocktails, she would plead, 'I am going to take my clothes off.' This would be ignored, such – we supposed – was the urgency of our consultations. Or she might be reading a book in bed in one of her away-day nightgowns when, after midnight, half a dozen men in black tie would pile into the room and start to discuss what next most urgently had to be done.

There will always be different versions of what actually occurred in Blackpool's corridors, and how far it bore on the final choice of Macmillan's successor. For one thing, there could be no official recording of what occurred. Government's affairs in London are closely monitored and minuted. The party conference is a party political affair, in which Civil Servants must take no part. They can provide facts for speeches in advance, but no more. Delegates – and Ministers – bear their own costs. Official cars may not be used. So once we were all in Blackpool, the recording hand was absent. We kept our own rough notes, which are bound to differ. The final outcome for Harold Macmillan, however, is firmly on record. I retain an early copy of his statement of 9 October, dictated to Blackpool from London. It is addressed to Alec Home, Foreign Secretary, who was also president of the conference:

I should be very grateful if you would tell the Conference assembled at Blackpool, of which you are President, how sorry I am not to be with them this week. I was especially looking forward to the Mass Meeting on Saturday, which is a great annual event and on this occasion likely to have special significance.

It is now clear that, whatever might have been my previous feelings, it will not be possible for me to carry the physical burden of leading the party at the next General Election. If the operation, which I am to undergo tomorrow, proves successful it is clear that I will need a considerable period of convalescence. I would not be able to face all that is involved in a prolonged electoral campaign. Nor could I hope to fulfil the tasks of Prime Minister for any extended period, and I have so informed the Queen.

In these circumstances I hope that it will soon be possible for the customary processes of consultation to be carried on within the Party about its future leadership.

I am writing to you as President of the Conference to ask you to announce this at the earliest opportunity.

So began another night of long knives. On the evening of Thursday, 10 October, at the Winter Gardens in Blackpool, Hailsham was billed to deliver the annual lecture for the Conservative Political Centre, a main event in the conference calendar. The Chief Whip and I had platform tickets. As we entered the Winter Gardens, Redmayne took me aside. He had been tipped off that at the close of the proceedings Quintin Hailsham would announce that his hat was in the ring for the Conservative leadership. This, Martin Redmayne anticipated, would lead to scenes of wild enthusiasm. People would rise from their seats and cheer. I agreed that this was likely. But, he went on, you and I, seated on the platform, will be in an exposed position. We shall be watched, and must not allow our feelings to show. It was a good example of the way Chief Whips are trained to think. Well, I said, if everyone is standing and clapping, and you and I remain seated and motionless, we shall look remarkably foolish. A compromise was reached. We would rise to our feet, but not clap too conspicuously.

Almost all the processes which then led to the choice of Alec Douglas Home as successor to Macmillan were invisible; and therefore held by those who disagreed with the choice to be secretive and deceitful. For those with any knowledge of the Tory party, it was a fairly predictable outcome. We had just come through a muddy patch. Tory choices of Leader tend to alternate between extremes. Alec looked a man everyone could trust. That was the uppermost consideration. Rab Butler was a better political all-rounder, he was a more experienced Minister and he carried all the equipment needed for No. 10. But, in this quest for a man whom bemused electors would instinctively trust, he came second. One of Alec's attractions, at that juncture, was that he *lacked* so many of the politician's attributes.

In the end, the delegates got their mass meeting on Saturday at 2 p.m. and it was addressed by Rab Butler with Alec Home in the chair. Rab had a heavy cold, which he might well have caught off me, and was on the drab side. I do not think it seriously affected the outcome.

At lunch time on Thursday, 17 October, the Chief Whip called me into his official residence at 12 Downing Street, gave me a glass of sherry and revealed the Conservative party's choice, stressing that no one else in the Cabinet yet knew. He emphasized that this was the fruit of the fullest 'processes' ever; that Home was first in his own right – by a margin. He also led the 'alternatives', and had fewer 'objections' than anyone else. The objections were not so much personal as the fact that he was the 14th Earl and so, as a member of the Lords, ineligible to be Prime Minister unless he disclaimed his peerage and fought a by-election. By every count it seemed, there had been the widest canvass ever made, and Home came out top; and this despite the fact that some did not think he was in the field at all.

Together with Harold Evans, the Chief Whip and I discussed the mechanics of all this. We agreed it would be best if Macmillan did not formally resign until the morning of the following day (18 October), and that we should try to get it all through that morning. In vain, as it turned out, I stressed the need to avoid any premature leak of Home's name. It would lead to an early counter-attack on him, newspapers being prone to attack what they have failed to forecast.

At 5.40 p.m. that day the Chief Whip called me to say that there would be a meeting at 6.30 p.m. in the Foreign Secretary's room, but that we would approach it by a subterranean route. There is – or was at that time – an underground tunnel which runs between 10 Downing Street and the Foreign Office. By this means, we reached the Foreign Office unobserved. The Chief Whip, Harold Evans, Philip Woodfield and I were then secreted in the ambassadors' waiting room. Alec (unsurprisingly) was ten minutes late. 'An unusual day,' he observed drily. We discussed the drill for next day, Friday, after Palace proceedings. There had to be a broadcast and a press conference. I pressed hard for a separate meeting with the Sunday newspapers and the lobby correspondents. The script for the broadcast was in draft and occupied three minutes. We ran through the questions that still had to be resolved. I wanted to know what Alec's wife would be doing with the press. There was the question of when exactly he intended to occupy No. 10. Then there was the essential by-election at Perth and Kinross ahead, needed to get him a seat in the Commons, and the arrangements for that. And when would he meet Parliament? That would be an early question, I warned. He proposed to see Harold Wilson and ask for a postponement.

Alec expressed himself shy on domestic questions, and was worried in case the press fired questions about education. Otherwise, he seemed surprisingly calm and in hand. I was due to dine with the headmaster of Harrow and deliver a speech. I left Whitehall at 7.15 p.m. and reached his dinner table forty minutes later. Everyone else by then had had a second gin. It was pleasing to be able to tell the headmaster of my old school who the next Prime Minister would be.

As so often happens in such situations, our manoeuvres

proved almost entirely in vain. Rab Butler's memoirs, *The Art of the Possible*, contain a succinct account of what had been happening on another front:

> By the Thursday afternoon the newspapers had smelt that things were going Home's way. A meeting took place that night at Enoch Powell's house at which Toby Aldington, Iain Macleod, Reggie Maudling and Freddie Errol were present. They were later joined by the Chief Whip. This was a meeting of revolt against the choice of Home. They telephoned me at the St Ermin's Hotel, where Mollie and I were staying while our house in Smith Square was under repair, to pledge their support. Quintin himself rang saying 'This simply won't do,' and Mollie answered him. She was superb throughout, counselling me to stay out, and this made my eventual decision all the more poignant.

I reached home from Harrow by 11 p.m. My telephone was ringing aggressively. Just after midnight the *Daily Telegraph* man, Harry Boyne, reached me. He was thoroughly disgruntled by news he had not anticipated. By 8.30 a.m. Harold Evans was on my telephone, worried by the headlines and not without reason. The *Express* and *Mail*, which got the first news of Home, were running in later editions news of the revolt.

I entered my office prepared for every contingency, but the morning was curiously uneventful. At 2.30 came a warning that Cabinet might be from 4 p.m. onwards. Soon after that Harold Evans rang me from No. 10. 'We haven't got a Prime Minister,' he remarked. In view of the revolt, Home had decided not to kiss hands, only to undertake to form an administration. He would be seeing Butler at 2.45 p.m., then Maudling and Hailsham. The hope was, said Evans, to settle it one way or the other by evening. In his sardonic mood, he had told the BBC to install machinery at No. 10 for 'one Prime Minister or another'.

At half-past six I went over to No. 10, which was ablaze with television lights and surrounded by a large crowd. In the waiting room I found the reassuring presence of Christopher Soames. Alec, calm but tired, told me, 'I asked the Queen not to make me Prime Minister. I said, "Let me try to form an administration."' He then sketched to me the form. Ten out of eleven Ministers so far interviewed had agreed to serve. Rab Butler and Reggie Maudling were reserving their positions and coming back later. Quintin Hailsham was doubtful and Iain Macleod was out. Enoch was still to come. Alec thought Macleod was in error. He feared it would be a blow to the young of the party, the young MPs especially. He then asked if I was happy. In different circumstances I would have proposed that a Minister of Information in the Cabinet, disguised as a Minister without Portfolio, was dispensable and would have offered to go. It seemed not quite the right moment.

We then discussed how the evening should close. I said that, if possible, it was important to tide over to the next day with an air of success, not doubt. I discussed this with John Groves. Enoch Powell and Freddie Errol were deep in talk. I suddenly felt enormously depressed. I pointed out to Groves that the four big fish holding back were four rivals for the job. It looked bad. For once, my invariably calm private secretary, Taylor Thompson, was also worked up. I ate some sandwiches, called Harold Evans and agreed to go back to No. 10. Evans met me at the garden gate and as soon as I got to his room went to see Alec Home. Rab Butler and Reggie Maudling were arriving for their second visits. The form, said Harold Evans, is that Butler and Maudling will not serve unless Hailsham serves. It was then 8.15 p.m. Hailsham was to return at 9.30 p.m. and was reported to be cheerful. Alec Home then made a statement on the doorstep of No. 10 – 'done a hard day's work. Going to get some food. Still talking to colleagues. Some out of town. Will be going on tonight and tomorrow.' I decided to draw stumps for the night.

14

1963–4

Our own little local difficulties apart, 1963 was a year in which a lot happened in the world. It had opened with de Gaulle's dashing of our hopes to join the European Economic Community. The Great Train Robbery, which netted £2.6 million, left a lot of people feeling uneasily that organized crime in Britain had entered a new dimension. Martin Luther King, addressing 200,000 people who had marched on Washington, declared, 'I have a dream . . .' We learned that Kim Philby was the 'Third Man'. On 22 November, President Kennedy was assassinated in Dallas. In December, Christine Keeler was sent to prison for nine months for perjury and conspiracy to pervert the course of justice. It had been a year, I reflected, that brought very little joy except to newspapers.

Early in 1964, after the break-up of the Central African Federation, Ian Smith took the helm in Rhodesia and defied us. International Beatlemania broke out. Closer to home, we set about persuading electors that under our new Prime Minister the Government had become easier to love. One of my duties was to chair what was called the Liaison Committee, which met weekly at Conservative Central Office and which was designed to keep the party in touch with what Government was doing. Ground rules were observed. I did not pass on Cabinet decisions, but I could warn of likely difficulties ahead or, less frequently, of glad tidings to come. The party chiefs, led by the new party chairman, Viscount Blakenham, thought the new

Prime Minister ought to look busier. They fretted about his week-ends off. They dreamed up an eight-day trip for him early in the New Year which would include the Woomera rocket range in Australia of all places, Singapore and East Africa.

The Chief Whip and I felt more protective. It seemed to us imperative to preserve him from overstrain. In a rare burst of confidence, Harold Evans supported us. He conveyed to me his anxiety lest the Prime Minister wore thin before the General Election. He thought he must be spread carefully. So there was a tug of war between those who wanted Alec Home to make the maximum impact quickly and those of us who thought it best to let him go at his own pace. I determined, insofar as it lay with me, to ration his television appearances, because I knew he found television's inquisitions, particularly on domestic topics, a strain.

In December 1963, Cecil King of the Daily Mirror Group summoned me to an audience. In the presence of Hugh Cudlipp, then editorial director of the *Daily Mirror* and *Sunday Pictorial*, he began to let fly at me on the arrogance of Ministers, their failure to consult him – or indeed to appear in the least interested in anything his newspapers had to say. He thought Ministers would benefit from the sort of advice his stable could offer. In effect he wanted to be closer to the inner ring of Government decision-making. Like Rothermere and Beaverbrook before him, Cecil King was seeking a dangerous bargain. As I noted at the time, his newspapers would support policies on which he had been personally consulted – and such consultation would then become a condition of this support.

To some extent, setting aside his extraordinary vanity, King was a victim of social change. The days had passed when senior politicians and newspaper proprietors could count on meeting together fairly regularly round London's dinner tables. In any case, such dinner parties formed no part of Alec Home's routine. When invited by King to luncheon in order to discuss television, of which the *Daily Mirror* claimed to have much knowledge and experience, Alec Home had refused. There was no other channel through which they could meet socially. King wanted occasional signs that what his newspapers said weighed with the Government. In that case, I retorted, they must stop demanding that this Minister or that be sacked – as the *Daily Mirror* often did. No Prime Minister in his senses could take such instructions from a newspaper. I had difficulty in persuading Cecil King even of this. We parted with a low opinion of each other, though I was heartened to hear from Cudlipp in the lift that the Labour party were experiencing the same difficulties with King.

I have sometimes reflected on this experience, which goes close to the root of relationships between newspapers and politicians. Of course a man who owns a national newspaper wants to feel he has the power to influence political events. At the very least he likes to think that the Government takes him, his newspaper and the influence it wields seriously; and to that extent is prepared occasionally to meet with him, and perhaps even treat him to certain confidences. And of course this proprietor is likely to have political views of his own and will wish occasionally to see them reflected by Ministers. Much depends on how this game is played. Newspapers have got noiser but, in my view, less dangerous than they were in the heyday of Lords Rothermere and Beaverbrook in the late 1920s and early 1930s. There was no television then to balance things up, and not a great deal of radio. Newspapers had virtually a monopoly of media power. In the famous attack he delivered on newspapers in 1930, Baldwin made a fair point: 'The papers conducted by Lord Rothermere and Lord Beaverbrook are not newspapers in the ordinary acceptance of the term. They are engines of propaganda for the constantly changing policies, desires, personal wishes, personal likes and dislikes of two men.' We have all grown up a bit since then. In the Tory leadership struggle of 1995, most leading newspapers advised MPs against voting for John Major. He won comfortably.

Insofar as we had any theme to justify our continuation in government in 1963–4 it appeared to be the 'modernization of Britain', and I was called upon to disseminate supporting evidence of this. Unfortunately the programme of modernization began to look like a course of pills, which the public found increasingly hard to swallow. There was, for example, the Resale Price Maintenance Bill, which had the effect of driving this nation of shopkeepers up the wall. The Minister responsible for this colossal pill was Ted Heath, the burden of Europe off his back, and endowed by Alec Home in his 1963 reshuffle with the resounding title of Secretary of State for Industry, Trade, Regional Development and President of the Board of Trade. That made him virtually unstoppable. I think a more experienced conductor of the orchestra, like Butler, would have moved Resale Price Maintenance into a later chapter, preferably after the election. Alec Home found it harder to put his foot down on the home front.

Then there was Dr Beeching, a discovery of my friend Ernest Marples, at this time Minister of Transport. Beeching was directed to modernize our railways. He recommended concentrating our resources on inter-city passenger and freight traffic, while at the same time shutting down many uneconomic rural and branch lines. The cries of those not yet sufficiently well off to buy a motor car drowned the applause. Another pal of Ernest Marples, Professor Buchanan, made his contribution to social unrest with a report entitled *Traffic in Towns*. It foreshadowed certain restraints on the uncontrollable motor car. This caused uproar among motorists. As an election-winning idea, the modernization of Britain presented drawbacks.

About this time in the Ashford constituency I became involved in the strange episode of the poisoned dog. Within a year it had engulfed several Government departments and, as

Minister without Portfolio, I found myself in the extraordinary position of having to quench a fire that I myself had started. Early in August 1963, a man came to see me about the death of his dog. It had eaten part of the carcass of a cow which had died in mysterious circumstances. A local vet took a strong interest in the case. It emerged that, on a farm near Smarden belonging to Jull and Sons, cows had died on 16 May and the rest of the herd had been in a poor state of health. On a neighbouring farm, belonging to a Mr G. H. Lowe, sheep had died in the same week.

Lowe, whose London address was Mount Street in Mayfair, was no country hick. At the end of August he wrote me a letter which included this passage: 'I understand that my neighbour sold one of his twenty-three chronically ill cattle this week for dog food. Subsequently two or three dogs died almost immediately after eating the animal's liver. According to my information, moreover, my neighbour could have sold all his cattle to a slaughter house for human consumption – with possibly fatal consequences.'

I wrote urgently to my colleague Christopher Soames at the Ministry of Agriculture. He dispatched a team of scientists and chemists to investigate. They concluded that the animals had died after drinking water contaminated by fluoroacetamide. The finger pointed to the activities of Rentokil Laboratories Limited, which had a small factory adjacent to the farms. Poisoning by factory effluent, Soames pointed out, was for the Ministry of Housing and Local Government. The wheels began to grind very slowly. By October cleansing operations on the ditches and ponds of the afflicted farms were in progress. The spoil had been dumped on the factory's land. Solicitors for the factory complained that the harbour authorities on the coast refused to permit the dumping of this spoil on the foreshore. Eventually more than 2,000 tons of soil surrounding the factory were put into sealed drums and dumped in the sea beyond the continental shelf, where they could do no harm to fish or marine life. At that point the Minister of Transport was called in, because his officials had to advise Rentokil on methods of loading the contaminated soil into containers, about conveyance by road and how to overcome shipping difficulties. Because he represented the Poisons Board, the Home Secretary had also become involved.

Meanwhile, as Government scientists and analysts scrambled round the farm, it remained frozen. The owners grew a crop of barley, but were not allowed to sell it. Southern Television ran a programme about the hundreds of sparrows which had died in the barley straw. Parliamentary questions were asked and headlines appeared. In February 1964, Christopher Soames had to make a statement to the House of Commons. After a meeting of the Home Affairs Committee of the Cabinet, it was proposed that the Government's Advisory Committee on Poisonous Substances should be given a wider remit to cover the whole field of pesticides. For different reasons this involved consultation with the Secretary of State for Scotland, the Minister of Health, the Minister for Science and the Secretary of State for Industry. So at this point the dead dog of August 1963 had involved about half the members of the Cabinet. Matters rolled on well past the General Election of 1964. In April 1965, as a back-bench MP, I staged an adjournment debate in the House of Commons, which Labour's Minister of Agriculture, Fred Peart, had to answer.

While I prepared to do this, I received a personal letter from a former Cabinet minister, Alan Lennox Boyd, by then the Viscount Boyd and chairman of Guinness. 'A little while ago,' he explained, 'we, through our subsidiary Twyford Laboratories and together with our partners, Philip Duphar, the pharmaceutical side of Philips Electrical of Holland, bought the business of selling pesticides under the name of Midox from the Rentokil company.' There would, he assured me, be no recurrence of the 'unfortunate accident when a number of cattle were killed through the escape of poisonous material . . .' He invited me to inspect the premises at Smarden and then set about reassuring local opinion. By that time no turn in the Smarden poisoning affair could cause me surprise. I simply added his letter to a huge file on the subject which I have kept to this day.

On the morning of 14 May 1964 I left London early for a short Whitsun holiday with my wife in Yorkshire. As I closed our front door, I glanced at a morning paper on the doorstep of the house next door, and saw we had won the Devizes by-election. It made for happier reflections on the road north. In York I bought an evening newspaper. We had won the Bury St Edmunds by-election as well. I think it possible, I told my wife cautiously, that this Whit holiday will be less anguished than last year's – which had been interrupted by Jack Profumo's confession.

In truth, the gap between Conservative and Labour had narrowed, and winning a fourth General Election no longer seemed altogether beyond our reach. In some ways this made life harder because people got jumpier about small things that looked like going wrong. My Sunday of 7 June 1964, of which I kept a log, was a good illustration of this. At the end of April there had been an outbreak of typhoid in Aberdeen, involving more than a hundred people. It was traced to a consignment of corned beef from Argentina. In the same year Rootes, the motor manufacturers, who had moved to a new plant at Linwood near Glasgow, reached a deal with the American firm of Chrysler. This was the background to a call I received from the Prime Minister at Chequers early Sunday morning. He was worried by a speech from Harold Wilson, which had been reported in the *Sunday Times*. It alleged that the Government had known since March about the corned beef being manufactured in Argentina without chlorinated water. He was also worried by the *Sunday Times* version of the Rootes–Chrysler deal. I promised to get in touch with the appropriate Ministers.

After attending the village Sunday School, which in those days received what passed for instruction from me, I rang the

Chief Whip. He pointed out, shrewdly, that what had probably upset the Prime Minister was a third story in the *Sunday Times*, a snide piece by its then political correspondent, James Margach, which declared that Ministers were relaxing over the week-end and letting Harold Wilson get away with it. I then called the Chancellor of the Exchequer, Reggie Maudling, and found him willing to converse with any newspaper steered his way on the Rootes issue. Walter Terry of the *Daily Mail* then called me about Rootes. I directed him to the Chancellor. At noon Ted Heath's private secretary called up. The President of the Board of Trade was worried about the *Sunday Express* version of the Rootes deal. Would I telephone him at his hotel in Geneva? I set the Downing Street telephone exchange (which was also having a hard day) to work on this. I then found that he was returning to Heathrow that evening. I suggested he forget the *Sunday Express*, and dished out some sharp answers to Wilson. I then called the Chief Whip to report that both the Chancellor of the Exchequer and the President of the Board of Trade were lined up for action. The *Daily Telegraph*'s political correspondent rang me about Rootes. He was directed to the Chancellor.

As I contemplated a delayed lunch, Selwyn Lloyd, whom Alec Home had restored as Leader of the House, rang to say that the Prime Minister had also been on to him. The main worry at Chequers had become the *Sunday Times* version of the typhoid story. As I started lunch, the *Daily Telegraph* man was back. Had I the Chancellor's home telephone number? During the afternoon I ventured to take a short break. On my return, a Mr Barrah of the Ministry of Agriculture was on the line with a note of urgency in his voice. How was he to deal with inquiries about typhoid and the bully beef? After reflection, I told him that an authorized statement would be a mistake. We did not yet know all the facts. I confirmed this line in a long telephone call to Christopher Soames, the Minister of Agriculture. I then made reassuring noises to Barrah. Before supper, I telephoned Selwyn Lloyd and reported the evening's work. 'Total for the day,' I noted at the time, 'fifteen outgoing telephone calls. To what end, it is hard to say. If this is a sample of what is to come before the General Election, heaven help us all.'

As a postscript, the truth about the typhoid scare turned out to be roughly as follows. An inspector from the Ministry of Agriculture on tour in South America notified his department early in March that a plant in Argentina was not chlorinating its cooling water. A principal medical officer of the Ministry of Health was informed. He took the view that it was reasonable that no further shipments should be accepted. But, as there had been no illness arising from this product, it would not be reasonable to have withdrawn stocks of corned beef from the plant which were already in circulation. Keith Joseph, Minister of Health, gave that decision his full support. It is not only facts that count. Sometimes the interpretation put on facts matters as well.

On personal grounds, I found the Rootes affair altogether more distressing. I had known both brothers, William (the entrepreneur) and Reggie (the engineer), for many years. They were Men of Kent or Kentish Men. Reggie Rootes and his wife had given me much help and comfort in the Ashford constituency. In 1963, the company made its last throw by moving into a new plant close to Glasgow where it was to produce the Hillman Imp. I had flown up for the opening ceremony in company with Roy Thomson the Canadian press magnate who acquired *The Times* in 1966. Depressingly, he was on a diet of orange juice. 'You're missing some good things,' I told him. 'I still have a lot to do in my life,' he retorted. The Linwood plant was to employ mainly Scottish engineers put out of work by the shipyards. Those were the days when companies which wanted to expand were directed north and given special allowances to mop up unemployment. I thought at the time that the prospects looked unpromising. Later it was said that Rootes made the wrong arrangements for remunerating the workforce. Whatever the reason, the project soon ran into the sands.

In mid-June the Chief Whip confided to me over dinner that he thought fatigue and anxiety were dimming the Prime Minister's spark. What depressed Alec Home, he said, was the lack of loyalty among his colleagues. We discussed whether the possibility that we might still win had reached enough influential folk, including Iain Macleod. Too many, I had sensed in recent weeks, seemed to have a vested interest in Home's failure. They had become more interested in the succession than in victory. Martin Redmayne then asked me about a *Sunday Times* piece predicting that Ted Heath would be made chief of staff for the General Election – or the Prime Minister's *alter ego* while he was in Scotland. I pointed out that the *New Statesman* had made such a prediction ten days earlier. The Sunday press had followed. What was new? Martin then disclosed secretly that some such arrangement had been discussed at No. 10. Thus the tip had come from a highly sensitive source. I explained to Martin that many fed the newspapers not simply from an urge to reveal secrets, which possesses most of us, but because it provided a form of security against press criticism. Indeed it sometimes led to positive enhancement. A lobby man kept well informed will not bite the hand that feeds him, but will discreetly succour it. Furthermore, I pointed out, the Opposition would be close to this network. Confidential information was a form of currency in the lobby, and fortune went to the man who spent it wisely.

'Rootes and typhoid still haunting us,' I noted at the time. 'More and more, this job becomes "bomb disposal".' Scotland complained that the typhoid epidemic was having an adverse effect on the tourist trade. Nothing was gained by being gloomy about it, I replied to a delegation that came to see me. Moved by their sullen features, I suggested that the Prime Minister be asked in a Parliamentary Question what the prospective losses were so that he could belittle them: low percentage of total bookings, 'sure sensible people will realize no risk ...' and so on. Not a smile lit the gathering. An hour later, Oliver Poole, with his strong City sources, came on with a warning to Selwyn Lloyd and myself that the Rootes–Chrysler deal was not as foolproof as it looked. He urged caution. I entered a meeting of Ministers at No. 10 to review the Tory party election manifesto with a sinking feeling.

Take 25 June as a characteristically happy day. At 10 a.m. there was an urgent meeting about some echo from the spy Guy Burgess which was troubling press officers. Then Gavin Astor, pillar of the Commonwealth Press Union complained that there had been a muddle over the Commonwealth Press Conference, the apple of his eye. No party had been arranged. Very well, I said grandly, I will give a party at Lancaster House on 8 July. Let details care for themselves. Officials put on their doubting look. Get on with it, I said. At 10.30 a.m. yet another meeting took place with the Prime Minister and Christopher Soames about typhoid. We agreed to stiffen up regulations for countries which exported to us.

The Chief Whip then told me of the Prime Minister's concern about a letter Clem Attlee had written to *The Times*. The gist of it was that because Churchill had invited Attlee to Potsdam in 1945, the new Labour leader Harold Wilson should be invited by Home to the Commonwealth Prime Ministers' conference. 'A try-on,' I said. Harold Evans reported that Charles Hill, then Independent Television boss, had banned Granada's *World in Action* programme on the Olympic Games. 'That's for him,' I said. The more Government involves itself with other people's affairs, I was constantly reminded, the more it becomes bogged down by grievances. We had done too little to wind down the involvement of Government in almost every department of human life, a legacy of total war 1939–45.

As luck would have it, this particular day included a dash to Brighton Kemptown on behalf of the Tory MP there, David

James. He travelled with me, talking incessantly of the Loch Ness monster, with which he was obsessed. His wife, worth three of her husband, met us in Brighton and sped us to the lunch, which was chaotic. I had to catch an early train to London. The chairman proceeded to speak for fifteen minutes. I gabbled a few words and left. The spirited Mrs James had the engine running. We made the train by two minutes. I was just in time for a meeting at which both British Rail and London Transport conveyed a proposal to raise fares.

At 5.30 p.m. the Prime Minister saw me alone at No. 10. Did I have views on how things were going? Generally, I said, I thought we should talk more about people and to people, and less about ourselves to ourselves. Quentin Hailsham, he said, thought we must attack. Yes, I agreed, but we need some constructive stuff as well. The triumph of the British people, I argued, lay in what they had done for themselves. On that we agreed. I urged him to take a proper holiday, but he plainly did not intend to go before the end of August.

Later in the evening, as I slowly drew breath and started to work on arrears of the day, David James slithered into my room. His chairman, he reported, considered I had shown signs of impatience during his speech, and had behaved rather abruptly. Would I be good enough to send him a letter of apology? I drew several more deep breaths. It's rather a marginal seat, pleaded James. Marginal, because you spend your time on the shores of Loch Ness hunting a non-existent monster, I snarled.

At next day's Cabinet I raised the sudden and subtle plan of British Rail to join the London Transport bandwagon and add 7½ per cent to fares. It was to include commuters' season tickets eighty miles round London. Ernest Marples was told to ring Dr Beeching and discover what the hell was going on. He returned at noon, admitting that the decision was unexpected and unknown to him. 'A more damaging move at this point', I noted, 'is hard to imagine.' The Beeching school of thought, I reflected grimly, will strike wherever traffic will take an increase. The commuter with his house in the suburbs or further afield, who works in London, had no alternative but to pay. So the increase led to no diminishment in traffic. But for this very reason the commuter feels ill-used and powerless. At first Cabinet argued for intervention, but then saw the red light. It was decided that Marples and I should meet Beeching and discuss presentation.

Dr Beeching and his top wages man appeared at 2.45 p.m. in Ernest's room. The doctor was in his cynical mood. He knew exactly what he was doing and realized there would be a howl from Ministers rolling towards an election. As for presentation, Beeching declared, the commuter will refuse to see the point anyway, however hard we try. No, he would not attend a press conference. The London evening newspapers, said Beeching, will have billboards: 'London Fares Shock'. They will then write and behave as champions of the commuter. I perceived that we were engaged with a man of broad and rather dangerous sympathies. Having foreseen – accurately – the reception he would receive, the intelligent doctor was disinclined to take any pains to change it. 'Give a dog a bad name and hang him,' he observed calmly. I drew a reluctant promise from him to convey some of his thinking to the serious press.

The task of approaching the General Election guiltlessly began to take on the look of an Alan Ayckbourn farce. The final touch was supplied by the *Sunday Mirror*, which on Sunday, 12 July sported a headline: 'Peer and a Gangster: Yard Probe – Public Men at Seaside Parties'. The storyline was that a top-level Scotland Yard investigation into the alleged homosexual relationship between a prominent peer and a leading thug in the London underworld had been ordered by the Commissioner of Police, Sir Joseph Simpson. The thug concerned, it said, had been involved in a protection racket in London's clubland that had cost club proprietors thousands of pounds. Later in the week, the *Sunday Mirror*'s stable companion, the

Daily Mirror, ran an editorial about police and crime and gangsters. I perceived signs that part of the press, with or without encouragement from the Labour party, intended to revive scandal (from which in recent days we had been relatively free) for election purposes. On a hunch, I called Hugh Cudlipp, then chairman of Daily Mirror Newspapers. He was abroad. John Beavan (later Lord Ardwick), political adviser to the Mirror Group, agreed to see me – before reporting to Harold Wilson. If he had anything to tell the Government, I urged, I was willing to hear it. There followed some embarrassing exchanges. The leading article in question, said Beavan, was not intended to mean what I read it to mean. I did not press the point, but declared that if the *Daily Mirror* had a story it thought we should know about, I was all ears – unlike Profumo times (when we were accused of burying our heads in the sand).

Beavan said he could not go further without authority from Cecil King and Hugh Cudlipp. Did I desire this? I desire nothing, I replied, but the *Mirror* is hinting that it has in its possession something Ministers ought to be aware of, and I am here to receive it. At dinner that night with Selwyn Lloyd and the Chief Whip, we discussed the implications of all this and decided it must be put before Cabinet. When I did this, the Prime Minister suggested a ministerial committee, with the Home Secretary, Attorney-General and so on.

Before this could meet, the *Sunday Pictorial* of 19 July had fired a second barrel: 'Pictures we can't print'. The *Sunday Times* was in with 'Brooke [Home Secretary] and the unpublished picture'. After a late talk with the Attorney-General, we agreed to meet at the Law Courts on Monday morning. The meetings continued all that week. On the night of Wednesday, 22 July, Lord Boothby entered the House of Commons smoke room about midnight. He had a talk with the Chief Whip. Then he declared he wanted to talk with me, and recited his version of the affair. He had been advised, he said, that damages of between £50,000 and £100,000 might lie. I responded cautiously.

On Sunday, 26 July, the *Sunday Mirror* appeared to climb down a bit. Lord Boothby called me at home and sought advice. I cannot advise, I told him, and never attempt to do so when other people's money is involved. I then promised to consult the Attorney-General. On Monday I found that Boothby had rung my office and talked to my private secretary. The Attorney-General, correctly, said he could not advise anyone privately but that Gerald Gardiner (who had been advising Boothby) was an old friend and was probably right. There was then a meeting of Ministers under the Home Secretary. It seemed clear that the *Mirror* had nothing in substance to justify its claim. But had it given up? The Attorney-General was nervous about August, when the House rose and allegations became harder to counter. Cecil King, it was said, had declared at some dinner that he had material to blow the Tory party sky high.

On the following day the Chief Whip sent for me on some pretext and declared that my own name was now involved with the Boothby rumours. People caught up in rumours, he said, were always the last to know. I agreed that my meeting with Beavan could be made to look compromising. The Home Office had asked for a full note about it and the police now wished to question me. Should I release the note on my talk with Beavan? I sought the Chief Whip for advice but failed to find him. I dined with the Attorney-General and consulted him. I should not release the note, he said. The following morning I instructed my private secretary so to inform the Home Office. If the Home Office didn't like it, I said defiantly, they could come and talk to me. Various people then rang me to say that the German papers had picked up the story – with names. On 1 August, an extraordinary letter from Lord Boothby appeared in *The Times*. It began:

On July 17 I returned to London from France and found, to
my amazement, that Parliament, Fleet Street and other

informed quarters in London were seething with rumours that I have had a homosexual relationship with a leading thug in the London underworld involved in a West End protection racket; that I have been to 'all-male' Mayfair parties with them; that I have been photographed with him in a comprom-ising position on a sofa; that a homosexual relationship exists between me, some East End gangsters and a number of clergymen in Brighton; that some people who know of these relationships are being blackmailed; and that Scotland Yard have for months been watching meetings between me and the underworld thug; and have investigated all these matters and have reported them to the Commissioner of the Metropolitan Police.

Boothby went on to say that, because television had made him well known, he had been photographed with people who claimed to be 'fans' – 'and on one occasion I was photographed, with my full consent, in my flat (which is also my office) with a gentleman who came to see me, accompanied by two friends, in order to ask me to take an active part in a business venture which seemed to me to be of interest and importance'. He was satisfied, Boothby added, that the source of all the rumours was the *Sunday Mirror* and *Daily Mirror*. 'If either ... is in possession of a shred of evidence – documentary or photo-graphic – against me, let them print it and take the consequences.'

Behind all this nonsense lay a tale of our times in the Sunday newspaper trade. Certain Sunday newspapers at that time had working arrangements with senior policemen, whereby 'tip-offs' were traded on both sides. There was no actual bribery, but there were good meals and good relations. At this particular time, the *News of the World* had by these means scored some good hits. Its main competitors, the *People* and the *Sunday Mirror*, became a shade desperate, and 'bought' a story at a low level, which was dangerous. The *Sunday Mirror* got a 'bum steer' to the effect that Lord Boothby's relationship with the Kray brothers was being investigated by Scotland Yard. No doubt the police were pursuing certain inquiries, but after this disclosure the decision was taken at the Yard to back off – fast. A statement by the Commissioner left the *Sunday Mirror* holding the baby.

Meanwhile, Boothby, who had gone abroad, got wind of this, felt a tweak of anxiety and returned. Among people he got in touch with was a director of the *News of the World* named Allen whom he reckoned would know what was going on. Boothby declared he was a victim of character assassination and asked for help. Damages, he thought, would be huge. Allen said this was beyond him, but suggested Boothby tackle the *News of the World* on his own account. Boothby said, 'I cannot go to Bill Carr [then the proprietor of the *News of the World*] because Carr sacked me.' (At one stage Boothby had written a column for the *News of the World*.) The approach was made then by Allen. At this point Mark Chapman Walker, who held a senior position on the newspaper, entered the scene. He had formerly been director of publicity at Conservative Central Office. He told Boothby that the *News of the World* could not assist him against another newspaper. They would, however, give him access to such legal advice as they had. This included Arnold Goodman, who was acquiring a legendary reputation as Mr Fixit. A conference was arranged. Goodman heard the story but because of the facts doubted if an action for damages would succeed. He suggested a 'halfway house' to 'flush' the Mirror Group. Lord Devlin, then chairman of the Press Council, was consulted. He declared that the Council could only follow up a specific complaint. A letter from someone declaring that the peer being mentioned by the Mirror Group was Boothby would not suffice. So Devlin pulled out. At that point the idea of a letter to *The Times* came up. With Lord Devlin behind it, could Sir William Haley, then editor of *The Times*, be persuaded to run the letter? Haley's puritanical instincts won. The letter appeared and was repeated in most newspapers on the following day.

The missing evidence was the photograph in question, which showed Lord Boothby sitting on a sofa with Ronnie Kray and a young man. Kray was presumably inviting him to 'take an active part in a business venture'. The photograph, I learned, had been sold to the *Daily Express* by Ronnie Kray's girl friend for the absurd sum of £100. She had been heard boasting in the West End of London that Ronnie had a picture of a peer. The *News of the World* would have paid five figures for it. The 'flushing' exercise, however, proved successful. Cecil King then decided to settle with Boothby.

Well, some will exclaim, what a storm in a teacup! But it was rather more than that. It illustrated the way in which thoroughly dirty linen is used as General Elections draw nigh. It also illustrated what a loose cannon in politics Bob Boothby had become. No doubt at all, he had got himself mixed up with the Kray brothers when he should have run a mile from any such association. Boothby was drawn to trouble as babies are drawn to milk – and he never grew up. According to the rough log I kept at the time, this bizarre affair had several Ministers on red alert for about a fortnight. These and other uncharitable thoughts passed through my mind at the end of March 1995, when on behalf of the *Daily Telegraph* I reported the funeral of Ronald Kray at St Matthew's Church in Bethnal Green – and his brother Reggie urged us all to pray for his soul.

15

Immigration

After a General Election which most people expected Labour to win easily, the Conservatives finished up with 304 seats against Labour's 317. But for disappointing results in Scotland, we would have run them close. Selfishly, I thought the result of the General Election of 1964 had turned well for me. Two years in the Cabinet was a useful experience, but enough. I also reckoned that my nebulous job as Minister without Portfolio had gone well past its sell-by date. I could see why in the desperate hours of 13 July 1962 Macmillan had suddenly hauled me out of a newspaper office into his Cabinet. He wanted someone whom he thought could put a professional gloss on things. When Macmillan departed in October 1963, so did that delusion. But Alec Home, a controversial successor, needed all the support he could get from the existing Cabinet. So I was kept on, and that was lucky. In terms of human vanity, it is better to leave office after losing a General Election than to be required by the Prime Minister to depart.

Except in time of war, the British political system is unsuited to Ministers of Information in any guise. There is a healthy suspicion of political propaganda, and a wonderfully well-developed perception among all classes of the tricks that go with it. It is one reason why our parliamentary democracy in this century has proved more durable than most of Europe's.

Of course, departmental Ministers must present their policies convincingly. In days past they did it by making political speeches, an art which has fallen into decline. Because so few want to hear or read political speeches nowadays, they are rarely reported. Only the politician who drops a clanger gets a headline. But that does not alter a cardinal rule that experience taught me. All Government departments must tell their own story, and must be persuaded that no Minister of Information is going to do it for them. If a department embarks on controversial policies, it is for the Minister to devise with his professional advisers ways of defending his policies. He can talk to editors, brief his departmental press officers, offer interviews to reporters and editorial writers whom he knows, take part in appropriate television programmes and so on. Thus I finished my career in Cabinet welcoming the thought that I was superfluous.

Back in Opposition and free to do what I chose, I discovered the advantages of being a Privy Councillor – as all Cabinet Ministers are required to be. It puts you up in the pecking order, moves you a couple of places nearer the chairman at any top table. For a journalist this carries advantages. When, after the war, I had joined Hugo Wortham on the *Daily Telegraph*'s Peterborough column I found he had established a useful rule. When invited to any lunch or dinner, he stipulated that he or any member of his staff should sit, not at the press table, but among the guests. This was not snobbishness but professionalism. A columnist is unlikely to hear anything useful from other journalists; but, if he is any good at his job, he will always discover something he did not know from his neighbours at other tables. A Privy Councillor who wants to speak in the House of Commons is a degree more likely to catch the Speaker's eye, though he is wise not to seek it too often.

And 1964 was a good time to get back to newspapers. I do not believe social history falls neatly within particular decades, but the 1960s had a strong flavour of their own. The Beatles were in orbit, Auntie BBC had become mischievous, Carnaby Street was the place for gear, and Mary Quant accused the Paris fashion show of being out of date.

Dear Bill

While holding office with some tenuous responsibility for political appearances, I had found some aspects of the 1960s, particularly a more mischievous BBC, troublesome. David Frost's brilliant *That Was the Week that Was* tended to make politicians look ridiculous. I felt like a maiden aunt at a fun fair; everyone seemed to be on the swings, except me. While still a Minister, I had said a few halting words in favour of the Beatles and was furiously attacked from the left for sycophancy.

But to be a reporter of more lively times was bliss. Both the *Daily Telegraph*, to which I returned, and the *Sunday Telegraph* were in the market for pieces on social and political issues. Life in Government had given me insight into some of these. Insofar as I had developed any political philosophy of my own it was that in the long run 'prosperity politics' would fail to give people lasting satisfaction. Just before the General Election of 1966 I discussed this in a piece for the *Daily Telegraph* which was headed: 'Not by bread alone . . .' I drew attention to words Winston Churchill had used in his foreword to the Tory political statement of 1949. 'Man is a spiritual creature, advancing on an immortal destiny, and science, politics and economics are good or bad as far as they help or hinder the individual soul on its eternal journey.'

This was hardly the thinking of these times, and no blame to the talented young men who stitch together the modern-style Tory manifesto for steering clear of souls on eternal journeys. Yet, I argued, if during relatively prosperous years we had moved so much closer to the all-powerful state, where were we likely to end up in a period not of rising but of falling expectations? It seemed to me that in most of life's adventures we find ourselves alone. Man entered this world alone, would leave it alone and was alone now.

'For the young there was a touch of magic in the air, which seems elusive now,' I wrote in a foreword to the *Daily Telegraph*'s chronicle of the 1960s, which was published in the early 1990s. But it was not all sweetness and light. A new spirit also prevailed at some of the universities, and it was markedly unfriendly to Tory speakers. A strange experience befell me at Essex University, where I had agreed to give a talk – unwisely – on race relations. Just before I left the House of Commons for Colchester a warning reached me: 'Apparently it is likely that a large number of students may turn out on the basis that it is suggested you are a friend of Mr Powell . . .' Enoch Powell had had five university meetings broken up in the course of that year.

As I entered the Essex lecture theatre with the local Member of Parliament for Colchester, Tony Buck, a small brass band took the company into 'God Save the Queen', sung extravagantly. For the next thirty minutes, through an unexpectedly efficient microphone, it was never possible to utter more than half a dozen words audibly.

Through the entrance, like small part actors, fresh groups arrived at intervals to be greeted boisterously. Almost the last, playing a solo, was a well-known student, sent down from Essex some time earlier, whose presence on this occasion was therefore puzzling. He received the sort of welcome accorded to the last cabaret star of the evening. But cabaret is not the right analogy. The comic hats, the painted moustaches, the bizarre clothes, the bold youths suspended like trapeze artists from the gallery, the concave shape of the lecture hall brought straight to mind the circus tent, in which clowns and audience had simply been transposed. The impression was heightened by the number of both sexes who had painted their faces in weird colours, as clowns do.

After declining to be garlanded with a black silk bra, and after the lights had been switched off, I suggested to the young chairman that we might withdraw. That was the start of more serious trouble. My strategy was to move away by easy stages, via the students' bar and the library, in hope that our main adversaries would get bored and depart. The library was a mistake. 'It is damn wrong', hissed one of the ringleaders in my ear, 'to involve the library. It is out of bounds to disorder. You are a bloody fool.' Then, as we moved round the quadrangle, they began to jostle us. 'You struck my friend! Tory bastard! Are you going to apologize?' Some of them were spoiling for a fight.

Just as it became plain that we were hemmed in, I encountered (for the first time) a senior member of the University staff. He was faintly green round the gills. He begged us in the interests of our own safety to delay our departure and wait in the porter's lodge. I was tired, hungry and cross. 'Either you call the police to secure our safe exit,' I said, 'or we leave and take our chances.' The police, he said miserably, were out of the question. 'Then we walk to our car,' I said. The mob was waiting outside, and stalked us like wolves. As we reached the car, half a dozen students threw themselves on top of it. We were in fact using Mrs Buck's car – her husband's had been put out of action during an earlier visit to the University. Somehow, we got the car into motion without injuring anyone.

An account of this experience – 'In the eye of the student storm!' – made a good piece for the *Sunday Telegraph*, which incensed the authorities of Essex University. Dr Albert Sloman, then vice-chancellor of the University, later told the Commons Select Committee on Education that the demonstrations against Enoch Powell and myself were aspects of student concern with wider issues and 'with the quality of society'. He argued firmly that it was in the interests of society that universities should criticize it. During the war Sloman had won a reputation as a gallant night fighter pilot, but I felt unsupportive of his declared aim to run 'a university without rules'. After that experience I became more selective in my acceptance of students' invitations. Scotland was the place to go. I recall a thoroughly productive evening at St Andrews University, where I learned more from the students than they from me.

I had returned to the back benches at the end of 1964 with plenty to occupy my mind. One of the biggest – and most mismanaged – political issues of the 1960s was our policy on immigration from the Commonwealth. It is a chapter of our history with which I became closely involved and to which I eventually gave a lot of parliamentary time. As a junior minister in the Home Office 1955–7, I learned something about the history and ethos of immigration here. Above the white cliffs of Dover we have long kept our own, invisible Statue of Liberty. The settlement of about 80,000 French Huguenots (after the revocation of the Edict of Nantes in 1685) in a population of around six million was probably the largest single influx since the Norman invasion. In modern times we had rescued 60,000 refugees from Nazi oppression between 1933 and 1939. After the war, at Churchill's decree, we took in about 120,000 Poles. At any one time, we had about 400,000 people registered as aliens in this country. They entered at the rate of 15,000 to 20,000 a year and about 4,000 became naturalized every year.

After the Second World War we had pursued a dual policy. The settlement of foreigners was restricted, permitting about one in 150 who entered the country to stay. Citizens of Commonwealth countries, however, were free to enter as they pleased. As Andrew Roberts points out in a chapter of his book *Eminent Churchillians*, the Labour Government's British Nationality Act of 1948, which was an attempt to define British citizenship, effectively gave 800 million Commonwealth citizens the legal right to reside in the UK. Yet no official record of their numbers was kept. For this reason it is impossible accurately to trace the rate of Commonwealth entry before the Commonwealth Immigrants Act of 1962. In 1953 the House of Commons was told we had no power to keep records. As late as 1958 we kept no check on arrivals by air.

It was the Labour Government which first thought of closing the loophole. A Cabinet sub-committee under Home Secretary Chuter Ede reported early in 1951 that, while no restrictions were immediately necessary, any substantial inflow 'might produce a situation in the UK rendering legislation for its control essential'. After the General Election of October 1951 responsibility for this fell on Churchill's Government. It was the last item on the agenda of the Cabinet meeting held on 25 November 1952. A working party was established, inelegantly entitled Working Party on the Social and Economic Problems Arising from the Growing Influx into the United Kingdom of Coloured Workers from other Commonwealth Countries. It took thirteen months to report. The Home Secretary reported to Cabinet in January 1954, 'there is no effective means of stopping this influx without legislation . . .'

Much of the work was perforce done in the dark, because of the absence of reliable figures. However, it was reckoned that under Churchill annual immigration from the Commonwealth had risen roughly from 3,000 in 1953 to 11,000 in 1954 and 42,650 in 1955.

In 1955 the Conservative campaign guide put the total coloured population in Great Britain at between 60,000 and 80,000, which I have always reckoned was a considerable underestimate. From 1955 to 1957 entry from the Commonwealth was estimated at between 40,000 and 50,000 a year. Troubled by this trend, a group of Ministers examined the subject in 1956–7. They stopped short of recommending control, because it would be complex and controversial; but proposed an appeal to Commonwealth governments to restrain emigration by voluntary agreement.

Unsurprisingly, this failed. There then followed what Rab Butler called a 'slight recession in the UK' and the entry fell to about 30,000 in 1958 and 21,000 in 1959. Ministers found this a welcome pretext for withholding further action, but their respite was brief. In 1960 entry had almost trebled to 57,700 and in 1961 it soared to 136,400. The Queen's Speech to Parliament of that year signalled a major shift of policy: 'Legislation will be introduced to control the immigration to the UK of British subjects from other parts of the Common-

wealth and give powers for the expulsion of immigrants con-
victed of criminal offences.'

With hindsight, it is not difficult to observe, as Andrew
Roberts has done, the flaws in our policy up to this point.
Cabinet papers show how short-term political expediency
guided Conservative government attitudes for the best part of a
decade. We totally failed to grasp the economic forces which
lay behind the influx. This was the United Nations estimate of
per capita incomes in 1958:

India	$60
Pakistan	$70
West Indies	$180
United Kingdom	$750

It explains Britain's magnetism. Thus hopes of securing from
leaders of the principal migrating countries agreement to
restrain the outward movement by voluntary means were never
very bright. There was furthermore not only push but pull. The
post-war demand for labour led to active recruiting in the West
Indies by British employers. In this the British Transport
Commission, with its large demand for unskilled labour, played
a notable part. London Transport, the National Health Service
and J. Lyons, the teahouse chain, also sought recruits.

So the appearance of the Commonwealth Immigrants Bill
in the autumn of 1961 had come as a shock. It soon ran into a
storm. Commonwealth leaders condemned the lack of consultation. Labour, led by Hugh Gaitskell, assailed the Bill furiously,
and a minority of Conservative MPs expressed reservations
about it. This was despite the fact that Ministers had to report
that net immigration from the Commonwealth amounted to
113,000 in the first ten months of 1961 (by the end of the year,
134,000), comprising 57,000 from the West Indies and 36,000
from India and Pakistan. It had taken eight days and the
guillotine to secure the Bill's committee stage on the floor of

the House. Ireland was excluded from its provisions, largely because control of the border between North and South was impossible and would have led to passports for the citizens of Ulster – 'an intolerable imposition', Butler called it.

The Bill's main feature required immigrants from the Commonwealth either (A) to hold a voucher from the Ministry of Labour which satisfied immigration authorities that they were coming to a specific job in the UK, or (B) to possess 'training, skill or educational qualifications likely to be useful to this country'. Those in a third, open category (C) were subject to any limit which the Government from time to time determined. Its effect, of course, was to impose the same restrictions on Canada, Australia and New Zealand, though everyone was aware that their citizens did not constitute a problem. It created resentment in the older Commonwealth which prevails to this day.

This hotch-potch of a Bill, on which countless concessions had to be made in order to secure its passage, was never likely to attain its main objective – as Labour soon found on taking office in 1964. The Act had become operative in July 1962. In November 1963, Labour voted against its renewal. Yet in September 1964, Labour's election manifesto declared: 'Labour accepts that the number of immigrants entering the UK must be limited.' By November 1965 Labour had not only to renew the Act but to make public compelling reasons for doing so.

The then Home Secretary, Sir Frank Soskice, reckoned that there were by then, 800,000 immigrants in Great Britain. Between the Act of July 1962 and November 1964, about 120,000 had arrived, 50,000 of them with vouchers, accompanied by 62,000 dependants. Ministers had also to disclose a serious number of evasions: 'a degree of evasion', declared Harold Wilson in March 1965, 'almost fatally eroding the Commonwealth Immigrants Act'. These arose from false passports, impersonation and false statements. In the preceding two years, it was disclosed, some 53,000 had entered the country as students under the Act. Many had never reached the educational establishment at which they had enrolled. They had simply entered the labour market.

So Labour turned full cycle. It sent Lord Mountbatten on a Commonwealth tour to discuss our difficulties with political leaders. In August 1965 it produced a White Paper which showed that the rate of entry was still running at about 60,000 a year. It cut back the issue of vouchers to 8,500 a year, discontinued category C, curtailed the right of children between sixteen and eighteen to enter freely to join one or both parents, withdrew concessions for young relatives, proposed stricter controls over students, put a limit on *bona fide* visitors of up to six months, and gave immigration officers the right to require individuals to register with the police in line with aliens.

None of these steps was really effective, for we had passed the point of no return. No doubt awareness of that was a factor in the explosive speech which Enoch Powell chose to deliver in April 1968 – a speech which led to his instant dismissal from Ted Heath's shadow Cabinet and to much else. Immediately, it produced 100,000 letters in his support. In the longer run, politics being what it is, it made matters worse – and over a friendly lunch some years later I told Enoch why I thought this was so.

For one thing, it put Ted Heath, then Leader of the Opposition, on the wrong foot. Having sacked Enoch Powell for – as he saw it – overstating the case for curbing Commonwealth immigration, he could ill afford to be seen giving the case for stronger control support of his own. The speech also cut the ground from under the feet of some of us who were seeking, in less emotive language, to alert both Government and Opposition to the mess we were getting into. We had drifted into accepting large numbers of Commonwealth immigrants without giving any serious thought at all to the social consequences in this country – both for them and for our own population. A growing restiveness was by this time making itself felt in certain cities, particularly where immigrants were settling in large numbers. The Labour Government's main response to this restiveness was to embark on Race Relations Acts making a wide range of discriminatory acts against coloured immigrants unlawful.

My own unshakeable conviction was that firm control over the rate at which immigrants entered the country was an absolute condition of good race relations. I deplored race discrimination and reluctantly accepted the need for legislation, though aware that it would infringe a principle we had long upheld. Since the eighteenth century Parliament had deliberately steered clear of legislation against the expression of particular views. As Gladstone had put it in 1871, 'In this country there is a great and just unwillingness to interfere with the expression of opinion that is not attended with danger to public peace.' Given that we had to break with this tradition, it is wise in a democracy like ours to seek as much public support as possible for controversial measures. There was by now widespread public feeling that we had virtually lost control of numbers entering the country. We would improve our chances of getting fair play for the immigrant, I felt, if at the same time we assured our own population that we could and would effectively control entry. No such sign was made.

Something like a million immigrants had entered the country in under a generation. Entry was still running at 50,000 a year, though by now most of them were dependants. The central question had become: how many more? I felt particular concern about the youngsters (under sixteen) who were entering the country as dependants. As the Labour Home Secretary concedes, after the admission of 13,000 children from Pakistan in one year:

This worries me quite considerably. Many of the boys are very nearly sixteen. If they go to schools for a short time they present a great problem of absorption in the schools. In any event, they soon find their way on to the labour market, and they do so with very little UK background, educationally or in other ways. They had come at almost the worst age from the point of view of successful integration, and furthermore they come, to a large extent, to join only a single parent, almost invariably the father, while the mother stays in Pakistan or India.

Of course it could be argued, as many did, that the indecisiveness of British governments since 1948 had already sold the pass, that the movement had become unstoppable, and all that remained was to wring our hands, as Enoch Powell had done in his speech of April 1968. I rejected this policy of despair. I foresaw serious problems arising in the schools, in the workplace and in the inner cities as a result of prolonged political fumbling. Though late in the day, the essential task was to strive to ameliorate some of these problems. I agreed to join the House of Commons Select Committee on Race Relations and Immigration, working until 1970 as deputy chairman to Arthur Bottomley, Labour's former Commonwealth Secretary, and thereafter as chairman of the Committee until my retirement from Parliament in 1974.

I also wrote a pamphlet for the Conservative Political Centre, about which they reported to me minor misgivings by Ted Heath, but which I declined to alter. It ended on this note:

We still do not know where we are going. What *is* our policy? To declare that immigrants shall be treated without discrimination is not in itself a policy. Should we, for example, continue to allow new arrivals to drift, without guidance and advice, into areas of their choice which will almost certainly be areas of heavy immigrant concentration...?

Answers will only be sought and discussed when we

accept that we are experiencing, not a transient social phenomenon, but a permanent change in the structure of our society; and are prepared to declare openly that this is so.

Our Select Committee was not set up by the Labour Government until the end of 1968. We were called on to look at the workings of Labour's Race Relations Acts, and at Britain's immigration policies. Arthur Bottomley and I got on well. We never had a cross word. From a reporter's point of view, we proceeded to discover a lot that people did not know. In political terms, we achieved little, for we were merely advising the shutting of stable doors through which horses had bolted long before.

In the course of six years, we visited India and Pakistan twice, Bangladesh once, and the Caribbean twice. After all these expeditions I sent papers to Ministers or members of the shadow Cabinet outlining our discoveries, some of which amounted to serious abuse of the law. They were acknowledged, but largely ignored. Suddenly to admit that we faced grave problems would have been political suicide. Had our committee been appointed at the time of Labour's British Nationality Act in 1948, or even a decade later, we might have been useful. But it is not granted to politicians to see that far ahead. Winston Churchill, who could peer into the future, did indeed have misgivings, but only during his final days in office.

At one extreme was a minority reluctant to accept any effective control and ready to turn a blind eye to illicit entry. Vainly did I stress the injustice done by illegal immigrants to those who played it by the book. At the other extreme were those embodying the National Front attitude, who expressed their resentment against all immigrants offensively. They were counter-productive. At the same time, I came to accept, there were grounds for resentment. At no point, we were repeatedly told by witnesses who came before the Select Committee, had any Government bothered to consult them about a fundamental change in the nature of our society. Andrew Roberts makes the point that all seven Ministers at the Home Office during the decisive years, including myself, lived in the country. In other words, none of them lived in areas that were starting to change dramatically as a result of mass immigration. But there was more to it than that. Until 1962 Ministers dealt with the problem defensively. They hoped it would go away. There was no looking ahead, no constructive policy. The Conservative Party's campaign guide for the 1959 General Election declared that it was not possible, as the law stood, to prevent people who were British from entering the country. 'Any legislation which sought to alter that position would be both complex and controversial.' There was reluctance to appear to be taking the matter too seriously. We were in the throes of granting independence to a large colonial empire. It was no time to upset them.

Now, for the sake of argument, let me put myself on the side of the liberals. These people had an absolute right to come. We had encouraged them to augment our labour force. All that is true. But correspondingly we had a political obligation to make provision for their arrival in large numbers; to perceive difficulties that were bound to arise in some of our schools; to take the language problem seriously; to consider the impact on local authority waiting lists for houses; to perceive that many dependants, including young children, must follow and would need provision made for them. As I sometimes argued with my liberal friends like Mark Bonham Carter, who was the first chairman of the Race Relations Board 1966–70, if a corresponding number of whites had suddenly descended on India's principal cities, there might well have been a stir of resentment.

But nobody in authority wished to acknowledge that there were difficulties to be resolved. After Enoch's speech, the subject was virtually out of bounds. There was in effect a conspiracy of silence among those called on to meet this main social challenge. Our Committee would ask school teachers to be open with us about their difficulties, particularly in the realm of language. They preferred to live with them in silence. Any admission of 'problems', they thought, would offer a cudgel to racists.

At one point when Margaret Thatcher was Education Secretary in the Heath Government, I invited her to give evidence to our Committee and urged upon her the need to quantify the challenge. How many Asian and Caribbean children with a language problem, for example, had entered our schools? How could we provide adequately for them, unless we knew the numbers involved? Margaret Thatcher fully accepted this and undertook to deal with it. She came back to us to report failure. The teaching profession had dug in its heels against revealing numbers. Their thinking, I surmised, was that any figures they produced would be pounced on by supporters of Enoch Powell. We got nowhere.

The teaching profession, I guessed, strongly supported by the Department of Education, held its ground. I have never doubted this had serious consequences for education as a whole. Some schools with large numbers of children who had a language problem effectively adopted the convoy system. To avoid any appearance of discrimination, that is, against children with a language problem, the class moved at the pace of the slowest vessels. And this at a time when grammar schools for the more able were out of favour, and the more egalitarian comprehensive school prevailed. As the Select Committee chairman at the time, I found these implications alarming. I was fortunate with my colleagues on the Committee. They included two or three Labour left-wingers, but when confronted by facts they invariably supported our duty to publish them.

They unanimously agreed that we should publish our findings on the refusal to quantify the problem in schools. Describing Department of Education figures as 'useless' and 'unreliable', we predicted disaster unless education authorities faced up to realities. 'For reasons we accept as sincere, though we think them misguided,' we wrote, 'there is a strong temptation to "play down" the challenge to our schools which immigrant pupils have posed.'

We went on: 'In the short term it may seem prudent to keep this subject in a low key ... In the longer term, we believe that such obscurantist attitudes may prove disastrous. They could have the effect of concealing the consequences of launching into our society children ill-equipped in language and general education to compete with their contemporaries in an advanced society.'

A quarter of a century on from there, we are wringing our hands over the failure of schools to provide the basic disciplines of literacy and numeracy. Of course not all of this can be laid at the door of misjudgements in the 1960s and 1970s; but they have been a factor. The 'convoy concept' requiring all to travel at the pace of the slowest, the linguistically handicapped, was damaging. We ended our report by saying: 'If, after our inquiry, one conclusion stands out above all others, it is that we have failed to grasp and are still failing to grasp the scale of what we have undertaken.' In London, we reported, the number of West Indian schoolchildren in educationally sub-normal schools was 'wholly disproportionate both to the numbers of other immigrant children in ESN schools and to the West Indian population'.

Our report, endorsed by all Labour's left-wingers, produced vivid headlines, some of them unfriendly to Margaret Thatcher's Department of Education and Science. I felt moved to send a line to her:

This is only a personal line to say that I am sorry if the report of the Select Committee – and the media's handling of it – has added in any way to your already heavy burden at DES. It is a pity that, rather superficially, the Press have dwelt so heavily on this vexed question of statistics and their compilation, because I think there are wider matters of greater concern raised by this small report – not all of which lie at the door of the DES. In certain interviews, where opportunity has arisen, I have tried to stress that. It is debatable whether the DES, however lavishly endowed, could or should be expected to find all the answers to a policy which, over many years, has given unrestricted right of entry to these Commonwealth children, regardless of age, capacity, language. Perhaps I had better stop there.

I am consoled only by the knowledge, shared by many, that a Select Committee, whatever it says, is not likely to diminish the very high regard felt for you and your work as Secretary of State.

Margaret Thatcher's handwritten reply to this effusion was stoical. 'Thank you so much for your personal letter about the press handling of the Select Committee's report. The whole of DES feels that it has been very unjustly treated. We politicians are used to that! It was kind of you to write.'

To make sure we had the facts right, both Bottomley and I sometimes submitted passages from our reports to overseas posts; and sometimes they had corrections to offer. But I drew the line at submitting drafts to Government departments for their approval. Late in 1973, I was pressed by ministerial colleagues in the Foreign Office and Home Office to do this. 'It would be helpful', they said. 'They want to doctor our report!' I told our Committee. My left-wing colleagues on the Committee played the hand beautifully. 'Tell them', they said, 'that we are thoroughly untrustworthy fellows, and will certainly leak to the press any attempt to interfere with our agreed report.' I duly passed this on and we heard no more. Our report appeared as written.

During my six years on this work I learned an important fact about parliamentary life. Taken away from the cockpit of Westminster and confronted by the facts of life, MPs of widely different opinions will often see eye to eye. We covered a variety of subjects: the school leaver, education, employment, housing, police and immigration itself. All our reports were unanimous. We made surprising discoveries. The Governments of both India and Pakistan differed from the liberals in this country, in that they fully accepted our right to control entry. India held no brief for its sons and daughters who wished to leave the country. The Pakistanis treated migration here primarily as a bread-winning exercise. The proportion of males to females was three or even four to one. Remittances from Pakistan's immigrants here were reckoned by the British High Commission – and this was a quarter of a century ago – to be upwards of £50 million a year. Nearly all immigrants from the sub-continent came from relatively tiny areas for particular reasons. In Pakistan, for instance, the building of a dam had caused a huge displacement of population. In Bangladesh, partition had cut off the port of Calcutta. The town of Sylhet, a traditional birthplace of sailors, was left empty-handed. In India, the high price of land round Gujarat had compelled many to seek a living elsewhere; and it was from there that many had emigrated to East Africa.

Our entry certificate officers who worked in the sub-continent had a hard time of it, particularly in Pakistan, where records were non-existent or unreliable. Documentary proof of identity simply did not exist. We admired their patience and professionalism. In New Delhi I was present during the examination of a woman who claimed to be a widow. Her brother-in-law in this country, she claimed, would look after her. I was mildly surprised to see her refused entry. 'She was wearing jewellery,' the entry certificate officer explained to me, 'a sure sign among Hindus that she is married and not a widow.' Agents were busy everywhere preparing papers and passports and travel arrangements – often for enormous fees.

On return from this particular expedition, I sent a long memorandum to Ministers. 'The question', I said, 'is not whether the system of entry is foolproof, which it never can be; but whether it still permits evasion on a scale we ought not to tolerate, and there can be little doubt that it does.' By contrast, the entry systems into Canada and Australia, which I studied, were stricter than our own and more efficient.

Given a choice between escorting a handful of Members of Parliament round India or fifty children round Disneyland, I would always opt for Disneyland. Taking a small party of MPs anywhere can be a maddening experience. The arrangements are made, the schedule of meetings agreed. Invariably one of the number then says that when travelling between X and Y, he wishes to make a small independent detour to Z in order to visit a friend who may be the next Prime Minister but three. The diversion invariably runs into unforeseen difficulties. So here we are on Monday morning, due to take evidence from the British High Commission and one short of a quorum. When about to leave some modest hotel, the Clerk of the Committee would approach me with an anxious face and declare that Messrs A and B had failed to pay their laundry bills. Treasury largesse does not run to laundry bills. Getting the bills paid meant twenty instead of forty minutes before the flight.

Our failure to handle the immigration issue more honestly and efficiently sprang mainly from an inability to understand what was going on in the world. Soon after the First World War ended, Field Marshal Smuts observed, 'Humanity has struck its tents. We cannot tell whither they are journeying.' What happened here was not simply a post-imperial spasm. Much of the world was on the march, aided by air travel, and it still is. America has acknowledged this generously. Europe has a huge influx of immigrants from other lands. We failed to read the signs in time. We were unprepared. It was a failure of statecraft.

With the young scholars of Bosnia, 1997.

On the satellite phone belonging to Diana, Princess of Wales in Bosnia, 1997.

With Clare Crawford in the mysterious Plain of Jars, Laos, 1997.

Blowing up a bomblet in Laos, 1997.

Where Christians in the desert near Khartoum come to worship, 1998.

In Hemingway's favourite bar, Cuba, 1999.

Fidel Castro's Havana, 1999.

Shopping in Lahore, Pakistan, 2001.

Above: With the desolate people of Darfur, 2004.

Opposite page: With the pupils of St Joseph's Primary School
in Sierra Leone, 2003.

In memorium, Normandy, 2004.

16

Censorship and Drugs

Between leaving the Government at the end of 1964 and retiring from Parliament in 1974, I spent ten years as a relatively senior back-bencher, six of them, 1964–70, in Opposition and four of them, 1970–4, on the Government side of the House. Some Members of Parliament on leaving or losing office feel the best is behind them and prepare to bow out. I found my last ten years the most pleasurable of all. Experience enabled me to be of modest public service, which is partly what being an MP is about. I returned to journalism with the *Daily Telegraph*. I had freedom to write what I wished, to say what I liked.

Early in 1965 Churchill died and lay in state in Westminster Hall. Michael Hartwell, chairman and editor-in-chief of the *Daily Telegraph*, rang me up in the office. He wondered if there was a chance of my assistance as a Member of Parliament in enabling him and his wife, Pamela, to attend the lying in state without queuing. We agreed to meet at his house in Cowley Street that evening. Before setting forth, he and his wife and I took a drink together. We said very little to each other, but I felt that the occasion sealed my return to the *Telegraph*, that I was back in harbour after a stormy passage on the high seas.

The *Harrovian* invited me to write something on Churchill as an orator and a prophet. Unquestionably, in his prime, Churchill saw further ahead than any other politician of this century. He combined his historical vision with practical inventiveness. The first was illustrated by his speech at Fulton in

1947 when he spoke of the Iron Curtain that had descended between East and West. The speech was criticized by some as alarmist, but he was right. Consider again his contribution to the invention and use of the tank in the First World War and the design of Mulberry Harbours in the second. As far back as 1925 – twenty years before Hiroshima – he predicted a bomb no larger than an orange with stupefying explosive capacity.

I recalled an Old Harrovian dinner, an annual event attended by Harrovians in Lords and Commons, not long before Churchill retired. President Nehru of India was in the country and, since he had spent a year at Harrow, was invited to attend. He and Churchill sat next to each other in company with the headmaster of Harrow, the school's head boy and the captain of cricket. It was at first not quite easy between them. Nehru could recall times in the earlier history of Britain's relations with India which Churchill did not wish to remember. At one point, as Nehru reminded him at the dinner, Churchill had been instrumental in ensuring his imprisonment. However, when the company rose and sang 'Forty Years On', they drew close to each other and Churchill became tearful.

As I have mentioned, Churchill took infinite pains with all his speeches. He was not, like Lloyd George or Aneurin Bevan, good at speaking off the cuff. Most of his speeches were set down on quarto sheets of paper with the left-hand margin of each line staggered, and so easier to read at a glance. It is a method I have copied for fifty years.

In this same year, 1965, Alec Home retired as Leader of the Conservative party. Under the new rules, which Home had himself devised, there was an election for his successor. Ted Heath emerged as winner with 150 votes, Reggie Maudling, his main rival, got 133 votes, and Enoch Powell received 15 votes. I thought it was an election in which my constituents should have a say. I set aside two or three evenings when I telephoned as many officers of Ashford's Conservative Association as I could find. Maudling got a few more votes than Heath in this poll so, good to my word, I voted for him.

On the parliamentary front, the first main item to engage me was the proposed abolition of capital punishment. A talented if troublesome Labour back-bencher, Sydney Silverman, came forward with a Private Member's Bill to this effect. To this the Labour Government gave full support. My Home Office blood tingled. I was not an absolute retentionist, but I thought there were offences for which capital punishment ought to be retained. It is an issue, I must add, on which I have changed my mind in recent years. It would be virtually impossible to secure even a majority verdict of guilty from a jury today if we still had capital punishment. There would be perverse verdicts and men guilty of serious offences would walk free.

But in 1965 the proposal to abolish hanging seemed risky and was highly controversial. It was something everyone could understand and on which therefore everyone was ready with an opinion. My parliamentary friends and I tabled a number of amendments to the Bill. We sought to retain hanging for murder in furtherance of theft, for a second murder, for the murder of a policeman or prison officer, or for murder by shooting or causing an explosion. All this was in vain. The Bill went through. As I wrote at the time, it would be churlish to deny Silverman his place in history. Against the intentions of the Labour Government in 1948, he had added a clause to the Criminal Justice Bill suspending the death sentence and got it through the Commons. The Lords threw it out. He tried again in 1953 and in 1955. In 1956 he introduced another Abolition Bill and got it through the Commons. The Lords again rejected it. In 1965, his hour had come. The execution of Timothy Evans in 1950, the discovery three years later of six bodies at Rillington Place and the subsequent trial of John Christie had converted many to abolition.

Dear Bill

From Home Office experience I retained doubts about the likely duration of life sentences which were to replace capital punishment. Gwilym Lloyd George, under whom I had worked at the Home Office, tended to agree with Sir Alexander Paterson, the great prison reformer, who had said twenty-five years earlier: 'It requires a superman to survive twenty years of imprisonment with character and soul intact . . . I gravely doubt whether an average man can serve more than ten continuous years without deterioration.' I was also doubtful, at the time of the Silverman Bill more than thirty years ago, whether the review of life sentences should remain in the hands of the Home Secretary. It seemed to me that, even with the best of advice, the Home Secretary would be faced with a series of decisions less privately agonizing but hardly less socially responsible than his exercise of the prerogative towards those sentenced to death. The longer life sentence which I assumed would follow abolition of the death penalty seemed to me to fall emphatically in the realm of justice and ought not to remain a private decision by one member of the executive.

While all this was going on, the Conservative party set up a committee to assess post-war trends in crime and to examine the treatment of offenders. I gladly agreed to serve. It afforded a close study of one of the subjects I wrote about in the two *Telegraph* newspapers. We were becoming troubled by the rapid rise in crime and puzzled by the fact that it coincided with a steady rise in living standards.

The BBC invited me to take part in a series for the *Listener*, on the BBC's duty to society. I glanced over this essay again recently. It had not the remotest bearing on what has come to pass! It was about this time that I became closely acquainted with Mary Whitehouse. I did not agree with all she said, but I formed a growing admiration for her persistence and her courage. Furthermore, I shared her frustration in the face of the BBC's refusal under Greene to have anything to do with her. They ignored her. The 1960s were rough times for people with the message Mrs Whitehouse sought to deliver. Being sexually explicit had become a newly discovered freedom. She suffered some bruising encounters, particularly with students. As Mary Kenny observed in a piece about her in the *Spectator* many years later, 'Look how we treated her – and look at us now!' I met Mrs Whitehouse quite often for morning coffee or lunch, and I would listen to her recitals, often painful, of what they had done to her on some university campus. I supported her partly because things were running fast the other way; and, in my book of Tory philosophy, arriving at the right social balance matters. Nothing in excess, as the Greeks had it.

We had abolished censorship of the stage. Television, a more random form of entertainment, was taking its cue from there. In a famous and much quoted essay on liberty, John Stuart Mill had a passage emphasizing our duty to protect children from corruption. I thought we were becoming careless about this, and, insofar as those who were being most careless also despised Mrs Whitehouse, she seemed a person to support. I spoke for her in Birmingham at an early gathering (1966) of her organization VALA, the Viewers' and Listeners' Association. I was on friendly terms with her supportive Member of Parliament, Jasper More, who occasionally conveyed her problems to me. What I most admired was her unchanging nature. People constantly in the public eye seldom remain unaltered. From start to finish of her long campaign, Mary Whitehouse remained entirely herself – same small faults, same great virtues.

Her enthusiasms occasionally made her embarrassing company. One evening she telephoned me requesting an immediate meeting at the House of Commons. Something shocking had come into her hands. We agreed to meet in the central lobby. She then drew from her bag a glossy magazine, opened the centrefold and invited my comments. It was a startling picture in high colour of a bonking scene. As I gazed at it, thinking of something appropriate to say, I observed that we had aroused the interest of one of the policemen who guard the lobby. Who on earth was this woman exhibiting pornographic literature to a Member of Parliament?

None of this dimmed my affection for her. While editing the *Daily Telegraph* in later years I received a request from her over the telephone which, had it come from any other source, I would have rejected. Her daughter's broken marriage, she told me, was about to be sensationalized in one of the Sunday newspapers. Had she not been the daughter of Mrs Whitehouse nobody would have been interested. Could I help? After thinking about it, I broke every rule in the book and called the newspaper's top man, with whom I was friendly. I told him the tale. He promised to call me back, and half an hour later did so. 'I've killed the story,' he said, '*not* because of your request but because, on inspection, it is not a very good story.' We shall both carry the shame of that episode to our graves.

I developed a taste for looking at what the rest of the world was doing, for I felt that our day among world leaders was passing. New ideas, solutions to old problems, were to be found overseas. On a visit to Germany I visited a new prison at Stuttgart in which modern technology had made escape virtually impossible. It greatly improved relations between prisoners and warders, the Governor assured me. Both sides could relax. It was the year, 1966, in which Lord Mountbatten was asked by the Labour Government to look into an epidemic of prison escapes in this country. They included George Blake, the spy, from Wormwood Scrubs and Ronald Biggs, the train robber, from Wandsworth. Had I sent my account of the Stuttgart prison to the Home Office, I would have received a polite acknowledgement, and that would have been the end of it. Instead, I wrote a piece for the *Sunday Telegraph* on 'The prison that *does* hold them', and it attracted attention. An advantage of combining journalism with politics, as Churchill knew, is that one can ventilate thoughts and ideas as one goes along.

Having become a member of the Government's Advisory

Censorship and Drugs

Committee on Drug Dependence, I thought a visit to the United States would be useful. I spent three weeks looking at crime and drug abuse on America's east and west coasts. It was a time when the computer was beginning to be useful to the police. Road patrols could obtain instant information about doubtful-looking vehicles. In California, where Ronald Reagan was Governor, they teemed with new ideas in the realm of what they called 'Corrections' – in our language, penology.

To my lasting regret, none of my travels included Vietnam. I had more than one opportunity to visit the war there. Each one coincided with some small but unavoidable engagement in my constituency. I regretted the omission because I have more sympathy than most with America's decision to fight that war. The spread of Communism through the East loomed larger then than it does today. That was why – under a Labour Government – Britain had fought in Korea. Today, we have forgotten this. Perhaps influenced by a generation of young who abhorred that war and marched against it, we have come to see America's adventure in Vietnam as an aberration, a wasteful folly. As it turned out, I did not set foot in the country until 1993, when I spent some days in Hanoi, with which by then America was contemplating re-establishing relations.

The oddest of my journeys around this time was to Brazil. I went with two parliamentary colleagues, the late Neil Marten and Marcus Worsley, who had been my long-suffering parliamentary secretary while I was in the Cabinet. We went ostensibly to support an independent British airline that was seeking to make its way in South America with VC10 aircraft. On our final night in Rio, we returned to our hotel to find a small delegation awaiting us. They wished to buy the liner *Queen Elizabeth*, which was on the market. She would, they explained, make a fine British trade ship in the harbour of Rio de Janeiro. For good measure they would also purchase two of our then novel hovercraft, which could ferry visitors to and from the liner. Their credentials were surprisingly good. One of their backers was the Bank of Boston. Secrecy, they stressed, was imperative, for there were rival purchasers in the field. Would we pursue their case with the liner's owners, Cunard, on our return?

Back in London, Marten and Worsley found better things to do. I pursued the matter with the Board of Trade, Cunard and other interested parties. Astonishingly, the negotiations seemed to go well. I appeared before the Cunard board, and won support. Lord Brown, who was Labour's Minister of State at the Board of Trade, backed the sale. I emphasized that I was acting out of pure altruism, since it would be wholly improper for a Member of Parliament to receive any consideration for the deal. The idea caught on. Enjoined to secrecy, I felt unable to consult anyone else and became the sole negotiator in Great Britain. The principals in New York and Brazil kept in close touch by telephone. All went swimmingly until the question arose of a deposit on the agreed purchase price. This involved Brazil's currency, which was shaky. Cunard got cold feet. Suddenly I was summoned by the House of Rothschild in London. They had received an SOS from New York, where it was perceived that the deal was slipping. 'You are not a great businessman, are you?' a Mr Rothschild said to me reproachfully. Why had I not consulted them? I explained that I had been sworn to secrecy. They shook their heads incredulously.

Another purchaser, presumably able to satisfy Cunard's anxiety about the deposit, won the day. But there was some hoodoo over that ship. Some time later, I found her languishing in swampish water in Florida and went over her. Then she was conveyed to the Far East and perished in flames. Serve them all right, I said to myself.

I do not remember what first provoked my concern about addictive drugs, though I fancy it was because nobody else in Parliament showed much interest in the subject. In a book I eventually wrote on the subject, *The Drugs Epidemic* (published in 1970), I set mid-1964 as the beginning of our concern about drug abuse in this country. There had been a huge increase in the use of drugs which affect the central nervous system. An inquiry under Russell Brain (later Lord Brain) in 1958 showed that the amount of barbiturates prescribed by general practitioners in the National Health Service had reached the staggering level of 162,000lb – 7 per cent of all NHS prescriptions. When these were added to other sedatives and analgesics, the total rose to almost 19 per cent. Some 5.6 million out of 214 million NHS prescriptions in 1959 were for amphetamines. This was attributed by the Brain committee to the 'accelerated tempo and heightened anxieties of modern life'.

In those days most of the heroin was being supplied to users by a handful of doctors – Brain put the total at no more than six. One of them, Brain found in his second report, had in 1962 prescribed 600,000 tablets of heroin, amounting to six of the forty kilograms being consumed that year in this country. I came to know most of these doctors. They may have been misguided, but they were not villains. By prescribing to those addicted to heroin – which precious few doctors were willing to do – they were discouraging illicit traffic and keeping addicts out of criminal hands. They felt they were keeping the party clean. So did the police. Brain's committee recommended a less liberal system. It was decided that all heroin addicts should be notified to a central authority. New treatment centres would be established, especially in London. Nobody seemed in much of a hurry over it, and twenty months elapsed before this new regime was made statutory by the Drugs (Prevention of Misuse) Act. The Government's Advisory Committee on Drug Dependence was not set up until the end of 1966 – eighteen months after Brain had reported.

In 1967, Sir Harry Greenfield, chairman of the Permanent Central Narcotics Board, came to see me and proposed a national, non-governmental institute for the study of drug dependence. He was accompanied by Frank Logan, who had wide experience of government service overseas. I agreed and the three of us formed what became the Institute for the Study of Drug Dependence. We secured the service of Dr Tom Bewley, then consultant psychiatrist at three London hospitals, and Dr Philip Connell, who was consultant adviser on drug addiction to the Ministry of Health. Others joined us. I left the Institute when I came out of politics in 1974. By then it had become one of Europe's major reference centres.

The Government Committee was chaired by Sir Edward Wayne, who earlier in life had chaired a committee that introduced breath tests for motorists. It set up two sub-committees, one of them under Lady Wootton to report on cannabis. A second, of which I took the chair, was called on to examine police powers of search and arrest. Lady Wootton, whose politics were well left of mine, drew the short straw. Her committee recommended a more liberal line on cannabis. This was thunderously condemned by the Labour Home Secretary, Jim Callaghan, whose performance in that hazardous office I came increasingly to admire. My report got off relatively lightly.

I began to receive invitations to talk about drugs at public schools, where they were beginning to take drug abuse seriously. Accompanied by a competent doctor, I spent a day at Eton, Downside, Cheltenham, among others.

When I entered the business in 1964, I felt confident there were obvious solutions to drug addiction if we applied our mind to the subject. When I finished in 1974, I had at least learned that there were no obvious solutions. I hope we do not legalize cannabis because we do not yet know the long-term consequences of constant use. We should inform the young of risks involved in all drugs, but never lecture them. Drug abuse belongs to these times. We shall never stop it. We can only strive for better ways of containing it.

Of the eight General Elections I fought at Ashford, the most surprising came in 1970. Up to polling day, the Labour party seemed to be cruising back to office. The opinion polls showed consistent and growing support for a Labour victory.

My experiences on the doorsteps pointed that way. At 4 p.m. on polling day, while touring the constituency, I entered the committee room of my smallest village, a hamlet of 112 people. 'I foresee victory,' said the chairman confidently. In such a tiny place, where everyone knew each other, they had been able to carry out a full canvass and claimed to know how everyone was voting. By comparison with the 1966 General Election (which Labour had won) they had detected a clear swing back to the Conservatives. I smiled indulgently. We old hands knew all about canvassing returns and the false dawns they produced. But the chairman was right. Furthermore the reported swing of votes in his village closely corresponded to the final result in which the Tories won 330 seats against Labour's 247. When the result became known, I took the superior smile off my face and wrote to the chairman, congratulating him and his team on such accurate canvassing.

My friend and neighbour Lord Aldington had also reckoned that Labour was likely to win. Being a close friend of Ted Heath, he thought it would be kind to hold at his home in Aldington, close to mine, a small consolation party on the following Sunday morning. My wife and I were to be the only other guests. 'What am I expected to say?' she asked dismally after I had explained our role. As it turned out, the problem did not arise.

17

Northern Ireland

One evening in August 1969, I received an urgent telephone call at home from Robin Chichester-Clark, who was Ulster Unionist MP for Londonderry. Belfast was burning. 'Come over quickly,' he said. 'We need witnesses.' His brother, James Chichester-Clark, later Lord Moyola, was then Prime Minister of Northern Ireland. For personal reasons, I found the invitation unattractive. After a keyhole operation on a dud ear in the London Clinic, I was taking a fortnight's convalescence. On professional grounds, I found the invitation irresistible and booked an early flight next morning. I was vice-chairman of the Conservative party's Home Affairs Committee; and Ulster's troubles were then the responsibility of the Home Secretary, who was Jim Callaghan.

There had been a week or more of sectarian fighting, in which five had been killed and hundreds injured. There were gun battles in Belfast between the Falls Road, predominantly Catholic, and the Shankill Road, a Protestant zone. British troops had arrived and were being welcomed. Prime Minister Chichester-Clark's Cabinet had asked for them to prevent a breakdown of law and order. It was, British Ministers thought, a limited operation from which soldiers could be withdrawn once order had been restored.

With one or two other parliamentary colleagues that August, I dutifully toured the harsh triangle in Belfast bounded by the Falls and Shankhill roads. During a night patrol with the

Army, I experienced for the first time since the war that visceral sensation we get when unsure who is shooting at whom. The first thing which struck me was the exceptionally high density of those streets in Belfast. I could think of no other city in the United Kingdom, except possibly Tyneside – they lived 180 to the acre in South Shields – where people lived so closely together. I speculated on how far this overcrowding was intensifying animosities.

The root of the tension in Ulster stretched back 800 years. But the more immediate cause of this outbreak lay in the persistent failure of the Unionist Government to do its job properly. It had held office continuously since the Government of Ireland Act of 1920. In consequence there was no effective parliamentary opposition – or alternative Government. Unchallenged power corrupts. The Unionists had become complacent, and the opposition which had taken shape was a civil rights movement, fragmented and bitter. A main failure had been to remedy wretched housing conditions – or to allocate housing fairly.

On top of that, we had the classic problem of a 'double minority'. In Northern Ireland itself, with about a million and a half people, two-thirds could be loosely described as Protestant (the majority) and one-third as Roman Catholic (the minority). Yet, taking the whole island of thirty-two counties, the Roman Catholics were in a majority and the Protestants in a minority by a ratio of three to one.

A third factor was the extraordinary nature and structure of the Northern Ireland police. At this time only 11 per cent of the force had been recruited from the Roman Catholic minority; and the Royal Ulster Constabulary was widely seen as the armed instrument of the Unionist Government. The RUC was largely self-administered and was led by an inspector-general who was answerable to no representative body.

One day in Belfast I ran into Robert Mark, whom I had come to know well when he was Chief Constable of Leicester. Three years later he was Police Commissioner for London. In

Northern Ireland, he was working with Sir James Robertson from Scotland under Lord Hunt to advise the Northern Ireland Government. Why on earth, exclaimed Robert Mark to me, was the RUC patrolling the streets in armoured cars to which Browning machine guns were attached? What were the guns expected to do? Mark thought it essential to separate the paramilitary role from duties as a national police force, and from duties as traffic cops. In many ways, the police of Northern Ireland had a 'colonial' flavour.

After the partition of Ireland in 1920, the RUC was set up with an establishment of 3,000. Because of Ireland's violent history, they had both a soldier's and a policeman's role to play, with emphasis on the former. Thus, when terrorists were at work, they were seen especially by the Catholic minority as a Protestant army and an instrument of repression – natural descendants of the Black and Tans – the notorious irregulars recruited in 1920. On top of that, the Ulster Special Constabulary was made for trouble. Originally, there had been established three classes of enlistment: Class A, which involved full-time duty; Class B, involving part-time duties; and Class C, comprising volunteers who could be called up in an emergency. In 1969, only Class B – 'the B-Specials' – remained. They were allowed to keep their arms at home. There was not a Catholic among them. Having relieved the RUC of their machine guns, the Hunt Committee dealt with the B-Specials. They were disbanded. Many then joined the locally recruited part-time force called the Ulster Defence Regiment, which came under command of our own General Officer Commanding in Northern Ireland.

I found it difficult to judge the merits of the Northern Ireland police. After August 1969, they suffered a lot of public obloquy. Some newspapers could not find enough bad things to say about them. The B-Specials were painted as undisciplined, partisan and dangerous. Yet all these men were called upon to perform their duties in conditions of unremitting danger. They were prime targets for the IRA. Repeated attempts were made to blow up police stations. They were brave men, but they suffered the same handicap that I encountered later in South Africa before 1994. They lacked legitimacy. They were seen as instruments of an unrepresentative government, rather than protectors of the people.

On my return, Ted Heath, then Leader of the Oppsition, invited me for a talk. It was holiday time, and I said he would do better to have it in writing. My observations are of only melancholy interest today because we were then only on the threshold of a quarter of a century of pain for Ulster. I offer a summary of what I wrote to Ted Heath, because impressions at the time are worth more than recollections twenty-five years later.

> From Stormont [The Northern Irish seat of government] it is difficult to avoid the impression that the Prime Minister is out to reduce the regime to chaos by a variety of tricks from his extensive repertoire; by agreeing one thing with his Ministers, by saying another on television, by leaks calculated to inflame mistrust.
>
> Physical damage in Belfast is extensive. Probably the homeless there run to 4,000, which adds a large problem and a potentially explosive one. With the exception of the Ardoyne [a relatively modern Roman Catholic area] the worst disorders occurred in the worst housing districts. The so called 'No-Go' area, still heavily barricaded and alleged to contain IRA in the triangle formed by Falls and Grosvenor Road is the worst of all. High densities, slum housing, all the ingredients for city disorder are there. Fire has also destroyed some work places and jobs, so precious to Belfast. Much of this was done mindlessly, because at the height of the panic some buildings were associated with snipers.

I then turned to the problem of the B-Specials and their disbandment. I urged caution. Threatened by loss of arms, I said, some would resort to guerrilla fighting. Then I entered some thoughts about the RUC. 'The single force is controlled from Belfast by an Inspector-General (Anthony Peacocke) who may be gallant but is certainly incompetent ... His second-in-command, Shillington, who twenty-five years ago would have been Chief Constable of a small county here, is better but hardly adequate.'

A main failure, I added, was Intelligence. It was difficult to discover what Ulster had by way of Special Branch, though presumably the mainland Special Branch was working over there. I thought it would be instructive to see what effect the infinitely superior Intelligence of the British Army might have. Much later on, it was to prove invaluable. Then I discussed the police and suggested that the armoured cars might go.

From then onwards, I became a regular visitor to Northern Ireland. A year later (1970) I sent a further set of impressions to Reggie Maudling, who after the June election of that year had become Ted Heath's Home Secretary. I thought hatred between the communities was worse than a year before. The Stormont regime was being steadily undermined by extremists in the constituencies. Our own Ulster MPs at Westminster were being torn between support for Westminster/Stormont policies and the demands of the Orange diehards and Paisley admirers who were gaining ground and boldness. The real battle, I thought, was at the grass roots, where moderates were losing ground.

We should ask ourselves, I added, whether the moderates would stand a better chance if they declared their independence, leaving the extreme right to hive off under Ian Paisley, William Craig or another. It might put together an alliance of moderates, and draw in some of value now keeping out of it. At least it would end the tug-of-war going on, which would (I predicted) destroy first the Unionist party and then Stormont, leaving us with no option but to step in. I concluded my letter, written on

17 August 1970: 'I see us heading for direct rule, with incalculable consequences (in Dublin too) and the Army committed more deeply than now, unless we (a) aim for a moderate coalition calculated to make the hard-liners hive off – and reckoning they would not be as many as we now fear; and (b) frame a long-term replacement for the Army on fairly bold lines.'

It was not a bad prophecy. Early in 1972, after Bloody Sunday, Heath ordered direct rule for Northern Ireland. Willie Whitelaw became the first Secretary of State for Northern Ireland.

I find among my papers the programme for a 'Monster Meeting of Orangemen and Loyalists at Newtownhamilton on Monday, 13th July 1970. The 280th Anniversary of the Battle of the Boyne'. It was an odd experience. I travelled over on Sunday, spent the night with my host, was called with a large whisky instead of early tea, and set forth with the local marchers. The event attracted 16,000 of them, with 150 bands. During this adventure I was spotted by a *Guardian* man. He reported my presence, adding: 'Was Deedes observing for Ted or was he spending a day of carnival with old friends? Once reporters had seen him, he didn't stay long enough to answer.'

I repeated this Orange Day expedition the following year and kept a note of what went on. It conveys the flavour of those times, which hardly belong to this century:

Ulster, 13 July 1971. Sunday night with Mr Sprock, maker of fine Irish sausages. Scotch in the study immediately after breakfast. Tour with McGuinness, Ulster Unionist MP, McCreedy, rose grower. McGuiness offers an account of his life as an Ulster MP. [He has to go through] a primary election – five weeks of constant meetings and all his election expenses to pay [out of his own pocket]. Saves £200. No organization. Says it is all he can do to raise £85 a year.

Required to head the subscribers' lists and generally treated as a door mat. Felt quite ashamed, wondering if a cheque for £750 would cover it. [His the] only seat needing a primary, but the only seat paying [his own] expenses. Not a penny raised by the locals.

At Portadown in rain by 0830, banners and sashes were in rich display. . . .

Then a march-past to the buses; 3,000 strong, ten bands, marvellous banners at £100 or so each. 'Secret of England's greatness': Queen Victoria giving a Bible to a creeping Indian. William III, Disraeli, Ridley, Protestants. Many young and children. Clearly not an old man's organization – though very old men walking. Fixed, determined-looking Ulster faces. Whoever thought they could stop! Round to the buses and on board for Newtownhamilton. Very orderly. Very narrow roads, but arrive by 11 a.m. in good order. De-bus and happily remeet MP. Sidle up the mainstreet ahead of the procession – alas, carrying two bags! Street filling up. Two Army wireless cars and a helicopter overhead. MP reckons worth of Portadown equipment – it included a silver band – at £33,000.

At Newtownhamilton I enter a lodge for 'refreshment' at noon.

Women clearly indispensable. After eating, adjourn to neighbouring shed, carefully guarded, where in semi-darkness perhaps fifty brethren sit on forms drinking beer, Guinness and a little Scotch. Harangued in good-humoured way by one who has clearly partaken. Whisky and orangeade! Then back to the field. Platform on a wagon. Divine Service, fairly punctual at 2 p.m. Longish address. Hymn cut for Psalm XVIII, and noticeable that most can sing without words on paper. Not a great number in the field, perhaps 2,000 out of 3,000. Then resolutions. Meet up with McGuinness (mercifully). Part from him and head for the nearest bus. Leave in punctual and orderly style.

On most expeditions I spent time with the Army in different parts of the country and came to admire their style and method. They made no complaint about the strange task they had been asked to undertake, but saw it as their duty to adapt to whatever their country asked of them. Since they were thin on the ground, every soldier carried responsibilities above his rank. A corporal in Belfast, for example, would patrol with his section an area which one might expect to find in the hands of an infantry company. As senior officers quietly conceded, it was fine training for junior non-commissioned officers.

I became closely acquainted with Brian Faulkner, who succeeded James Chichester-Clark as Prime Minister of Northern Ireland in 1971. Through his brother, Robin, James Chichester-Clark had had opportunities to meet back-bench MPs in London. I thought that Faulkner should have the same opportunities, and invited him to come over to Westminster. This was picked up by the Home Office and caused a flutter. I wrote reassuringly to Reggie Maudling. 'I think it will do no harm. We propose to give him a small dinner, with one or two chairmen of committees. My private feeling is that he ought not to be allowed to feel any disadvantage vis-à-vis his predecessor, when it comes to meeting back-benchers at Westminster.' The Home Office calmed down. 'I am sure', Maudling wrote back to me, 'Faulkner will impress your people greatly. He is a very good man to work with, clear-minded and incisive. I have asked him to look in at the Home Office for a general talk when he is in London for your meeting.'

In the long run, stronger forces prevailed over Faulkner. He held office for less than a year before Bloody Sunday and direct rule in 1972. In 1977, he was killed in a hunting accident. I have always been glad I extended a hand to him. He was not blind to the faults of the Unionist administration. He was simply too late to remedy long-standing grievances which had poisoned wells and made IRA gunmen appear to some of the Roman Catholic community gladiators against oppression.

There were other missions, some of them difficult. In March 1971, the Tory party suddenly developed a mood of restiveness about Northern Ireland. There was a feeling that the aggressors were gaining ground, and the Tory Government was losing it. As chairman of the party's Home Affairs Committee since the 1970 General Election, I presided over a large meeting of Tory MPs at Westminster, attended by both Reggie Maudling and Peter Carrington, Defence Secretary. The restiveness made itself felt. Ministers were roughly handled. Next day, the *Daily Telegraph* wrote of the Home Secretary being 'roasted'. I immediately arranged with James Ramsden, a close colleague and former Secretary of State for War, to go to Belfast quickly. There we went to see Lieutenant-General Harry Tuzo, then General Officer Commanding. He revealed to us that fresh orders to the Army had gone out. He showed us the document, which we discussed. We spent the whole day talking to senior officers. It became increasingly plain to me that there had been a significant change in tactics and that much of the misgiving expressed at the party meeting in London had been misplaced. I found it difficult to understand why Ministers had not revealed this to us. The new orders, Tuzo assured us, had gone out on 25 March. The salient points were (a) the Army and the police would work more closely together than hitherto, (b) there would be no more stone-throwing without response, (c) the Army was now patrolling actively by day and night. The virtue of these patrols was that it enabled soldiers to make contact with the local population, which restored their confidence and increased willingness to co-operate and provide information. It also courted confrontation with the IRA. It nipped incidents in the bud before a crowd could gather.

As I reported back to Members after this visit, there could be no doubting the resolution of all ranks to encounter and tackle the enemy – though there remained limitations. There was no martial law. We were not at war. The General's new instructions did not override the yellow card, which imposed conditions on opening fire. The aim was not to engage the IRA in gunfights, but to squeeze them out and get them into court. The troops, I added, were on a knife edge. They were on the offensive against the gunmen, yet needed help and co-operation from the Roman Catholic population among whom the gunmen dwelt. Too many Catholics had been terrorized into silence. The main task was wooing the population against the extremists – on both sides. It was our best long-term hope. There had, I reported, been a shift of balance from the passive to the active, yet one calculated to turn the population on, not off. As we all now know, these were vain endeavours, though through no fault of the armed forces. We moved inexorably towards direct rule.

We have since learned from peace-keeping operations in other theatres that we were pursuing an unattainable objective. We wanted Ulster to continue business as usual. We sought to woo the population most likely to be sympathetic to the IRA. Yet we were confronted increasingly by Loyalist as well as IRA violence, while seeking by peaceful means to bring determined terrorists in both camps to book. We were pursuing what was out of reach. At one time I thought our senior commanders in Ulster, whom I came greatly to respect, might have made this plainer to their masters. They understood the nature of the task on the ground better than our politicians. It did not lie with the military to remedy the social grievances which had fired this tinder. The best they could do was to disregard religious affiliations and act in an even-handed way towards the community.

But soldiers do not argue with politicians. Haig learned that lesson from Lloyd George in 1917–18. Alexander and Montgomery learned it from Churchill in the Desert battle before Alamein. As a junior commander, I learned it myself in the battle for Europe 1944–5. In uniform of any rank, you obey orders.

In October 1971 I led an all-party delegation on a visit

which included 'Places of Internment in Northern Ireland'. Among them was the Crumlin Road prison and the Long Kesh internment camp. It was basically a visit to those who nursed strong grievances. I found it hard going to suit all parliamentary tastes and value a letter I received at the end from Kevin McNamara, then Labour spokesman on Northern Ireland. 'Just a brief note to thank you for your unfailing courtesy and splendid leadership during our brief tour of the Internment Camps in Northern Ireland last week. If I may say so, I thought you were very fair indeed and handling a very disparate [his secretary had typed "desperate", but he corrected it] group of Members with considerable tact and continuous courtesy. It was a pleasure to be with you.'

One of the things that endeared the people of Northern Ireland to me was their courtesy under great provocation. We were developing an uncouth minority on the mainland – which has grown. In Belfast, manners held up. Guards at every important building would search you in the spirit of 'We're all in this together.' I admired the staff of the Europa Hotel, where we sometimes stayed. They had suffered repeated attempts to blow it up, some of them overthrows as it were from the Unionist headquarters in Glengall Street near by.

On one visit just before Christmas 1971, we arrived to be told by the Army that our hotel had in fact just been bombed. We were moved to the Woodlands Hotel in Lisburn, from which I subsequently received this letter: 'Dear Sir, Regarding the payment of your account at the above hotel on 21 December 1971, we find that you have overpaid us by £2.00. Please find enclosed the amount and accept apologies for any inconvenience caused. Yours faithfully, Angela M. O'Kane (Manageress).'

With the coming of direct rule from London, priorities changed. In March 1972, I wrote to Willie Whitelaw in the Northern Ireland office about future democratic representation in the province. It seemed logical to some of us at Westminster that with the ending of government from Stormont, Ulster's representation at Westminster required fresh attention. Whitelaw was opposed to integration with the United Kingdom, on the reasonable grounds that we could not hope at Westminster to cope with the minutiae of day-to-day business in Northern Ireland. But I did not think we should seek to have it both ways. 'If we determine that the Parliament which formerly represented the interests of the North is ended,' I wrote to him, 'then we have to consider what parliamentary representation there is to be at Westminster.'

I persuaded myself later in 1972 that my duties as chairman of what had become the Northern Ireland Committee called for a day or two in Dublin. I had always found myself at home there because my mother, a Chenevix-Trench, had been born there. I had inherited a certain feeling for Irish attitudes. On this particular visit I acquired insight into their dilemma. The last thing the Irish Government wanted was responsibility for the North, which reunification would bring. The objectives of the Sinn Fein and Irish Republican Army would not be fulfilled simply by reunification. Tail would wag dog. A disruptive element would enter the administration of Ireland. At the same time, attitudes towards mainland Britain prevailed. When you dine with them, play golf with them, drink with them, the Irish are wonderful company. But privately they nurse reservations about us British, and they always will.

On this visit to Dublin in September 1972, I stayed with our ambassador, Sir John Peck. He left a book by my bed with this note attached to it: 'If you are addicted to reading in bed, may I commend to you certain excerpts from this book which I have marked as being basic to an understanding of Anglo-Irish relations, as well as having both comic and tragic aspects. They also reinforce my belief that the elements of Anglo-Irish misunderstanding antedate the Reformation by many centuries and have little to do with religion!'

I had a talk with the Taoiseach, John Lynch, at Parliament

House. We were to confront each other a little later at the Oxford Union, where we spoke from opposite sides. The evening was memorable for two reasons. There was a railway strike, so we all went to Oxford in limos, commissioned by the enterprising president of the Union. As is customary after these debates, we retired for refreshment. In honour of his distinguished guest from Dublin, the president of the Union had ordered up an Irish whiskey called Paddy. Lynch consumed it without turning a hair. We shared a limo back to London. He spoke eloquently of the Republic's inner thinking about Ulster. I slept.

The final event of my visit to Dublin was a courtesy call on the provost of Trinity College, Dublin. He turned up a little late, having spent the earlier part of the evening fishing near by. It made a good end to the day, he observed. I was left with the feeling that I was leaving a country in certain respects more civilized than my own.

Soon after my return to London, we invited some leading Unionists to come over and talk to our Committee at Westminster. It was a depressing evening. They spoke of the isolated farms, both Catholic and Protestant, in Co. Fermanagh where brutal murders had occurred. Telephone lines had been routinely cut, security forces were stretched, many inhabitants had been forced to desert their farms, but would receive no compensation.

At the close of 1972, I went over to speak at Newtonards to what was left of the Unionist leadership. According to a letter I wrote to Willie Whitelaw reporting this event, I tried to discourage their hopes from rising too high and warned them that a forthcoming White Paper would disappoint them. It was a superfluous warning. They knew what was coming. Just before Christmas, Whitelaw talked to me about aspects of security in the province. He spoke of the possibility of rockets and mortars which could reach Government House and Army headquarters. It was a melancholy postscript to our first year of direct rule.

Most people have forgotten what an ordeal the people in cities like Belfast and Londonderry had to suffer during that period. To many of them it seemed a one-sided war. The bombing continued indiscriminately. The British Army could respond only with the utmost discrimination. In July 1972, something like twenty bombs exploded in seventy minutes, all within a mile of Belfast's city centre. Nine were killed, including two children, and 130 injured. Morale in the province plummeted. I marvelled at the patience of junior Army commanders, who were called on by the circumstances to take considerable personal risks.

I do not pretend I was a detached observer of this one-sided encounter. Wartime experience made me sensitive to what soldiers were being called on to do. They worked in continual danger. I did not relish even brief excursions with them. At the same time, they could be brought to book for shooting back in defence if it led to casualties. 'A soldier who goes to Northern Ireland on his third unaccompanied tour of four months', I wrote early in 1972, 'will mark the sharp upward gradations which over two years have changed his duties from peace-keeping to life in the front line . . .'

'You find', said a corporal in Londonderry, a day or two before the Prime Minister visited him there, 'that when you finish your two hours [on guard] you are pretty tense. It can take you an hour to unwind, so you don't sleep for much more than half the four hours off.' There were compensations. The soldier who knows he is doing a good job on the streets of Belfast or Londonderry has something which millions of his safer contemporaries on the factory floor are without. Nobody is insensitive to public approval. My only doubt was whether there was sufficient recognition over here of what we were expecting our soldiers to do.

An operation undertaken in August 1972 was an example of this. It was decided that no-go areas in the Bogside and Creggan must be cleared. They had been under control of the IRA for so long that they appeared to be enemy territory. There was anxious discussion on how best to achieve this without heavy casualties. Thanks to brilliant soldiering this Operation Motorman was carried out successfully without casualties. In four months up to Motorman there had been some 3,500 shooting incidents, involving ninety-five deaths. During the next four months this total of incidents was halved. Along with this went other initiatives. One was designed to give effect to what was called the Border Pledge. It was an article of faith that Northern Ireland should remain part of the United Kingdom until the majority of the population agreed otherwise. It was decided to put this to the test, thus disposing of the IRA line that the British Army was keeping an unwilling people under a colonial yoke.

The Border poll took place in March 1973. I led a party of observers from Westminster to see fair play. We travelled round the polling stations and attended the count. There was a good turn-out with no disorder. Of those who voted, 591,820 were in favour of remaining united with Britain and 6,483 were against it. Some 425,000 abstained. So 58 per cent of the whole electorate voted in favour of Ulster remaining in the United Kingdom. It was an instructive few days. As the polls closed, we watched the presiding officer in one of the Belfast polling stations apply his seal to soft wax on the tapes which sealed the boxes. 'Let us hope,' I said lightly, 'they have a safe night in the Floral Hall!' This had been chosen for storage of boxes over-night. 'Floral Hall!' exclaimed the presiding officer. 'It was easier to get out of Colditz than this place. Why, they have troops out on the surrounding hills!'

Throughout the day, which involved countless irksome checks, searches and delays, I heard no voices raised in anger, witnessed no officiousness or impatience. A tolerance, a gentleness even, prevailed inside and outside the schoolrooms converted into polling stations; and this was not submissiveness. People are often kinder and more considerate to each, as we learned in the 1940s, when circumstances are disagreeable and dangerous.

Whitelaw's next step was to move towards re-establishing a legislative assembly of eighty members for Northern Ireland. The proposal got a mixed reception – predictable opposition from Ian Paisley and the Democratic Unionist party, broad support from Faulkner's Unionists and the mainly Catholic SDLP. It also led to a fatal split in the Unionist party. William Craig hived off with a new party quaintly named the Vanguard Unionist Progressives. They set out to make the new Assembly unworkable.

Polling day was fixed for 28 June. It was Whitelaw's fifty-fifth birthday and I arranged for our party from Westminster to present him with a box of golf balls. We might have saved our money. While Secretary of State, Whitelaw achieved one round of golf in Northern Ireland.

The outcome of the elections, which were fought on a system of proportional representation, was ominous. The SDLP won nineteen seats, the Alliance party eight. The Loyalist coalition led by Paisley and Craig took eighteen seats and the Faulkner Unionists twenty-two. This presented problems in the creation of an executive. After exhaustive negotiations, Whitelaw hammered out an agreement between the parties and announced this to the House of Commons on 22 November. Alas, his efforts were brought to naught by violent industrial action taken by the Ulster Workers' Council early in 1974. As if that was not enough, Ted Heath's Government staged the General Election in February 1974 over the miners' strike. Leading personalities in Northern Ireland, drawn into tenuous co-operation by Whitelaw, were called on to fight each other in the Westminster election.

Not surprisingly, at the close of that election campaign,

Whitelaw physically collapsed and was ordered to bed by his doctors. I had seen a lot of him during his two years of office in Ulster. I reckoned the ordeal would have crippled a less robust character. It was probably a factor in his minor heart attack of 1988, which put him outside active politics.

More than thirty years on, we can see what a demanding test Ulster was and still remains. As one who had only a minor part to play in the years 1969–74, I look back on the experience gratefully. It introduced me to the difficulties of modern peacemaking, which I have since witnessed in other parts of the world. It brought home to me the limitation of politics and the virtue of modesty by those who practise the trade. That, in truth, was Whitelaw's strength. He failed but he had never misled anyone into thinking that he would succeed. Later, he became a dependable counsellor to Margaret Thatcher. But above all Whitelaw has been a wise counsellor to himself. Like Rab Butler, he knew that politics are the art of the possible. The aspiring young politician should study Whitelaw's performance in Northern Ireland 1972–4. He would learn the supreme importance, in triumph or disaster, of keeping both feet firmly on the ground.

18

Editor

Towards the end of 1973, Ted Heath's Government ran into trouble. Middle East oil producers announced a price hike of around 70 per cent which brought a threat of petrol rationing. An overtime ban by the miners' leaders had cut coal supplies to power stations. Industry and commerce were reduced to five days' electricity consumption in the last half of December, and with the prospect of a three-day week in the New Year. In presenting his emergency Budget barely a week before Christmas, the Chancellor of the Exchequer talked of 'the gravest situation by far since the end of the war'.

Early in February Heath and his Ministers took a bold – and, it turned out, fatal – decision. They called a General Election on the 'Who governs Britain?' issue. I said good-bye to my colleagues at the *Daily Telegraph* and prepared to fight my eighth General Election. 'At a time of acute difficulty caused by events in the Middle East,' I told my constituents, 'there has arisen a challenge to the authority of Government and Parliament which the Prime Minister and his colleagues feel they cannot shirk. Upon the outcome will turn not simply the immediate future of the Conservative party but, beyond that, our national fortunes.'

Beyond that, again though I did not know it at the time, lay my own fortunes. Early in the campaign I received a letter from our faithful secretary on the Peterborough column, Dorina Paparritor, to the effect that the *Daily Telegraph* was running a crisis of its own. The deputy editor, Colin Welch, had been told that he would not succeed to the editor's chair, then occupied by Maurice Green. Colin was a beautiful writer, rooted in strong political principles which carried great influence at the *Telegraph*. He had had a hand in appointing talented young men of like thinking to the leader-writing staff. One of them was John O'Sullivan, who became editor of the *National Review* in America, was at one time head of Margaret Thatcher's research team at No. 10 and later adviser on her memoirs. The other, Frank Johnson, later became editor of the *Spectator*. In terms of what the *Daily Telegraph* was seen to stand for, Welch was the most influential opinion-former in the office. But, like many another genius, he was erratic in his personal life and, when he drank too much, was apt to get into scrapes. I surmised that Lord Hartwell, the owner, had decided that Colin lacked the gravitas needed for the editor's chair.

A General Election campaign cuts you off from almost all the normal features of life. It supplants everything else in your mind, especially if you are working alongside as good and single-minded a political agent as mine. Robin Coombes, my third and outstandingly talented agent, put all he had into fighting an election, and he expected his candidate to do the same. I was called on to enjoy a heavy programme of house-to-house canvassing during the morning and afternoon, meet delegations and speak at two or three meetings every night. On top of this, because Ashford was considered to be a reasonably safe seat, I agreed to give two or three evenings to Conservative candidates in marginal seats. So I had little time to think about the *Daily Telegraph*'s difficulties. Insofar as I thought about them at all, I felt worried lest in his disappointment Colin Welch decided to leave the newspaper altogether. As our election campaign reached its climax John O'Sullivan called me to say that a round robin was going to Lord Hartwell urging him to ensure that Colin Welch did not feel obliged to resign. Would I sign it? I felt doubtful if my intervention while absent from the office fighting an election would greatly assist the cause and declined. In the event, he did not resign.

We were pleased with our result in Ashford, but as the night of 28 February wore on it became clear that the Government was in trouble. Two early results from Salford and Guildford had shown a small but unmistakable swing to Labour. When all the results were gathered, Labour had won 301 seats and the Tories 297. Neither party had an overall majority. During the week-end, as he often did, Ted Heath came over for a talk with my neighbour, Toby Aldington. I felt moved to give Aldington a call and say that, while negotiating at No. 10, Ted Heath should keep close to his party. Some of my supporters, wryly digesting the result, were observing crossly that the Government had got its election strategy wrong. I rang again, to say that on reflection I thought Heath had two battles on his hands: to salvage his Government, if possible; but also to safeguard his own position in the party. Point taken, said Aldington.

After some unproductive wrangling at No. 10, the Liberals refused to help Heath, and Labour returned to office. The Tory party's 1922 Committee was summoned for the following Tuesday. A few of us met privately in London the day before and found the mood against Heath strong. Who then? My note at the time says among names discussed were those of Edward du Cann, Sir Keith Joseph, Margaret Thatcher and Peter Rawlinson. I said I thought that, if Ted Heath wanted to go, that would be one thing. But for the party to be seen to push him out would be damaging. Reggie Maudling, who had lost the 1965 leadership contest to Heath, was a steadying influence. 'Keep the chaps calm!' he said characteristically.

Back with the *Daily Telegraph* on Friday, 22 March, I encountered Peter Eastwood, then managing editor of the Telegraph Group, who was lunching in the same coffee house. Why, he asked me, had Alec Douglas-Home just announced his retirement from Parliament? I explained that this was the time when MPs had to decide whether or not they would fight the next General Election which, because of the narrowness of February's result, could not be long delayed. Eastwood then asked if I had made any decision of my own. I said truthfully that I had not thought about it. He pointed out that there would soon be vacant chairs on both the *Daily* and the *Sunday Telegraph*. Maurice Green of the *Daily* and Brian Roberts of the *Sunday* had given notice of retirement. 'You would get my vote,' said Eastwood unexpectedly. Eastwood relished power, and no doubt saw in me an amenable partner. But my mind then took a rather different turn. I had represented the Ashford constituency since 1950, or for almost twenty-five years. The short gap between General Elections afforded a rare opportunity to change course smoothly.

I had witnessed enough by-elections necessitated by the Member's translation to some other appointment to know that such elections usually ended in tears. Conservative constituency workers in General Election campaigns are loyal, efficient and wonderfully supportive. Key workers will cheerfully alter holiday dates to take part in a campaign. But when a by-election is suddenly thrust upon them because their Member of Parliament wants to improve his position, they are apt to become broody. I had always known that such a course was out of the question for me in Ashford. There were too many close supporters to whom I was in debt. So, I mused, here suddenly was an opportunity. I seriously doubted if Lord Hartwell would want me as editor of either newspaper. Since entering politics I had worked on the Peterborough column. I was unfamiliar with other parts of the newspaper. But a life devoted entirely to the newspaper, and not divided between Westminster and Fleet Street, offered attractions.

There was not much time. During the week-end I drafted a letter to the editor, Maurice Green, offering more ample service, which I delivered to his office on Sunday. On Monday they told me that he was away for a fortnight. I had sent my private letter to him in two envelopes. His secretary gave me back the inner letter, unopened. The intelligent Dorina Paparritor questioned me closely. Was this really what I wanted? I thought about it, and on 25 March drafted a fresh letter to Lord Hartwell. I said I ought to decide soon whether I would stand again or ask the Ashford committee to look round for someone else. I was tempted to go on for another term because as a senior Member of Parliament one had a spoiled life and, thanks to his indulgence, a comfortable job in his newspaper. Before deciding, I wanted to know whether I could be of more service to the newspaper if, at this point, I chucked politics. I doubted it, but his family had been kind to me over many years, and I had given little back.

Silence fell until Thursday, 4 April. Dorina Paparritor, the only other person who knew of this exchange, then told me that a letter would be coming down to me from the fifth floor, seat of authority at 135 Fleet Street. It was a friendly and reassuring reply from Lord Hartwell.

Thank you so much for your personal letter. I would like, first of all, to talk to Maurice Green before giving you a sensible answer.

I appreciate that in the present political situation you have to decide quickly whether or not you are going to stand for Ashford again at the next election.

In the meantime, you are much too modest about your past and present contributions to the paper. There is nobody with whom we could replace you.

On 30 April I received one of Michael Hartwell's scribbled and almost indecipherable notes asking to see me on 1 May at 5 p.m. For the first five minutes – this was characteristic of Michael Hartwell – we discussed some minor political issue. Then, our engines warmed up, he turned to business. Normally, he said, the newspaper arranged promotions on a family basis and within itself. That is to say a deputy succeeded the head. Colin Welch, he went on, was not suitable – 'too argument-ative'. There was pause. 'I would like to offer you the job.'

I perceived the significance of the phrase 'too argument-ative'. Colin Welch had certain political convictions which he would forcibly express and from which he would never will-ingly retreat. Later I was to become eternally grateful for them, because, while he remained deputy editor, his were the colours under which we rode. I supported his political principles, but lacked the intellectual equipment to formulate them. Hartwell's politics, however, were not altogether those of Colin Welch. On leaving the Army after the war, Hartwell had written a book which appeared in 1948. It came out when many of us were reassembling our political ideas and was called unexcit-ingly *Party Choice*. Michael Hartwell was a political pragmatist. He had a certain disdain for the 'party game'. He was sceptical of all ideology, whether of the right or the left.

Before I took on as editor, I read this book carefully and sensed that we had a certain amount in common. Like Hartwell, I have always doubted if our affairs can be sensibly run for long on any rigid theory or doctrine. My Tory party is more a party of balance than of doctrine. When things swing too far one way, you throw your weight in the opposite direction in order to maintain stability.

Furthermore, life in the Army for five years had given me unfashionable respect for authority. When the Colonel gave his orders, I thought it right to obey them. I construed my task as editor of the *Daily Telegraph* to fulfil as far as possible the wishes of its owner – though, when called upon, to defend the young Turks who wrote editorials which sometimes ran con-trary to his point of view. I have never seen why the man who owns a newspaper should not have a voice in its policy. I was happy to become an intermediary between Hartwell, with his political pragmatism, and men like Colin Welch, T. E. (Peter)

Utley, John O'Sullivan and Frank Johnson who thought differently and felt they had a serious political message to deliver. To some extent all of them were prophets of what eventually Margaret Thatcher sought to do and so permanently change the political landscape.

I had anticipated something less responsible than the editor's chair. I thought I could make a competent deputy and leader writer and could write signed pieces on subjects I knew something about. A quarter of a century in politics had made me a well-informed journalist. When Lord Hartwell said he wanted me to be editor, I began a laboured explanation about what my letter had been meant to convey, aborted it, and said in effect, 'Oh well, given my age, if you've made a mistake you won't have to wait too long too correct it.' He then begged me drily not to apply for the Chiltern Hundreds (which offer immediate release from Parliament) and so suggest that the present editor had suddenly gone off his head. I then told Toby Aldington, president of the Ashford Conservative Association, of my decision. He eased the way. It was a lucky bit of timing.

I ended my years as Member for Ashford with a constituency case which was a tragedy for one family, yet brought home to me that the MP can be of service to humankind. In July 1973 a young girl of sixteen was murdered on the outskirts of Ashford. It was such a horrible crime that the police put a lot of work into solving it. As a result of their exertions, a man was arrested and charged. Before the case was heard, consultations took place and in consequence a charge of manslaughter was preferred. The accused was then sentenced to four years' imprisonment. Part of the defence evidence was that the girl had invited the man to take liberties with her. So the parents, Mr and Mrs Swaffer, lost their daughter – and her good name.

After the sentence, letters of protest poured into me, insisting there had been a miscarriage of justice. Some came from parents of children who had been friends of the girl at school, and found the allegations incredible. Senior police officers involved in the case and dismayed by the verdict came to see me. Neville Sandelson, my old Labour opponent in the General Elections of 1950, 1951 and 1955, and by then a Member of Parliament and a barrister, wrote out of the blue offering me every assistance. He had reason to know the family well, because in the village of Great Chart, just outside Ashford, the Swaffers had been among his stoutest supporters and my strongest political opponents. At every one of my eight General Election meetings in that village I had had to cross swords with one or other of them. It lent piquancy to my endeavours.

After consulting the police, I wrote to the Lord Chancellor, who was then Quintin Hailsham. In a long reply, Hailsham declared that the judiciary was entirely independent of the Lord Chancellor, and insisted that my criticisms were ill founded. I found it painful to convey this verdict to the parents of the girl. I knew enough about law to perceive that Quintin Hailsham, with experience of forty or fifty murder trials, was on strong ground.

I consulted a friend in the House of Commons, Peter Rawlinson, who was then Attorney-General and a law officer of long experience. He promised to make inquiries. Neville Sandelson made similar representations to Sam Silkin, a heavy-weight lawyer on the Labour side. Meanwhile, unknown to me, the police were pursuing a line of their own with the Director of Public Prosecutions, whose department had handled the case.

At this critical juncture, February 1974, the Government changed hands. Sam Silkin became Labour's Attorney-General. Spurred by my old opponent, Neville Sandelson, as well as by me, he pursued his own inquiries. On 24 September 1974, just before the second election of that year and my departure from politics, dawn broke. Sam Silkin sent me a letter which I reproduce in full:

Editor

My dear Bill,

On 11th January you wrote to Peter Rawlinson about the prosecution's handling of the case, which came up for trial at Maidstone Crown Court on 1st November 1973. On 9th April I wrote to assure you that I would continue the enquiry which Peter Rawlinson had begun. This letter is to inform you that, after making the fullest possible investigations, I have now completed the enquiry. I have informed Peter Rawlinson and the Director of Public Prosecutions of my conclusions and they agree with them.

My conclusions are that the charge of murder ought to have been left to the jury and that Yvonne Swaffer's moral character ought not to have been impugned in court in circumstances which gave no opportunity for the allegations against her character to be traversed or even questioned. I deeply regret the pain which must have been caused by what occurred and I very much hope that the mistakes made can be regarded as isolated, though deeply regrettable, errors of judgement.

I should be grateful if you would inform Mr and Mrs Swaffer of the result of my enquiries, and offer to them, on my behalf, both personally and in my capacity as Attorney-General, my deepest sympathy for the tragic death of their daughter and my profound regret for the pain of their experience at the Crown Court.

In view of some of the observations contained in your letter to Peter Rawlinson, I feel it only fair to the Director of Public Prosecutions and his staff to add that the errors to which I have referred above cannot fairly be laid at their door.

As you are aware, Neville Sandelson also has interested himself in this case and I am therefore writing to him in similar terms.

Au revoir

Yours ever,

Sam

I called at the Swaffers' house in Great Chart to show them this letter. 'Nunc dimittis . . .' I murmured, as I drove away.

Maurice Green, I sensed, had entertained other ideas about his successor; but he took Hartwell's decision in good part and we had a smooth hand-over. Our first talk, I recall, not long before Christmas, involved discussion of names of office messengers and other acolytes who traditionally received half-bottles of whisky from the editor at the festive season. After he left, Maurice Green continued to write occasional pieces for us and, for some years, wrote the editorial on Budget Day.

I inherited a system at the *Daily Telegraph* with which I had become familiar before the war. The managing editor had charge of the news pages. The editor presided over the rest of the newspaper, was the senior editorial figurehead, and occupied by far the grander room. Mine was panelled with oak veneer. Lord Hartwell, like his father Viscount Camrose before him, was effectively editor-in-chief. His custom was to hold a brief discussion with the managing editor before lunch, and another with the editor around the hour of 6 p.m. It was not an ideal way to run a newspaper, but it was the Berry family way; and if you held one of the top jobs you went along with it.

When I joined the newspaper in 1937, after it absorbed the *Morning Post*, this system was already in place. A sharp newsman formerly with the *Daily Mail*, Oscar Pulvermacher, was managing editor. He held the post jointly with Seymour Berry, Camrose's eldest son, who later inherited the title. Pulvermacher was the driving force, Seymour Berry was the ideas man – and it worked well. Arthur Watson, editor from 1924 until 1950, occupied the grand room which I inherited.

Peter Eastwood, managing editor when I took on, was a Northerner who guarded his territory jealously. He was also a disciplinarian on company sergeant-major lines, who found my way of running things deplorably lax. From time to time he would bring to my notice what he judged to be lapses by members of my staff. Abstemious by nature, he detested the pub next to the office, the King and Keys (as it was then), to which members of my staff and his resorted during the lunch hour and later in the evening. He found it hard to accept that, whenever clear of other engagements, I liked drinking beer with them. It was one of the unspoken areas of disagreement between us. Eastwood's sense of discipline led also to fierce and absurd quarrels with some of his own staff. At some point in the battle, the victims would forward the correspondence to me and demand justice. This called for tact on my part.

Early on, I came to the conclusion that my placid nature had been a factor in my appointment. I was expected to get on with Peter Eastwood. Now and again I became exasperated – and so did he – but we never had a serious quarrel. Eastwood had been a first-rate night editor, whose performance on the demanding night of President Kennedy's assassination was still an office legend, and he remained a first-class newsman. But he had developed a shameless weakness for promoting his own small interests. Stories about his yacht club on the River Crouch in Essex appeared from time to time in the news columns. I kept my sense of humour uppermost, but I sometimes wondered what on earth Hartwell made of them.

The editorial staff I inherited from Maurice Green, on the other hand, presented no problems. New editors often feel the urge to hire and fire, in order to put their stamp on the newspaper. It was not a course likely to appeal to Lord Hartwell, and I saw no need for it. It was not the staff, but the musty appearance of most pages in the *Daily Telegraph* that provoked my attention. To change them proved to be an insuperable task. Colin Welch, who loyally agreed to soldier on under my editorship, was a reliable guardian of our editorial line on things that mattered. Peter Utley – blind, but wise and able to write magisterial editorials – also helped to keep us on course. He was assisted by a succession of lovely and intelligent young women who adored working for him. Most of them went on to enjoy successful careers of their own. They would type the copy which he dictated out of the top of his head, read relevant matter aloud to him and take him on their arm wherever he wanted to go. He smoked continuously and dangerously, with cigarettes in one pocket and loose matches in another, so that the girl working in his small office lived in a tobacco-laden fug. None complained. During the lunch hour they would accompany him to the King and Keys next door, buy his tipple – invariably whisky and water – with currency notes he kept confusingly in every pocket – and then, with a soft drink of their own, attend the court he liked to hold of young men, colleagues and friends where issues of the day were seriously discussed.

Utley had a wonderful ear for young talent. A number of journalists who have climbed Fleet Street's greasy pole owe their first chance to him. 'There's a young man not long down from Oxford whom I'd like you to meet,' he would begin. 'Peter,' I had invariably to reply, 'we are already over-strength – and I simply have not a vacancy for him.' 'Quite so,' he would reply blandly, 'but I do think you should see him. I think you would like him.' They were always fliers, for whom I would sometime seek a temporary berth in the Peterborough column.

For obvious reasons, Peter Utley's hold on his financial outgoings was tenuous. He had a wonderful wife in Bridget Utley, but financial control was not a strong point with either of them. From time to time the office secretary and chief accountant would seek audience with me about Utley's financial condition. I never mastered the subject, nor did I make great efforts to do so. Men with great minds often clash with accountants. 'A lot of it goes down his throat, you know,' Peter Eastwood (who invariably got wind of these crises) would say to me. 'Yes,' I would reply, 'and to very good effect.'

I had first met Utley early in my political life when he was writing leaders for *The Times*. He became a friend and sage adviser. I never met a man who offered counsel more disarmingly. I did not always go with his line on Ulster, on which his views were entrenched, and where at one point he fought an election in order to give them expression, but he made serious discussion such fun even if you failed to agree with him. When I think of him now, there enters my mind's eye a picture of Peter Utley at 10 Downing Street, where with my knowledge and consent he would sometimes assist in the composition of Mrs Thatcher's speeches.

It was an arrangement I had persuaded Lord Hartwell to accept on special grounds. 'At fifty-six,' I wrote to him, 'because of his blindness, he can never advance from his present occupation. Without this handicap, he would on every count be near the top of your hierarchy. I find it significant that Mrs Thatcher chooses him now [1978], since he is by far the best balanced of our team.'

It proved a good arrangement. Utley was eventually made a CBE and, some time later, I asked him to be my joint deputy editor. In return for the wisdom, the Prime Minister put up with the smoking, but she was troubled by the ash which invariably hovered on the end of an Utley cigarette until it fell on the carpet. I treasure the portrait someone gave me of Mrs Thatcher, in the throes of speech-making, grasping an ashtray, with the determined air of catching the Utley ash before it dropped.

I recall a scene at New Scotland Yard, where a senior officer handling pornography asked me to inspect his wares. Peter Utley came with me with a leading article in mind. As we glanced through some of the material, there were involuntary 'Oohs!' and 'Ahs!' 'I wonder', said Utley after a while, 'if I could be given some idea of what you are all all "oohing" at!'

John O'Sullivan and Frank Johnson represented the voice of the under forties. Frank Johnson's gifts as a humorous writer brought me nearest to a serious quarrel with Peter Eastwood. While covering the General Election of 1979, Frank Johnson wrote a comic sketch for the news pages on a day's electioneering with Denis and Margaret Thatcher. It dwelt on the then undiscovered qualities of Denis Thatcher, and Johnson in his favourite vein of comic writing declared that only Margaret Thatcher could lose the election for her talented spouse.

Eastwood took the view that the piece was unhelpful to the Thatcher cause and ordered it to be spiked. It was brought to my attention. I liked it, and decided to print it on one of *my* pages as a leader-page article. There were volcanic consequences. The flow of Eastwood lava stopped just short of seriously damaging those living near me.

Reginald Steed, who had been an experienced foreign correspondent, Michael Hilton and later John Miller (who had worked in Moscow) looked after the overseas editorials. 'He will be a writing editor,' Eastwood had told his friends cheerfully, in the hope and expectation that I would leave the running of the newspaper to him. Given the leader writers I inherited, I felt shy about writing anything at all. I threw in ideas and a certain amount of political experience; but that experience had left me chary of fixed political attitudes. I had for many years been a member of the One Nation group, which I have mentioned earlier. Towards the end of my time there I became its chairman. Strongly influenced by Keith Joseph, who was also a member, I subscribed to One Nation's philosophy and felt closer to the Tory traditions of Disraeli than to the doctrines of the right-wing Monday Club. With a small group of One Nation members, Keith Joseph and I gave expression to our philosophy in a pamphlet called *The Responsible Society*.

Early in 1975 Mrs Thatcher was elected Leader of the Conservative party. We found no difficulty in rallying round her. One of my first tasks as editor in 1975 had been to commission declarations of faith from contestants in the Tory party leadership election. Heath's contribution, I recall, seemed to be the work of many hands. Mrs Thatcher's was a seamless garment which required virtually no attention from the subeditors. Many years later I mentioned this in print, and received a pained letter from an old parliamentary friend, Angus Maude (later Lord Maude of Stratford-upon-Avon), who in 1975 was deputy chairman of the Conservative party and one of her strongest supporters. A first-class journalist, who at one point had edited the *Sydney Morning Herald*, he had given her contribution the professional touch.

I soon came to the conclusion that the most valuable contribution I could make to the *Daily Telegraph* lay in man management and personal relations. Journalists are sensitive birds, the best of them in constant doubt about themselves and in need of encouragement. When drinking together in pubs they spend much time discussing sorrowfully with each other the ill-treatment of their copy or, even more sorrowfully, the prospect of losing their job. I remembered Malcolm Muggeridge, who had been deputy editor in the 1950s before going to *Punch*, outlining to me what he considered to be his most important function. It was, he said, loitering on the staircases wearing a friendly face and allowing journalists you encountered time to unburden themselves.

Soon after he took over Express Newspapers in 1977, I invited Victor Matthews (later Lord Matthews) to drop in to my office one evening for a drink. Sipping Coca Cola cautiously, he discussed sadly with a small group of us his problems at the *Daily Express*. Journalists, he observed, seemed interested only in their own work and their own grievances. The company's achievements meant nothing to them. If the dividend went up at the parent company Trafalgar House, everybody cheered. The journalists took no interest in such things, but only in themselves. We tried to explain to Victor why this was so, but in vain. It struck me that he had joined the wrong ship.

There were several other reasons for my decision. Five years in the Army had taught me something about getting the best out of people. Relations between the editorial and management floors struck me as uneasy, and that was damaging because the gathering storm with the print unions made us increasingly interdependent. With Lord Hartwell as the fountainhead of all decisions, management had no cause to consult or inform us on the editorial floor. We worked in separate compartments. I knew and liked the managing director, H. M. Stephen, who had had an outstanding war with the RAF. He needed very little encouragement to join me for a drink in my office around 7 p.m. from time to time. We became close allies, which helped in the troubles that lay ahead.

I also perceived that in our family – one might say feudal – business we had a problem at the top. It lay in Seymour the 2nd Viscount Camrose, who had succeeded to his father, creator of the modern *Daily Telegraph*, in 1954. In pre-war years, when he was joint managing editor, the family plan seemed clear. He would inherit ownership of the *Daily Telegraph*, probably assisted by his brother Michael Hartwell, who was then managing editor of the *Financial Times*. I became an admirer of Seymour Berry, and enjoyed chasing his ideas. At some point in 1938 he asked me to give time to Virginia Cowles, who was about to become an outstanding, as well as beautiful, war correspondent. She wanted to know more about our civil defence in which I was then specializing. Cowles was a light in Seymour's eye, and I have always reckoned that if only they had hit it off, things might have turned out differently for Seymour. He had a good war in North Africa and Italy, and was mentioned in dispatches. He returned briefly to be elected Tory MP for Hitchin in a by-election of 1941, a seat he lost in 1945. Thereafter nothing went too well for him. I saw him occasionally in the office after the death of his father. He drank heavily, though not without remission. He fought hard against the enemy and enjoyed spells of freedom. But Michael effectively took over.

Seymour was the more extrovert of the two. He did not suffer from his brother's shyness, was a good listener, and was polite to everyone. His death early in 1995 confronted me with a challenge. I had gone to South Africa to look things over just before the Queen's visit. It was a bad flight and I arrived feeling well below my best. 'We will', I said to my travelling companion on arrival at the Sandton Sun Hotel, 'take two hours' snooze by the pool before starting work.'

When I reached my room, the telephone was ringing urgently and the floor was papered with messages. Alec Russell, our staff correspondent in South Africa, was on the telephone. 'I do hope', he said breathlessly, 'that this will not be a shock to you, but Lord Camrose is dead. The office want to speak to you most urgently.'

I called London. The Camrose obituary, I was told, had been condemned as inadequate by the editor, Max Hastings. I was to freshen it up with a personal appreciation of my own, and the copy was wanted at once. I opened the minibar in my room – this was about 10 a.m. local time – and uncovered a very strong beer. Then I sat down and spent the next two hours writing and telephoning. 'One cannot tell', I concluded about Seymour, 'whether, if his health had held up, he would have been among the great proprietors. He would certainly have ranked among the most courteous of them.'

19

Dear Bill

A question every editor has to decide is what his political relations should be with senior political figures. Examples from the past strongly influenced me. In the days immediately before the Abdication of King Edward VIII, I thought my own editor at the *Morning Post*, H. A. Gwynne, was too close to the Prime Minister, Stanley Baldwin, and so too beholden to Baldwin's wishes. He was persuaded by Baldwin to keep quiet about the affair, which was almost certainly the right Downing Street policy, but not necessarily the right line for our newspaper.

I was even more strongly influenced by what happened to *The Times* in September 1938. At the height of the Czechoslovakian crisis as I have already described, Geoffrey Dawson, the paper's editor, wrote a leader urging the Czech Government to arrange the secession of 'that fringe of alien populations who are contiguous to the nation with which they are united by race'. It was, as our man in Prague, Lord Runciman, observed at the time, 'recommendation to *Anschluss*'. Worse, it was widely held to reflect the Government's policy. As historians of *The Times*, Oliver Woods and James Bishop later observed with commendable candour: 'By the publication of this article *The Times* identified itself in the most dramatic way with the "guilty" leaders in the eyes of contemporaries and posterity. The image of *The Times* as the arch-appeaser was carried into the post-war era and proved impossible to shake off. *The Times* history published in 1952 put on sackcloth for its sins.'

A question never fully resolved was whether this disastrous editorial was written by Dawson just after a visit to the Foreign Secretary, Lord Halifax. Rab Butler, then parliamentary under secretary at the Foreign Office, was convinced that Halifax had had a hand in it. 'The two Yorkshiremen were very close and I saw Dawson leaving the office on the 6th after a long interview with the Foreign Secretary.' That version has been disputed, but that the Foreign Secretary and Dawson were close is undeniable. As I observed in a piece I wrote about Munich for the *Spectator* in June 1988: 'It was no end of a lesson for editors to keep a hygienic distance between rulers and themselves.'

In weighing up what relations between Margaret Thatcher and the *Daily Telegraph*'s editor ought to be, these thoughts transcended the affection and admiration I felt for her. Many years earlier, we had been parliamentary candidates together in Kent. While I was preparing in 1948–50 to fight the relatively safe seat of Ashford, she was tackling the Labour seat at Dartford, occupied by a noisy Labour MP called Norman Dodds. One of the duties of Conservative candidates in those days was to attend week-end seminars. I have recounted earlier one of these in the late 1940s at which she shone. She was not smartly dressed, but when she posed a question everyone turned their eyes on her. I was bored. It was a warm summer Saturday afternoon, and I longed for my garden or the golf course. As we drove back together, the chairman of my Conservative Association – who was then Viscount Allenby – delivered reproaches, later expanded over a lunch. Why had I not been on the ball, like that bright young woman from Dartford – at that stage he did not even know her name. I would have to pull my socks up if I wanted to win the Ashford seat. After what had seemed to me a wasted summer afternoon, this was too much. I felt resentful of this bright, eager woman who had put me to shame by asking all the right questions.

Thereafter we met infrequently. I sat behind her during her maiden speech in the House of Commons because I was speaking in the same debate. By 1975, when she was elected Leader of the Conservative party we were on friendly terms, but mainly as neighbours in Kent. After that, we exchanged correspondence, met from time to time, and occasionally she discussed with me privately thoughts about her colleagues. Her thoughts remain private. While she was Leader of the Opposition, my wife and I joined one or two Sunday lunch parties which she and Denis gave in their home at Scotney Castle in Kent. Once or twice, after I became editor, I invited her to an evening drink in my office at the *Telegraph*, where she discussed her thoughts with the leader writers. We gave her a chance to expand her thinking over a private supper party at the Savoy. She looked stunningly pretty and gave our intellects a sharp canter. The dinner was a success. What I admired was the constant quest for self-improvement, by reading, by seeking experts to talk to, and by listening. It continued through the Downing Street years.

One of her early moves on becoming Leader of the Opposition was to ask me for the services of Richard Ryder, then working for me at the *Daily Telegraph*. She wanted him to be her private secretary. While speaking in the North during the autumn General Election of 1974, I had encountered Ryder dining in Newcastle's Station Hotel. Assisted by Cambridge friends, he was fighting the Labour stronghold of Gateshead. Soon afterwards, he asked me for a job on the Peterborough column – the only corner of the newspaper that lay within my gift. They were days when leave of the journalists' union had to be sought before making editorial appointments. I was granted permission to employ Ryder on the Peterborough column. Somewhere among my papers, I have Mrs Thatcher's receipt for Ryder. It was an auspicious choice. He remained with her until 1981, married her closest aide, Caroline, won a seat in Norfolk in 1983 and went on to become the Government's Chief Whip. With him I established the custom of discussing Mrs Thatcher's political affairs at regular intervals. After he moved up, and Mrs Thatcher became Prime Minister, I did the same with whoever was her parliamentary private secretary. It saved her time. I got all the political guidance I needed. It was done with her full knowledge. It put neither of us under any obligation.

At no time, I must add in fairness, did Mrs Thatcher seek any political or personal favours from the *Daily Telegraph*. Our relations were such that, when her daughter Carol applied for work with us, the Woman's Page editor deliberately gave her a trial without informing me. 'I thought it would make it easier for you,' she said. 'We seem powerless in this matter,' I reported to Lord Hartwell, who was fiercely jealous of the newspaper's independence. He looked thoughtfully at me for a while and then gave his shoulders a consenting shrug. I was not unaware that relations between Margaret Thatcher and Michael and Pamela Hartwell were cool. After her appointment as Leader of the Opposition in 1975, Pamela had invited her to one of her evening parties where politicians and senior members of her husband's staff mixed. Mrs Thatcher sent her apologies. Pamela upbraided me. Who did she think she was? Did she not realize that as a relatively untried figure she needed all the help she could get? 'Why is this Leader of yours not here?'

Pamela's relations with the Tories were complex and went back to the days when her father, F. E. Smith, later the 1st Lord Birkenhead, experienced difficulties with the Tory party.

In 1985 Mrs Thatcher went to Washington to deliver an address to both Houses of Congress. Her parliamentary private secretary, who was then Michael Alison MP and whom I saw regularly, asked if I would try to put a speech together for her. I agreed, but decided that Lord Hartwell would be happier to remain in ignorance of the arrangement. One evening soon after the speech had been delivered, Hartwell asked what I had thought of it. 'Not at all bad,' I said carefully. He concurred. The Berry family were endowed with an invaluable sixth sense. Before the war a friend of mine in the reporters' room received an offer from the *Daily Herald* of £15 a week, which was £3 more than the *Daily Telegraph* wage. He reported this approach to Viscount Camrose, Michael's father. 'What are they offering?' asked Camrose. 'The figure is £16,' said my friend. There was a pause. 'I will raise your salary here to £15,' replied Camrose.

There was another consideration behind my wish to keep a certain distance between myself and Mrs Thatcher and her colleagues. Nothing is more aggravating to those who work closely with an editor than a constant reminder that he is better informed than they are. Sir Colin Coote, *Daily Telegraph* editor from 1950 until 1964, suffered that weakness. He had been briefly in politics as a Liberal MP after the First World War, and had countless political friends. 'You are not quite right,' he would say on receiving some juicy piece of inside information. 'I happen to know the truth of the matter, which is . . .' If you say that too often to your staff they will cease to bother, and your Intelligence system suffers. I also enjoyed a certain advantage. I had come to know all the principal Tory figures as a Member of Parliament. I felt no social urge to meet them round a lunch table. I liked to feel that whenever it seemed necessary the *Daily Telegraph* could attack any one of them without any shadow of betrayal on my part.

I made an exception of Whitelaw, who was a friend of long-standing, a golfer and a lovely companion. By a bit of luck I had a lunch engagement with him just after Michael Fagan entered the Queen's bedroom on 7 July 1982. As Home Secretary, Whitelaw had offered his resignation, which had been refused. Glancing at his face as he entered the Savoy Grill, I ordered up a glass of champagne. It went down without touching the sides. Over a second glass, he outlined the grisly chapter of mishaps which had led to a man sitting on the Queen's bed and asking her for a cigarette. My note on the episode runs as follows:

Man seen climbing the [Buckingham Palace] wall. Reported.
Patrol (police) out in the grounds. Nothing found. Nothing
reported. No alert. When he climbed the wall, he jumped
over the electronic system. This was close to the wall, lest it
interfere with the parking of cars. So warning system did not
work. All this in early summer morning. Light. He entered
the Palace. Policeman on duty outside the Queen's bedroom
off duty at 6.30 a.m. Place taken by footman. His first duty
to take the dogs for a walk. So absent. On first receiving the
intruder, the Queen rang (ostensibly for a cigarette). Her
voice was recognized on the exchange. Someone informed,
who informed Control, who informed a policeman, who
informed another policeman. Delay long enough to cause
Queen to ring again to the exchange. By this time the footman
back from doggy walk and took charge. Man apprehended.

As a golfer, Whitelaw had been in a different class from the
rest of us who played for the Parliamentary Golf Society. He
had been in the Cambridge side and played top amateur golf.
While Ted Heath's Chief Whip, he had scored in the 70s on the
Old Course at St Andrews. On every round of golf in later
years Whitelaw was accompanied by two men from Special
Branch, whom he encouraged to take an interest in the game.
Loyal supporters of their boss, they accompanied Whitelaw and
myself in a year we were playing together in the Parliamentary
Golf Handicap. As we set out, rain began to fall. We elected to
get comprehensively wet, handed our umbrellas to the Special
Branch men and asked them to mark our respective cards for a
Stableford competition. At the close of the round they handed
over two very soggy cards. Whitelaw: 33 points: Deedes: 32
points. There's loyalty for you, I said.

Mrs Thatcher's cheerful response to my ungracious stand of
independence on behalf of Lord Hartwell's newspaper was to
be generous with invitations to dinners and parties at No. 10. I

invariably accepted whenever I could, not least because the Thatchers were outstandingly good hosts. Parties at No. 10 bring together insiders and outsiders, not all of whom know each other. I have never known a couple better than Margaret and Denis at making strangers to No. 10 feel immediately at home. They had the gift of leaving guests at even the largest parties with the impression that they were being entertained by their own friends.

I can recall only one evening at No. 10 when, during a national emergency, the system went awry. On the night of 19 May 1982 the Prime Minister gave a dinner at No. 10 for the Duke and Duchess of Kent and Prime Minister Muldoon of New Zealand. We were on the eve of the Falklands War. On arrival, shortly before 8 p.m., the Prime Minister was missing. I was told to talk to Muldoon and to keep talking. At dinner, which was very late, I sat at the Prime Minister's table between her and the New Zealand singer, Kiri Te Kanawa (Mrs Park). She was an easy companion because she took a passionate interest in golf.

As we reached the main course, a long message arrived for the Prime Minister, who read it, made some pencilled notes and returned it. 'United Nations on the telephone at 9.45 p.m.,' she said. 'Awkward.' It would clash with the speeches. Unknown to me, she had told them to put the call back to 10.30. Then she found that her watch, unwound, had stopped – which implies in all of us a preoccupied state of mind. She and Muldoon discussed favourite and unfavourite figures on the international scene. He had just visited Charles Haughey, Prime Minister of Ireland, whose government had pulled the rug from under sanctions against the Argentine. He had not wished to do this, Haughey explained to Muldoon, but 'his people had insisted on it'. Mrs Thatcher's face during this recital was a study.

Then a further message arrived at the table from the UN. The call would come at 10.30. After consulting a piece of paper in her handbag, the Prime Minister rose and delivered a spontaneous speech of welcome, quoting only from a scrap of Foreign Office paper about the anniversary of our first import of New Zealand lamb. At this somewhat fraught moment Muldoon, not invariably the most graceful of speakers, caught the right note. It was a family business, he said, and dwelt on the good fortune of the British people to have the right leader at the right time. He then offered the Prime Minister a New Zealand destroyer. Many of us, I reflected, had sent flowers to our hostess after a good dinner; a destroyer was original.

We then adjourned to a reception, from which Mrs Thatcher and Francis Pym, who was Foreign Secretary, vanished, presumably to deal with the United Nations. Mrs Pym suggested that I took on a bit of hosting. I gathered up Mrs Charles Douglas-Home, wife of the then editor of *The Times*, and introduced her to the Duke – superfluously, since they knew each other well – and Mr Muldoon, then looked round for fresh conquests. That sort of thing is harder than it looks. Half an hour passed, and it struck me that the Duke and Duchess of Kent were thoroughly enjoying themselves and not moving. So none of the other guests could leave. Charles Douglas-Home consented to have a word in her ear. We left not long before midnight to find the Prime Minister and Denis on the doorstep of No. 10 saying farewells.

At the head of the stairs as I left I encountered an elderly lady from New Zealand, who squeezed my left hand and said: 'I do wish you well. I so feel for your burden.' She had mistaken me for Denis.

That was not the only occasion I did a boy-scout act at No. 10. There was a large lunch party, attended by among others the Archbishop of Canterbury, who was then Robert Runcie. He and I were friendly because he kept pigs at a charity home bordering our garden in Kent. One of these pigs, about which I had kept readers of the *Daily Telegraph* fully informed through my column, had been named champion at the Kent Agricultural Show.

The lunch at No. 10 came not long after an unfortunate incident within the Church of England. The traditionally anonymous author of the Introduction to *Crockford*, troubled by the fuss created by his contribution, had committed suicide. Runcie was therefore something of a target for well-intentioned guests at No. 10 who desired to express their condolences. I decided whimsically to rescue him with pig talk – to which, perceiving my intentions, he readily responded. We discussed earnestly how much water should be added to the pig meal and kindred matters of importance to pig breeders. As a guest surged forward to discuss the suicide, feeling more and more like P. G. Wodehouse's Earl of Emsworth, I raised a fresh pig topic. By the time lunch was called, frustrated guests in our vicinity reckoned that both of us were off our heads.

My relations with Denis Thatcher were on a different footing. With two mutual friends we had played a good deal of golf together at home and abroad. When his wife's advancement began to make life serious for him we saw it as a national duty to give Denis golfing holidays. So one or twice a year we would travel together to Portugal, Spain, France or America and spend a week playing golf together. Even on holiday, Denis was ever watchful of 'beloved Margaret's' best interests. He signed autographs cheerfully, entertained the chatter of total strangers politely and moderated his language on the golf course. In the evenings we would all drink gin together and laugh. I think it did him good.

These were times when *Private Eye* was running the Dear Bill letters, invented by Richard Ingrams, then the editor, and John Wells. Ingrams, who has long been a personal friend, claimed that Bill was a man who lived in Folkestone and was out of touch with everything. At the same time, he occasionally inserted in the letters items, such as the name of my golf course at Littlestone, which linked them to me. At my daughters' insistence, Ingrams had played the church organ at their weddings. While writing a book about the Romney Marsh, he occasionally stayed with us. So he was familiar with small details of my life, which occasionally went into the letter like crossword-puzzle clues. I took the Bill in Folkestone with a pinch of salt.

Privately, I thought the letters did Denis no harm at all. Among news media people, who read *Private Eye* avidly for gossip about themselves, Denis was established as a pantomine figure, with a love of golf and gin, and a mind for very little else. This made it impossible to see him as a figure who might be influencing the Prime Minister behind the scenes. It is the sort of story certain newspapers relish. Denis's views on issues such as South Africa and the politics of the BBC were pretty well known. Newspaper reporters were 'vultures'. Thus, when his wife stood out against a desire by the Commonwealth Prime Ministers to impose sanctions on South Africa, he could well have been labelled as the *éminence grise*. But the *Eye* had established an identity with which this simply would not wash. There was a lot of Denis in *Private Eye*, as Carol Thatcher observed after the first night of the dramatization of the letters *Anyone for Denis?* at the Whitehall Theatre in 1981, which we both attended. I think Margaret also saw the point, but it was not an altogether flattering portrait, and when holidaying with Denis I kept off the subject.

Denis Thatcher was not the only victim of Richard Ingrams's curious sense of fun. It came close to getting me the sack. In 1976 Jimmy Goldsmith issued over sixty libel writs against *Private Eye* and applied to the High Court to bring an action of criminal libel against the magazine. It was a weird and wonderful case, which *Private Eye* managed to survive; and in 1979 Richard Ingrams wrote a short book about it, entitled *Goldenballs*. I thought it merited a main-page feature and wrote it myself. One evening soon after it appeared I paid my usual visit to Lord Hartwell. 'I have news for you,' he said as I walked into his room. 'I have just been asked by Sir James Goldsmith to sack you.' Later Goldsmith made it up. Sensitive to personal criticism – who is not? – he insisted that there existed what he called a 'symbiotic relationship' between *Private Eye* and certain individuals in our City office. We sorted that one out as well.

One lives and learns. Not until relatively late in my tenancy at the *Daily Telegraph* did I discover the danger of using irony in an editorial. My failure to observe the rule in October 1983 played its part in the resignation of Cecil Parkinson, who was then Mrs Thatcher's Secretary of State for Trade and Industry. It also caused a lot of unnecessary pain. During one of our leader conferences, John O'Sullivan suggested a leader on the Parkinson/Sara Keays affair. A week earlier, Parkinson had made an announcement to the effect that he had withdrawn his offer to marry his mistress Sara Keays, his former secretary, and that he and his wife had decided to stay together.

Naturally, this led to controversy – and to O'Sullivan's desire to write a by no means unsympathetic editorial. The fatal passage, which I cheerfully passed, ran like this: 'Then it is said that not the adultery, but the embarrassing fact that it resulted in a pregnancy, is the issue. But the moral logic there is that a quiet abortion is greatly to be preferred to a scandal. That hardly seems a moral advance . . .'

On reading this, Sara Keays got in touch with *The Times* late on the night of 13 October with a long and explosive statement. I give the opening passages:

> I agreed for the sake of my family that we would not discuss with the press the statement made by Mr Parkinson last week. I hoped that it would not become necessary for me to say anything. However I now feel I have a duty to do so.
>
> On Friday October 7, *The Times* said that 'Mr Parkinson had made a sad and silly blunder.' Like the Government, the editor believes this should have remained a 'private matter'.
>
> For the *Daily Telegraph* (Monday October 10) 'the moral logic is that a quiet abortion is greatly to be preferred to a

scandal'. I was not aware that political expediency was sufficient grounds for an abortion under the 1967 Act, quite apart from the fact that I could not have contemplated it . . .

Early news of this explosion, which covered much of *The Times* front page, was conveyed to the Imperial Hotel, Blackpool, where both the Prime Minister and Cecil Parkinson were staying. Parkinson arrived in Mrs Thatcher's suite at 2 a.m. and told her he would have to go. That resolved, Mrs Thatcher looked round the room, where she had been finishing her conference speech, and said to her private secretary, 'And now I think we can all go to bed.'

'There is just one other thing, Prime Minister,' he replied. 'Mr Parkinson was due to open a helicopter terminal at Blackpool airport tomorrow morning.' There was a pause. 'Denis will do that,' said his wife. Standing in front of a plaque with Cecil Parkinson's name on it, he did just that. Meanwhile, I thought it imperative to set our own record in the matter straight. With Hartwell's approval, I sent a letter to *The Times* which Charlie Douglas-Home, then editor, gladly agreed to print the following day. After quoting the relevant passages, I concluded: 'While I appreciate that Miss Keays' statement was made under emotional stress, I have to point out that by misreading the argument and then ignoring the last sentence she has drawn and attributed to us a conclusion precisely opposite to what we wrote.'

Barely had this been dispatched to *The Times* than I learned that in the course of the BBC's *Any Questions* that evening Shirley Williams had declared that the *Daily Telegraph* had advised Miss Keays to get rid of the child. I called Douglas-Home and said that in the circumstances I would have to give my letter to the Press Association for wider circulation. He agreed. Then I called the BBC's duty officer. He took the point. In the repeat of *Any Questions* the offending passage was excised. At 2.30 a.m. next morning the *Daily Telegraph*'s night editor called me to say that mine had climbed to the top of *The*

Times letter column, but that most of the day's newspapers were cheerfully continuing to misrepresent what we had said.

Jean Ritchie in a 'Personal View by *Sun* writer' remarked: 'Any man who can stay silent while the *Daily Telegraph* suggests she should have had a quiet abortion to save his political career has no compassion for her or for the child.' Diana Hutchinson of the *Daily Mail* opened: 'It started in *The Times* with the writing off of the affair as "a sad and silly blunder". Worse was to follow in the *Daily Telegraph* when it was suggested that "the moral logic is that a quiet abortion is greatly to be preferred to a scandal".' Sandra White of the *Star* had it: 'It was a bad day for Sara. She had started it by reading a *Daily Telegraph* editorial that suggested a "quiet abortion is preferable to a scandal". Only a man could write that . . .' The *Daily Mirror* plastered page 1 with a heading: 'I was not aware that political expediency was sufficient grounds for an abortion.' Since this was not attributed to us, the night staff entered only the mildest rebuke, which the *Mirror* acknowledged, while declaring that an industrial dispute with the printers rendered any change in later editions impossible.

Amid this *galère* Katharine Hadley, woman's editor of the *Daily Express*, stood out as a good reporter – the highest award in my book. She had checked her facts:

> 'According to the view expressed in the *Telegraph*, I should have sacrificed my baby's life for Mr Parkinson's career and the Government's reputation.' But the *Telegraph* said no such thing. In the course of outlining several suggestions made in public discussion, it said that one had been made that an abortion might have been best. The *Telegraph* leader rejected such a suggestion quite firmly as 'hardly a moral advance'. It was attacking the 'moral logic' of an abortion suggestion.

Bernard Levin began a humorous piece in *The Times* by declaring:

The one figure in l'affaire Parkinson for whom I have no sympathy at all is Sir William Deedes [sic – journalists do well to check titles as well as to avoid irony], Editor of the *Daily Telegraph*. I could have told him (but he didn't ask me) that the gentle irony of his paper's leading article . . . was, like all irony, a weapon more dangerous to the hand wielding it than to anyone against whom it might be directed. It took Miss Keays a mere three days to work out a method of misunderstanding it (the technique included excising the last sentence altogether) and there she was, as white as Mother Teresa of Calcutta . . .

It is hard to quarrel with Bernard Levin in that mood, and I thought privately he had a point. On the other hand, Auberon Waugh took my side. In a piece for the *Spectator* – not then owned by the *Daily Telegraph* – which was headed 'Book of Golden Deedes', he delivered his own verdict:

But amid all the boredom and gloom of it, amid all the blacks and whites merging into sludgy grey, one hero and one villain can be clearly seen. The villain is Mr Charles Douglas-Home, who published Miss Keays's statement, unchecked, as a 'scoop' for his worthless newspaper. The statement contained an extremely damaging misrepresentation of his rival newspaper, the *Daily Telegraph*, which anybody within ten miles of Fleet Street would have known to be untrue. This did not stop all the other newspapers reproducing the statement next day, of course, but the initial dispensation came from *The Times*.

Waugh then gave the text of our exchanges and went on: 'The person to emerge as a hero from this ugly episode, straight out of Arthur Mee's *Child's Book of Golden Deeds*, is the editor of the *Daily Telegraph*. His letter written, with no apparent sign of rancour, should be used as a model for anyone who feels he has been misrepresented in the press. There is no bluster, no threat to sue, no mention even of the Press Council ...' Quoting the final sentence of my letter to *The Times*, Waugh concluded: 'Not a word of rebuke to Douglas-Home, but what a mammoth snub one reads! Mr William ("Golden") Deedes, now 70, cut his teeth as a cub reporter with Evelyn Waugh nearly 50 years ago in Abyssinia. Twenty-five years later, he helped guide my faltering footsteps in the Peterborough office of the *Daily Telegraph*. I am proud to have known him. Sense and decency still exist in this land.'

One hesitates to contradict such a generous fellow, but I think Bernard Levin may have been nearer the mark. In the light of this episode, I offer two bits of advice to all who aspire to be future editors. Watch out for irony – and before commenting on anything another newspaper is supposed to have done, check the original copy!

Soon after becoming editor, I decided that the best way of combining newspaper business, social duty and pleasure was to invite guests to my office for a drink at around half-past six in the evening. No two editors use the same routine. I chose to reach the office at about eleven in the morning, take the news conference and leader writers' conference in the early afternoon, and stay in the office long enough to see the leaders in proof and the first edition of the newspaper on its way. I left the office, with luck, at about ten o'clock. So a break at half-past six was welcome.

It had other benefits. Any leader writer who wanted to join me and the guest for a drink was welcome. I found ambassadors, company chairmen, trade union leaders and others surprisingly pleased to be invited. I kept Michael Hartwell informed of anyone who might interest him. He sometimes joined us, though insisting rather chillingly on drinking only soda water. If a leader writer appeared with his copy, I dealt with it there and then. Visitors found all this rather original. Sometimes they came at their own request. The Russian embassy periodically invited themselves and treated it like a bottle party. They would present me with gifts of their own vodka. I thought this rather compromising, so accepted the gift, but left the vodka undrunk. It still sits in my cellar. On suitable occasions, I invited management to join us. This made a pleasant change from evenings when the office was being convulsed by some dispute with the printers and I was invited to drink with management.

No editor has ever had an easier owner to work with than Lord Hartwell. He rarely interfered or gave a direction, yet he took a close interest in everything that went on and was a demon for detail. Extremely shy by nature, he found main office events a trial and left most of them to me. His wife, Lady Pamela Berry, did the entertaining at their house in Cowley Street. She was a character over whom people took sides. I found no difficulty in taking her side. When I learned that she was dying I went to see Lord Weidenfeld, whom I did not know well. He probably thinks I want to write a book for him, I reflected on my way to his house; I must be one of the few people to have commissioned him. I asked if he would write Pamela's obituary for me. In accepting my request, he made a good point. Pamela Berry, he pointed out, had the knack as hostess of making members of her husband's staff attending her parties appear a degree more important than any of the political luminaries present. She could make a Prime Minister or Leader of the Opposition feel glad to meet one of her husband's correspondents or leader writers. For that she could be forgiven a great deal, including her propensity for stimulating controversy round her lunch table.

Soon after Mrs Thatcher came into prominence, Pamela held a lunch party where the guest of honour was Katharine Graham, owner of the *Washington Post* and a considerable Washington figure. Another American guest at the table asked Mrs Graham what she thought of Mrs Thatcher. She described her contemptuously as a 'fishwife'. At this I felt the temperature around the table rise, and there followed an instructive display of very British politics. Both Roy Jenkins and Shirley Williams, then senior members of the Labour party, who were present, flew to the defence of Mrs Thatcher. They addressed Mrs Graham in terms I would not dare to have employed – Mrs Graham was a long-standing friend of both Michael and Pamela Hartwell. I mumbled approvingly at Labour's reaction. Mrs Graham began to look displeased. The lunch ended on an exceptionally cool note. Michael himself, mercifully, was not present.

My plot with George Weidenfeld to do Pamela Hartwell justice was only partially successful. On the morning of her death Michael Hartwell called me up with the news. 'I have asked Kenneth Rose to write her obituary,' he said. Kenneth was Albany of the *Sunday Telegraph* and, after his biography of King George V, a literary celebrity. I could think of nobody better, but felt cornered. With tact, I was able to arrange for George Weidenfeld's contribution to appear in the *Sunday Telegraph*.

Throughout our time together I can recall no occasion when Michael Hartwell asked me to appoint any friend of his to our staff. On the other hand, he showed indulgence over some of my appointments. For reasons of my own, for example, I employed the controversial figure of Alfred Sherman to write leaders two days a week. I thought he had an original mind and stirred things up. He was hostile to cosy thinking, which I thought valuable. He was also extremely right wing. Our owner found Sherman a tremendous pill to swallow. Because he presided over the *Sunday Telegraph* on Saturdays, Hartwell was absent from the office on Mondays, a day on which a Sherman leader was apt to appear. 'I take it', he would remark gloomily on Tuesday evening when I went to see him, 'that the leader on so-and-so was Sherman's work.' I would look suitably contrite. There came a day on which Edward Pearce, a talented political commentator but moody, threw an ashtray at Sherman. It missed. When Hartwell heard of the episode, his face lit up.

In the summer of 1979 I received a note from Mary Ann Sieghart, who was about to go up to Oxford. Did I have a holiday vacancy? Alas, I said, the summer vacancies had been filled. In 1980, she applied again. I said she would be welcome in the long vacation of July–October to a mixed bag of duties. She began with a dull spell of sub-editing on the radio and television page, moved on to the Peterborough column and, as a treat, finished up with Features. I knew and admired her father, Paul Sieghart, a public-spirited member of the Bar, for whom later I did a little work at Justice, a public-spirited body which produced occasional reports on the working of the law. Let loose on the leader page, Mary Ann wove a sometimes startling liberal thread through the *Daily Telegraph*'s blue tapestry. But what impressed me most about this talented young woman were comments that floated back from co-workers on the radio and television page. She was a lovely person to work with, they said.

Newspapers have plenty of clever journalists, but are not over-endowed with people whom other people find attractive company. At one of my conferences she proposed a leader on the Greater London Council's new 'Fares Fair' policy, which had slashed ticket prices. 'I couldn't work out why there was so little enthusiasm,' she told me later, 'until I looked round the room and realized that I was the only one there that day who didn't have a free Tube pass!' In another leader about Mrs Thatcher, who had been talking about morality and religion, she declared that preachers should stick to preaching and politicians to politics. Distressed by this, Mrs Thatcher tackled my colleague Peter Utley. 'Ah, yes,' he said mischievously, 'it was written by a nineteen-year old we have working there at the moment.'

In the summer of 1981, I encouraged Sieghart to go to New York to write a piece about IRA funding there. In the Easter vacation of that year she persuaded me to accept a leader-page article on the virtues of popular music, then her passion. 'Not everyone may enjoy the noise it makes, but we can no longer dismiss the whole thing as a useless triviality.' This came as a surprise to our readers. When she finished at Oxford with high honours, I offered her a job, while urging her to seek elsewhere for her own good. She went to the *Financial Times* and soon joined the Lex column. My son, working for Eddy Shah at the time, after consulting me, then invited her to become City editor of *Today*. The *Financial Times* was cross. Sieghart felt the challenge of entering the world of new technology, recruiting and managing a team of journalists – eight women and one man – in an office of her own irresistible. She was then twenty-four.

When *Today* went down, Sieghart sensibly moved to *The Economist* and buckled down to two years' apprenticeship to serious politics. She found it hard there to follow Simon Jenkins, who had gone to edit *The Times*. 'He seemed to play tennis with half the Cabinet. I knew nobody.' But she met Tony Blair and made friends with him. Blair and his wife were guests at her wedding in the summer of 1989 when Mary Ann married David Prichard. Called on to propose the bride's health, I missed the marriage and was lucky to make the reception. On the morning of the day, a bee from my wife's hive, misled by the smell of Mr Trumper's Eucris, for which I have a weakness, stung me on the head. I suffered a collapse. Happily, my doctor, Norman Corfield, lived nearby. He took a cardiogram and declared it was a near-run thing. 'But I have to be at a wedding in London this afternoon,' I said. He agreed to come back after lunch and do a second cardiogram. He then consented to my attendance at the London wedding, providing my daughter Jill, visiting us from Australia, drove me there and back and I drank no alcohol. Throughout my speech on behalf of Mary Ann, I thought mournfully how much better it would have sounded on a glass of champagne. Later, Guy's Hospital told me that I had become highly vulnerable to bee – and wasp – stings. It is a common condition. You can either undergo a prolonged and dreary cure, or carry the wherewithal to inject yourself with adrenaline.

By then *The Times* had claimed Mary Ann. We agonized together over that move, but it has turned out well for her. When in 1995 the BBC revived the *Brains Trust* and put Mary Ann in the chair, she was described in the hyperbole of our times as 'among the twenty most intelligent women in this country'. As one who remains deeply fond of her, I sometimes reflect that the most useful thing I did for her was to send her at the age of nineteen to sub-edit at a humble level. Thereby I discovered her gift for concealing 'the effortless superiority of Balliol' behind lovely manners. In fact, she went to Wadham.

One of my few appointments which Lord Hartwell received with enthusiasm was that of Jock Bruce-Gardyne as writer on economic affairs in 1977. A product of Winchester and Magdalen, Jock had begun life in the Foreign Service, switched to journalism, won a parliamentary seat in Scotland in 1964 and lost it in 1974. He was an exceptionally quick writer and had a sharp eye for economic folly. While working with me, he went in pursuit of another parliamentary seat. I followed his endeavours with an anxious and sympathetic eye. Eventually, he landed Knutsford and won the election there in 1979. Mrs Thatcher, who thought highly of him, made him Economic Secretary to the Treasury in 1981, and we temporarily parted company.

During the Falklands War, political disaster struck him. In a bread-and-butter letter to Sam Brittan of the *Financial Times*, Jock added a postscript unfavourable to Mrs Thatcher's line on the war. The rest is a tale of our times. Brittan showed the letter to his editor, in support of his own line about the war. It was spotted on the editor's desk. The incriminating passage then appeared in the *New Statesman*. Jock was embarrassed. Ridiculously, he was omitted from Armistice Day arrangements in his own constituency. On redistribution of his seat, he lost out to Mrs Nicholas Winterton. In 1983 Mrs Thatcher sensibly made him a life peer – a duty which he took more seriously than I have ever done. After the *Daily Telegraph* upheaval of 1986, he was welcomed by my successor Max Hastings. One day he found that he could not co-ordinate the keys on his typewriter. On learning that he had a mortal brain tumour, he wrote an account of experiencing the approach of death for the *Spectator*.

Called on to deliver the address at his memorial service, I found myself occupying the front pew in St Margaret's Church, Westminster Abbey, with Margaret Thatcher. 'The trouble about being in front', I murmured to her – rather prophetically, as it turned out – 'is that you cannot tell what those behind you are doing!' She received this with a perfectly straight face. We both held Jock in deep affection and shared distress over his affliction. I have done my share of *in memoriam* addresses, but on this occasion I found it hard to speak calmly. I spoke of his passion for travelling everywhere in London on an ancient bicycle – 'They steal new bicycles,' he would declare. I ended my talk about Jock with a reference to his love of fishing, usually in Scotland. 'I do not fish,' I said, 'but I shall forever think of Jock on that river of his. And I shall think of that because, when it came to the widest of all rivers, and the hardest to cross, we none of us saw him out of his depth, nor make a false cast. He showed us how to ford the river. He helped us all to understand.' As Margaret Thatcher and I left the church, I reflected sorrowfully on Jock's misfortunes. Some people have all the luck in the world, others no luck at all.

I spent a long time preparing that address. Memorial service addresses are in my experience the hardest of all to prepare. You know the family of the departed will be there, and feel that you cannot take enough trouble to find words that will be of comfort to them. I acquired a certain amount of practice as an editor in Fleet Street, because there was usually a service of thanksgiving for departed colleagues in the Church of St Bride's. The most rewarding memorial address I ever made was for Henry Cotton's Memorial Requiem Mass at the Church of the Immaculate Conception in Farm Street. His generous step-daughter, Chicki Moss, presented me with a twenty-four-carat gold-plated Ping putter, which I regard as an heirloom. Two of the exacting occasions I encountered were on behalf of Charles Hill in Westminster Abbey, where Lady Plowden and I shared the honours, and on 26 February 1991 when Malcolm Muggeridge was remembered in Westminster Cathedral. Such addresses to large audiences are disconcerting because you get no playback from them – unless you give them something to laugh at. And when you leave the pulpit or lectern there is dead silence. That, for anyone who has been a politician, is worrying. You wonder where you went wrong.

20

Fleet Street Revolution

Always overshadowing our efforts to turn out a better newspaper were the Fleet Street print unions and the incorrigible behaviour of their inflated membership. At this distance, more than a decade after the Wapping revolution, it is hard to convey the damage some of these men inflicted on national newspapers and the burden they imposed on our lives. Soon after I took over as editor, an episode occurred which conveys the atmosphere. This is the note I made of it at the time:

> Men on the foundry [where the plates that printed the paper were shaped] paid until 3 a.m. By custom they pack up and go at 1 a.m. leaving a skeleton crew. When (because of some internal difficulty) Saturday's paper did not begin until 1 a.m., the foundrymen declared that they would be working 'normally' – that is until 1 a.m. Printer said, 'That is not working normally. 3 a.m. is your normal.' They then demanded overtime for two hours. This was refused. On this they called a chapel [local branch] meeting, ignoring the printer's request to weigh in and discuss it all later. Chapel met, delaying production for another twenty minutes, losing tens of thousands of copies, before deciding to take printer's advice.

This sort of performance, which in the argot of those days went under the casual heading of 'custom 'n' practice', occurred somewhere in Fleet Street pretty well every night of the week. The hardest part, that of negotiating with the unions and their representatives in response to outrageous demands, fell on management, which aged visibly. It lay with them when some trifling grievance threatened the night's production to trace the union's bosses and seek their help. When serious trouble threatened, however, the bosses were invariably hard to find. There was a room where management usually met on the third floor of our old building in Fleet Street, and where on bad nights I would sometimes join them. It came in my mind to resemble more and more a scene from Sherriff's play about the First World War, *Journey's End*, complete with the sort of dug-out officers occupied in the front line, shells falling around them, candles trembling on the table, and bottles of whisky for consolation.

My own difficulties began when a union branch official approached me, either to object to something about to appear in the newspaper or to persuade me to put into the newspaper some letter, correction or statement that his men desired. I sought with only partial success to establish a rule at the *Daily Telegraph* whereby such requests could be made only in respect of matters directly affecting their own affairs. Protests about South African advertisements, for example, were in my book off-side. Even this was hard to enforce. In the 1970s, for example, there was a notorious dispute at the Grunwick film-processing laboratories. Fierce demonstrations took place in protest against the firm's refusal to recognize trade unions. In June 1977, the National Association for Freedom placed an advertisement with us. It was pungently worded:

> The outstanding courage of the Grunwick workforce in continuing to work against unlawful odds should be an inspiration to all who wish to see freedom both to join and not to join unions survive in Britain.
>
> We hope that all who are outraged by this display of mob

rule will help us to continue to help the beleaguered staff at Grunwick.

The 260 Grunwick staff do NOT want to be unionized. They voted 86.4 per cent against any form of union . . .

And so on. Next morning I received a note from the publisher in charge of the night's production. One of the print unions had approached him and made a protest. At 2.30 a.m. the father (head) of the chapel had come to see him and spoken gravely of hotheads who were talking of shutting down. (Talk of hotheads who were proving impossible to control was a familiar gambit from chapel officials.) They had spoken about the 'right of reply', which the publisher had advised might be open to them, subject to my consent. He concluded in his note to me: 'I did expect a letter this morning, but this has not been forthcoming. Maybe they will give me one tomorrow. We'll see.' The letter eventually materialized. I passed it for publication, though it was on the extreme borderline of my ruling. This had a sequel. To cheer them up on the management floor I sent some account of it under personal and confidential cover. Here it is:

In the light of last week's talks about letters from Fathers of Chapels, you may like to hear of this exchange between myself and Mr L of the machine minders, who wrote a letter last Friday. He approached me on the stone [where type was put together] last night and the conversation went something like this:

'Mr Deedes, I want to have a word about the letter which you were so kind as to publish from me last week.'

'Yes.'

'Mr Deedes, I think you should know that I have as a result of that letter received a number of letters, all of them very horrible indeed.'

'I am sorry to hear that.'

'Mr Deedes, I did not realize that such people existed. You cannot imagine the language they used towards us.'

'Well, Mr L, we are men of the world – we must make allowance for the excitement Grunwick has generated. Don't take it too much to heart.'

(Indignantly) 'Mr Deedes, are you aware that some of these people have threatened my private parts?'

'Now, Mr L, as you know, your colleagues do come to see me from time to time with letters. When I suggest to them, as I often do, it might not be in their best interests for their letter to be published, they think I am trying it on. You know better now, Mr L?'

'We certainly do, Mr Deedes.'

'Perhaps you could mention this to one or two . . .?'

'I certainly shall, Mr Deedes.'

In the three-month period ending March 1977, we lost some 6.5 million copies of the paper. *The Times* lost 1.7 million, the *Daily Mail* 3.0 million, the *Sun* upwards of 24.0 million and the *Daily Mirror* 12.5 million – a total in all of some 48.5 million, and there was worse to come.

About this time, Sir James Goldsmith visited my office – ostensibly to complain about a member of my staff alleged to be in league with *Private Eye*, which was permanently at war with Goldsmith. The individual involved had resigned the night before, thus shooting Goldsmith's fox, but he had lit a huge cigar, and chose to remain for a while, chatting amiably about life at the *Daily Express*, in which he was taking a tentative interest. He said that his accountants had been staggered by the Express Newspaper accounts. It had led him to believe that Fleet Street was the most prosperous and worst-managed industry in the country. He foresaw that if it was run efficiently, it would turn into a gold brick. Only an enormously prosperous industry, he assured me, could survive such over-manning, over-paying and inefficiency. I must be feeling happy, he observed as we parted. Long experience, I retorted, had taught me that no one stayed happy in Fleet Street for very long.

The storm was gathering fast. In November 1978, BBC's *Panorama* ran a fifty-minute programme entitled *Behind the Times*, in which Michael Cockerell spoke to both sides in the dispute which was about to shut *The Times* down for a year. Our television previewer, Ronald Hastings, wrote an anodyne curtain-raiser. Next morning I found a note on my desk from the night editor: 'A P [a printer's leader] and one of his NATSOPA [a print union] came to see me at 12.10 a.m. to demand the removal of Hastings's comments on tonight's *Panorama*. I refused, pointing out that the [offending words] "dubious, even corrupt, customs of Fleet Street . . ." to which particular exception was taken were in quotes and attributable to Michael Cockerell. Also offered usual letter to Editor, which didn't go down too well. It is now 1.40 a.m. and nothing has happened, so perhaps it was just a try-on.'

It was the way we lived then.

Around this time, after consulting Michael Hartwell, I drafted a leader which admitted to our readers that most of the newspaper industry was giving its readers an indifferent service. If any other industry had done as badly, I added, what a scolding it might have expected from Fleet Street's omniscient leader writers!

In October 1978, we experienced total disruption in London. This particular dispute had begun for complicated reasons. Members of the telecommunications and electronics section of the composing and reading room of the National Graphical Association – one of Fleet Street's principal unions – refused to handle telephone equipment installed and operated for many years without extra payments. On 4 October, other sections refused to handle any material that would normally come through the telecommunications and electronics sections. This meant, among other things, that we lost the City pages. Hartwell determined, rightly, that we could not print the newspaper on those terms; and furthermore that, if the newspaper failed to appear, no payments would be made to members of the chapel involved. The following day was spent negotiating a claim by the NGA chapel involved that these threatened stoppages of pay be withdrawn. Management offered to restore half the pay if men would resume normal working. This was turned down. The newspaper then went out of production in London.

On 17 October, Hartwell addressed an open letter to all the staff which appeared on the front page of the newspaper – still being tenuously produced in Manchester. After seeking to explain the reasons which had stopped the printing of the newspaper in London for eleven days, he concluded: 'In short, The Daily Telegraph Ltd, which comprises both *Telegraphs* and the Magazine, is in danger of bleeding to death. Alone in Fleet Street, we are not part of a great conglomerate. Oil, shipping, paper manufacturing will not come to our aid. We spend all our energy and all our resources on our newspapers. This used to be taken for a virtue. Now, if you do not rally to us, it will be our downfall.'

In referring to our limited resources, Hartwell had put his finger on it. Over the years, newspaper proprietors had been playing a dangerous game of poker. When printers made outrageous demands of any particular newspaper, other proprietors would sit round the table at the Newspaper Publishers' Association in Bouverie Street, off Fleet Street, examine their own hand and consider the consequences of knocking weaker players (who were also rivals) out of the game. Ours has always been a furiously competitive industry – and a ruthless one. I attended one or two of these poker schools, because Hartwell took Mondays off. Occasionally, I would stand in for him on that day. I came to see clearly how far this lack of solidarity among newspaper owners delivered us into the hands of powerful unions who enjoyed regimental discipline within their own ranks. Over and again, they made ridiculous demands of one newspaper or another, witnessed the failure of the industry to close ranks, and scored. *They had never lost*. They believed they could never lose.

Another baleful factor was the extent to which Fleet Street newspapers, like the London docks, had come to depend on casual labour. In the docks, the demand for labour depended on how many ships came in for unloading on any particular day. In Fleet Street, particularly on Saturday nights when the Sundays were being run off, the demand for labour depended largely on how many pages the newspaper wanted to print. There was an invisible but close affinity between the printers' families and dockers' families. They came from much the same districts of London. They had learned to fight through hard times, and they knew how to milk employers who appeared to have money to burn. Casual labour did to Fleet Street what dry rot does to old buildings. Loyalty to a newspaper is unlikely to be given by men who can never be sure in whose premises they will be working on any given night.

Our constant failure to give readers a fair return for their money had a lowering effect on editorial morale. The journalists themselves were subject to union disciplines and I was expected to recognize that. The larger of the two journalists' unions, the National Union of Journalists, had what could be called a symbiotic relationship with the print unions. The smaller union, the Institute of Journalists, was a degree more flexible and moderate; but, depending on its leadership at the time, could be touchy and difficult.

Journalists as well as printers therefore were virtually in a 'closed shop'. Nobody could work as a journalist at the *Daily Telegraph* without belonging to the appropriate union. There were rare exceptions, but I took care not to know about them. I wangled small compromises, whereby I could give young men and women of high promise a run on the Peterborough column, which had a staff of five or six. By this means we got a foot in the door for people like Charles Moore, later editor of both

Sunday and *Daily Telegraph*, Martin Ivens, who became a senior figure with Times Newspapers, Mary Ann Sieghart, also with *The Times*, Graham Patterson, Angela Gordon and others.

Our private secretaries were not spared. They were required to join one of the print unions, NATSOPA, pay their dues out of slender earnings, and attend without fail mandatory chapel meetings on pain of fines for absence. My own secretary, Susan Davey, was not exempted. Duties compelled her to absent herself from one or two meetings. She received warnings.

One secretary, working for our books editor, David Holloway, came to me and explained tearfully that she had been summoned to a disciplinary meeting for failing to attend some gathering or other. She was, she told me, permitted to take one companion to this 'kangaroo court'. I invited her to submit my name. The union was flabbergasted and complained to our management, who were horrified by my irresponsibility. They begged me in the wider interests of the newspaper to withdraw my offer. I had become fed up with the bullying of secretaries, including my own, and dug my heels in. If the union chose to withdraw the disciplinary charge, I said, I would also withdraw. Management thought this risky, but I held out and nothing more was heard of the matter.

In this perpetually warlike atmosphere, I occasionally felt glad of experience in the Army. I had learned something about sustaining morale when everything went wrong. When I had no lunch appointment, I went next door to the King and Keys and drank beer with the colleagues – mainly because I like a pint or two at lunch time. It taught me a lot. The reporters had a strong and justified sense of their vulnerability. They were, after all, trained to see round the next corner. I found the business of reassuring people who had every reason to be gloomy about the future a hard but indispensable part of an editor's duties.

In the last quarter of 1978, *The Times* ran into the heaviest seas of all. By the end of October it had lost 3.9 million copies and its sister paper the *Sunday Times* 6.3 million copies. The threat of suspension became a reality. There were always superficial reasons for disruption, but behind this gathering storm on the shop floor lay awareness among printers that elsewhere in the world systems were being developed and practised that would eliminate whole production processes – and a lot of cosy jobs.

When travelling abroad, I made a point of visiting friendly newspaper offices. At the *New York Times* at this period, I saw the new dawn – direct input through the computer by journalists and advertising staff that would transform the industry. I saw other versions of it at the *Sunday Times* in Johannesburg and the *Age* in Melbourne. In fairness, union rebellion against this prospect was not confined to our own shores. New York had had its problems and shut-downs during transition. Katharine Graham, formidable owner of the *Washington Post*, had an exceptionally hard time. I happened to be in Washington when some of her print workers were in court for sabotaging plant.

On 1 December 1978 *The Times* failed to appear. It had a day or two earlier published a farewell editorial headed: 'There will be an interval'. William Rees-Mogg, editor, and Marmaduke Hussey, chief executive and managing director, found themselves on the bridge of a sinking ship.

After exactly six months' closure, on the evening of 31 May 1979, Rees-Mogg called me on the telephone. He did not want, he began, to hand me a poisoned chalice. But the *Observer* had commissioned an article from him to coincide with this melancholy anniversary and, on viewing it, had chickened out. Might I be interested? He promised to deliver it himself later that evening. I invited our managing director, H. M. Stephen, to look it over with me. 'Print it!' he said. I then sent it to Hartwell with a strong recommendation that we ran it as a leader-page article on the following night – unexpurgated. He agreed, but wisely advised me to telephone to the boss of the main print union, the NGA. I did so, assuring him of a right of reply. We set the article up under a heading, 'Where *The Times* stands'.

Around 8.40 that evening, while entertaining guests from the Defence College in my office, I was told that visitors awaited me. There entered my room four imperial fathers of the National Graphical Association, two from *The Times* and the *Sunday Times*, two of our own. It was the closest you could get in our wild world to a royal straight flush. They began by declaring that the reply from the NGA boss must run alongside Rees-Mogg's piece – a physical impossibility, apart from the fact that it had not yet been written. I offered to put a notice under the Rees-Mogg article, indicating that the NGA would be responding. They then came up with the familiar line that their hotheads would become indignant and uncontrollable. They were unsure if they could hold them back. It dawned on me that this bluff was designed to ensure that their reply took the form of an article, and was not confined to the Letters column. I immediately gave assurances on that score. We would run the article in full. As we sat talking, I caught the welcome sounds of the machine room starting up and the presses running. They also heard it, and after an hour or more of close engagement left my room smiling.

Next day, 1 June, I spent my birthday at Walton Heath playing in a triangular golf match between the club, the press and the Lords and Commons. At lunch I sat next to Brian Nicholson, then managing director of the *Observer*. 'I read that article with interest,' he told me. 'I caught it off the end of your bat,' I told him smugly. He looked astonished. 'It shall go no further,' I promised – and it hasn't until now.

The Times reappeared on 13 November 1979, but eight months later was hit by a journalists' strike. The Thomson organization which owned it decided enough was enough and pulled out. After a short period of acute uncertainty for my friends at *The Times*, Rupert Murdoch purchased it.

Dear Bill

I have always taken the view that the absence of *The Times* for a year indirectly did the *Daily Telegraph* a good deal of harm. It was a time when we should have been undergoing a facelift – and, if necessary, paid the printers' price for it. One of my minor ambitions was to import a strip cartoon. With the help of Ian Ball, our man in New York, I trawled America for a suitable strip. I persuaded artists in this country to experiment and paid them for their efforts. In the nicest possible way, Hartwell rejected all my offerings. He thought they would take the newspaper down market. There were other areas I thought due for a change. The page opposite our leader page remained a ragbag of not very exciting news. I wanted to use it for news features from home or abroad. This was an invasion of Peter Eastwood's territory. His professionalism drew him towards the idea, but he could not bear to part with territory. He was not enthusiastic. So we remained as we were, purring over a circulation – temporarily boosted by the absence of *The Times* – which bordered on 1.5 million.

They were days when the smallest change anywhere in the newspaper led instantly to print-union demands. They pounced like cats on any fresh editorial initiative, however minor. Those directly involved in any change got more money. Those indirectly involved then complained that their differentials, jealously guarded by all the unions, had been eroded. Disputes would follow. Late one night there was a 'go slow' in our foundry. 'Why?' I asked. It was because the four-day week had been granted to some other section and to maintain their differential the foundry was demanding a three-day week – in return for £12,000 a year. Not surprisingly therefore management dreaded innovation and did all they reasonably could to discourage me from burdening the newspaper with it. In my travels I became increasingly jealous, not simply of what was being done in countries like America, but in smaller countries as well. I visited Finland. Their principal newspaper made us

302

look drab. This is where, looking back, the print unions did us lasting injury.

A check done in 1980 showed that the wage drift – that is money paid out above the going rates – among the production workers amounted to something like 40 per cent. No business could long survive on those terms. On top of that, there was a good deal of downright swindling. At one point the Inland Revenue found themselves with 16,000 names for casuals on Saturday nights. They whittled this down to 7,000. In reality there were some 2,000 men involved in Saturday-night production. The discrepancy arose through men giving a different name at every attendance in order to avoid tax. Some, it was said, signed themselves in as Mickey Mouse. At one point, I recall, the militants demanded a fire drill in working hours. It was pointed out to them that this must involve calling a roll. The proposal was dropped like a hot brick.

In 1982, we ran into a new sort of dispute over the Health Service workers' strike. The print unions demanded that we print statements in support of the strike. The TUC staged a 'Day of Action' which printers were required to support. Failing editorial backing for their support in this *Alice in Wonderland* world, there was disruption. I wrote an angry editorial:

> On at least one day this week, our readers will be deprived of copies of this newspaper ... The failure to deliver will be due, not in the language of our trade to 'production difficulties' but to the decision of the TUC to stage a day of action, ostensibly on behalf of hospital workers. In support of this, leaders of two print unions have instructed their members to withdraw labour. The decision is unashamedly political. By no stretch of the imagination can it be seen as furthering the interests of their members ... Given the financial state of national newspapers just now ... earnings will be lost ... in

the longer run jobs will be endangered. For the second time in recent weeks, Fleet Street newspapers collectively will be hit to the tune of about £2 million. No member of the nursing profession will be a penny better off . . .

It helps to convey the atmosphere of those times.

In July, I learned from the night editor and general manager of an arrangement whereby the print union SOGAT paid £250 for an advertisement, which was well below the rate, and at the time stipulated that the cheque be sent to Bart's Hospital. In effect, we gave them the space for free. I put this to Hartwell, who bravely ordered all those concerned to put their foot down and refuse the demand.

In the November of 1982, things reached a point where the general manager felt impelled to send a warning of impending disaster to all departments. In the preceding year, he pointed out, Fleet Street had collectively managed a surplus of some £8 million, less than 1 per cent of total revenue. In the current year, he went on, costs had risen, a world recession had continued, and Fleet Street's collective losses had amounted to £29 million. Disputes, it was reckoned, accounted for £10 million. Days of action and prolonged railway strikes had added to production costs. The future, he warned, was grim. Not unnaturally, our readers were becoming fed up with a lamentable service. I got a sense of this through the letters they wrote to me. One of them from a working-class family is worth reproducing:

Dear Sir,

We have read your newspaper daily for about ten years, putting up with the appalling spelling mistakes and paragraphs which have words missing or complete lines misplaced or left out.

Recently new neighbours moved in next door. The husband who is in his thirties told us he is a copy-reader at the

Daily Telegraph. Our first amazement was the amount of time at home he enjoys. He told us quite unashamed he works a three-day week. Officially he is on a four-day week. He is at present off work for a week, holiday we thought. Apparently, he is home sick, as it is his turn on the 'sickness rota' which he told us is arranged in the reading room so that the wages of all the men in the reading room can be supplemented by sharing out weekly a sickness fund ... This particular man is one of approximately thirty copy-readers who are bringing home wages of £350–£400 a week. I wonder if the reading room is a unique institution or if management is turning a blind eye throughout the building. I feel sickened by the power and greediness of men who work on a newspaper I have in the past unwittingly supported by buying each day, so now I have stopped ... I understand for obvious reasons my letter will not be printed, but I feel so angry I intend trying other avenues like a radio phone-in to inform *Telegraph* readers of the kind of men and newspapers they are supporting.

One of the last of these humiliations occurred during the miners' strike of 1984. Our industrial correspondent warned me that the miners would be marching down Fleet Street and would expect to meet editors and discuss their handling of the dispute. Granada Television telephoned to my secretary and asked if I would be willing to account for my own performance with two miners' representatives in a filmed interview. Originally, the miners' representatives had required editors to leave their offices and meet them in the street. I drew the line at that, and said we would meet, if at all, in my office. This was allowed to pass as adequate penance. In fact, I found my interview with a group of miners instructive and at times moving. What I objected to was having to hold it under duress.

The night is darkest, they say, just before the dawn. Eddy Shah, a figure unknown in Fleet Street, was engaged in a crucial battle at Warrington. Pickets, organized by the National Graphical Association, were trying to stop publication of his group of newspapers, and in particular the *Stockport Messenger*, because he was employing non-union labour. The battle of Warrington began to attract national attention. In another corner of the world there was planted in the minds of Rupert Murdoch and his henchmen the seeds of Wapping. As Clough put it:

> For while the tired waves, vainly breaking,
> Seem here no painful inch to gain,
> Far back through creeks and inlets making
> Comes silent, flooding in, the main.

I knew nothing of what lay ahead, as I greeted rather wearily the start of 1985, and what turned out to be a decisive year in the life of the *Daily Telegraph*.

21

Resignation

In 1985, it seemed to me, our troubles at 135 Fleet Street came as 'not single spies, but in battalions'. On top of the anarchy of 1984, we had early in 1985 been given notice to quit Withy Grove, the Manchester plant where we printed our Northern editions. That meant that, as well as building a modern printing works in East London, we had also to find a new home in the North. Taken together, the cost of modern facilities in the Isle of Dogs and at Trafford Park, Manchester was put at £104 million. And this, as Kenneth Fleet, our former City editor, then with *The Times*, remarked in his column, was 'an investment way beyond the company's own capacity'. We also expected to spend another £38 million buying out superfluous labour and costly practices. (The scale of these payments ranged from £25,000 to £37,000 a head.) Such outlay spelt the beginning of the end for the Berry dynasty in Fleet Street, which went back to 1915, the year William Berry, later Viscount Camrose, purchased the *Sunday Times*.

Withy Grove was a huge warehouse in Manchester, converted into one of Europe's largest printing plants. Together with the *Daily Mirror*, the *News of the World* and others, we rented its facilities from the Thomson family, which was pulling out of the country. With its closure went 876 printing jobs. On my occasional visits to Manchester I had grown fond of the place. Its sheer ugliness was endearing. One day during my time as editor, I was asked by a friend in America to entertain a prominent woman journalist when she came over to London. We were to meet at 135 Fleet Street at one o'clock. At quarter-past-one with no word of her, I walked down to our hall and found her sitting patiently on a pile of matt boxes destined for our Manchester office. The porter at the lodge had simply omitted to call me. Full of shame, I began a grovelling apology. As we walked out, she slipped a comforting arm through mine. 'Don't worry,' she said, 'all the great newspapers of the world come out of slums.' Whenever I visited Withy Grove, I thought of her.

Our position at the *Daily Telegraph* early in 1985 was confused and disheartening. We had gone to the City of London in search of fresh capital. We were in the throes of installing an expensive new photo-composition system – without securing agreement on whether it would be mainly in the hands of journalists or printers. We were still turning out a paper full of blemishes, though by some miracle the circulation was holding at around 1.25 million copies a day.

At the back of the shop, we were in effect playing a gigantic game of musical chairs. Our new printing plant in the Isle of Dogs was designed to ensure that when the music stopped hundreds of production workers would find themselves without chairs to sit on. Our faltering movement towards that brave new world reached its nadir in the third week of May 1985. My note for that week read as follows:

Chaos. (1) Line in the hands of temporary operators (some of whom did not speak the language) while six at a time train on the new machines. (2) Management invite these customers, flushed with the new deal, to take time out to discuss their income tax problems. Thus, a two-hour meeting 7.45–9.45 p.m. left the stone bare. Deputy printer and overseers rushed around with metal. Tax settled, men return and sling the paper together two hours late; 120,000 copies lost. Tuesday not much better. Encounter deputy printer, for once not trying to push cock-up over to editorial. 'This is the worst I have ever known.' Transpires that Express Newspapers next door were paying their temps £750 a week, or £36,000 a year, and so collecting the best. We limp along with our bottom rung on £500 a week, a mere £24,000 a year. Clearest signs since I took over that (a) management has lost control of the workforce downstairs, (b) the dissidents, who don't like the agreement and want yet more money (including chapel officials), are determined to screw it up. Just as the DT is in the City for £100 million!

Week's efforts produce 504 letters from readers enraged by the type mess and literals. Show to Hartwell on Friday evening and suggest an apology or statement. He moves this over to the deputy managing director. 'Yes, sir!' But an hour later has second thoughts; it might interfere with some mythical new understanding. Hartwell rings me, and says 'Not yet!' Meanwhile dummy pages arrive which are designed to give the DT a much needed stronger impact; but the leader and op-ed pages remain in limbo. There will never be a moment when those pages, skilfully redesigned by Liz O'Hanlon at my request, are ripe. Yet, as have said over and over again to H, new tech won't make us look less grey. Visual impact comes from us, not the machines!

In his endearing way Hartwell appeared unperturbed by the grey mists swirling round him, and kept me on the hop with his zest for detail. Our daily entry on Birthdays was very important to him. Every month the social editor sent to me for discussion with Hartwell birthdays that had appeared in *The Times* but not in our own newspaper. We had certain club rules attached to these birthdays which took me a year or two to master. After that, I began to submit my own suggestions. They all had to be good chaps, so it was sometimes a struggle to secure a woman's entry. Our methods were of course hidden from the readership. One evening in 1985 Hartwell handed me a letter from a peer who had had the temerity to ask for his birthday to be included, and asked me to reply to him. I was pleased with the result: 'Our Birthdays are in charge of our Social Editor, a lady in whose hands I am as clay to the potter's wheel. All I can do, in return for your letter, is to approach her tactfully. That I will do.'

This was not too far from the truth. In all matters of protocol and etiquette our social editor, Maureen Laker, was unchallengeable. The Speaker of the House of Commons once asked to see me privately. His private secretary was puzzled to find that when he submitted to our social page his list of those who were dining with Mr Speaker, the *Daily Telegraph* printed the names in a different order. As editor I knew better than to summon Miss Laker, but the next time we met I made tactful inquiries. 'But of course,' she said, 'the names I receive from Mr Speaker's secretary are not in the right order.' Mr Speaker's office took note of her ruling.

I persuaded myself there was wisdom behind Hartwell's sharp eye for small detail. It bore some relationship to the way good commanding officers, when inspecting my company during the war, found tiny and unlikely things at fault – and then somehow conveyed to me that they reflected gravely on my fitness to command. Another area which grabbed Hartwell was any reference by the BBC to our Gallup poll which failed to mention the *Daily Telegraph*. There was also sense in this. We were paying large sums of money for the Gallup service, partly to promote the *Daily Telegraph*. Hartwell saw those who pinched our Gallup service without attribution as thieves.

Behind these light skirmishes with Hartwell, who rarely discussed family matters with me, I sensed that a bigger and perhaps decisive battle was looming. Early in the summer of 1985 other newspapers reported that our attempts to raise £30 million of fresh capital in the City were meeting with resistance from institutional investors. Unknown to the rest of us at the time, Hartwell and his senior managers flew in Concorde to

Resignation

New York, held a brief meeting with Conrad Black, a wealthy Canadian industrialist, and flew back on the same day. In return for a 14 per cent stake in the *Daily Telegraph* and a seat on the board, Conrad Black had agreed to provide £10 million towards our complex refinancing package. It was a shrewd move, for as the *Financial Times* reported in June:

> Mr Conrad Black, the Canadian financier, who emerged this week as a 14 per cent shareholder in the *Daily Telegraph*, has been granted an unusual option, which could lead to his taking control of the newspaper group.
>
> In a deal with Lord Hartwell, the 74-year-old chairman of the Telegraph, Mr Black, 40, will be able to match any bid from a third party, should Lord Hartwell and the Berry family wish to sell their 60 per cent controlling share block.

Naturally this led to headlines such as one in the *Guardian* 'Pact on Berry shares could win Black control of Telegraph'. As editor, I found the next few weeks strenuous. Naturally, colleagues wanted me to explain everything. I knew better than to cross-examine Hartwell about his business, and I refrained from doing so now. I felt no resentment about his reticence; it was part of the compact an editor made with Hartwell. Having appointed you, he left you to edit the newspaper and you left him to manage his business.

He was also generous in allowing me to follow my nose on likely stories overseas. I found short intervals of being a reporter again indispensable. Early in the summer of 1985 a senior figure in the Japanese embassy in London gave me an expensive lunch. He had a message. The collapse of the regime in the Philippines, run by President Ferdinand Marcos and his extraordinary wife Imelda, seemed imminent. That would put a question-mark over America's Clark Air Force base and the Subic Bay naval base in the Philippines. If they went, Japan would be concerned because the balance of power in the Pacific might shift. This was around the time when President Gorbachev had spoken of the Pacific as a lake that must be shared. I pricked up my ears at this, and obtained brief leave of absence from Michael Hartwell.

Then I got in touch with Ian Ward, who was our roving correspondent in the Far East, based in Singapore. He knew the Philippines well, and had influential friends there. I flew out via Kuala Lumpur, where there was a meeting of Asian ministers and met Ward in Manila. He set up rapid arrangements by telephone. Within an hour or two he had set up a dinner party with Imelda Marcos at the Palace and an interview there with the President on the following morning. There was a background to this unexpected welcome. America, which had hitherto courted the Marcoses, largely because of the bases there, was growing restive. It had wind of what my Japanese friend had told me in London. President Reagan had been warned to be careful. In these circumstances, a newspaper editor from London was a welcome guest.

On the appointed evening Ward and I appeared punctually at the Palace and were joined in an enormous gallery by what they called a Blue Lady, otherwise a lady-in-waiting. She was Carmen Nakpil, mother of the first Filipino beauty queen. She had the good sense to order both of us whiskies and sodas. But, before these could arrive, doors were flung open, lights blazed and we were led into the presence. It was a large drawing room, full of flowers and signed portraits of the world's leaders. The place was brilliantly lit because the cameras were turning. I sat on a sofa next to Imelda, longing for my whisky. The television men outnumbered the guests. It had been a 'terrible year', she told me. Drought, floods, financial difficulties, the Americans behaving badly, her husband's illness and the killing of Aquino. 'A political disaster,' she said, looking me in the eye. Benigno Aquino, opposition leader and main rival to Marcos, had been shot dead at Manila airport on his return from America in circumstances that stank. Fearful of interrupting Imelda's tale of woe, the servants withheld my whisky for twenty minutes. On the strength of it, I sustained a forty-five-minute *tour d'horizon*. At most dinner parties the banter takes place over cocktails, the serious talk over dinner. Imelda Marcos reversed this convention.

Seven of us eventually sat down to dinner, Imelda, her Blue Lady, the British ambassador and his wife, the deputy governor of Manila, Ian Ward and myself. Over five courses and four wines, she told us the story of her life. She was one of eleven children, all of whom played different musical instruments. When she married Marcos, without parental consent, he was relatively poor. She had spent half of the housekeeping on flowers, because their love had to be surrounded by beauty. Occasionally during this recital I glanced at this astonishing figure in her short black silk frock adorned by a single jewel, and pinched myself. Soon, surely, I would wake up and discover that it was all a dream.

She spoke of her aunt, with whom General MacArthur had been in love. Once as a child she had seen them from an upstairs window on the beach in a passionate embrace. We heard of her encounters with Colonel Gaddafi, whom she found 'macho' and who had implored her to embrace the Muslim faith. He had sent her a romantic telegram. But when they had been alone together, her line had been, 'You are a good man and a religious man . . .' Although he was 'very macho', that had kept him at bay. So it went on.

At midnight, in the best tradition of the Foreign Service, our ambassador pushed his chair back a little and murmured, 'First Lady, we have to thank you for a delightful evening.' Mrs Marcos ignored him. When eventually the evening came to a close, and we were waiting for our cars in the early hours of the morning, our ambassador approached me. 'I am indebted to you for an unusual experience,' he said. 'Not one we are likely to repeat in our lifetime, Excellency,' I replied. Ward and I returned to our hotel at 2 a.m. and decided to spend another hour jotting down everything we could remember of this experience before going to sleep. Next morning we paraded for a formal interview with the President. It was not nearly so entertaining.

I returned, refreshed, to the toils of the *Daily Telegraph*. In mid-July Hartwell wrote a long explanatory letter to our readers which appeared on our leader page. It sought to explain our difficulties in raising enough money to take the *Daily Telegraph* into the twenty-first century. Travel often alters the set of one's thinking, and at this point I began to wonder privately, as speculation about Conrad Black's further intentions grew, just how much Hartwell wanted to stay on. He had lost in 1982 his talented wife, Pamela, who was a fighter. She might at this point have put out a strong supportive hand. But neither of Hartwell's sons, Adrian and Nicholas, showed any desire to succeed their father on this bed of nails – small blame to them. We had at one point dabbled with the Fairfax group in Australia, but they had plunged into a crisis largely of their own making. No one else was on hand. Hartwell was seventy-five and suffering from a painful back. Most of those closest to him, including myself, were very senior citizens.

On the evening of 19 June, when I went to see him he shed enough of his reserve to say: 'We have a pack of trouble.' We had indeed. The bankers were still mulling over the deal. There had been a breakdown in talks with our journalists in Manchester – a constant trouble spot. Journalists in London, looking for extra payments for work done to make up the printers' deficiencies, were disappointed and threatening to withdraw goodwill. The engineers downstairs were having a row with their own union about who should sweep the machine-room floor. A union official had been called in, but was too drunk to conduct the business. There was a picket line in Shoe Lane. The general manager reported that because of this only one lorry had been able to deliver newsprint. The other lorries with deliveries to offer were running out of tachograph time. I noted drily at the time: Lord Hartwell's patience, if it lasts out, is to be admired.

Next morning, bless his heart, I received a typewritten note: 'No doubt you are investigating why the caption to the Peterborough cartoon this morning was omitted. As it was, it made no sense.' Around this time I took a telephone call from Eddy Shah, who had his own plans for the new era, and was preparing to launch his newspaper *Today*, based on new technology. Because my son Jeremy was working closely with him, we were on friendly terms. Shah called to convey to me that if he could be of service to our newspaper he would do all in his power. This, he said, was out of personal regard for Hartwell. Any such gesture would remain strictly private. After his battle at Warrington, Shah had become a seasoned soldier in a field where the rest of us were still in training camp. I conveyed the message, though I sensed we had passed the point when such an offer counted. I felt deeply pleased that my son had chosen to work for such a man.

By September we were making slow progress in the transfer to photo-composition. We had, I reflected sadly, acquired new technology but retained the old problems. A senior friend on the business side of the newspaper came to see me. Our loss in the first half of 1985 had been of the order of £5 million. Wage drift had cost us £3.5 million – £400,000 of it to journalists. We had no overdraft facilities. Everyone was too optimistic. 'They're always on the optimum,' he said sadly, 'which never materializes in Fleet Street.' Heavy spending cuts, he warned me, lay ahead. He was right. By November we were in financial crisis.

On the afternoon of 21 November someone rushed into my news conference to say that Lord Hartwell had collapsed at a board meeting. A coronary unit had been called. I had by then some experience of Hartwell's sudden collapses. Called on to address a staff lunch many years earlier, he had fainted. At a small private lunch for the Fairfax brothers in his own dining room at 135 Fleet Street, he had suddenly fallen unconscious. So when news of this collapse reached me, I was economical with alarm. 'Well,' I said, 'let's give him a good newspaper tomorrow,' and carried on. A little later Peter Eastwood, managing editor, returned to my room to say it had been a false alarm. It had been one of his fainting fits. My relief was short-lived. Half an hour later Hartwell's faithful secretary, Eileen Fuller, was at my door. Lord Hartwell, she said, had been taken home, looking grey. The family had gone to Cowley Street.

At this point in our fortunes, my mind switched to public relations. *The Times* called me on the telephone. There were ambulances outside our office. What was amiss? Management descended on me. I suddenly felt extremely bossy. Draft a statement, I ordered, and issue it. What was it to say? they asked. I proposed suitable words – 'And put it out on Press Association (PA) creed,' I said. As soon as my room was empty I called up Adrian Berry's sensible wife, Marina. She was faintly reassuring. Her father-in-law went to bed too late, she said, and smoked too many cigarettes. He sat up waiting for the first edition to start up, staring into the distance and smoking up to 1 a.m. Later, Adrian called me. We recalled past collapses. Yes, he said, but he had not liked the noise his father had made as he went under. Ah, I said, recalling my own experiences, it is alarming!

As autumn drew about us, I sensed final days for the old order. In the light of our losses, stringent economies were announced. There was talk of imposing editorial budgets – something unheard of at 135 Fleet Street. Coopers and Lybrand, the accountants, had moved in. Andrew Knight, editor of *The Economist* since 1974, came on the horizon as a likely chief executive. At the smell of a wage freeze, the journalists grew restive and began to pass resolutions. Late in November they passed a motion of no confidence in their management, which they declared had brought the newspaper to the brink of ruin. Other people's headlines became gloomy about us. A message came from Hartwell's floor that his Christmas lunch had been cancelled, presumably on grounds of economy. This annual feast was held upstairs for around fifty relatively senior members of the newspaper. By tradition, the editor proposed the health of the proprietors, Lord Camrose welcomed newcomers of the past year, and Lord Hartwell replied wittily to the editor. I sent Hartwell a note, suggesting that he reinstate the lunch and allow us all to pay our share. When I saw him, he insisted that he and his brother Camrose paid. 'You two pay your whack,' I said, 'and let us do the same.' He asked to defer the subject. I did not press him and the lunch did not take place. 'He is a proud man,' someone said at the time.

Still the grip on detail was maintained. I find among my papers a memorandum dated 12 November and addressed to Hartwell which is headed: 'World Chess Championship'. It begins: 'Further to your memorandum to Mr W. F. Deedes dated 11 November 1985, we have investigated the possibility of producing a book reproducing all the games in the Championship.' By early December it became clear that Conrad Black was on the brink of winning total control. I saw Hartwell on the evening of 5 December. 'I seem to have lost out,' he began, adding that he would become a minority shareholder. He took me over the ground, starting with the original deal with the banks, the unexpected load of Manchester's new plant, bringing the total of capital needed to over £100 million. He spoke of the shortfall of £15 million, the visit to Black in America, and Black's later statement that if more money was needed, he would wish to have the option. He then showed me the official statement about to be made. He would remain for the time being chairman and managing director. H. M. Stephen, then managing director, would go early in the new year. Andrew Knight would become the new chief executive.

It was an embarrassing question, he admitted, but did I think the staff wanted him to remain on? I said that although the journalists were displaying resentment against management, particularly over the new technology deals, there was no animus against him. If he were to go, the change would be too abrupt. Both staff and readership would be reassured by his decision to stay on, I advised; adding that he should find a way of lightening the burden on himself. The business and the journalism of both newspapers were too much for one man. He smiled and said nothing.

We then turned to Andrew Knight, with whom Hartwell knew I was acquainted. I was in fact personally indebted to Knight for showing great kindness to my youngest daughter Lucy while she was working at *The Economist*. Hartwell pointed out that as well as being editor, Knight had also been chief executive of *The Economist* – which had a turnover of £60 million – and had found it too much and become editor only. I said I thought he would make a better chief executive than editor, because his political views had struck me as pretty middle of the road. I ended by saying that the Berry family had long been part of the *Daily Telegraph*'s ethos. At seventy-five, he would not wish to go on much longer, but if he stayed for a while it would make the break easier.

A week later I received an urgent call from him. He was distressed by an entry on our Court and Social page. There we had contrived to print twice an exceedingly long list of names attending the annual dinner given by Atlantic Richfield, then owners of *The Observer*. I promised to investigate. Taking second place on our agenda was the statement to come at the end of the week, which he showed me. He had decided to hold a press conference.

I told him that Max Hastings, who was writing a main feature about us for the *Sunday Times*, had asked to see me and that I had consented. This was some months before Hastings was asked to succeed me as editor. I proposed, I told Hartwell, to give Hastings my version of what had gone wrong. He, Hartwell, had got into difficulties because he had sought to put the *Telegraphs* on the right basis for the twenty-first century. To pull that off he had put at risk and partly lost his own autonomy. Hartwell affected not to understand what I was saying. I duly conveyed these reflections to Hastings. That same evening I attended a party and was struck by the kindness so many conveyed towards us. It stemmed, I reflected on returning to the office, from a feeling that the *Telegraph* under the Berry family had been an honourable paper. Dull perhaps, badly made up, ill-delivered; but, in times of doubtful standards, perhaps more valued than it had been in earlier years.

On Friday, 13 December, I wrote a long leader about ourselves which Hartwell passed without much fuss. The company's statement duly appeared, with very little new to me in it. Perry Worsthorne and I adjourned to the pub next door, as we had done many times before, and wallowed in speculation. Peregrine Worsthorne had joined the *Daily Telegraph* in 1953 and had been deputy editor of the *Sunday Telegraph* since its inception in 1961. We met regularly, often discussing the main leader-page piece which he wrote every Sunday. Arguing with Perry sustained my interest in serious politics. He expected Knight to take command whenever Hartwell went. He asked what I intended to do. I said that I had been ritually submitting my wish to retire as editor to Hartwell; and at the age of seventy-three I expected that wish would now be fulfilled. Whoever succeeded me, I added, must have control over the whole newspaper. (This eventually came to pass.)

Our next hurdle was the introduction of Andrew Knight to the troops. For this unpredictable event I was urged to take the chair. Knight's future role was still a matter of speculation. He was not to meddle with the editorial side, Hartwell assured me. Some hope, I thought; and reflected on the risk of battle lines being temporarily drawn up with Hartwell and myself on one side and Black and Knight on the other. It was reassuring to receive a note from Hartwell: 'Opera and Ballet. Whoever is responsible has forgotten this morning to put a cross-reference on the penultimate page stating that Opera and Ballet are on page 10.' I clutched it to my heart.

On the evening after Knight's address to the staff, Hartwell asked me for a report. The one area over which he intended to keep control, he repeated, was the appointment of the next editor. Had I views on who should succeed me? I mentioned Ian Ball, our New York correspondent and a senior figure – a card I had played before when offering my retirement. Too long in America, said Hartwell. Then he asked about our City editor, Andreas Whittam Smith. I replied cautiously, which was as well in the light of events about to unfold. Pressed on my choice, I named Charles Moore, who was by then editing the *Spectator*. His youth was against him, I agreed – he was not yet thirty – but that would do the *Telegraph* no great harm. I stressed 'character' and said it was important. During the Falklands War, though a relatively inexperienced leader writer on the *Telegraph*, Moore had forced his way to the front by his clear thinking. Hartwell remarked that he too was much impressed by him. Would Andreas Whittam Smith be expecting it? He had, I said, strong views about the way in which we were conducting our affairs. He had told management that they had cocked it up. I felt he was disenchanted with us. Hartwell and I then looked steadily at each other without saying anything.

After this, Christmas libations were welcome, but they were exceedingly short-lived. On 27 December I returned home after a jolly Christmas with my son and his family. As I entered my house the telephone was ringing in a threatening manner. It was Andreas Whittam Smith, asking if I had seen that day's *Financial Times*. No, I said truthfully. He then read aloud a story headed: 'New Quality Daily Is Planned'. He together with two of my leader writers, Matthew Symonds and Stephen Glover, were off to form a separate newspaper with City backing. He asked how I thought he should now proceed. I thought he should prepare a statement, and invited him to call me back with it, after I had talked to our own office. Gradually we sorted it out. The operation was confused by telephone calls from both Lord Camrose and Michael Hartwell, asking if I could explain to them what was going on. In the evening Hartwell called me again to ask if I thought that Whittam Smith might try to recruit staff from us. I thought it unlikely. My difficulty during many telephone calls from the different parties was to refrain from declaring what I thought I knew.

At some point during our crisis at 135 Fleet Street, Andreas Whittam Smith with the best of intentions and considerable knowledge of the City had approached Hartwell with his own ideas. He had been rebuffed – or felt he had been rebuffed – because Michael Hartwell was a very private individual. There was always an area in which those of us who thought we knew him well never ventured to enter. Rebuffed, and observing the amount of water entering the *Daily Telegraph* holds, Whittam Smith jumped ship, taking two of my closer colleagues with him. I felt no resentment, so I have never expressed it. The plight of the *Daily Telegraph*, which I have described and for which I bore some measure of responsibility, helped to explain why people felt the urge to jump ship. There might have been better ways of doing it, but in seeking to escape from what must have seemed to someone close to the City an impenetrable madhouse, run by geriatrics like myself, Whittam Smith had his reasons.

Fleet Street, as it was then and remains now, is a market place. Loyalties have never been deep there, not since my earliest days. Being conservative and unadventurous, I had remained with the same house most of my working life; but that did not lead me to despise those who played the market. The worst Whittam Smith and Co. could be accused of was naivety. They thought their plan would remain secret until they chose to reveal it. But people cannot keep such secrets now. Confidentiality is a lost virtue. Hartwell, who counted a lot on loyalty, was wounded. That distressed me. As for the rest, I fell back on a little nugget of philosophy which in the darkest days of Fleet Street I had picked up from our printer, Peter Turnage. 'Don't take it to heart, sir,' he would urge on our darkest nights. 'It's all part of life's rich tapestry!'

Some months later Glover and Symonds invited me round to City Road to inspect the new premises of the *Independent*. I was pleased to be asked, and felt rather jealous of their location. Compared with our isolation in the Isle of Dogs, they seemed enviably close to the heart of London. What they did by founding the *Independent* was good for journalism and journalists.

Early in January 1986 Hartwell asked Jock Bruce-Gardyne and myself to lunch with him and discuss a replacement for Andreas Whittam Smith. There was need to step warily for Andrew Knight had invited me to lunch on the following day to discuss the same subject. I felt uneasy about the strategy I saw developing. Hartwell would remain a nominal but reassuring figure at the top while the new regime was an unknown quantity; but the main decisions would be taken independently of Hartwell, who would then simply be confronted with a *fait accompli*. My thinking was about to be confirmed in dramatic fashion.

Over lunch next day at Brooks's, Knight and I went over the same ground without reaching any decision about the City. Then he asked about my own position. I spoke of the occasions when I had urged Hartwell to find a younger editor. Knight seemed to have persuaded himself that I wished to leave immediately. 'We need some glue,' he said. I resolved the matter by saying rather sententiously that I was a servant of the company and would do whatever they wanted. I spoke critically of the past editorial dichotomy and said it was imperative that the new editor was given overall control. We spoke of Hartwell and the strain imposed on him in recent months. His fortune as well as his control was threatened, for the family had used their own resources to finance the new production units. Knight then warned me that Hartwell might soon be faced with decisions he did not like. Within reason, I said, I would try to smooth the way.

One bright morning in mid-February just before noon I was called to Knight's room on the fourth floor. He began, uneasily, by saying he wished to impart a confidence unknown to Hartwell. My successor was to be Max Hastings. I signalled cautious affirmation. Perry Worsthorne, he added, would take over the *Sunday*. That delighted me. There followed a certain amount of shuffling by Knight. Was I free for lunch? Max might be free. Max was anxious I should stay with the newspaper. It would be good if we could talk soon. He then addressed himself to the main plot. Hartwell, so far kept in the dark about all this, would be informed by a combination of Knight himself, Rupert Hambro and Lord Rawlinson (both new *Daily Telegraph* directors) just before the board met at 2.30 p.m. It crossed my mind that, if they could startle Hartwell into resignation at that point on grounds of lost authority, they would not worry overmuch. But I had to agree that for the moment it would help things along if Hartwell did not explode. I would do my best to ease matters, I said. I left Knight's office sensing that the timing of all this had for some reason been brought forward. They were in a hurry.

Back in my room, Max was on the telephone, as if on cue. Lunch? He wanted to go to his club, which was Brooks's, but that was also Knight's club. I urged the Paradiso e Inferno, an Italian restaurant in the Strand where I had lunched guests for many years. On this of all days they had closed the basement, which is best suited for an exchange of confidences. So I found Max upstairs, concealing his immense height behind a very small table. He looked harassed but was full of goodwill. He had a book on the Korean War in hand, which he had to finish. I said he could count on any help I could offer.

On return to my office, I presented the picture to my

admirable secretary Susan Davey. She was unamused. At 6 p.m. I paid my usual visit to Hartwell, who opened: 'Have you heard the Black diktat!' Then he read me a long letter from Sir Frank Rogers, by then deputy chairman to Conrad Black, which was addressed to shareholders. Every line in it strengthened my hunch that developments elsewhere, perhaps Murdoch at Wapping, had created something like an emergency. John Thompson, who was leaving the *Sunday Telegraph* as editor, joined us. I concluded that Hartwell was upset, but still there. As we finished, I said gently in my unexpected role as peacemaker, 'Don't talk about Black diktats!' He smiled unresentfully.

My room that evening became like the VIP lounge of an air terminal. New chiefs and old chiefs turned up to offer me their version of events. I dispensed drinks to them all, so tongues wagged faster. It emerged that both Hastings and Worsthorne had been flown to Toronto for inspection by Conrad Black. As one might expect, Perry had a good tale to tell about his trip. Arriving at the wrong entrance, he had trudged up the Black mansion drive in snow, and arrived much the worse for wear with a bad headache. He asked for aspirin. Black made it clear that the house contained no medicaments, but a police car was sent humming to a pharmacy in the city. My final telephone call of the day came from Maggie Brown, then media correspondent of the *Guardian*. She made my departure sound part of the plot – which, in respect of Hartwell, it was. I decided to pull her leg. 'How many have you on the *Guardian* who have passed the age of seventy-two?' At this there was a burst of laughter from the guests in my room. 'It sounds as if you are having a champagne party,' she said. 'No,' I said, 'not champagne . . .'

It became even plainer to me that Rupert Murdoch's coup at Wapping had caught the *Daily Telegraph* on the hop. As Lynda Melvern explained in her excellent study, *The End of the Street*, it was the summer of 1984 that pushed Murdoch to the limit of his patience. By the start of 1985 he had drawn up his battle plan. Behind a tight ring of security his men worked on it through that year. A new plant was built under wraps at Wapping which was designed to bypass the print unions. By January 1986, they were ready to roll the presses there in a new world for British newspapers that had taken too long to be born. It was a revolution, and like most revolutions it became violent. There were furious clashes between print workers and the police at Wapping; but nobody could long doubt the outcome. In their different ways, Murdoch and Eddy Shah had turned the crazy world of Fleet Street upside down.

At the end of February, in my last week as editor, I attended a Newspaper Press Fund lunch. David English, then editing the *Daily Mail*, had been on a conducted tour of Wapping. It was unnerving, he said. There were eighty-five men dealing with the distribution of around 5 million copies of the Murdoch papers. The *Daily Mail* had been running 350 men for 1.5 million copies. They thought they had done well to reduce this to 150, but were still well out. At lunch I found myself sitting next to Sir Frank Rogers. Yes, he said, Wapping had changed things overnight.

On 7 March, I bowed out. I did my utmost to avoid a ceremonial exit, but only partially succeeded. There was a gathering in the Cheshire Cheese at lunchtime. Beer was served from barrels. Hartwell appeared. Peter Utley made a generous speech. I responded in the vein of Sydney Carton in the final lines of Dickens's *Tale of Two Cities*. I dwelt on the revolution going on about us and on the new city I saw arising. In the middle of the afternoon I received a call from 10 Downing Street. Could I possibly find time next day to help the Prime Minister with a speech? Mrs Thatcher needed no help at all. It was her kindly way of intimating that I would not be left out in the cold. Nonetheless I immediately accepted her invitation, and next day put in a hard two or three hours. 'Now who will pull all this together?' she exclaimed as we drew to a close. I explained that on the following day I would be leaving for a break in Australia, where my wife already was. Mrs Thatcher thought there would be no difficulty in getting a government office to transmit my work; but other counsels prevailed. The episode has stayed in my mind as displaying a side of Margaret Thatcher of which too little has been said. It was well put by Adam Lindsay Gordon, the nineteenth-century Australian poet:

> Life is mostly froth and bubble,
> Two things stand like stone
> Kindness in another's trouble,
> Courage in your own.

Many years later, at a dinner at Claridge's attended by the Queen and the Duke of Edinburgh to mark Margaret Thatcher's seventieth birthday, it gave me satisfaction in proposing her health to dwell on this unfailing 'kindness in another's trouble'.

After a day or two with my daughter in Melbourne I began to breathe through my nose again, but not for very long. Very early one morning soon after my arrival Andrew Knight was on the telephone. Mrs Thatcher, he said, wished to give a dinner party for me at No. 10. Half the guests would be hers, half would be mine. Would I therefore consider suitable names and submit them? It was very early in the morning. I had not entirely thrown off my jet-lag. I was in pyjamas, which creates an inferiority complex when you know the man on the other end of the telephone is fully dressed. This plan, I told myself unworthily, had more to do with the social aspirations of Andrew Knight than anything else. I became unreasonable and obstructive. There was an argument on the telephone, which I lost. At that stage, Andrew Knight was riding high. Most people lost their arguments with him.

22

Life under Max

I came back to England from Australia with no firm idea of what I most wanted to do. The *Daily Telegraph* had settled generously and endowed me with a pension. I did not feel much drawn to the House of Lords. Charles Moore, who was editing the *Spectator*, suggested one or two ideas for future articles. Both Andrew Knight and Max Hastings had written to me earlier, asking me to stay on as an editorial writer. But the newspaper under Max, I reflected, was undergoing a long-overdue shake-up and rejuvenation. I wondered where someone of seventy-three could usefully fit in there. Furthermore, this need for a drastic shake-up reflected to some extent on failures of the earlier regime. I did not see myself as a very good advertisement for the *Daily Telegraph*, but rather otherwise.

All this was settled for me soon after my return by a note from Max, hoping I was back, and asking when he might expect to see me in the office. I found the peremptory tone of the letter reassuring, and reported for work on Max's staff as leader and feature writer. He had already appointed half a dozen new editorial figures, among them John Keegan, the military historian, who joined as defence and military editor. Neil Collins had been brought in from the *Sunday Times* as City editor, Kathleen Samuel from a magazine to be fashion editor, Don Berry from the *Sunday Times* to give the paper an overdue facelift. Others were working out their notices elsewhere and due to arrive. They included Veronica Wadley from the *Mail on Sunday*, whom I came to admire as our features editor, Mark Boxer from the *Guardian* as pocket cartoonist. Max raided other newspapers ruthlessly for the staff he wanted, as well as firing freely. He earned the encomium he later received from Conrad Black for being 'good at drowning kittens'. But he was not altogether confident of his own political judgements – who is? – and found it comfortable to have someone around with whom he could occasionally share thoughts on the political scene. Only a few days after I got my feet under the table, an international event occurred which threw an unexpected political challenge to the Hastings regime. US Air Force bombers, using British air bases, raided Colonel Gaddafi's Tripoli. Max, who was nothing like as gung-ho as he sometimes made himself out to appear, was critical of the raid and wrote an editorial on those lines. He asked me to rustle up fast a signed article on the raid's likely impact on our relations with America.

I thought there were mitigating circumstances and said so. Conrad Black, who claimed the right to express a view when American affairs were on the agenda, was, as P. G. Wodehouse so felicitously expressed it, if not disgruntled very far from gruntled by the leader. Max was made aware of his feelings. With endearing candour, Max confided to his leader-writing staff that he was anything but flavour of the month with Black. The episode gave my self-confidence, which was low, a small boost.

Early in June 1986 Mrs Thatcher gave the dinner party at No. 10 to mark my retirement as editor on which Andrew Knight had been so insistent. The dinner took place on the 5th, which coincided with Floodlit Beating Retreat on Horse Guards. So after dinner on this warm summer night the upstairs windows of No. 10 were thrown open and the guests were able to enjoy the spectacle as well as chatting among themselves. There were roughly twenty-five of the Prime Minister's guests and twenty-five of mine. At some point during the evening, Eddy Shah, one of my guests, struck up an understanding with

Andrew Knight, a consequence of which was an agreement that my son Jeremy should leave Shah and join Conrad Black's *Daily Telegraph* as editorial director. I am not especially good at being a guest of honour, and found it difficult to respond to Mrs Thatcher's generous words adequately. I defy anyone not to find such an evening a strain. Happily, everyone else seemed richly to enjoy another demonstration by the Thatchers of kindness to their friends.

From then onwards, life at the *Daily Telegraph* gradually became for me more enjoyable than at any time in the previous fifty years. Max Hastings offered me every encouragement to write special articles, as well as leaders, some of them from overseas. I think every journalist needs to take to the road from time to time. I thought up several expeditions; Max proposed others. For his own reasons, he was unenthusiastic about editorials on South Africa, which had long interested me, but he gave me a free hand to go there and write under my own name. Towards the end of June 1986 I went to Johannesburg and Durban and wrote one or two long pieces. The country was approaching an hour of decision about apartheid, but different people were at different stages down that long road.

As a fairly sensitive visitor to South Africa, I had detected from the late 1970s onwards among intelligent Afrikaners awareness that things could not go on much longer as they were. Those whom I had come to know well would privately explain their misgivings to me. I became increasingly moved by the tragedy of it all: this most beautiful country arousing fierce passions in the world as well as within itself. I had the luck early on in my association with South Africa to become a close friend of Tertius Myburg, who was then an outstanding editor of the *Sunday Times* in Johannesburg and a respected figure. His appointment as South Africa's ambassador to Washington surprised nobody. I found his sudden death before he could even take up the post hard to bear. Under his editorship, the *Sunday Times* was uncomfortable reading for the Nationalist

Government; yet in private conversation Tertius always saw both sides sympathetically. It made him a valued counsellor.

On one of my visits, our correspondent there for many years, Chris Munnion, urged me to visit the Voortrekker Memorial in Pretoria. It would give me insight, he claimed, into the nature of the Afrikaner. A contemplative hour there would clarify my mind. I took his advice. Taking an unhurried look at the ox carts, the giant bibles, the story of the great trek and so on told me more in a short space of time than a dozen books. Chris Munnion and his wife Denise had by then become close friends – he and I had worked together in Rhodesia during Ian Smith's final years of defiance.

Life under Max was like the war again. There was always a risk of getting wounded, but there was also the chance to win medals. How fortunate, I told myself, to come under Max's command at this stage in my life and not during the war. He would have made a fine and fearless brigade commander and would have been highly decorated, but casualties in the brigade would have been high. As it was, my telephone might ring early in the morning: 'I don't know how you feel about this, but I would tremendously like to see a piece about . . .' Max also possessed a fine sense of mischief. Someone, letting their imaginations run a bit, would make some outrageous suggestion at his leader conference. 'Why don't we say that!' Max would exclaim. Oddly enough, it usually came off.

My missions were diverse. At one point I went off to Morocco for a week to report the filming of Evelyn Waugh's novel of the Abyssinian War, *Scoop*. The producer, wisely, had decided that his cameras would not be welcome in Abyssinia which since the revolution of 1977 had become Mengistu's Ethiopia. After an extensive search, he hit upon a downtrodden village close to the Sahara Desert which on a dull day could be mistaken for parts of Addis Ababa. We occupied a surprisingly comfortable hotel on the edge of the desert, said to be popular with honeymoon couples who desired to see dawn over the

Sahara. It made a good news feature. In September Max sent me off to Washington to report Congressional hearings on what had been happening in the White House during the Iran War. Too many acolytes in the White House had been exceeding their authority in President Reagan's name. A patriotic but wayward figure named Colonel North had been waging an undercover war of his own.

Instead of the dismal business of trying to produce a newspaper in the teeth of a gale from the print unions, I was back in front-line reporting – with an editor willing to make the most of what I sent him. No journalist could ask for more. I developed a sharp ear for Max's wishes. 'Latin America,' he would muse at our conference. 'Lot going on there ... we ought to look more closely.' 'Would you like me to have a go?' I would murmur. 'I wish you would.' By lunch time the flights would be booked.

Less ambitiously, I suggested a sentimental journey back to what in pre-war days were known as the Distressed Areas – Tyneside, West Cumberland, Liverpool, South Wales. I had seen a lot of them in the mid-1930s. Half a century on, I went back to Newcastle and Jarrow and Maryport. We had a splendid girl working up there as our Northern correspondent, Chris Tye. She made most of the arrangements and we travelled round together for ten days. I found it a moving experience to be back in the shipyards of Jarrow. We did the tour in winter. The hard young men of Newcastle stood at certain points in the City in their shirtsleeves. 'I don't know what they are trying to prove,' said Chris Tye. Nor did I, but it carried my mind back to 1939–45, when 50th Division, based on the Tees and Tyne, produced some of the hardest soldiers of the Second World War. They were used in every one of Montgomery's main assaults from the Desert through to D-Day.

Early in 1987, Max suggested a return to the Philippines. The revolution had taken place a year earlier. The Marcoses had been noisily but bloodlessly removed. In romantic circumstances Mrs Cory Aquino, widow of the assassinated Leader of the Opposition, had become the people's choice as President. When travelling overseas, I rarely sought interviews with top people unless I happened to know them. It can waste a lot of time in return for very little. Presidents rarely say enough to justify the time taken in keeping the appointment. On this occasion I was asked by Mrs Aquino's staff to make a private call. I thought her an attractive woman and admired her courage. But to be called upon suddenly to take over the reins from the corrupt Marcos regime, in a capital seething with political intrigue, was asking a lot. I doubted if she would remain – or wish to remain – in office very long. It was the first anniversary of the overthrow of Marcos, when people had assembled at the big Highway Junction in Manila, had halted the Marcos tanks by sheer weight of numbers and given power to Aquino. I joined the vast crowd which reassembled there to mark the anniversary with Mass led by the Archbishop, a speech from President Aquino and a pop disco, in that order.

I also revisited the Palace which – not without difficulty – had been kept more or less intact since the departure of Ferdinand and Imelda Marcos. It took ten minutes to walk round her wardrobe rooms, which resembled a large department store. She had innumerable pairs of shoes, including shoes for the disco. Dazzling lights in the high heels came off a little battery. Lord Acton was right when he said that power corrupted and absolute power corrupted absolutely. Towards the end of their time the Marcoses had ceased to be aware that they were doing anything wrong. Power had rendered them amoral.

Early in 1987 Max and Peter Utley parted company. Max found his trenchant views on Northern Ireland unacceptable. Utley went to *The Times*. I was asked to take over his Monday column, called Commentary, which appeared on the leader page. It was supposed to consist of four different items, preferably with a light-hearted finish. I kept a notebook in my pocket and jotted down ideas that occurred to me from reading the newspapers, from personal experience, or from casual conversation. I found the column an outlet, especially when travelling abroad, because on all journeys there are small episodes which have no place in the news columns but are worth recounting because they illustrate the human comedy. *Daily Telegraph* readers love to write, 'Your recent experiences when flying to Katmandu reminded me of an incident which befell me in Chichester many years ago, and which you may like to hear about . . .'

Late in life, I learned under Max to write quickly – a feat much assisted by the advent of the word processor. During all my years in journalism, my ill-ordered mind had found it essential to scribble a draft of what I wanted to say on copy paper before typing it out. I recall the exciting day, soon after we had been introduced to the direct-input system, when I found I could put 1,200 words straight on to the screen, with a considerable saving of time – much enhanced by my touch-typing.

It helped, because Max was a sudden editor, apt to get good ideas late in the day. He could also write as fast as any journalist I have known and expected the same of us. During my brief training programme on the new machines, with Adrian Berry as my tutor, I received a visit from Conrad Black. Decent of him to call and find out how I was getting on, I thought; but he wanted to talk about something else after class. It turned out to be a trifling disagreement with something I had written from Washington about the President's relations with Congress. I knew better than to argue with Conrad about North America. At least he had read the piece, I told myself consolingly.

I was probably the only person working at the *Daily Telegraph* who saw Conrad Black in the improbable role of a fairy godmother. I had been closer to the Berry family than anyone else left on the newspaper. I felt gratitude towards them and affection for them. It followed that, during the closing years of Michael Hartwell's stewardship while I was editor, I suffered more private anguish about our doubtful future than most other people. As editor of the *Daily Telegraph*, I felt I had at least some responsibility for the future welfare of those who worked for it. Yet, because of our funny set-up, I could do little or nothing for them. In some ways, I found the ordeal of watching printers draw blood from an already anaemic patient of which I was fond more distressing than most of my wartime experiences. I found the final ruinous years of Fleet Street painful. Conrad represented the new order. I think Rupert Murdoch has debased the quality of British journalism and have often written to that effect, but I give him best over Wapping. As for Conrad, why look in the crystal, when you can read the book? – as Aneurin Bevan once exclaimed. He has presided over the making of a far more attractive newspaper than it was in my time. His politics are well to the right of Hartwell's and probably those of Max Hastings. But that does not appear to have altered the politics of the *Daily Telegraph*. It was in my day that critics dubbed the newspaper 'The Daily Torygraph'. The advent of Conrad Black has had the effect of putting a more powerful engine behind a very good newspaper. 'He's a tough cookie,' some of my friends tell me. When I look round the battlefield over which this country's national newspapers choose to conduct their business, I say devoutly, 'Thank God for that!'

Towards the end of 1988, Max suggested I revisit Ethiopia. He thought it might be fun to discover such landmarks as remained and I remembered from the Abyssinian War of 1935. It was a fairly hazardous undertaking, for the country was then in the hands of the tyrannous Lieutenant-Colonel Mengistu Haile-Mariam, General Secretary of the Central Committee of the Workers' Party of Ethiopia, President of the People's Democratic Republic of Ethiopia and Commander-in-Chief of the Revolutionary Armed Forces. It would be difficult to cram more Marxist crap into a single title. A civil war against the 'rebels' was still in progress and Addis Ababa had all the apparatus of a police state. I installed myself at the Hilton, which was then the only habitable hotel. It was comfortable in a limited way, but difficult to leave. Every journey in a hotel taxi had to be ordered in advance and registered at a booking office. For some reason the taxi was not allowed to wait at your destination but had to be resummoned by telephone when required. This proved expensive and time-consuming. Photography was dangerous. If you stopped to look at something and took out a notebook, the odds were on someone appearing suddenly and asking you to move on.

Notwithstanding the difficulties, I felt the journey should include a trip on the French railway which runs from Djibouti on the coast to Addis Ababa. In 1935 it had been the sole means of entering or leaving the country. After patient negotiations with the tourist office, I arranged to fly down to Diredawa, visit the walled city of Harar and return to Addis Ababa on the train. For this exercise, of course, I had to take a minder. This is a fragment from a long piece I wrote for the *Daily Telegraph* Week-End section:

So here we are, 50 years on, in Harar again on a golden afternoon, searching for traces of times past. When Evelyn Waugh first saw Harar in 1930 he was enchanted by its magic. Returning five years later for the war against Italy, he was disappointed. Much of the old beauty, he thought, had faded. Therefore I did not expect too much and was not disappointed.

One of Harar's few entertainments was to go at sundown to the outskirts of the city and watch the hyena man. He carried a bucket of raw meat and summoned the hyenas with the sort of cry piemen used to offer. A few of us stood in a group round him and the trick's climax came when he tossed a piece of meat only a few feet in front of us and the bolder hyenas would come forward and scrabble for it. Our return journey to Addis Ababa was memorable. I could hardly believe that the railway would be less comfortable than it had been in 1935, but it was. At one of many station stops my minder bought a bunch of greenery that turned out to be kat. He chewed this vigorously for the rest of the journey. By the time we arrived in Addis Ababa he was stupefied, and soon vanished. But, as Max had surmised, the adventure made a good piece. 'Lord Copper was right,' I thought irreverently when I saw it displayed on the front of our Week-End Telegraph. 'Lord Copper is *always* right.'

The requirements of Max Hastings apart, there were, at least in theory, duties to be performed in the House of Lords, which I had joined in 1986. When Mrs Thatcher had first proposed this, I was in two minds about it. I had spent the best part of twenty-five years in the House of Commons. My heart was in journalism, and that was where I most wanted to be during my remaining years. I wanted to feel free to travel wherever I chose. I doubted if I would find much time to attend the House of Lords. I therefore begged to be excused. This did not go down well. I had Mrs Thatcher's trouble-shooter, Willie Whitelaw, on my telephone. I was made to feel that I was behaving badly. 'Oh, well,' I said.

That resolved, I had to consider how much time conscience required me to give to the Lords. The matter was decided for me when on grounds of penury the *Daily Telegraph* took itself off to the Isle of Dogs. Communications with inner London via the newly built Docklands Railway were tenuous – and, at inconvenient times of the day, non-existent. There was a brief struggle in my mind between Max Hastings and the Chief Whip. Max won in the first minute of the first round. I made a maiden speech in the House of Lords. Thereafter I used the Lords as a platform for things I cared about, such as anti-personnel mines. On the rare occasions I have attended the taxpayer made a small saving. As a penance for neglect of duty I claim none of the attendance allowances.

Neither South Quay, where we began life on the Isle of Dogs (which was later blown up by the IRA) nor the tower of Canary Wharf itself where we eventually settled, I have to add, were ideal perches for newspapers, simply because it took so long to get anywhere. Given a thirty-minute journey each way to, say, the Strand, the Isle of Dogs added an hour to time taken for lunch. Max Hastings felt this keenly. Conrad Black for good business reasons remained firm. Early in 1989 Max gave a lunch at Wiltons in Jermyn Street for Conrad and invited two or three of us to join it. The talk turned to our place of business and the problem of getting to or from it. Conrad asked how I got on. 'No problem for me,' I replied blithely, 'I travel on public transport. It is the men with limos who have problems.' (This was before the Limehouse Causeway had been built, and the narrow road to the Isle of Dogs was frequently gridlocked.) Conrad looked amused. Max, who foresaw a possible cut in executive cars, looked troubled. As we left Wiltons, Conrad pointed to his own limo, which was then an ancient Rolls-Royce. 'That is my limo, Lord Deedes!' I eyed it scornfully. 'I shall be back at the office before you are,' I retorted. Max's fears about executive cars proved groundless. A day or two later, he reported to me that Conrad was still laughing.

Even without travel, life with Max was never dull. One day he performed his 'drowning kittens' act by firing Carol Thatcher. She had worked successfully under me on the women's page. Her dismissal led to predictable repercussions. Andrew Knight supported Max's decision, but invited me to quieten things down a bit. I did my best. Carol herself behaved irreproachably. Eventually, with a sigh of relief, I enlisted the help of my son, Jeremy. Settling with drowned kittens was part of his responsibility.

There were consolations. Around this time, in the late

1980s, I made the acquaintance of Robert Runcie's pig, to which I have already referred. The then Archbishop of Canterbury kept his pigs next door to me, partly to assist a charity which cared for mentally handicapped adolescents. One of the pigs was named Harriet. All news of Harriet excited readers of my Commentary column. This was how it ended:

> Harriet, most charismatic of the Archbishop of Canterbury's prize-winning Berkshire pigs, is dead. She fought another younger and leaner sow called Poppy at the Archbishop's pig headquarters at Aldington in Kent, exhausted herself and suffered a heart attack. The verdict was death by misadventure. The Archbishop has been informed.
>
> At the time of her death, Harriet was two and a half years old. Due to an oversight at her birth, she was never registered and so could not enter for Show prizes. She then unselfishly concentrated her efforts on producing prize-winners, first with Basil, who proved an unsatisfactory husband, and later with a boar named Butch Cassidy.
>
> Harriet first entered the lives of our own household [writes W. F. Deedes] in November 1987. My wife purchased her as a wedding anniversary present. When her bulk rendered her unmanageable as a household pet in our modest sty, we returned her to the Archbishop's minders next door. Although unshowable, she was widely admired in pig circles, and much enjoyed being photographed.
>
> This proved to be her undoing. Her death came about after a photographer had arrived to take pictures for a magazine. Harriet and Poppy were released from their respective homes for the benefit of the camera. Jealousies were aroused. Innumerable children survive her.

Such was Harriet's fame by then that they refused to let me keep this for my column. It was treated by the *Daily Telegraph* as front-page news. So was the triumph of one of her progeny at the Kent Agricultural Show. The Archbishop's winning pig appeared on our front page, in company with her attractive trainer, Tracey Davidson.

The fiftieth anniversary of the outbreak of the Second World War, which fell on 4 September 1989, led to a request that Clare Hollingworth, a highly distinguished war correspondent, and myself should appear on breakfast television. 'Not— likely!' I said. The *Daily Telegraph*'s promotions ladies applied pressures. Overnight in London? No problem. We would both be installed at the Savoy Hotel. We were due to appear at the BBC Television Centre at 8 a.m. We signed hefty bills for our Savoy Hotel suites and climbed into a limousine stacked with the day's newspapers. On arrival at the Centre, a wispy girl appeared and said: 'You both know the form?' No, we did not, and it dawned on me that nobody was altogether clear why we were there. The wispy girl explained that we were invited to select two stories from the day's newspapers, one about the war and one about something else. I had encountered this zany world before. Clare Hollingworth looked puzzled. We mulled over the newspapers together. I selected a *Sun* leader on Vera Lynn's complaint that youth was ungrateful to the war dead. Out of loyalty to my own newspaper, I also selected a *Daily Telegraph* exclusive about deadly catapults. Clare chose a story about the Auschwitz monastery, and a tale about Hong Kong.

It seemed already to have been a long day when at about 9.45 a.m. a blonde who had been reading the news moved from her desk to ours. She did her best, but was unable to conceal her cluelessness as to who we were or why we were there. All three of us suffered embarrassment in our different ways. I did my *Sun* leader turn. Clare spoke briefly of the monastery. I was embarking on the catapult story when the blonde called time. Clare, unaccustomed to the culture, looked put out. 'It is how breakfast television runs,' I tried to explain. 'They have very short attention spans.' She refused to be mollified. My attitude to performing on television or radio has always been co-operative. We are brothers and sisters under the skin. Do as you would be done by. So when I can, I do; but there have to be limits. One of mine is breakfast television, which is too early. The other is *Newsnight*, which is too late.

23

CARE

Late in the autumn of 1989 I found a fresh dimension to overseas travel for the *Daily Telegraph*. I formed a friendship with CARE (International) UK in London. In sub-Saharan Africa and in Asia, war and famine were attracting public attention. What aid and development organizations did in these emergencies was news. When in the summer of 1985 Bob Geldof put together the Band Aid concerts, they were watched by 1.5 billion people in 160 countries on television and raised an astonishing £40 million. I watched it with awe from the airport in Kuala Lumpur.

CARE, which was everywhere in the developing world, could spot situations which might also interest the *Daily Telegraph*. There were advantages in working with an organization that could offer fast access to sudden emergencies, transport over rough country, charter flights and a safe place in which to sleep at night.

CARE had been founded in the United States when the Second World War had ended. Europe, as I had seen at the time, was destitute, hungry and swarming with displaced people. CARE raised funds to dispatch millions of food parcels. From that beginning it grew into one of the largest aid and development organizations in the world, working in sixty countries.

My first acquaintance with CARE was fortuitous. On the last day of a visit to Ethiopia in 1988, a message came to me from Santha Faiia, wife of CARE's country director, Scott Faiia, inviting herself to tea. She sought my help in promoting an exhibition of her photographs. In return for tea, she asked me to dine that evening at their house in Addis. There I met Charles Tapp, then overseas director of CARE in London, later its UK director. I learned more about the condition of Ethiopia from Scott Faiia and Charles Tapp during that evening than I had gathered during my restricted week in Addis Ababa. We agreed to keep in touch.

In 1989 Frances Carroll, then responsible for fund raising and communications in the CARE London office, suggested a story in a south-west corner of Ethiopia. In this remote quarter of Africa lived the Borana people. A pastoral, semi-nomadic tribe, they occupied about 6,000 inhospitable square miles not far from the Kenya border. During the dry season, the human and livestock population became entirely dependent on a network of forty or so deep wells, some of them going far back in time. To bring water to the surface a chain of men was spaced at intervals of roughly six feet down each well. Supported by rough platforms of wood struts across the well, they rapidly passed water up from hand to hand in small leather buckets. At the top of the well water was tipped by the last man into a holding pond just above his head. Thence it was thrown up one final stage into long watering troughs. From these the camels, horses, cattle and small stock took their daily fill. They were led to the troughs in orderly processions by their drovers with the precision of a well-run international airport. Roughly built of earth, the troughs were liable to break down. One of CARE's projects was to make them more durable.

The Borana people and their livestock lived on slender margins. They could possess only as many animals as this primitive system at the wells could provide. Why, you may ask, was the water not pumped up? Apart from a liability to break down in inexperienced hands, water pumps would have destroyed this delicate balance on which the Borana people lived. It was one of those harmonious human systems which so many have sought and so few have found.

After a day or two at our embassy in Addis Ababa with Sir Harold (Hooky) Walker, then our ambassador there – and later our ambassador in Iraq – we trekked south in two CARE Land Rovers. I remember our journey for the variety of bird life we saw. That region of Africa has something like 400 different species, some of brilliant colouring. Santha Faiia and I took two days to reach the Borana people. There had been a tremendous fuss about my photographer from the *Telegraph Weekend Magazine* in London. All such magazine editors like to believe that there are only four photographers in the world whose stuff they are ready to use. Santha Faiia, I insisted, ranked with professionals. Moreover she possessed a fine head for heights and would stand on the brink of the deepest wells, and then tip forward on her toes to give the camera a direct shot down the shaft. I could hardly bring myself to watch her. We toured the wells, shooting scores of pictures and staying uncomfortably with CARE's local director, an amiable Indian and his wife who occupied a minute residence. Santha slept in their only spare corner. I slept on the floor of a tiny kitchen. There was, I recall, a hole in the mesh covering the kitchen window. Through this at dusk flew droves of hungry mosquitoes.

We decided on a forced march back to Addis Ababa in a single day. On arrival I seized the telephone in the Faiias' home to send my weekly column. I put in a collect call. The features editor told the operator that he had no idea who I was and my call was rejected. After half a century with the newspaper, I took this hardly. The bill for telephoning the column direct on a bad line cost more than £100, which I refunded the Faiias in American dollars. The *Telegraph Weekend Magazine* graciously accepted the pictures. CARE was happy. Santha consolidated her reputation as an international photographer. A year later, the Princess Royal opened an exhibition of her photographs of Ethiopia in London. 'Ethiopia is a very poor country,' I said.

'Not as poor as Bangladesh,' replied the Princess Royal firmly. I never argue with women.

In 1990, travels for the *Daily Telegraph* through Eastern Europe, South Africa and South America left no time for CARE trips, though in Lima, Peru I spent a day viewing its work in a deeply depressing shanty town. CARE was lighting bright candles in the darkness there by offering loans to tiny enterprises. The idea spread to a point where CARE was funding innumerable small businesses with loans totalling $11 million in twelve countries.

Towards the end of 1990, CARE urged me to look at what was happening in Sudan. It would need a minimum of ten days, the organization's staff thought, and suggested early in the New Year. I put it at the back of my mind. Then on 1 February 1991, a press release reached me from CARE: 'According to an urgent telex received today from CARE staff in Sudan, over 1 million people are facing starvation in the drought-affected area of North Kordofan.' CARE procured a visa for me. I consulted Sarah Errington, whom I had met through CARE and who was among the top international photographers. She knew the Sudan well and was about to go there. Her reputation satisfied the exacting standards of the *Weekend Telegraph*. They wished me joy. Alexander Heroys, then overseas director at CARE in London, arranged our itinerary. He had held command in the Brigade of Guards, which demands a lot of its soldiers. Sarah Errington and I met in Khartoum and, after a day or two's briefing, got ourselves into El Obeid. As soon as we reached the heart of the famine in North Kordofan, I saw the size of the story. The only professional competition came from the BBC. Jonathan Dimbleby had flown down there with a team, but Sarah Errington and I reckoned we were more mobile and could file faster.

Reporters need to be in the right place at the right time, and I have been lucky with the timing of some expeditions. We reached the scene in El Obeid just before the first big trucks carrying wheat came thundering down the long road from Port Sudan. They had been delayed by difficulties in reaching a deal with the drivers. We saw them off-load, then set off to watch the distribution of food to starving people. I remember with what dignity gaunt women came to the distribution centres to receive their portion.

Nothing in journalism lasts for long, but at the time this was serious news and we worked hard at it. I began to long for means to send something back to London. We finished up in Bara Town, from which Alexander Heroys, with his Guards Brigade ideas, had arranged for us to travel by our land cruiser across the desert back to Khartoum in a single day. We left before dawn, barely stopped, got briefly lost and stuck in the sands, and eventually staggered into the Khartoum Hilton around nine o'clock at night. We were unusually thirsty, because we were in Ramadan and our Muslim driver, while observing a strict fast between dawn and dusk, had been splashing himself liberally from our container of drinking water. My first test of any hotel in the world is how Reception behaves when you arrive exhausted after a long journey. The Hilton in Khartoum stands alone. Perceiving our condition and alcohol being out of bounds in Sudan, they served up long icecream sundaes on the counter while we re-registered.

Then they produced an ominous-looking message from my pigeonhole. On our first days in Khartoum we had lunched with the British ambassador. He noticed my interest in the Battle of Omdurman which had taken place near by and in which Winston Churchill had joined a cavalry charge. 'When you return here,' he said, 'I will take you out there.' Sucking down my icecream sundae, I glanced at the note. Our ambassador would be at the Hilton at five o'clock the following morning, so that I could see the Omdurman battlefield at dawn, the hour at which most of the battle had taken place. I made arrangements to ensure that I was woken at the right time. All of them broke down. Three minutes after my telephone rang just before 5 a.m. to say that I had a visitor, I was dressed, unshaven, unwashed and downstairs, ready to greet his Excellency and bodyguard. He was a wonderful guide. I forgot my weariness and relished his graphic description of the battle. We returned to breakfast at the embassy, which tasted delicious.

Meanwhile, CARE's experienced country director in Sudan, Rudy Ramp, thought that before writing I should talk with someone who could put the Sudan Government's case. I have always felt glad that I agreed to do so. Yes, the spokesmen told me, the Government faced a crisis in this famine which it could not, single-handed, resolve. It needed outside help, and was grateful to the aid organizations. But – this was said with great emphasis – once the Government gave the impression that it had surrendered responsibility for famine relief to aid organizations, it was finished. It could not therefore allow young enthusiasts from aid organizations to bang the table and give orders. Having been in government myself, I saw his point. I also saw the wisdom of Rudy Ramp in persuading me to hear the other side of the story. It was reflected in what I wrote. Jonathan Dimbleby in his film version charged the Sudan Government with gross incompetence and gave one of its Ministers, who was persuaded to talk, a roasting. Naturally, I preferred my version. When reporting emergencies from any country, I think it best to give the facts, but without screwing it up unduly for those who have helped you to get the story and have to stay on.

It was not quite the end of our adventure. Because Sarah Errington was staying on to make a documentary, she asked me to carry back to London the rolls of film she had shot for us. I thought nothing of it until the day of my departure, when our vigilant ambassador asked if I anticipated any problems on leaving the country. 'None,' I said airily. 'I'm just taking a few rolls of film for Sarah.' He looked thoughtful. 'I think,' he said, 'I will collect you from the Hilton late tonight and put you through the VIP channel.' I begged him to do nothing of the kind, because the flight was at some unearthly hour after midnight. He insisted and, with the full escort, collected me from the Hilton at around 1 a.m. and piloted me through the VIP channel. I was about to board the plane, carrying Sarah's films in my hand luggage, when a disturbing figure stepped up to me. 'Excuse me,' it said, 'but may I know your credentials for travelling through this channel?' Out of the corner of my eye I saw our ambassador looking anxious. One must never let the Foreign Service down. 'Peer of the Realm,' I replied loftily but truthfully. He stepped aside. Ten seconds later I was safely in the plane, hugging my hand baggage and Sarah's pictures. On my return to London and our office on Friday night, I found Max Hastings was in one of his gung-ho moods. To hell with the *Weekend Telegraph*. The story would run on the front and back of Monday's newspaper. I got some sleep at home and returned on Sunday to write the story, while shedding tears for Sarah's great pictures. A few appeared in black and white with the news story. The best of them never saw the light. A true professional, she forgave us.

In the last week of August 1991, I went to Moscow with the idea of a *Daily Telegraph* piece in mind. It was another lucky bit of timing, for the idea had arisen at one of Max's conferences in July. 'Would you like me to go?' I asked. 'Yes,' he said. So I booked a ticket for the first free space in my diary. A week before my flight, President Gorbachev was toppled in a coup. Boris Yeltsin, President of the Russian Republic, entered the stage, climbed on to a tank and defied the rebels. Violence broke out on the streets. The foundations of the Soviet Union began to quiver. I arrived in Moscow to find the *Daily Telegraph* staff of three, led by John Kampfner, working round the clock. I thought it well to trouble them as little as possible. It struck me that, because of what was happening, people in Moscow might feel willing to talk openly for the first time in modern history. I booked into the Hotel Savoy and hired an interpreter from the business section. We took to the streets and during the next three or four days spoke to a wide variety of people. 'After hours of such talk,' I wrote later in the *Daily Telegraph*, 'I have reached one conclusion. Women have borne the brunt of Russia's pain: while their men were in armies or Stalin's prisons, they have coped alone; have learned not to depend on men. Women speak from the heart, men from the head.'

On a sunny Sunday morning the interpreter and I went out to the monastery town of Zagorsk. There, among others, we found Lena in a park, rocking her baby's pram. 'A fine pram,' I said with grandfatherly intuition. Sad smile. 'Yes, but I can get no shoes for my baby. I can sew, I can knit, but I cannot make shoes!' – a cry heard from every mother in the country. We talked of her husband, a computer engineer in a fruit depot. She laughed. 'That is why you find me eating this apple.' Her mother-in-law in the next town had two cows. 'So twice a week we get milk.' But her mother-in-law had to fetch water and was growing old. 'So I am not typical. We exchange milk for food.' She had taken higher education, was a specialist in haematology. We discussed Communism. 'My mother understood it, said it was just a game.' Then the young. 'Our young people are not bad, many good.' Then suddenly her heart burst out. 'We must influence our system so that people are not afraid to show their feelings like patriotism, generosity. To write a love letter, I need feelings.' She turned her head away. 'Communism goes with all the other -isms, but the human spirit does not. Oh, it is so easy to command people when they are poor and depressed.'

On my return from Moscow, Anne Allport, who had recently become CARE's director of fund raising and communications, came to see me and asked if I thought there was work for CARE to do in Russia. I did not offer much encouragement. CARE saw it as a matter of conscience. There was acute human distress. In such circumstances, should an agency working in the Third World get involved with what might be termed the Second World? I saw it differently. The

Soviet Union was falling apart, with unforeseeable consequences that might overwhelm even so strong an organization as CARE.

In December of that year I lunched with Sarah Errington, my Sudan companion. After describing the grim civil war in Mozambique from which she had just returned, she urged me to get out there. She spoke of the 'boy soldiers' and how they were being exploited. CARE liked the idea, Max gave it his blessing. I planned the trip for early 1992. It fell to Anne Allport to make the arrangements with CARE in Mozambique; and because of the hazards involved she decided to come too. We flew to Maputo, the capital, via Johannesburg in mid-February and found that CARE's American director of operations in Mozambique, Joe Kessler, had chartered a small plane. In this, accompanied by his wife and Harlan Hale, a highly experienced African hand, we flew north for three days with stops at Inhambane, Quelimane and Nampula. Hale, jolly and rotund, was called 'Radio Harlan', because he knew so much about Africa. His optimism was welcome, for it turned out to be a more hazardous expedition than we had anticipated. In search of the mobile war round Quelimane, we never knew whether our plane was landing in Renamo- or Frelimo-held territory. To reduce the risk of small-arms fire our pilot, a very cool young man, spiralled down on to landing strips in the approved manner. On the ground we found in progress an exceptionally cruel war. Villages were changing hands frequently. There were nightly raids on enemy territory. Men, women and children were seized, brought back and corralled in pens, sometimes without clothing, food or water. Seldom have I witnessed such human degradation.

In theory peace talks were in progress somewhere; but, as we learned later in Angola and former Yugoslavia, peace talks often provoke the fiercest fighting, because both sides strive to establish a base line from which to negotiate. I reported to the *Daily Telegraph*: 'One listens to endless tales of rape and pillage, of children kidnapped and then trained to return and kill their parents, of what amounts to the destabilization or depersonalizing of children . . .'

This was what Sarah Errington had talked to me about. At the same time, I began to see some of the world's aid workers in a fresh light. They could not stop the fighting, they could only try to ease the pain. They lived in permanent discomfort and frequent danger. I was moved to write: 'The killing keeps up, the terror persists, plans fail, roads are cut off, convoys are lost, but the work goes on. For there is a spirit behind it which will never die.' As usually happens in these civil wars, countless families were torn apart, children were lost. At this juncture, early in 1992, the Family Tracing programme in Mozambique had documented nearly 10,000 unaccompanied children.

Our final port of call at Nampula was the last straw. Its main streets were pitted with enormous potholes, so that the shortest journey took a long while. We dined late with a large party in a noisy restaurant, dazzled by imported strobe lighting that ill-fitted the scene. Dog tired, Anne Allport and I were quartered in a run-down guest house. As I made my arrival in the dark, there was a power failure. For breakfast next morning we sipped hot water – which was the only available refreshment.

As often happens when one is very weary, I suffered acute depression and began to persuade myself that I might never see England again. Perceiving our plight as we flew south again, the pilot made an unscheduled stop on our flight from Nampula to Maputo which we had planned to do in one hop. We swooped unexpectedly – and fairly dangerously, because someone's knee got in the way of the pilot's controls – on to the little-known Ilha Magaruque, not far south of Beira. 'Paradise Found', the brochure said, and for an hour or so it did seem like that. From a small beach hotel, we bathed, relaxed briefly in the sun, ate a delicious lunch of prawns and rice, watched the fishermen coming in from the sea, took photographs, bought silly T-shirts and wound down. I admire aid workers who can give their services unremittingly amid scenes of human distress. The visitor who is not in training for such work needs an occasional break.

I filed my account of the war from the home of Chris Munnion in Johannesburg. It ran to 2,000 words that they were not expecting in London. As often happens when reporters think they have chanced their necks and earned a pat on the back, I received no glad acknowledgement, only a faint muttering about lack of suitable pictures. We had sent rolls of film by air; but it is never useful to argue about these things. Anne Allport contrived to raise a striking photograph from the CARE office in London. The piece ran in full over two-thirds of a page. It had the effect of drawing people's attention to the suffering and, when adapted by Anne Allport for a CARE appeal, raised a lot of money for relief.

We followed this up with a short and calmer trip to Lesotho, and returned to Johannesburg at the end of the month, thinking gratefully of a flight home early next morning, England, home and beauty. There was a message to call my office. 'If you are not feeling too done in,' they said cheerfully, 'Max thinks you might like to look into white feeling in South Africa while you are there.' At that point my telephone in the Holiday Inn Hotel at Jan Smuts airport broke down in despair. I spent a dispiriting couple of hours on Anne's telephone calling every acquaintance I thought I had in South Africa. They responded generously. Next morning after Anne Allport had flown back to London, I moved to the Carlton Hotel and spent three days taking white pulses. Max was right. It made a good piece.

It may well be that during this trip I felt, without being fully aware of it, a twitch on the thread. My uncle, Brigadier Sir Wyndham Deedes, after distinguished military service before, during and after the First World War, had decided while still a relatively young man to turn from public life towards the poor of Bethnal Green, and later to do what he could for persecuted Jews of Germany. I had resided with him in Bethnal Green during the years 1931–9 – without feeling, I have to say, the slightest compulsion to join him in good works. But his example may have lingered in the blood.

Up to this point I had seen these emergencies and the response to them simply as good news stories. With clear recollections of our last colonial days and the struggle of so many territories for independence, I began, as I have mentioned earlier, to see the aid organizations and the cohorts of workers from the UN agencies in a curious light – a new form of 'colonialism', I suggested to Anne, who disagreed. She emphasized the international and essentially humanitarian character of the work, and thus its distinction from colonialism. My view of aid and development as practised by non-government organizations like CARE is uncomplicated. The parable of the Good Samaritan applies. In all wars, all emergencies, innocent people suffer, and the prime function of NGOs is to reduce the suffering. How far aid workers may at the same time be fulfilling inner needs of their own seems to me beside the point. Most of us have mixed motives in anything we do.

Nor am I persuaded by the argument that aid organizations perpetuate conflicts by succouring one side or the other – and sometimes both sides. Most of them recognize this danger, and take steps to avoid it. In a world as open to the roving camera as this one has become, human disasters which would have stayed unnoticed half a century ago can no longer be hidden. To some degree aid organizations have to respond to the public conscience. What the public sees and deplores on television screens and reads in newspapers demands a response.

I recognize that the ethics of fund raising in emergencies sometimes raises awkward questions. A civil war breaks out. A famine suddenly occurs. News media focus on the event and report it vividly. People are distressed by what they see. The aid organizations tap this emotion to raise money, sometimes large sums of money. Okay? I think so, but it needs thinking about.

In these respects, on this and other CARE trips Anne

proved an illuminating companion. In fund raising for CARE, she was wholly professional. She could also stand back from time to time and survey with critical detachment the work in which she was strenuously engaged. This led to long and inconclusive discussions between us. The more I saw of Africa and its problems the more I found myself in the position of the apocryphal British judge who went to administer justice in India. After his first year, he wrote to a friend saying he was learning a lot about India. After ten years, he wrote saying he found there was a lot to learn about India. At the end of his time, he confessed he knew nothing about India.

In the summer after our return I was invited to become chairman of CARE's corporate council, which comprises British companies supporting CARE with four-figure subscriptions. It was a sinecure, but I thought carefully about it. As a rule, journalists should stay outside organizations on which they may have to report or comment. But one can be too sanctimonious about these things, so I agreed. CARE staff in London did most of the work. I occasionally lunched with company chairmen who showed an interest in CARE's work. But I knew that I had committed myself to an organization whose work I had come increasingly to admire.

Anne Allport and I chose a less venturesome expedition in Africa for early in 1993 and took a look at CARE's work in Zambia and Zimbabwe. They were territories which I had first visited at the time of the ill-starred Central African Federation. Recollections of those early days floated through my mind as we arrived in Zambia at the end of March 1993 in what we were assured was the first Boeing 747-400 to touch down at Lusaka's airport. We always travelled at low cost, but we also travelled sensibly; and under Anne Allport's guidance I learned to bring the right clothes. Over and again we found ourselves at occasions with Africans in their smartest clothes. From the humblest of dwellings, African women would appear beautifully dressed in high colours. They deserved better than

T-shirts, jeans and scruffy trainers. Anne turned out in the best from Harvey Nick, and I sought the equivalent.

In Lusaka we gazed spellbound on Kenneth Kaunda's colossal party headquarters. I was pounced on while taking pictures of it, but escaped with a caution. We flew in a charter plane to the Zambia–Angola border. The Meheba refugee camp there for Angolans was unusual in that its occupants had been made self-supporting. CARE ran the camp under contract with the United Nations High Commission for Refugees (UNHCR). Stretching over a considerable area, it afforded every family enough space to grow its own produce. A notice at the entrance to the camp signalled the end of all free food supplies from outside sources at an early date. Most of the 25,000 inhabitants had been exiled there since the start of the Angolan civil war in 1971. As I recount later, I met some of these refugees again in dismal circumstances early in 1996 when I travelled to Angola with Clare Crawford of the Mines Advisory Group to look at minefields.

We spent a couple of mornings visiting three of Lusaka's compounds, a euphemism for slums. That is where you find the salt of the earth. In the worst of them was Cari Whyne of Toronto, twenty-three, who had graduated in mechanical engineering at Queen's University. This was her first assignment for CARE. She had coaxed some 500 inhabitants of the Kanyama compound into setting about what amounted to their own resurrection. 'They long to help themselves,' said Cari. 'Just show them how.' 'Your degree is a help?' I asked as we watch teams of women making up impassable roads, building latrines and containers for garbage. 'This is about organizing people,' she replied.

In the next urban slum, the George compound, we found Cathy Snow from Halifax, Nova Scotia, who graduated as a civil engineer at the Technical University of America. She took us to the solitary medical clinic which served 200 customers daily but had no running water, no latrines, no sanitation.

Under Cathy's direction a dozen women were cheerfully building a latrine. Inside the clinic, another dozen ladies were learning to be health workers. Like Cari, Cathy had some 400 women working four hours a day on rain-ravaged dirt roads. 'You find out what they most want,' said Cathy, 'you give them the tools and it happens.' Writing about this later, I described both girls as shining lights in a world of unending twilight.

What Cathy said had the ring of truth. There are two golden rules for aid organizations. One is to keep in with the government, however difficult, because without its consent no useful work can be done. The second is to find out what people most want and show them how to do it themselves. Then the charge that aid and development organizations merely increase people's dependency on them falls.

There are signs in many parts of Africa today of a new wind blowing across the continent. Macmillan's 'wind of change' in 1959 proclaimed *independence* – and much of it fell into the wrong hands. This fresh wind carries more promisingly *self-dependence*, and there lies the future in Africa. I saw it when travelling through Rwanda with International Red Cross late in 1996. This is a country struggling to rise from the abyss of genocide. Red Cross, which has a big presence there, was employing a thousand Rwandans on its staff, all of them working actively in different fields towards their country's resurrection. I had seen it also in Uganda and Kenya earlier in 1996 when Anne and I went to look at the African Medical and Research Foundation (AMREF), a charity of which we are both directors. It is better known as the Flying Doctors Society of Africa, founded forty years ago. Today it employs 800 skilled hands working in different spheres of health and medicine. All but a handful are Africans.

Back in Lusaka in 1993, we spent a depressing hour with the Minister of Health, who was unexpectedly open about problems on his doorstep. A high proportion of hospital beds in Lusaka were occupied by Aids patients. 'They are too sick to be left in the homes they occupy,' said a doctor; 'but not sick enough to be taking up a hospital bed.' Aids, it has seemed to me when travelling in Africa or Asia, is a difficult subject for aid workers and cannot be dealt with in isolation. Precautions against it and propaganda about it enter the wider realm of sexual customs, which differ from one country to another. The most successful small enterprise in anti-Aids propaganda I have encountered was undertaken by CARE in Phnom Penh, Cambodia. It made an inexpensive film about the perils of Aids, built round a simple story everyone could understand. When I last heard of the film, its soundtrack was being adapted for use in Vietnam.

After a spell in Lusaka, a week-end at the Victoria Falls came welcome. I have an affection for these Falls. In a world ruled by safety first, the Victoria Falls afford – or did at this time – total freedom to fall in and drown anywhere you please. There was a glorious absence of warning notices. The Falls were at their most spectacular after heavy rain in the north. The spray descended on us like a rain storm. We walked over the bridge, got soaking wet, visited the Victoria Falls Hotel, with its fine Victorian dining room. At our own hotel, monkeys took charge. They lurked in the foliage surrounding the premises; leaped on to breakfast tables along the open terrace, stole food and grabbed keys and even credit cards. It was a refreshing week-end and demonstrated what I find so attractive about Africa. Monkeys have no opportunity of stealing your food in the clubs of St James's.

I had not been back to Zimbabwe since Christopher Soames as the new and last British Governor wound down the old regime early in 1980, declared an amnesty for black guerrillas and set in train the General Election which Robert Mugabe won. We decided to make a rapid visit to the mysterious ruins of Great Zimbabwe, one of the world's treasures. In a dozen earlier visits, I had never made it. We rattled down in a car at breakneck speed. No matter how fierce the fighting in Africa, I have learned to recognize the fast driver as the biggest physical risk you run. We reached Great Zimbabwe to see the sun go down and the moon rise slowly over the ruins. I reckoned the risk had been worth while. Over supper at the Great Zimbabwe Hotel, I overheard Judith Collins, CARE's temporary country director in Zimbabwe, plotting with Anne Allport a return to the ruins at dawn. To this I turned a deaf ear; but then awoke early, heard sounds of movement around me and joined them under the fading light of the moon for a second visit. Dawn was even more rewarding than dusk. Early sun on the ancient stone produced a magical effect.

There was an emergency feeding programme at the local school in what had until recently been a bad famine area. We arrived late. Nobody seemed put out. If you work in a newspaper office and suffer as I do from train fever, plane fever and deadline fever, there is something wonderfully relaxing about 'African time' once you adjust yourself to it. It constitutes a holiday on its own. The school choir sang 'Ishe Komborera Africa'. Anne and I made short speeches. I marvelled, as I always do, at the way poor children in Africa dress for school, usually in uniform. They dress up, I have come to see, for something they value highly.

'Africa time' is lovely, but once you fall behind a day's schedule there time runs through your fingers like sand. The distances are always longer than you hope, the tracks always bumpier and slower. Back in Harare we were due to take a sundowner with the high commissioner and his wife. As the day wore on, that prospect receded. I telephoned the residence to that effect. 'Well, come if you can,' said the high commissioner's wife cheerfully. Our driver, like a horse returning to its stable, began the journey home at breakneck speed. I sat in front, so the women mercifully could not read his speedometer hovering round the 140 k.p.h. mark, though we slowed for the suburbs of Harare.

'Late though it is,' said Anne suddenly, 'I think we should

go to the high commissioner's party just as we are, dirty and smelly. They'll appreciate our effort.' She was right. We sat with the high commissioner and his wife, sipping consoling drinks and sharing sandwiches off which they were eating a late supper. It illustrated the unstuffiness of our overseas posts, which I experience everywhere I go. It is time journalists ceased to present the Foreign Service as stuffed shirts. We ended our mission with a very late night in a Zimbabwe dance hall, ostensibly to hear African music – to which I am tone deaf. The bands were non-stop, the noise mindbending. I eased my nerves with copious draughts of African beer from the bottle.

Michael Cockerell of the BBC added another loop to my travels that year by making one of his documentaries about my life. He wanted to film me on a trip I had planned to take with CARE in Angola. The war was still on. Our visas arrived an hour or two before Cockerell and I left for South Africa, where filming was to start. We flew up from Johannesburg to Windhoek, thence in a charter plane to Lubango in Angola, which was the only way in. For a reporter it was a rewarding visit. We saw wounded from a nearby battlefield being brought into Lubango airport by helicopter and met there a smartly dressed brigadier from the Government forces. He travelled stylishly with his pet monkey on a chain, which reminded me of the pet monkey Evelyn Waugh had kept in Abyssinia. CARE in Lubango seemed grateful for our attentions and rewarded me with a real bow and three steel-tipped arrows. I wondered what the men who frisk you for arms at airports would make of this. Happily, the arrows which formed the controversial part of the package just fitted obliquely into my suitcase. Carrying the bow merely made me look daft.

Back at Jan Smuts airport in Johannesburg, where Cockerell and I had to arrange our return to London, a lovely girl in the navy-blue uniform of South African Airways approached me, her brass buttons gleaming. How did I rate the future there? she wanted to know. Did I think there was a future? We discussed South Africa's chances. I did my best to cheer her up. She looked forlorn and my heart melted. Her eyes were faintly misty when we parted – at which point Michael Cockerell pounced. 'Now, what about an upgrade for us?' he asked. 'You are incorrigible, Cockerell,' I said later with mock dismay. 'That lovely girl . . .' 'And you', he retorted brutally, 'are flying back with me to London first class.' I thought of the bow and arrows and swallowed my pride. As my travel companions of recent years have sometimes sorrowfully observed, I am chronically bad at seeking favours. In countless air journeys I have never had the nerve to ask for an upgrade. 'You are frightened of rejection,' one woman declared bluntly after some failure of mine to ease our journey. I suppose so.

In terms of copy for the *Daily Telegraph* the most reward-ing journey Anne Allport and I made came in 1993, when we made a trip to Hanoi. There was a CARE International meeting in Sydney which Allport had to address. I had a daughter in Melbourne. We decided to break our journey in Vietnam.

Before leaving for Hanoi I consulted that doyenne of war correspondents, Clare Hollingworth, who knew the region well. 'Talk to Kathleen Callo,' she advised. Kathleen had been head of Reuters bureau in Hanoi. We lunched together. The story in Hanoi, Callo explained to me, lay in a psychological problem. Many in America remained convinced that the Viet-namese were still hiding numbers of American prisoners who had been reported missing in action. Callo then faxed letters of introduction for me to some of the principal witnesses in Hanoi.

On our arrival at the Thang Loi Hotel in Hanoi, we spent a day or two on CARE duties. When we turned to America's problem, it suddenly became clear to me that I was chasing a gigantic ghost story. No American prisoners were being hidden in caves, or anywhere else. Yet so persistent was the legend that Americans who had lost kin in the Vietnam War were still flying in, hiring helicopters at inflated prices and chasing false clues. We spent an afternoon with Colonel Cray of the United

States MIA (Missing in Action) office in Hanoi. He gave us a straightforward account of his work, which was tracing the graves of unknown soldiers, sifting through the evidence, striving to reach the truth.

Once again, the timing of this visit was lucky. We were in time to see one of the last of the world's unspoiled cities. Hanoi, with all its past suffering, had escaped the swathe of tower blocks, mirror-clad banks and penitentiary-style architecture that has swept through the world and turned its cities into clones. We spent a day travelling by Highway 5 from Hanoi to Hai Phong, where CARE was helping to resettle the poorest Vietnamese on tiny smallholdings. The landscape, looking its shining best on a sunny day, excited me. So this had been the scene of a terrible war that had laid waste to a beautiful land – and to thousands of American soldiers who fought there. I had brought with me Graham Greene's tale of that war, *The Quiet American*. I am not unduly sensitive to atmosphere, but I felt suddenly consumed by melancholy.

After business with the Provincial Association of Vietnamese Food Horticulturalists in Hai Phong, we ate an astonishing lunch of many delicious local dishes. Surprisingly, through the long warm afternoon that followed I felt no urge to drop off. We parted from our friends of the PAVFH with glasses of apricot lemonade. I longed for the recipe, but felt that to ask for it would be to lose face.

Back in Hanoi, we toured the back streets buzzing with human activity. Nobody seemed idle. We took a look at French colonial buildings from another age. The story I was hunting came together slowly. I know of few sensations more pleasurable than drawing together the threads of a story you think the newspaper will be glad to see. I decided to reflect on what I had discovered, and did not try to set it down on paper until we had reached Australia. The *Daily Telegraph* treated the piece generously. Headed 'Ghosts of War', it made a Saturday front for the *Weekend* section.

A Sunday gathering of Ministers at Chequers. 1963.

Receiving guests (Viscount Camrose pictured entering) at No. 10 at a dinner party
Mrs Thatcher gave for me when I ceased to be editor of the *Daily Telegraph*.
Summer 1986.

Left: Dialogue under Bow Bells during a lunchtime gathering in Bow Church.

Below: Peregrine Worsthorne and WFD at a farewell party for John Thompson, *Sunday Telegraph*, and WFD, *Daily Telegraph*. 1986.

Right: Garland salutes the new peer. 1986.

Below: *Scoop*. Making the LWT film of Evelyn Waugh's novel in Morocco. 1986.

27 Heath Hurst Rd
London NW3
15 June 1986

My Dear Bill,
Many congratulations

Yours ever
Nick G.

Modelling golf clothes for Hilary Alexander, Fashion Editor of the *Daily Telegraph*, at Littlestone Golf Club. July 1988. (*Daily Telegraph*)

End of Lino Line, 1988. (*Simon Grosset*)

Left: Hippy. A *Daily Telegraph* pantomime organized by Hilary Alexander. Christmas 1994.

Below: Golfing quartet. Left to right: Denis Thatcher, Ron Monck, WFD, Len Whitting.

Above: Working with Victoria Combe.

Below: With CARE International staff in the Angola war. 1993.

Lunchtime pint at the Blacksmith's Arms. Isle of Dogs.
(*Ken Mason, Daily Telegraph*)

It was, I explained, about pain felt when a long war has been lost and also about a sense of guilt. With the end of the Cold War, America's war in Vietnam, at the cost of 58,000 American dead – and many more Vietnamese – is seen by most of the world as an appalling aberration. That is a history trap, easily fallen into. 'How could Americans bomb and napalm folk like this?' I exclaimed to my companion, as we walked among gentle, friendly people in the markets of Hanoi. They did it in days we have forgotten, when it seemed likely that much of South-East Asia would fall behind the Iron Curtain. The Vietnam War left wounds, as all wars do, but also hindsight and blame and an inner desire for revenge, which helped to explain the MIA (Missing in Action) issue. The task of Lieutenant-Colonel John Cray, leading America's MIA task force, I wrote, was to 'strip away, bone by bone, button by button, ghost by ghost, America's last pretext for refusing to forgive a smaller nation which defeated her'.

Max Hastings generously sent me a note which I kept: 'I hope you will not think it presumptuous of me to offer my warmest congratulations on a superb Weekend front from Vietnam. Again and again, you demonstrate that you remain by far the best journalist of us all. I would have been very happy to write that piece myself, on a topic on which I entirely share your sentiments.' It is not hard to hit on good stories if you are given the freedom, as I was, to follow your nose.

At some point in the summer of 1994 I ran into Sarah Hogg, who was then working in the Prime Minister's office. We had earlier worked together under Max as leader writers at the *Daily Telegraph* and were friends. A year earlier, I fancied, she had been instrumental in persuading John Major to mark my eightieth birthday with a small dinner party at No. 10 – nursing a hope, perhaps, that it might mend some fences between the Prime Minister and the *Daily Telegraph*. I had jibbed at the idea, but Max persuaded me that it would be helpful. Very well, I determined, you will do it my way. Men are such bores round a political dinner table. I invited Max and my son Jeremy, who was then executive editor at the *Daily Telegraph*, and two Members of Parliament who were chums, Tim Yeo and Michael Trend. But I insisted on four women in the party. To join Sarah Hogg, I prevailed on Veronica Wadley, then our features editor, Hilary Alexander, our fashion writer – and later fashions editor – and Anne Allport to join in. I thought it would be jollier for the Prime Minister, and discourage table talk devoted exclusively to politics. It was a happy evening. I felt grateful to John Major and also to Sarah Hogg.

So when I met her a year later – and this explains the above diversion – I felt under an obligation. Sarah explained that her son Quintin was using an interval between Eton and Oxford to work with CARE International in the Meheba camp which Anne Allport and I had visited in 1993. Recalling that he was the great-grandson of the first Lord Hailsham, whom I had known in the 1930s as a lobby correspondent; grandson of Quintin Hailsham, a former Cabinet colleague; and son of Sarah, to whom I was indebted, I felt special measures were called for. I arranged a lunch for Sarah and her son, Anne Allport and myself. Hogg junior got his money's worth. Anne told him what to take and what to wear. He was also prevailed upon to take two bags of little woolly garments for refugee children. His baggage might be overweight, the CARE ladies said, but it would ensure goodwill. He was also urged to take paper wipes, which Anne carries on all expeditions. I commend them. 'So much hand-shaking . . .' We explained the lay-out of the camp to him, and gave him snapshots of it. 'If you are taken ill,' said Anne cheerfully, 'don't worry. CARE will look after you and evacuate you.' Quintin Hogg finished lunch looking dazed; but he survived and won high opinions from CARE for his work.

In 1994 Anne proposed a trip to Ethiopia, where CARE was busy. Nobody had to twist my arm hard to get me back there. We reached Addis Ababa early in July and spent a day or two with Robin Christopher and his wife at the embassy – which I had first set eyes on fifty-nine years earlier when it was our legation. We prowled round as many of the 1935 haunts in Addis Ababa as I could remember. Then we took a long sweep round part of the country with Robin Needham, CARE's country director. An Etonian, kinsman of someone in the British Government, endowed with first-class mind, Needham could have held a well-paid job in the City of London. Instead, he chose this uncomfortable vocation.

A spell of rough living is useful from time to time if you live in one of the Home Counties. Robin Needham supplied it. We returned to Addis Ababa by a spectacular mountain route. The road was slippery after heavy rains, and I am not brave about hairpin bends in high mountains. I closed my eyes. But, whenever I dared to look, the views were spectacular and the air delicious. Ethiopia, where few Europeans travel, is a beautiful country. When the rains cease and the flowers burst out in September, as I recalled from 1935, it becomes an enchanted land.

Reckoning it would be rough in Ethiopia, I planned a day or two with our feet up at the Windsor Country Club outside Nairobi. I had stayed there on my way to South Africa a year earlier. 'There's a rainforest and bird-watching,' I promised Anne. Barely had we arrived and settled down with a cup of tea than A. E. Housman's lines invaded our lives:

> On the idle hill of summer,
> Sleepy with the flow of streams,
> Far I hear the steady drummer,
> Drumming like a noise in dreams . . .

'Why are we here?' Anne suddenly exclaimed, 'and not in Rwanda?' The world was still learning about the massacre which had taken place there some weeks earlier. I knew better than to argue, and left her to make arrangements. She asked the

CARE country director in Nairobi to rent us a plane. Barely had we agreed this than we ran into the Windsor Club's board of directors who had been meeting at the club. One or two recognized me. We were drawn back to the terrace for drinks. Chairman of the directors was John N. Michuki MP, a prominent member of the parliamentary opposition to President Moi. He had much to tell us. Serious drinking continued until long after darkness fell. Braziers and snacks were brought out for our comfort. Eventually, some time after 10 p.m., supperless and with Rwanda plans unsettled, we retired to bed. I awoke with a headache, and recollections of talk about Rwanda, shuddered and went back to sleep. My hangover slowly dissolved; the shadow of Rwanda did not.

We flew first to Mwanza on the Tanzania border for immigration formalities, then an hour on to the Benaco camp, which had been quickly set up to cope with the torrent of refugees. Holding something like 250,000 of them, Benaco was an impressive creation, credit for which was shared mainly between Oxfam, Concern, CARE, Médecins Sans Frontières and Red Cross. But the darkest of spirits brooded over the place. I slept uneasily in one of the tents provided for us. Once or twice I woke to the sound of running feet and shouts of anger. Next morning I was told that I had missed considerable drama. We were escorted round the camp by a lovely black girl from CARE headquarters in Atlanta, USA. They had told her she looked too much like a Tutsi for her own good; and she was leaving us sadly to return to America. The visit was an ugly experience, but it made a good Monday column and a news story for the *Sunday Telegraph*. I was thankful to put the place behind me. Horrors apart, it depressingly confirmed my suspicion that, some sixty years after I had first set foot in Africa, I knew nothing about the place at all.

24

On Assignment

For some sixty-five years, as reporter or Member of Parliament, I have been a close witness of Great Britain's post-war winding down of Empire. Starting with India and ending with Hong Kong, the process has spanned virtually the whole of my working life. There is no point in arguing whether imperialism was a good or a bad idea. It is history. What I am ready to assent is that the way in which during the latter part of this century we British have dismantled our former Empire forms a highly creditable chapter. We have made mistakes. We moved too quickly. But, over all, converting the British Empire into which I was born into the British Commonwealth of Nations has been a tremendous achievement. The old Anglo-French state was broken by the sword of Joan of Arc. The Atlantic Commonwealth was defeated by George Washington. Our third Empire has been broken up and reformed as the British Commonwealth of Nations under the Queen of England. No other empire in the world's history has pulled the trick off thrice.

There are many reasons why this Empire had finally to go. America's hostility to it, born of its own history, made itself felt soon after the Second World War and at a time when we were heavily dependent on its goodwill. There was a stirring in many of our colonies which we tried to ignore but which became more insistent. What made the end inevitable in the long run were our losses in the First World War. We lost on the battlefield much of the generation willing and able to sustain our interests overseas. We lost the power to remain imperial. India was the cornerstone. Once India secured independence, the rest was bound to follow.

I can trace the exact date on which my association with India's prospective independence began. On 21 April 1933 the *Morning Post* ran a splash headed 'INDIA "GAG" AGAIN'. The first sentence by our political correspondent conveys the tone in which the *Morning Post* then addressed India's affairs: 'Desperate efforts are being made by those who control the Conservative party machine to hide the growing determination of the rank and file up and down the country to defeat the Government's policy of abdication in India.'

The single word 'abdication' says it all. The story lay in the fact that Earl Winterton, then MP for the Worthing constituency and a leading supporter of the Government's White Paper on India, had been put up in the House of Commons to reply to Winston Churchill – who, as I have made clear elsewhere, was a leading opponent of Indian independence. Barely had Winterton delivered his impassioned defence of the White Paper than the executive committee of his constituency Association passed a resolution condemning it. I was dispatched to Worthing to discover the truth of the matter. I asked the chairman of the Association if the report was true. No resolution, he insisted, had been put forward at the meeting. No vote had been taken. We then obtained solid evidence to prove that such a resolution condemning the Government's policy had indeed been moved, and furthermore had been passed by thirty-five votes to twenty-two. That put the fat properly in the fire.

From that point I developed a strong interest in the Indian story, not so much on behalf of India's destiny as because the political battle running between Westminster and the constituencies produced such good copy. I was made responsible for finding out what other constituencies might be doing. In May –

in my first splash for the paper – I reported that the Central Women's Advisory Committee of the Conservative party while meeting in London had condemned the Government's White Paper on India by 980 votes to 760. Of the 2,500 delegates gathered at the Queen's Hall, another 700 abstained. The *Morning Post* was cockahoop.

In the end, despite the weight Winston Churchill and his friends threw against Baldwin on this issue, the gigantic Government of India Bill with its 356 clauses was pushed through. Much of the work in Parliament fell to Rab Butler, who was parliamentary under secretary to the Secretary of State for India, Sir Samuel Hoare. It laid the foundations of his later career. Baldwin, who has suffered so much disparagement posthumously, deserves more honour for his stand on the India issue than he has been accorded. 'The man recovered from the bite. The dog it was that died.' The *Morning Post* breathed its last in October 1937.

It might be argued that my experiences in Abyssinia in 1935 represented, in negative form, another step away from Empire. It was certainly the most blatant, if not the final, attempt by a European nation to achieve colonial expansion by force. It gave imperialism a bad name – though not with Evelyn Waugh. He was going through a phase of admiring Mussolini's adventure in Abyssinia. There are passages in his book *Waugh in Abyssinia* which so vividly reveal his outlook in 1936 that he later expurgated them. He is describing the Italian labour force working at Axum:

> It was a new thing in East Africa to see white men hard at work on simply manual labour; the portent of a new type of conquest. To the other imperial races it was slightly shocking. To the Abyssinians it was incomprehensible. To them the fruit of victory is leisure ... The idea of conquering a country in order to work there, of treating an empire as a place to which things must be brought, to be fertilized and cultivated

and embellished instead of a place from which things could be taken, to be denuded and depopulated; to labour like a slave instead of sprawling idle like a master – was something wholly outside their range of thought. It is the principle of the Italian occupation.

After contrasting Italy's mission favourably with British colonization, Waugh concluded:

> But the Italian occupation of Ethiopia is the expansion of a race. It began with fighting, but it is not a military movement, like the French occupation of Morocco. It began with the annexation of potential sources of wealth, but it was not a capitalistic movement like the British occupation of the South African goldfields. It is being attended by the spread of order and decency, education and medicine, in a disgraceful place, but it is not primarily a human movement, like the British occupation of Uganda. It can be compared best in recent history to the great western drive of the American peoples, the dispossession of the Indian tribes and the establishment in a barren land of new pastures and cities.

It was not how many other people saw it at the time.

My first post-war stop-off on the road to decolonization was with a parliamentary delegation to Northern Nigeria in May 1959. Led by the Duke and Duchess of Gloucester and the Colonial Secretary, Alan Lennox Boyd, we went, rather prematurely as it turned out, for a week of celebrations to mark the North's independence. The smaller Eastern and Western regions had become self-governing in 1957. The North, three times the size of Britain and our largest colony, had followed suit in March. Our small parliamentary delegation bore with it a handsomely bound copy of Erskine May, the parliamentary Bible. It became customary at these events to present some symbol of the Westminster system – a Speaker's chair, a mace or Erskine May. 'It is a proud and proper act to hand over your instruments of government,' I wrote in a piece for the *Daily Telegraph* at the time, adding with prescience rare for me: 'It is unwise to expect others to wield them precisely as you have done.' When we arrived at the airport a congenial Nigerian took charge of our baggage. I wondered why such an apparently intelligent man had been appointed to such a menial task. 'Today,' he remarked cheerfully, 'I am baggage boy. Tomorrow in our new Parliament, you will see me as Mr Speaker.' So we did. The exchange has lingered in my mind ever since because it illustrates a main obstacle to an orderly transition. There was in almost all the former colonies a desperate shortage of locally trained administrators. 'Greatest of all problems, certainly in Northern Nigeria', I wrote in the same piece, 'will be to find and train administrators at every level. Even if many Europeans are encouraged and willing to remain – prospects are not disheartening – demand must for some years exceed supply. These rulers will face – as we did not so long ago – the demands of patronage, which is the companion of power, and the deficiencies of a qualified Civil Service.' Not long after we left Nigeria with our lofty hopes, darkness began to fall over the land and it lasted for a long time. Nigeria is a good example of a truth we overlooked while following Harold Macmillan's 'wind of change'. Man-made frontiers very seldom relate to tribal affinities and that is bound to be a source of unrest.

Returning from the celebrations. I drove with Earl De La Warr towards Kano airport. On our way, we ran into a devastating sandstorm. We battened down the hatches, but the sand penetrated every corner of our car and obscured our vision. We could see nothing, but sat waiting anxiously for the next phase of this phenomenon. We had no idea what would happen next or if we would be able to finish our journey. Later I came to see this episode as symbolizing the way in which we were driven forward, blindfold, by Harold Macmillan's 'wind of change'.

In April and May of the following year I took a long journey with Lord Balniel MP (later the Earl of Crawford and Balcarres) through the Federation of Central Africa. The invitation came from Cuthbert ('Cub') Alport, who was then Minister of State at the Colonial Office, and later became British high commissioner for the Federation. Our host was Sir Ronald Prain of Rhodesia Selection Trust, the mining corporation. In these days our visit would probably have caused a tremendous fuss – two Tory MPs travelling partly for free with a copper-belt corporation which had a vested interest in the Federation. Sleaze! In 1960 we suffered none of these inhibitions.

There had long been talk of a British East African Dominion which would incorporate Kenya, Uganda and Tanganyika and have close ties with Southern Rhodesia and South Africa. This came to nothing, but another idea took shape. This was to bring together Northern and Southern Rhodesia and Nyasaland. All three countries had enjoyed relative prosperity during the war years. Production on Northern Rhodesia's copper belt provided well-paid employment for black workers from Nyasaland; Southern Rhodesia prospered from its Wankie coalfields and the demand for tobacco, cattle and maize. By the mid-1950s Southern Rhodesia's white population was over 100,000 and by 1960 it was twice as many. The Federation came into being in 1953. It was primarily a white plan, over which black Africans were barely consulted. Many of them saw it was an arrangement designed to consolidate white power based on Salisbury. In that sense it clashed with the growing force of African nationalist opinion. That was its undoing a decade later.

At the time of our visit, however, everything seemed to be in place. Sir Roy Welensky had become the Federation's Prime Minister. Edgar Whitehead, a bachelor with a passion for cricket, had charge in Rhodesia. He lived untidily in a bungalow. When I visited him there one Sunday evening he had holes in both his socks and stuffing was coming out of the chairs. The

Kariba dam, harnessing power from the Zambesi on the Rhodesian border, seemed a good augury. 'Kariba', I wrote after my first visit there, 'is a project conceived and achieved on a scale which would have won the heart of Cecil Rhodes.' The Queen Mother was to open it. They asked if I would like to test the landing strip on which her light plane would arrive. It seemed a patriotic thing to do.

What forcibly struck both Balniel and myself was the unwillingness of the whites to yield power and, because their progress had been so retarded, the blacks' unreadiness to assume it. While in Salisbury I visited one evening the only black barrister in the city. He went to a niche in the wall of his home and drew out a bottle of whisky. 'Firewater!' he said with a smile. 'I am not supposed to possess it.' At that time the only hotel in Salisbury open to blacks was the Jameson, which is why the Monckton Commission were staying there while reporting on the future of the Federation.

As well as the gulf between white and black aspirations there were growing differences between the whites. Many of them were artisans, who were enjoying more comfortable lives than they would have done in Britain and were instinctively opposed to any advance by the blacks. Among the grandees, there were many who realized that change must come but also that blacks were not ready for it. One of these, I am happy to say, was my cousin Gordon Deedes, who had lived most of his life in Rhodesia and was at that time (1960) chairman of the Land Resources Board. As we travelled about the countryside in his twin-cylinder diesel-burning Mercedes, he spoke of his difficulties in improving African husbandry of the land. He was a 'working liberal'. There were not a great many of them, but they wielded influence, and sometimes they were well disguised.

Balniel and I attended a Sunday-morning party in the grounds of a wealthy white man. Not many liberals around here, I thought, as we sipped a rich assortment of drinks in the bright sunshine. Our host, in a panama hat and wearing an expansive smile, had all the appearances of a well-heeled white who intended to keep one of the heels firmly on African aspirations. I met him again on the plane returning to London. He was going to the City of London, he explained, to launch a scheme which might provide small loans for black African businesses. Appearances were sometimes deceptive. At white dinner parties I began a game of trying to discover the individual's private sympathies over drinks beforehand.

Gordon Deedes's twin brother, a former brigadier who lived in Bulawayo, shared none of his brother's sympathies. When Balniel and I travelled south, to visit Rhodes' grave in the Matapo Hills, I stayed a night with the brigadier. Garfield Todd, the former Prime Minister of Southern Rhodesia, whose liberal sympathies were pronounced, was holding a meeting locally. We decided to look in. During the course of Todd's speech the brigadier became violently agitated and attracted adverse looks from the predominantly pro-Todd gathering.

Later, Balniel and I travelled on to Nyasaland and spent a night with Sir Glyn Jones, then Chief Secretary and about to become Governor. He occupied a hut in wild country seven miles from the residence and 3,000 feet up in the hills. I kept notes of his talk with us. The Soviet Union, he told us, was pouring influence into Kenya. Our methods came nowhere near to matching this. We could not, he said, train Africans to telescope 500 years of parliamentary experience. India had taken 200 years to develop; Ghana was expected to do it in three years. The Central African Federation would require at least one generation. Parliamentary democracy (in Africa) was not understood and would not work. The aim had to be 'benevolent autocracy' with direct efforts to keep it benevolent. This was the only course which time allowed, and it called for fundamental rethinking. Glyn Jones was one of the most far-sighted figures I met during those years. Remarkably, he moved from being Governor of Nyasaland 1961–4 to being Governor-General and Commander-in-Chief of Malawi when the change came.

On Assignment

At this distance, it is not easy fairly to summarize post-war political feeling at Westminster about the future in Africa. After Macmillan had sent Iain Macleod to the Colonial Office in October 1959 to accelerate the winds of change, I recall one or two ugly meetings within the parliamentary Tory party. Some saw Macleod as a slippery fellow, betraying our imperial trust. I have already quoted Lord Salisbury's bitter comment, 'too clever by half'. The fact is that through the late 1940s and early 1950s we were largely preoccupied in making our own recovery from the ravages of war. Africa and its aspirations seemed a long way off, and not especially urgent.

I got a closer view of Africa's unreadiness to govern in the following year, 1961. A senior Labour MP, a Clerk of the House and I went to Uganda and Nyasaland to deliver some lectures on the ways of Westminster and Whitehall. In the light of what was to come in Uganda, our mission can be seen in retrospect as a frivolous episode but we took it seriously enough at the time and I retain the notes I prepared for my five lectures. They were on 'The Member and His Constituency', 'Parliamentary Questions', 'Parliament, Press and Broadcasting', 'Parliament and Control of the Executive', 'Parliament, Ministers and Civil Service'.

What our African audience made of the last lecture I cannot imagine, for our tour brought home to me once again the desperate shortage of experienced African administrators. This is what I had to say about it in the *Daily Telegraph* on our return:

> To spend three weeks with members of two new Legislatures discussing constitutional problems brings no answer to any local difficulty; but it suggests one or two fundamental issues which in the longer run will count for much. At the head of a long list stand Civil Service administration and financial responsibility. They are interrelated. We have laid tremendous stress on the Westminster model throughout Africa's new legislatures, and have excited Africans with romantic, if hazy,

notions about it. What of the Whitehall model? Though few Englishmen acknowledge it, having been brought up on a joke about Civil Servants playing, like the fountains in Trafalgar Square, from 10 till 4, reliable rule depends a lot on the experience and behaviour of a Ministry's Permanent Secretary – as well as the Mace and Erskine May.

Ultimately, I added, some of Africa's governments are going ahead without mace or May, and yet they may succeed. 'They will emphatically not succeed without a good Civil Service.' Africans, I pointed out, already perceived to what extent appallingly weak administration contributed to United Nations defeat and dishonour in the Congo. In Tanganyika Nyerere had openly appealed to senior British Civil Servants to save his Government from 'making a mess'. So I concluded:

Our failure is to convince ourselves and Africa that it takes much longer to make a reliable civil servant than a passable politician. Mr Macleod was a Minister two years after entering Parliament. There can be few Permanent Secretaries in Whitehall who got to their chairs in much less than 20 years.

Turning to finance – and the vast prospective debts that now burden the Third World – I drew attention to the host of liberal international agencies, apart from the British Treasury and the Colonial Development Corporation, that appeared ready at hand to drop in a million here or there with surprisingly few questions asked. 'Such sources', I remarked, 'offer a reassuring prospect, but they are not conducive to strict accounting.'

No doubt we shall have to continue to be reassuring for some time to come. The bill for reassuring Kenya, now blinking at bankruptcy, is in the post. But a few facts confront us: increasingly the competence or otherwise of Africans in financial administration is going to touch the British tax-payer's pocket. Loans will have to be properly serviced . . . Puzzling and painful adventures await some African politicians who, momentarily dazzled by emoluments of £1,000 a year as MPs and £2,000 or £3,000 as Ministers, reckon that the future beckons with a golden finger.

At this time, the Soviet Union was frequently being brought into the argument. Some African leaders were talking on these lines: 'We shall not wish to approach them, but failing all else . . .' On which I felt moved to observe: 'But the Communists make hard bargains, and, when they do fulfil all their promises, the terms make our financial arrangements look like charity. A few intelligent Africans have discovered this.'

Looking back on these predictions, some of which have been fulfilled, I think the *Daily Telegraph* got reasonably good value for my three weeks of absence. But amid the lectures we found time to enjoy two beautiful African countries. I rarely travel in Africa, even if there is a war on, without reflecting sadly on what joys could await the growing traffic of European holidaymakers seeking fresh horizons. Between lectures in Nyasaland, we practised water skiing on Lake Nyasa. I took Churchill's *My African Journey* to Uganda and compared notes on the sources of the Nile. We went out to see that mysterious range, the Mountains of the Moon, where the flora seem to be different from anywhere else in the world, and we took a day or two in the Queen Elizabeth Game Park. I found Uganda an enchanting country, for some of it will persuade you that you are back in the English countryside. Many years later, in 1996, I passed the Parliament Building in Kampala. 'My hat!' I exclaimed to my companion. 'To think that thirty-five years ago I came out here to teach those fellows politics.' She smiled, shook her head, said nothing.

Singapore under Lee Kuan Yew was a different proposition. I first visited it in 1963 to represent the Government at a Far

East Defence Conference. Thereafter I went back there several times. Cyril Horne, former professional at my own golf club at Littlestone in Kent, had gone out there to seek his fortune and had found it at the Royal Island Golf Club. He worked on Lee Kuan Yew's golf and got his handicap down to 10. This provided a certain bond between us. I played a few holes with Horne whenever I visited the island. He lavished hats and ties and socks on me. He had been born for this difficult transition. There came a time when his hitherto exclusive golf club came to admit Chinese members. Horne, with the best qualities of the Cockney, welcomed them in his own way. He would line up the Chinese learners on the great amphitheatre of a practice ground. 'Stick you bottoms in!' he would shout, waving a putter shaft at them. They thought he was wonderful. So did Geordie Selkirk, who was then Commissioner for Singapore and Commissioner-General for South-East Asia. For Horne's singular contribution to the winding down of Empire, we decided on one of my visits to put him in for an MBE. Alas, the Honours system is unaccountable.

Horne became a link between Lee and myself; and this produced sweetness and light until one painful visit which coincided with a decision by the British Government, in retreat from Empire, to close down our naval, military and air bases on the island. They provided a great deal of employment for Singaporeans. Lee Kuan Yew's industrial estate, planned for this contingency, was not yet ready. Some of his wrath was vented on me.

In the autumn of 1970, a parliamentary delegation visited the Services in Singapore, Malaysia and Hong Kong. By then the sun was well down in the imperial sky and there was conveyed to us the anxiety of Service families who wondered where their future lay. Where, for example, would the children go to school? On return I sent a long letter to the Ministry of Defence about the resettlement problem. It failed to produce much joy.

I remember how impressed we were with the Jungle Warfare school in Malaysia. It had offered the Americans, then fighting in Vietnam, a chance to train men there. Nothing came of the idea. It was not America's style, but I have wondered since whether acceptance of our offer might not have altered the course of that war.

A year later, five of us from the House of Commons paid an unofficial visit to Somalia, then under the presidency of Major-General Mohammed Siad Barre. It was a sharp reminder of the extent to which East Africa was then seen as a power base. The Soviet Union had a foot in the door. It had created an enormous fish cannery. China was contributing a water supply. The outlook struck me as precarious. Early one morning, accompanied by the British ambassador and his wife, all five of us flew in the President's plane from Mogadishu to Kismayo. For reasons never clear to me, the pilot of our plane received what might be termed a 'bum steer' into Kismayo airport. He therefore came in downwind instead of upwind. He hit the tarmac with a bang and at high speed. Reckoning that he had no chance of bringing the plane to a stop, he decided to get up again and try again the right way round. He missed the airport buildings by a coat of paint. On the second landing, he had to reckon with a damaged undercarriage, so it was uncomfortable. On the ground a medical and veterinary group had assembled to take us on a tour of their undertakings. Having seen more of the drama than us, some of them looked green round the gills. One of my companions was David Steel, the former Liberal Leader. The episode which might have precipitated five by-elections created a permanent bond between us. When it comes to life or death, political differences do not amount to all that.

Increasingly for me the centre of interest in the closing days of Empire became Rhodesia. The Central African Federation had broken up in acrimony in 1964. Ian Smith's Rhodesia then took a line of its own, defying Harold Wilson's Labour Government, which took office in that year, to do its worst. I find it difficult to explain why, contrary to all correct thinking at the time, I found myself in sympathy with Ian Smith. He had been in the forces with some of us. He was standing virtually alone against the world. He had made Harold Wilson as Prime Minister look fairly silly. He inherited a thin legacy from his white predecessors, who had done very little to advance the black Rhodesian. Unlike his neighbours in South Africa, he accepted that the future Government of Rhodesia must be multi-racial, and rather late in the day he worked towards that end. The war waged against him by Nkomo and Mugabe defeated all his intentions. I think a Tory should have an eye to striking a balance. If his party seems to be moving too fast in one direction, it does no harm to pull the other way for a while. Dissolution of our colonies had been proceeding apace under Macmillan, Macleod and others, like cars rolling off an assembly line. A setback seemed to me not altogether untimely. There had hardly been a ripple until Smith dug his heels in.

I came to know him fairly well and, perversely, to like him. He cared deeply about his country. He knew as well as anyone else that the days of white hegemony in Rhodesia were over but he desired to shape the future of the country himself, and to defy propositions from President Carter's State Department or Dr David Owen's Foreign Office. Smith felt he knew his country better than Western politicians, urging him for their own reasons to do what they wanted. The long procession of well-intentioned negotiators who made their way to Salisbury, hoping to persuade Smith to reach a compromise, had a hard time of it.

Some of his supporters, one must add, were anything but admirable. Many were artisans living a lot more comfortably than they might have done in Islington or Nottingham. They backed Smith because he was delaying the day when they would lose their jobs to black Rhodesians. On the whole, relations between blacks and whites in Rhodesia, by contrast with South Africa, were relatively amicable. How else could

Smith have defied the world as long as he did? Until internal war got the better of him he kept Rhodesia in surprisingly good trim. I never saw peeling paint in Salisbury during what was in effect a siege. As one writer observed during a visit I made in the 1970s, 'Eleven years of sanctions have transformed Rhodesia from an easy come easy go, happy-go-lucky country into an amazingly efficient, disciplined and diversified economy. The shops are filled with locally made goods of better quality than five years ago.'

One of Ian Smith's chosen vessels was the black Bishop Muzorewa, whom I also came to know fairly well. We had a remarkable meeting in London one day when he arrived with half a dozen of his entourage and invited me to give them lunch. We met downstairs in the Italian restaurant Paradiso e Inferno in the Strand. As we sat down the Bishop's bodyguard (whom I presumed was armed) placed himself on a corner of our table facing the staircase. His duties precluded his eating lunch, they told me. He did not, I observed uneasily, refuse the wine.

From time to time when I became editor, I made short expeditions to Salisbury. My routine was to leave London on a Saturday evening, catch a connecting flight to Salisbury on Sunday, and with luck arrive in time for Evensong in Salisbury Cathedral, which was magnificent. Chris Munnion, normally our correspondent in Johannesburg, at this stage spent most of his time in Rhodesia at Meikle's Hotel. He would set up useful appointments for three days. I would be back in the office on Thursday morning.

On one such journey to Rhodesia, I was sitting at Heathrow awaiting my flight when a former colleague at the *Daily Telegraph* encountered me. 'Going to Salisbury?' he exclaimed. 'There's a girl here who is flying out there to get married. Can I put her under your wing?' How does one refuse such an invitation? We were introduced. She had several pieces of hand luggage, one of which in a cardboard box contained her wedding dress. Barely had we become acquainted when they announced a long delay to our flight. It meant that we arrived at Jan Smuts airport in Johannesburg at around 4 a.m. The next flight to Salisbury was at 8 a.m. I proposed spinelessly that we sat there and waited for it, which is my nature. No, said the bride-to-be, we would go to Sun Airport Hotel, put our heads down for a couple of hours, get called, take a shower and set forth again looking our best. I saw the logic of this. How I looked to Chris Munnion on arrival was immaterial, but she was about to meet her future husband.

It proved to be entirely worthwhile for the sight of Munnion's face as we stepped off the plane at Salisbury. I was carrying the cardboard box with the wedding dress inside it under one arm, and giving the weary girl support with the other. What Munnion saw was his editor with one arm round a nubile girl and his other round her most prized possession. Perceiving the expression on his face, I could read the message: 'God! What has my editor become entangled with!' I felt it essential to take the tease a step further. I introduced them to each other. 'We are taking her to Meikle's with us,' I explained in matter-of-fact tones. 'She has a lot of telephoning to do.' We drove in grim silence in Munnion's car to the hotel. Over an egg and bacon breakfast in our suite, I put Munnion in the picture. We contrived to reunite her with her loved ones. Subsequently, she sent a lovely letter and an invitation to her wedding in Salisbury. I declined, but not simply because of the cost of flying to Salisbury. I felt I had had my hour.

Whenever I visited Salisbury, I saw Ian Smith and Ken Flower, head of his Intelligence, and was entertained by the Rhodesia Promotion Council, which was forging friendships with well-connected black Rhodesians. When the guerrilla war got going, I came to know Lieutenant-General Peter Wall, who commanded Rhodesian Forces. Chris Munnion was friendly with Lieutenant-Colonel Ron Reid Daly, who commanded the Selous Scouts, a group of valorous soldiers who performed extraordinary feats of daring, such as free-dropping at night from great heights over enemy territory. Daly had been a highly efficient regimental sergeant-major, but was not himself very well disciplined. He determined to put his own stamp on the Selous Scouts and make them famous. This made nonsense of their role as an Intelligence unit working in conjunction with Rhodesia's Special Branch. Munnion arranged a lunch in Daly's officers' mess, where we met one or two outstanding warriors. One of them had just been decorated with Rhodesia's Grand Cross of Valour, equivalent to our Victoria Cross. My soldiering blood tingled a little. I wonder what has since happened to those medals. To the right sort of collector, they would be worth a fortune.

On this same visit, Munnion thoughtfully arranged for us both to do the rounds in a Hercules, one of those wonderful transport planes which seemed able to lumber along at the speed of a motor car and fly low enough to drop off supplies reliably. The Hercules has great qualities, but when spiralling down in a war zone, as this one did several times, it is a challenge to queasy stomachs. Mine is not particularly queasy, but it was tested.

My final visit to Rhodesia took place in 1979, after the Conservatives had won the election. Mrs Thatcher had put Rhodesia near the top of her agenda and a settlement had been reached at Lancaster House. During these proceedings Ian Smith rang me up and, declaring that he had had enough of the food in his hotel, invited himself to lunch. We met in the Paradiso e Inferno, where he created a favourable impression by ordering his meal in Italian. I raised my eyebrows. Smith explained that, after he had been shot down in Italy during the war, he had spent a little time learning the language.

Lord Soames was dispatched to Salisbury for Rhodesia's last rites. We had been in the Cabinet together in the early 1960s and enjoyed each other's company. In the closing days, he suggested that two or three of us from the *Daily Telegraph* should dine with members of his staff and discuss the outlook.

None of us, so far as I remember, foreshadowed Mugabe's victory in the election. Politics is a funny business. Who could have guessed that a Conservative government under Mrs Thatcher, in one of its first strikes, would end Ian Smith's fourteen years of defiance and so lead to his replacement by a Marxist?

Early in 1997, from my window in the Mandarin Hotel, I could just glimpse the Union Flag fluttering outside Hong Kong's General Post Office. From the fourteenth floor, it looked minute, and somehow symbolic. By the time these words appear, it will no longer be there. We shall for the first time, in divesting ourselves of Empire, have handed over a colony not to its inhabitants but to another country of whose intentions we know nothing. A day or two later, while working in my room at the Mandarin, I was startled by the sound of a ship's gun. Out in the harbour HMS *Starling*, shrouded in gun smoke, was firing a twenty-one-gun salute to mark the Accession of Queen Elizabeth II on 6 February 1952. 'That', I said to my companion, 'will never been seen again in Hong Kong.'

Many will think it unfortunate that this task of converting the British Empire into the British Commonwealth of Nations should close on a controversial decision. There are those who view our readiness to yield Hong Kong to mainland China on the appointed day as a betrayal of its people. I sense that Chris Patton, our last Governor of Hong Kong, is troubled by this. It seems the right moment to urge that we do not altogether lose historical perspective. Throughout the difficult business of dismantling an Empire, we have acted honourably. We are entitled to put our own record against that of France (Algiers), or Belgium (the Congo), or Portugal (Angola and Mozambique). History, I predict, will grant us more honour for what we have done and the way in which we have done it than we now feel ready to accord ourselves.

25

Christian Soldiers

My account of Diana's death and funeral for the *Daily Telegraph* won a British Press Award. Reporters mustn't rest on their laurels, I said to Charles Moore, my editor, and outlined an idea which Victoria Combe, who used to work on the foreign desk in the newsroom, and I had discussed to mark the millennium which lay two years ahead. Given the frail state of religious observance in Britain, we thought some account of Christians suffering for their faith in certain parts of the world would make salutary reading.

We chose five countries. In Sudan, a complex war had caused prolonged suffering for African Christians. Russia was emerging from a long night of Christian persecution under communism. In Pakistan, the haphazard blasphemy law hovered like a sword over those who were not Muslims. China was permitting Christian worship but only on its own terms. In Cuba, under Fidel Castro, the tide was turning towards Christians, but slowly. We knew we were embarking on a huge subject with too little time to do it justice. Victoria was now the newspaper's religion correspondent. I was employed to write leaders, occasional features and a weekly column. 'But journalism, as someone generously remarked, is literature in a hurry,' I told Victoria. So we swotted up as much as we could before travelling, agreed to spend a week in each country and spread our travels over the best part of a year.

We got good advice from Lambeth, Oxford and other

sources and then went in at the deep end. Earlier expeditions to Sudan led me to think it would be the most testing of our missions. The chief enemy of the people there is isolation. The outside world is kept at a safe distance.

After consulting witnesses in Nairobi about the state of religious affairs in the oppressed south of Sudan, we made a promising start in Khartoum. 'Forty [US] dollars,' said the taxi driver taking us to the Hilton. 'Twenty,' said Victoria sternly, and twenty it was. Contrary to expectations, we had a run of luck; we found the Roman Catholic archbishop unwinding at home after release from a police cell. He had done no wrong but was held responsible for some debt the cathedral was alleged to have incurred. He saw it as another attempt to break his spirit. His was one of the biggest dioceses in the world, running to nearly a million square kilometres. Yes, he told us, there is harassment. The government suspected the Catholic church of siding with the rebels. 'People have to make a stand,' said this sad figure whose residence was a small shabby house down a dirt road, 'otherwise they will lose everything. I believe God has the final word.'

As we left the archbishop a message reached us that Dr Hassan el-Turabi, leader of the National Islamic Front would receive us early that afternoon. I had asked our embassy if they could arrange a meeting but had hardly expected one. Dressed in white robes in a cool white office, Dr el-Turabi spoke in the most fluent English to be heard outside our embassy. While imprisoned by the communists he had learned languages and studied law. The war? It was about Africa. Religion had little to do with it. 'I know the people who are fighting. It is tribal.' During our seventy minutes with Dr el-Turabi, he spoke fluently and incessantly. 'Americans know nothing about the world ... Africans are only expressing their nature ...' He made an impression on us both, though perhaps not the one he intended. In or out of office, even when in prison, Dr el-Turabi was a powerful influence on the course the government in Khartoum had determined to take against southern Sudan.

The following day we went deep into the desert that lies outside Khartoum, talked to refugees living like nomads and visited their simple church.

To write sensibly about the church we needed to know about conditions in Sudan and the United Nations Children's Fund (Unicef) gave us a briefing. Keeping children alive in the savage civil war was their mission.

Our departure from Khartoum early next morning required us to leave our hotel at 3.45 a.m. for a 5 a.m. flight to Cairo. Not until we reached the airport did we learn that our flight had not yet left Cairo. We returned crestfallen to our hotel where I rashly ordered a breakfast of coffee and two eggs which were very hard-boiled. Indigestion on top of frustration made me fretful. 'Strong coffee always gives me a fast pulse,' I complained. 'Same here,' said Victoria. 'Why drink it?' There is no answer to that sort of question.

Eventually we reached Cairo too late for an onward flight to London. My mood darkened. We had whacked these Egyptians in the war, I told Victoria in colourful language. She asked drily if she could pass on some of what I had said to her military husband. Good humour partially restored, I ordered a beer, then found I had no Egyptian money to pay for it. The Egyptian barman remarked to Victoria that her companion was not happy. Damn right, he was not happy.

Three months later we flew on the second leg of this jaunt into Moscow, arriving in time to take a walk round Red Square, which Victoria had never seen, as midnight was chiming.

Having read of the slaughter and torment the clergy had suffered under Lenin and Stalin, I was surprised to find any church in Moscow open. The Anglican church's incumbent, who we visited the next day, was a faintly stage figure prone to pressing his fingertips together before answering our questions. But he explained Russia's rules, enshrined in the 1997 law, with which all churches other than the Orthodox had to comply. The Kremlin had been in no mood to licence the sort of criticism Anglican or Roman Catholic leaders sometimes direct at governments in the West. Victoria rewarded him with two recent copies of the *Spectator* which she had brought with her.

Our dinner that evening was instructive. We drove miles with our man in Moscow to a restaurant of great beauty and enormous prices. There was nothing on the menu below the US$50 mark. We ate frugally and received a bill for US$405. I presented my Coutts gold card, which was returned as unsatisfactory. Slightly stunned, I handed the waiter the precise amount in dollar notes. He then looked stunned because fat tips were expected on top of a hefty service charge. Only later did we discover that such restaurants had sprung up to allow the new rich of Moscow to display their wealth.

Next morning we had a good hour with Father Martini, a famous rebel, sitting round a table laden with biscuits, chocolates, sweets and cake. Then to a monastery of great beauty and into the cathedral which was lovely but which gave me a sense of strong resistance to change in the Russian Orthodox Church.

Our last call of the day was to the Russian Orthodox Church's equivalent of the Vatican. At its external affairs department a young priest of thirty-two was refreshingly frank, though constant telephone calls to his desk made consecutive talking and thinking difficult. Russia's authoritative regime, he explained, had no anxieties about a church which remained as conservative as the Russian Orthodox. It was new arrivals from the outside world which might deliver unwelcome messages and stir things up that needed watching and controlling. Hence the 1997 law.

Seeking a breather, we visited a huge toy shop close to our

hotel where furry animals cost up to £200 each and dolls £400. Shades of Karl Marx, I felt moved to exclaim and not for the last time on this expedition. We agreed to give most of the next day, a Saturday, to culture rather than religion. We had been strongly advised in England to take soundings in St Petersburg as well as Moscow, so towards the weekend we took a short flight to that historic city. It seemed crazy to visit St Petersburg without exploring the Winter Palace. An excellent guide was available for US$20 and we spent a couple of hours gazing at the treasures which include French Impressionists galore. I glanced at some of the old dears sitting on chairs in every room, ostensibly guarding these treasures – the beguiling side of communism, I reckoned. Walking slowly back to our hotel we spotted St Petersburg's grand equivalent to London's Fortnum and Mason offering a wide range of expensive groceries. Well patronized by the political masters of the past, we reckoned, and left without making any purchases, but feeling we had been granted insight into how the old Soviet Union bosses had lived.

Our main assignation in St Petersburg was with Natalia Pecherskaya, an intellectual of renown and director of the St Petersburg Association of Scholars and School of Religion and Philosophy. They were holding seminars to explore what Auschwitz and the Gulag had done to religion and Natalia gave us summaries of the earlier discussions. Intelligent, charming and anxious to help, she offered a car, driver and interpreter for the following Sunday when stern duties lay ahead of us. The weather forecast left on my pillow said 'snow'.

Descending early next morning I found Victoria tackling bliny and red caviar for breakfast. I asked anxiously about the day's weather and our arrangements. 'Relax,' she ordered, 'and enjoy this breakfast.'

At a large Roman Catholic church nearby, we began with a brilliant show by an American priest who, combining the dignity of his Church with fun, quickly put the children present on his side. He preached on the parable of the Good Samaritan, concluding that from those to whom much is given much is expected. Sound thinking, I murmured sententiously to Victoria as we departed.

Natalia's driver and interpreter then raced us off to a disappointing evangelical service. First we had to mount a long flight of stairs leading to a large concert hall with a red motif. A gathering of about 120 people including forty-five children were talking among themselves and occasionally glancing at the platform from which emerged a confusing medley of words and music. As we left, Victoria and the interpreter encountered an elderly woman. Most of her family, she told us, had perished in a deadly siege. Living off a monthly pension of 300 roubles – about US$20 – she would be happy to die, she added quietly. Victoria felt we must give something, and I pressed 100 roubles into her hand. Not much religion being practised on this site, I observed unkindly as we moved on.

Then to a popular and fully attended Russian Orthodox church, close to a huge city cemetery in a wood. It was one of two churches never closed even in religion's darkest days because of its proximity to the cemetery and its role in burials. The church was timber-built and attractive. It was alarmingly cold and Victoria urged that our interviews be brisk. We chatted to people waiting outside the church, but my fingers were too numb to write down what they told us. Suddenly we were summoned to meet the priest, a dramatic encounter. Throwing his arms round me and the interpreter, he looked at me anxiously. Had I fought in the war? At least I could give satisfaction on that score. Why did Hitler not invade England? I mentioned the Battle of Britain. Wrong! 'It was because so many people were on their knees praying.' After more on these lines, recorded on film by at least two members of the congregation and witnessed by a score more, we parted amicably. 'Pray for peace,' he instructed me. I readily agreed and revised my earlier opinion of the Russian Orthodox Church – all ritual and no soul. This priest was over-endowed with soul, but in the shelter of his church my feet and hands had got warmer.

It was a mistake to plan our expedition to Pakistan during Ramadan. At Heathrow we found the world and his wife trying to gets seats on a PIA flight to Lahore. It was one of those days when you reach the head of the queue to check-in forty minutes after the plane is supposed to have left. Ramadan, which calls for a strict fast during the hours of daylight, is hard on the digestion. 'A man behind me,' Victoria whispered to me on the plane, 'has just eaten three suppers.' I tend to judge countries by how long they keep me standing at immigration. Pakistan scored well and we were in the Hotel Palm Continental an hour after landing. Our cicerone was Philip Lall, with whom Victoria had made arrangements before we left London, and our first encounter with him was encouraging.

After an hour's sleep, we sought our way to the Anglican cathedral for evensong at 5 p.m. 'It's near the Courts of Justice,' they told us. From there we groped our way in rapidly failing light towards where we hoped the cathedral stood. Three taxi drivers and two onlookers declared they had no notion where it was. By following a bell we got there to find a congregation of five. The bishop's chaplain took the service beautifully and delivered a first-class sermon. What faith, I reflected, to be able to take evensong (as some of us remember it too) and to preach a sermon so buoyantly before a congregation of seven. After the service we made ourselves known to him and he insisted on returning to his residence, starting up an old jeep and delivering us safely back at our hotel.

Talk next day with the National Commission for Justice and Peace left me aware how often religious intolerance springs from bad legislation. We spent ninety minutes going through a list of twenty-one Islamic religio-political groups in Pakistan, and another list of those who have been brought to book by the infamous blasphemy laws.

While talking to Bishop Malik, in whose Anglican cathedral we had attended evensong, Victoria asked him why Christianity seemed strongest where it is most harshly treated. Bishop Malik quoted the psalmist, 'When I am weak, then I am strong.' We learned the truth of that.

So far so good, but we were approaching slippery ice. Our next talk was with Air Marshal Cecil Chaudry, a man recommended to me by a friend in England. Chaudry ran a school for 2,500 boys – Muslims and Christians – and declared there was no discrimination. Our discussion roamed widely over the break-up of the Soviet Union, the end of East–West confrontation, the rise of Islam and the nature of extremism.

Back at the hotel, reception tendered the welcome advice that those desiring alcohol could call the butler service for a menu of what was available. My spirits rose; Victoria declaring herself to be in January training went off to the gym. When we met later, she had a startling tale to tell of what Conan Doyle might have called the Chaudry Episode. She had received a fax from the Chaudry we thought we had just met, expressing a wish to meet us. Assuming he sought to add a postscript to our talk, she rang back to find herself talking to a totally different Chaudry. This Chaudry was in fact the man I had been recommended to interview, Air Marshal Zafir Chaudry, who told Victoria he would be pleased to meet us. Philip Lall had arranged on our behalf an audience with Group Captain, not Air Marshal, Cecil Chaudry, the schoolmaster.

'Awkward,' I say. 'More awkward than you suppose,' said Victoria, who recalled that while the three of us were waiting for schoolmaster Chaudry, Philip Lall had pointed to a wedding portrait on the wall and observed, 'She used to be extraordinarily beautiful but has put on a lot of weight.' From where she was sitting Victoria observed that the door was ajar and

Mrs Chaudry was hovering behind it, and had entered only when Lall had stopped speaking. 'Crikey!' I said.

The most depressing encounter of our entire tour came next day when we contrived to interview a victim of the Blasphemy Law. In theory at least he faced the death sentence. What emerged from our talk was how open this law was to abuse. One neighbour has a grievance against another, so he accuses him of mocking Mohammed or the Koran, or of hearing one of his children doing so. Then it's one man's word against another's. Charges are laid. The death penalty seems rarely if ever to be invoked, but it casts a long shadow over lives.

We also met what Lall calls 'working-class Christians'. Good chaps all and we kept it going for ninety minutes but it was very chilly. A permanent pall seemed to hang over Lahore, as it does in many of the subcontinent's new industrial cities. We talked to the cathedral's organist and his wife who were, as one would have expected, discreet, but we got a sharp sense of the nagging worries Christians had about a prosecution for blasphemy. Supposing his son, who went to school every day, was found guilty of some lapse? The young did not always guard their tongue. What then?

Our day ended with a supper party chez the Lalls. 'Sorry I shall not be able to offer you a glass of wine,' I heard Philip Lall say cheerfully to Victoria as we entered the room and my heart sank. You don't have to be an alcoholic to find that an evening party at which you are called on to chat to a lot of total strangers in a rather chilly house goes easier with a small refreshment in the hand.

We took the next afternoon off for a look at Lahore's attractions including the cricket ground which I faintly remembered from an earlier visit. The railway station, a gigantic Victorian artefact, looks majestic from the outside but is squalid inside. I lazily left Victoria and Philip Lall to explore the interior with its wide and handsome platforms built 140 years ago. Lahore reflects the confidence of the Victorian age: magnificent buildings mingle with the slums; the Victorians gave India a grandeur unmatched in any other part of the Empire.

The great Chaudry puzzle was resolved by the appearance of the Air Marshal and his wife for dinner with us. 'This is the genuine one,' I murmured to Victoria. Philip Lall differed and insisted he was a spy. This Chaudry runs a human rights bureau which struck me as innocent enough.

We were about to say farewell to Lahore, where I had caught a cold and passed it on to Victoria. I felt a bit down but rallied to give Philip Lall and his wife a farewell supper in a place of their choosing. Victoria proposed a bottle of beer for herself and a bottle of whisky for the Lalls and me. This kindly thought fell at the first fence of the hotel's butler service. 'No Scotch,' they declared, 'only local.' My experiences abroad have taught me that local beer is often surprisingly good, but if you aim to finish the trip upright, give local whisky a miss.

A fortnight later we were in Fidel Castro's Cuba, politically chilly but with a more congenial climate. As we soon saw, the island holds two different societies. The tourist, Cuba's main source of dollars, lives well here. From that level there was a long drop to Castro's own people who were earning an average wage of US$10 a month and living in bad housing. Forty years of Castro have left much of Havana in a time warp. The shabby narrow streets of old Havana, the once beautiful but now decaying buildings that stretch along the waterfront are the same streets, the same buildings that Graham Greene saw when he was there in the 1950s to write *Our Man in Havana*. As I observed in the capitals of Eastern Europe in the 1970s, in Hanoi in the 1990s and now in Havana, Marxist governments preserve their old skylines longer than capitalist governments.

The exteriors are lovely to look at, the interiors often slums of the worst kind.

Winter in Havana with temperatures of an English July had attracted a host of tourists, many of them from Canada and Italy. The lobby of the Hotel Nacional where we checked in swarmed with visitors, most of them dressed for the beach and bringing Ogden Nash's lines to mind:

> Sure, deck your lower limbs in pants;
> Yours are the limbs, my sweeting.
> You look divine as you advance—
> Have you seen yourself retreating?

There were other joys for them. We visited the Hotel Sevilla where Greene did much of his work. Sumptuously restored, it had installed his portrait. La Bodegita del Medio, where Ernest Hemingway did some of his drinking, had become Havana's most celebrated bar. Tourists fell over themselves to get a glass of his mixture, Mojito, which is made up with fresh lemon, sugar, plenty of crushed mint, ice and Cuban rum. It cost US$3 and was delicious. Heightening this illusion of being back in the 1950s were Havana's taxis. These very old American automobiles were imported into Cuba before the revolution of 1959, carefully preserved and never replaced. All the great gas-guzzlers were represented: the Chevrolet, the Cadillac, the Studebaker. Outside the Hotel Sevilla stood an ancient cream-coloured Ford with a dicky seat.

On our first night in Havana we took a taxi to the Hotel Inglettara for a drink on the terrace before supper. Of all the pleasures to be drawn from travel I find the best is leaving England in a cold climate and only hours later sitting out of doors being caressed by tropical warmth.

The Pope had recently paid a visit to Cuba, been rapturously received and greeted by Castro wearing a dark suit instead of military fatigues. We joined a baptism in the cathedral and talked to some of the mothers whose babies were being openly baptised. A godmother whose two sons had been baptised eleven years earlier spoke of the change that had come about. She had told only her family at the time. 'The Church was less open then. I would have got into trouble if people had known. For me it was no contradiction being a Catholic and a communist, but other people did not understand me.' The child's mother spoke in the same vein, 'Now it is much freer than it was. A few years ago, if you were religious there was prejudice against you and you did not get promotion. Now it does not matter at all. The Pope's visit made a huge difference.'

But we noticed other straws in the wind. There were no Bibles in the cathedral, no hymn books, no service papers. There were still no church schools anywhere in Cuba. The only religious teaching children got was in the home. Were we witnessing a church permitted to exist on sufferance and still under severe restraint? Or was it a church slowly triumphing over a determined attempt to abolish it? We asked Father Miguel Angel Rene who said, 'One of the worst things that has happened is the closing of Catholic schools and hospitals. It was where young people discovered religion. In 1990 a change for the better began, but we still have no church schools. Revival? It is superficial.' Children were still forbidden to take religious items to school. 'It is the grandparents who pass it on. We are thinking of building a monument to grandparents because they have kept the faith alive.' Were people still afraid? 'The state is communist and controls everything,' replied Father Rene.

Orlando Marque, spokesman for the Archbishop, was a degree more sanguine. Things had been getting better before the Pope's visit, he thought, and it had given the Christian community a valuable lift. In the early years of the revolution people had expected religion to disappear from Cuba. 'This has not happened.'

Father Marque thought the revival was genuine. 'But some

people come to church with expectations learned from a communist society, and quite far removed from Christian ethics.' That was the challenge faced by the Church. In 1959 there had been 700 priests for 6 million people and 2,000 nuns. 'Many were expelled from the country, yet we have to acknowledge that we are not comparable to Eastern Europe. No bishops were imprisoned or killed and ordinations continued.' With the revolution, Father Marque thought, the Church lost its social trappings and surplus weight, which was human not divine. 'This has given the Church respect in society.'

We hastened on from the cathedral to Mass at Merced, the oldest church in Havana, where the numbers were smaller but the celebration impressive. The Presbytarian church which we visited next was unexciting; but the Methodist church was in full swing. The preacher looked distractingly like Groucho Marx, but was in tremendous voice. We felt we had caught the authentic note of religious observation in Havana.

Nearly everyone was careful of what they said in Cuba. It becomes a habit in authoritarian regimes and makes it harder to catch the authentic note. We caught it in the cathedral quarter while talking to a nun who had worked in the city's poorest quarter for ten years. 'Castro has not changed his mind,' she told us quietly. 'Only the passage of time had brought about changes in the Church.' There were benefits: the Church was closer to the poor; but it was a Church under surveillance and one false step could reverse the forward march. 'We must not rush; a big change could be damaging. We have to take small steps.' Theoretically, she told us, Castro's plan was perfect. In practice it had failed, and class differences had become more extreme. 'Nobody is homeless, but it depends on what you call a home. If you call it a twelve foot by twelve foot room, with eight people living inside it, then nobody in Cuba is homeless. Children sleep with adults, so they see everything, and this leads to promiscuity. The living conditions are at the root of prostitution.'

We took a look at Revolution Square where the Pope had spoken to a gathering of 500,000 people. They all look the same these revolutionary squares: lifeless asphalt monuments to human vanity. Our visit coincided with the opening of a new church nearby. Some 500 people or more had turned up for this event, kept happy by a nun with a selection of hymns. Police seemed light on the ground, though our interpreter spoke darkly of secret police being present. I took snapshots cautiously. There is a narrow margin between carefree reporting and photography, and the headline: 'Peer held as Spy in Havana.'

Where religion is suppressed people resort to a wide range of substitutes. The most popular in Cuba was Santeria, an African-based religion that mixed Catholic rituals with voodoo. We were told that 60 per cent of the population had used Santeria at some point in their lives, usually at times of acute personal stress. So we visited the voodoo museum, involving a long tour round incomprehensible objects. Then we met a friend of our guide who taught voodoo. An enormous black man with a blonde wife, he outlined the system, regretting that we could not meet the 'king' of the movement, an influential figure in voodoo circles.

Our final interview, with an articulate young woman who had grown up with the revolution, was revealing, 'As a youngster I was enthusiastic about the revolution and worked for it. I believed in it so much I neglected my faith. I stopped going to church and convinced myself that religion was the opium of the people. If you believed in religion, you were cut off. You had to be a member of the communist party. Now I feel deceived. I gave the revolution my best years. What have I to show for it? Nothing!' The turning point had been the death of her mother in 1992. 'I was so distressed I went to church. I still did not believe, but I was desperate. One day I took communion and after that I did not look back.'

Christian Soldiers

'What a lot there was to discover about that extraordinary country,' I said to Victoria as we drove to the airport.

The flight to Shanghai took eleven hours and it redounds to our credit that within an hour of arrival we were walking towards the cathedral not far from our hotel, stopping only to buy cashmere jerseys – it was piercingly cold – at a shop selling them at about a quarter of the London rate. Shanghai's cathedral is an imposing building, well kept and open to visitors, but our virtue went unrewarded. A man we approached threw up his hands, which seems the Chinese way of saying they cannot communicate. An hour later, when we tried again, all was sweetness and light. We were shown into a comfortable waiting room at the back of the cathedral and seconds later the Roman Catholic bishop of Shanghai walked in. This was a big slice of luck.

He told us of his long years in prison, his solitude, his reliance on God. It conveyed all the agony such people suffered during the Cultural Revolution. We returned to the hotel feeling that we had got off to a promising start.

There were a hundred people at Mass in the cathedral early next morning where we met an Anglican bishop. Born in 1915, he was a reminder that China's church leaders are either over seventy or under thirty because the Cultural Revolution left a long gap. He was on a visit to Shanghai from Nanking and had another good tale to tell in clear English. We asked about the intellectual quality of religious teaching in the Church. That, he said, is the subject of the conference that had brought him to Shanghai. So we had met two bishops in less than twenty-four hours and been spared an uncertain train journey to Nanking.

The guide book spoke highly of the Peace Hotel on Shanghai's Huang Pu river front, along which we strolled after lunch. On the opposite bank of the wide river, full of strings of barges, were some of Shanghai's latest and most spectacular creations.

'Dr Carey [former Archbishop of Canterbury] once preached here,' Victoria announced as we entered the Community Church next morning. We received another vivid account from the priest there of his fears and faith during the revolution. I began to find meeting people who suffered, kept their faith and felt strengthened by it, a humbling experience.

After three days in booming Shanghai, we moved to a drabber Beijing. But it was spring and brighter than the gloomy days in 1979 when I was last there.

Our Saturday treat was to be the Great Wall, which is a ninety-minute drive from the capital. I had walked the Wall before when I was twenty years younger. There now seemed to be a lot of steps, going up rather than down. Victoria thought the Wall offered insight into the Chinese mentality and we chattered away, pausing now and again to survey our majestic surroundings and aiming vaguely for a cable car to bring us down. A party of visitors moving towards us waved their hands and shook their heads. The cable cars stopped at 4 p.m. Panic-stricken, I envisaged a night on the Wall. We retraced our steps and eventually struck a pathway of stairs leading down. Talk about the Long March! Victoria goes to the gym regularly and is fifty years younger than me. For the last fifteen minutes of this ordeal, against which my knees rebelled, I was glad of her arm. We had promised the driver to return at 4 p.m. It was now nearer 5 p.m. and there was no sign of him. I sat down on a low wall and despaired. Relatively minor crises of this kind render me useless. Victoria found our driver who was searching for us. Oddly, after a very hot bath on our return, I suffered no stiffness, only sore lips from the sun and altitude.

Sunday posed a different challenge, for we planned to visit different church services and make discreet enquiries, starting with Mass at the cathedral at 7.30 a.m. The cathedral was impressively full despite being piercingly cold. While chatting up people outside we approached two women, one of whom turned out to be an official. We were warned off. 'You will get people into trouble if you talk to them.' Our fingers were numb with cold again, but we got that down in the notebooks and moved rapidly on. At the Methodist church there were at least 800 people present, the biggest congregation we had seen on the whole tour.

The last lap. Back in England it was Holy Week, when we hoped our five pieces would be running in sequence. We worked rapidly on the China story, called the office in London (yes, they were running our first piece), dined with our correspondent and his wife and discussed the loneliness of a foreign correspondent in distant Beijing. 'Wouldn't be my cup of tea,' I told Victoria later. David Rennie had a fine wife, she said, which made all the difference.

'I'm sad it's over,' I said, as we boarded the plane for London via Paris, 'but not in tears to be leaving China.'

26

World in Conflict

Of all the conflicts I have witnessed, Sudan's civil war has been the most grievous. Yet I felt no special interest in it until one Saturday early in 1998 when, reluctantly abandoning a round of golf, I travelled to London to lunch with Carol Bellamy, American director of the United Nations Children's Fund (Unicef), who was passing through London. She urged me to join a party that was going to look at a relief operation mounted by Unicef called Operation Lifeline Sudan. My companions would be Vanessa Redgrave, a band called Caliche comprising three South American musicians, a film crew making a feature about Vanessa's role as goodwill ambassador for Unicef and Marie Staunton, then Unicef UK's deputy director. As it turned out, only Marie and I made the trip due partly to the difficulty of procuring visas. It was an expedition that required the support of two visas, one from the government of Sudan, a second from the Sudan People's Liberation Army in Nairobi. The SPLA was prone to reject passports which bore the Khartoum stamp. Nothing much has changed, I reflected, since Evelyn Waugh's William Boot in *Scoop* ran into similar difficulties when seeking entry to Ishmaelia. Luckily, I carry two passports.

Operation Lifeline Sudan (OLS) had been set up in April 1989 after a famine caused by drought and civil war had killed 250,000 people. Its mandate, negotiated between Unicef, the government in Khartoum and their opponents in the south of the country was to deliver humanitarian assistance to *all* civilians in need, irrespective of which side they were on. Countless civilians were in need. Sudan's war had been running for upwards of forty years and was sharpened by Khartoum's imposition of Islamic Sharia law in 1983. Nobody knows how many lives it had cost: one estimate in 1998 was 1.4 million of Sudan's 27 million population; at least twice as many people had been displaced. Ostensibly it was a war between an Arab/Muslim north and an African/Christian or animist south. But as often happens in conflicts that go on for a long time, crosscurrents had developed and the pattern of a ruinous war had become almost indecipherable. Insofar as Unicef could make it so, OLS was an even-handed operation; but that did not prevent both sides from constantly calling 'foul!' and interfering with flights from the airbase, because the aim of both sides was to direct as much food as possible towards their own supporters and prevent it from reaching their opponents.

Marie and I flew to Nairobi, spent a comfortable night there, then took the short flight from Wilson airfield to the OLS airbase at Lokichokio on the Kenya/Sudan border. I am always content to fly economy class and by the cheapest routes when travelling with aid organizations, and while in the field to sleep rough, but I draw the line at cheap hotel accommodation where something better is available. The chances are next day's business will start at dawn. Sleep and eat well while you can is my motto.

Loki had become the base not simply for Unicef's air operations but also for innumerable non-government organizations that were working in remote parts of southern Sudan. Every evening at around 6 p.m. they met the security officer to exchange news of dangers in the region. One of Loki's functions was to keep in touch with everyone working out in the field and, if need arose, to rescue them by air. I found this evening ritual impressive, a reminder of the risks aid workers take as part of the day's work. There being no runway lights, all flights were restricted to daylight and one woke at dawn to the sound of Hercules and Buffalo planes thundering off the tarmac with supplies.

Marie and I took a Buffalo transporter loaded with grain to Panthou in the Bahr el Ghazal region. As we landed in suffocating heat, women and children gathered round the plane, seized loose grains and ate them – my first inkling of the famine surrounding us. We walked slowly through the heat to a Médecins Sans Frontières supplementary feeding centre nearby. There, under the merciful shade of a large tree, were gathered some hundred mothers with their babies and younger children. If the babies fell 70 per cent below the weight for height formula or an upper arm measurement, they got a slender ration of high-protein Unimix – beans, rice, milk and sugar. If not, then the mothers, empty-handed and uncomplaining, set off back home in the searing heat. I felt profoundly moved by the dignity the unlucky ones displayed. 'A cruel feature of any famine,' I scribbled in my notebook, 'is having to say "no".'

It was a snapshot of Sudan that lodged in my memory. Another was our visit to the Red Cross hospital at Loki, partly a base hospital for the war. A capable matron took Marie and I round the beds. The worse the wound, the keener she was to show us the treatment. We visited a woman who had suffered a rifle shot through her cheeks. She will recover? 'Oh, certainly,' said this formidable woman calmly, 'but she is in great pain and grumbles a lot.'

A year or two later, Marie Staunton and the *Daily Telegraph* managing editor Sue Ryan hit on the idea of a book about Sudan in aid of Unicef to which well-known authors would contribute. I sought, over lunch, to persuade Helen Fielding, inventor of Bridget Jones, to join the company. She had written a good novel about Sudan after filming there. But she told me her heart was with Comic Relief and she didn't think the book would come off. (In fact, it sold well and won the WH Smith prize for travel books.) Do it yourself, I thought, and headed for Sudan's burgeoning oil fields. As I read Unicef's brief on 'Oil and Conflict in Sudan', while sitting in the sun at the Muthaiga Club in Nairobi, my reporter's whiskers twitched. The search for oil had begun in 1959, but not until 1975 was it found in southern and south-western Sudan. Most of the active oilfields were in disputed territory round Bentiu in Western Upper Nile. As more oil was found, conflict in that region intensified. So did an oil-thirsty world's interest in concessions. To speed the flow a 1,000-mile pipeline was built by the China National Petroleum Corporation across cruel territory to Port Sudan.

We flew to Wichok and Nhialdiu which was as near to the oil as flights were allowed but close enough for me to spot that to protect the oilfields, a vicious cordon had been thrown round them: villages burned and people displaced. The scandal lay in allegations implicating Canada's largest private oil company, Talisman: it was letting gunships fly off its airstrip. I secured a copy of Canada's Assessment Mission which had been investigating the affair. Hot stuff! I filed a story for the *Telegraph* and wrote a tale for the Unicef book about an imaginary country which preached human rights but acted as Canada was accused of doing. Just as well I took it over from Helen Fielding, I told myself grandly.

Sudan got into my blood. A year later I went back with Sue Ryan to see the work being done by the UN's World Food Programme which was providing a third of Sudan's food requirements. Its ninety-two pilots were flying 2,300 hours a month on deliveries, more than the entire South African air force. We took a two-hour flight to Lankien, where they were awaiting their first big air drop for ten months. There we met two displaced women with lifeless eyes. All their children had been drowned while fording a river as they fled from gunships. Sue Ryan was superb, gently debriefing them through an interpreter. I was speechless. It was the sort of tragedy you encounter in doom-laden Sudan. We saw the big air drop before we left. A four-engined Hercules C130 deftly jettisoned 16 tons of wheat from 1,000 feet up. They said that 10,000 people had come to greet that plane, most of them women dressed in gorgeous colours. Celebrating!

Among Sudan's most inaccessible regions, there being no roads to speak of, lie the Nuba Mountains. There, rumour had it, unspeakable horrors had occurred during the civil war. I suggested to Clare Crawford, chairman of Landmine Action and an intrepid travelling companion, we should take a look. Yes, they told us when we had wormed our way in, there had been terrible loss of life and every school had gone but the curse laid on the Nuba Mountains was uncharted landmines planted by both sides. The SPLA laid them round the villages, the government of Sudan laid them on the so-called roads, which were dirt tracks. As well as mines there was unexploded ordnance everywhere. So we travelled circumspectly, watched Landmine Action de-miners at work and visited mine victims. By contrast with most of Sudan, I thought watching a stunning sunset one evening, it is a beautiful region concealing hideous secrets.

But it's not Sudan's most inaccessible region, I decided in the summer of 2004 after getting into Darfur with a guide from Save the Children and the talented *Telegraph* photographer, Abby Trayler-Smith. What America called genocide was going on there and one caught a glimpse of what lies behind the Sudan tragedy. This vast country, ruled from Khartoum, contains many oppressed and discontented people, in the north as well as the south. Khartoum's grip on them is tenuous. Any sign of unrest – and whack! Darfur's agony sprang fundamentally from the over-reaction of a deeply insecure regime in Khartoum.

When people ask me, as they sometimes do, 'Why on earth, at your age, do you want to go on these trips?' I answer them by saying truthfully, 'I have such engaging travel companions.' Marie Staunton, who left Unicef to become director of Plan UK and Clare Crawford, who has been associated with Mines Advisory Group and Save the Children, have borne the brunt of it, mainly because both of them have an eye for a good news story. Both are also more resourceful than I am in bad situations. Clare demonstrated this when, wearing her Save the Children hat, she persuaded me that child soldiers were one of the world's scandals and we should go to Sierra Leone's dirty little war to prove it. We went in through the back door, flying to Ivory Coast, thence to Monrovia in Liberia and hired a small plane to fly us up to the eastern border of Sierra Leone.

I sat alongside the pilot, Clare behind me with an African guide. Suddenly the pilot's compass in this grotty plane packed up and he lost his way over unfriendly country. Somehow we got him to turn about and fly on until he spotted a familiar landmark. We got back to base without much in the tank. I would have settled for a strong drink; Clare stormed back into the plane-hire shop. It was not nearly crashing that annoyed her, she told the slippery proprietor, but losing a day's engagements. She demanded another plane instantly and free of charge. The proprietor shrugged nervous shoulders. His only other plane was a Russian gunship with a crew of six. 'That'll do nicely,' said Clare, 'get it out quick.' The slippery proprietor, hypnotized by her anger, got it out. We flew comfortably to the Sierra Leone border. I forked out twenty dollars for locals to guard the gunship that night so the crew could get a good sleep on board.

One needs to be aware that when crusading against child soldiers – or landmines for that matter – that one is beating the air. Those who force children, drunk or drugged, to kill or maim their own kind don't care what the world thinks of them any more than those who make or plant uncharted anti-personnel mines give a damn for the consequences. But to care for the victims of these atrocities is a serious task. It is impossible for the layman to fathom the mental damage done to children driven to butcher people. Clare and I met one lad of eleven who had been soldiering since he was seven. Did he have any difficulty with the AK47 rifle, we asked. Oh none! 'If I had one now,' he boasted, 'I could give you a demonstration.'

They were a rum bunch. Removed from family influence, they had become malleable and ruthless. Given food, clothing and drugs, they told us, they were expected to fight without pay. One thirteen-year-old had been commanding men since the age of ten. Save the Children reckoned Liberia had some 6–8,000 child soldiers – a fifth of the factions' armed forces. At dinner with Unicef, I listened to aid workers discussing in troubled voices what seemed to them evil on an unprecedented scale: they spoke of children whose minds had been stolen.

Clare Crawford and I chalked up three and a half wars together, the half being a grim experience on the northern border of Angola as the ill-named Democratic Republic of the Congo erupted, and panic-stricken refugees flooded into Angola. The plight of the refugees had such an effect on us both that we felt driven to break training and at four o'clock in the afternoon sat together in rough surroundings sipping medicinal whisky. We visited Angola, a country laid low by civil war and corruption, a couple of times. The only happy recollection I have of that sad land is of Clare meeting her future husband, who was exploring its huge oil potential.

*

My blood tingled when in the summer of 2000 Clare proposed an expedition to Eritrea on behalf of Save the Children. Colonized by Italy in the late nineteenth century, it had been Mussolini's base for the attack on Ethiopia in 1935. Because I reported that war from Addis Ababa, Asmara was on my list of places to go some day. After Italy's defeat by British Commonwealth forces in 1941, Eritrea became a British protectorate, was then federated to Ethiopia in 1952 and became an Ethiopian province in 1962 – a recipe for disaster. It secured an uneasy independence from Ethiopia in 1993, but a long-running dispute over the frontier smouldered on, culminating in a ruinous battle in the summer of 2000. Clare and I arrived just after an Organisation of African Unity (OAU) brokered ceasefire. They were awaiting UN peacekeepers. The battle zone, where 1.5 million Eritreans had been displaced, was miserable and nerve-wracking because there were landmines everywhere, but Asmara was a treat.

We saw a complete art deco city, virtually rebuilt by the Italians between 1935 and 1938. As one writer had put it, 'Mussolini's world is not usually associated with beauty, but when the Italians built Asmara, they did it with the style and elegance for which they are historically renowned. Influenced by the beautiful landscape and desert light, and in the spirit of the age, they created a dazzling *international moderne* city which was well-planned and well-built, functional and of great aesthetic appeal.' This, I must add, was not how Evelyn Waugh saw it. Though at one time an admirer of Italy's endeavour to 'civilize' the wild Abyssinians, he wrote in *Waugh in Abyssinia*, 'Asmara may have been a decent enough little town before the [1914–1918] war when it was built to accommodate a white population of 2,000. Now there were 60,000 and it was hell . . . Every shop, restaurant and place of entertainment, even the cathedral, was unendurably overfull.' Waugh says he was bitten by fleas, which may account for his feelings. Furthermore, he was there in 1936 when Asmara was full of engineers, craftsmen and labourers.

The third war I visited with Clare was Kosovo in September 1999. With Martin Bell as a travel companion we shared the rigours of Pristina's five-star hotel, the Grand. The food there was tolerable but due to constant power failures the lifts were unreliable. Whenever I stayed there I found that when the lifts were not working, the room allotted to me was at the top of the hotel. Climbing ten flights to bed at my age was a trial.

Marie Staunton and I had first gone out to Kosovo in November 1998, when outright war merely loomed. Some 15,000 houses in Kosovo had been destroyed. Health conditions were dire. Marie wrote telling me that 200,000 people – a tenth of the population – had become homeless. Soon snow would add to their trials. She was going out to assess this human crisis for Unicef. Would I join her? One portrait of that visit lodges in my memory. Marie and I were on the first floor of a half-finished house in the village of Gloreva, not far from Pristina. The place had no windows or doors. There was snow on the ground and it was bitterly cold. Sitting round the bare brick walls in Muslim fashion was an extended family of some twenty-five men, women and children. Their only source of warmth was a tiny charcoal fire on the lid of a biscuit tin.

It was a young girl's face that caught my eye. There were no tears, no expression of cold or hunger, only a look of utter desolation. 'She was of an age,' I scribbled down as I watched, 'to have all the dreams of childhood, and all her dreams were gone.' The girl sat there with her arm round one of the youngest children, her sensitive face revealing a broken spirit. Feeling a brute, I asked the photographer with us to catch a close-up of her. As it turned out, my own snap of her taken with a cheap camera delivered a more moving message.

A woman in a white headscarf spoke for the group. 'We

would gladly go home to what is left of our house. The trouble is we do not feel safe. The West has been too late.' Three days earlier they had gone back to see their burned-out house in Obria. They found one of their pictures, a family group, in the ruins. 'The police,' said the woman in the headscarf, 'had shat on it. I cannot think that these people are normal.' Live with the Serbs? 'Never!' It was the voice of doom.

By Easter 1999, ethnic cleansing in Kosovo was in full swing. The Unicef office in London arranged for me to fly to Skopje in Macedonia with one of their stars, Sally Ann Burnheim. The only way in seemed to be via Greece, so we flew to Thessaloniki and motored to the Macedonian frontier, where on Easter Sunday Unicef picked us up. The crisis, we soon learned, was at Blace, a short drive out of Skopje. Thousands of refugees had poured into a field there since Good Friday, and were without food or shelter, waiting to be processed for entry into Macedonia. Clare Short, then overseas development minister, suddenly flew in from London. There was to be a small top-level meeting with her at 6 p.m. attended by Lieutenant-General Sir Michael Jackson (at that point head of the Allied Rapid Reaction Force) and Macedonian ministers. For security reasons, I had been made a Unicef special representative, so was eligible to attend. It was an hour before Clare Short reached us. She'd come, she said, at the urgent request of Prime Minister Blair. She wanted 10,000 refugees moved out of Blace that night. Some hope! There ensued a wrangle. 'I want a short meeting,' said Clare in a commanding voice, 'and these people out.' As the meeting broke up, I thought, 'solidarity abroad,' went up to her and said, 'Well done!' She looked embarrassed.

Next morning Sally Ann and I went to Blace. Below us in a muddy valley sloping down to the River Scupi were crammed some 65,000 refugees. Macedonian police manned the solitary exit, allowing one at a time to leave the field to be processed and moved off in buses. It was a grim scene. I heard a man shout, 'They're dying down there and dead bodies are going into the river.' It was not true, but in the circumstances it seemed likely. The crush and ruthless behaviour of the over-whelmed police meant that families were being torn apart, thus adding to the agony. I glanced at the hills on the other side of the road. Some of the trees were in blossom, 'wearing white for Eastertide,' as I wrote in my account for the *Telegraph*, scrib-bled out as we drove back to Skopje and dictated to London on Sally Ann's mobile telephone.

By June 1999, two months after NATO had started to bomb Yugoslav military installations, almost a million ethnic Albanians, or half the population had fled Kosovo. To look at the refugee camps in Albania, Marie Staunton, Gary Street MP, Opposition spokesman on overseas development, and I flew down to Tirana and thence by helicopter to Kukes. Refugees, I was reminded once more, suffer twice over: they experience the bodily discomfort of improvized camps, invariably over-crowded; they have nothing to occupy their minds except speculation on the likely fate of their homes and belongings, which have probably been trashed or destroyed. In one of the camps, I watched children running round in the sun, looking happy and getting brown. I remarked how closely it all resem-bled a holiday camp which most children love. 'Yes,' said my companion, 'but when holiday camp ends they're glad to get back to their pets and their friends. For these children, the pets will be dead and their friends flown.'

In one corner of this teeming camp the children were holding a sing-song. They were singing a well-known song about a mother whose children had been sent off to fight. She has just heard that they are dead, and she is crying. As they sang, I noticed a woman near me in tears. 'The children should not be singing this song,' she protested. 'It is too sad.' I felt like crying myself.

In one of the refugee camps Unicef had established what they called 'child-friendly spaces,' a naff title but an inspired idea. In this tent children could escape from their sorrowful parents for a couple of hours. There, with drawing books and pots of paint, Unicef were helping a few fevered minds calm down. Only a few, but it counted for something in the human experience. As an exhibition of their work showed, when they first arrived the children's drawings and paintings were of fighting, planes, tanks, fires, after a while, they painted gentler scenes – animals, trees, flowers.

We dined with a psychologist from the World Health Organisation (WHO). Ten per cent of these children, he said, were seriously disturbed and prone to panic. Those over eight years of age were the worse affected. He talked to us about the rape that had been going on, the importance of not cross-examining the victims, adding harsh words about reporters who had been searching for victims and their stories. I looked him firmly in the eye.

My seventh and final visit to that region was with Clare Crawford again to investigate an aspect of the war which troubled us. NATO had been dropping cluster bombs. Dropped by aircraft in huge containers, these were bomblets which, if they failed to go off, took on the role of landmines. The failure rate was as high as 10–12 per cent. Richard Lloyd of Landmine Action who came with us reckoned 8,000 unexploded bomblets had been picked up so far and that there were another 14–20,000 to be found and dealt with. Walking the fields, we came across one or two of these little yellow perils. 'Just the thing to attract a child's curiosity,' I observed.

I was discussing the legacy of the Vietnam war over lunch with Clare Crawford in London when she said, wearing her Mines Advisory Group hat, 'We ought to take a look at Laos. It's still full of unexploded ordnance.' Between 1965 and 1973, the United States Air Force dropped 2 million tons of bombs on the Ho Chi Minh Trail which ran through Laos, losing upwards of 500 planes. Laos was still infested with this ordnance, an alarming amount of it unexploded. The dangerous stuff was the live cluster bombs which the passage of time had concealed. We found a big American helicopter engaged in tracing where the USAF bombers had fallen so that the crews' remains could be sent home. The task was expected to continue for five more years.

We took one afternoon off from our melancholy business to explore the Plain of Jars. These heavy stone pots, each standing as high as a man, are scattered over two adjacent areas of the plain. Most but not all of them were smashed by American bombing. Nobody seemed to know what they had been or why they were there. 'I'll do some research when we get home,' I said to Clare, but I never did and I never shall. There are too few mysteries left in this world.

Our hotel, the well-named Auberge de la Plaine des Jarres, was otherwise unoccupied. It is delightful to have a hotel to yourself and exclusive attention from the staff. It was also a beautiful spot, close to the Plain, perched high on a hill and surrounded by dazzling flowers, though the flower beds were oddly decorated with empty shell cases. Sitting in the bright sunshine with Clare, I shared my dream of being enormously rich and owning such a place in this remote corner of the world, largely for the pleasure of my friends, particularly those recovering from illness. 'Yes,' I said, warming to my dream, 'and I would be rich enough to buy their return tickets to Vientiane, and they would share part of every English winter with me.' As Graham Greene discovered, this region of South-East Asia with its lovely landscapes, widespread poverty and gentle people is a good place to indulge dreams of the unattainable.

The Invisible Hand has been kind to me on all the overseas adventures I've undertaken in recent years. In the only mishap to befall me, it showed marked benevolence. The Indian earthquake early in 2001, which struck hardest in the heavily populated state of Gujarat, was a grim assignment. With two companions, David Bull, director of Unicef UK, and *Daily Telegraph* photographer Peter Macdiarmid I flew in a relief plane to Ahmedabad, which had been badly damaged. At first they told us that 100,000 people were homeless; I put the figure much higher. It was distressing to see so many people groping precariously through the ruins of their houses or apartments in the hope of recovering small treasures. A cheering drink might have helped, but it was not readily available in India and I had unwisely chosen that fortnight for one of my self-imposed spells of abstinence.

We took a long journey by car to look at damaged villages. There were gloomy bulletins. 'Blachou, population 60,000, stench of bodies. Could be 15,000 under the rubble.' 'Anjar, population 80,000, flattened.' 'Some 229 villages destroyed.' In Ahmedabad's civilian hospital they had undertaken 300 major surgical operations, most of them relating to the spine or head. In the children's ward we saw small children with crushed limbs. One little tot who stared at us with enormous sick eyes seemed to have lost a leg and an arm. Thank God, I thought, for the analgesics and pain killers which Unicef was rushing in. I ate a light supper, retired to my room and fortuitously wrote 700 words about our day's experiences.

Early next morning we flew by helicopter over the damaged zones. Our flight took just over five hours. As we took off after our final stop for fuel, I felt a slight numbness in my left arm. My two companions declared I was having trouble in turning the pages of my notebook and, when we landed at Ahmedabad, insisted on my going to a hospital for a check-up. It was late on Sunday evening but they seemed ready to receive me. In under an hour they had done a scan and X-ray, taken my blood pressure and delivered a reassuring report. There was no serious damage. If I behaved sensibly, the top doctor told me, I would return as good as new. Not a bad performance, I reflected drowsily, by a small hospital in a city knocked about by an earthquake. I felt slightly fraudulent. David Bull and Peter Macdiarmid took the copy I had providentially written the night before and dictated it to the foreign desk in London, checking an illegible word or two with me while the doctors fluttered round. Next day, the top doctor had me out of bed and standing on my two feet. By the end of the week, he had me walking round the ward. Stephen Robinson, our foreign editor, flew out from London to assist my return. We were joined by a splendid doctor who specialized in assisting walking wounded to return from foreign adventures to their base. We flew to London via Delhi. As we sat in the airport lounge, the good doctor took my blood pressure with a fingertip device, smiled and said, 'Would you care for a large gin and tonic?' Thus I broke three weeks of abstinence.

27

Pressing On

People find it odd that at the age of eighty-something I choose to work more or less full-time in a newspaper office. 'You go to the office five days a week?' they say in a tone of voice which leaves me with the onus of proving that I am not bonkers. 'You stay in London, of course?' 'Not if I can help it!' 'You surely don't commute from Kent every day?' I then try to explain that a train journey of seventy minutes in the morning gives me an opportunity to read the newspapers thoroughly and so sometimes arrive at the office with ideas for editorials or my weekly column.

I do not find it easy to explain even to myself precisely where the attraction lies of working in the Canary Wharf tower every day. There are in fact several professions where, granted good health, people are reluctant to give up. The stage is one of them. Music is another. Politics was once. Gladstone was older than I am now during his fourth and last premiership. But politics have become too strenuous for octogenarians. Writing applies no age limit. If I were suddenly given five seconds only in a television chat show to explain why, the *Daily Telegraph* permitting, I find working there compulsive, my answer would probably be 'not being sure what lies round the next corner'. That is one of journalism's enduring charms. Every day one enters the editorial floor with a faint flutter of expectation. What may be required of me today? Goodness, there have been some weird requests in recent times. 'Will you cover Ronnie

Kray's funeral in Bethnal Green?' 'Will you interview Richard [*One Foot in the Grave*] Wilson for us?' 'Will you go to Rwanda?' 'Will you do 1,100 words on the Princess of Wales's interview with *Panorama*? We shall need the copy, by the way, before she actually finishes the interview.' If you think as I do that you are as good as – and no better than – the last piece you wrote, then all such requests represent a challenge, particularly if they require you to write against the clock. If I put my mind to it, and depending to some extent on the subject, I can turn out a thousand words in a hundred minutes. I find being required to do so rejuvenating.

There is something else as well. As we grow older, our perspectives grow wider. We forget a lot, but we also gain a little more insight into things. In some situations, I now see aspects of human life that I would not have seen even ten years ago. With luck then, you can occasionally offer a new way of looking at old problems; or illustrate that what everyone thinks is a new problem is in fact an old problem. To do this calls for no great wisdom, but it helps to keep moving. Given the indulgence of the *Daily Telegraph*, I have travelled overseas more lately than I have ever done before in my life.

> Clay lies still, but blood's a rover
> Breath's a ware that will not keep,
> Up, lad, when the journey's over,
> There'll be time enough to sleep.

A. E. Housman conveys the right message, but when you get past a certain age the helping hand of a younger colleague becomes welcome. In this respect, I have been fortunate. Early in 1994, Trevor Grove, who was then deputy editor to Max Hastings at the *Daily Telegraph*, approached me with a new idea. Would I like to look at the political scene in Britain with Victoria Combe, who had come in from a long spell overseas, find out what she made of it through fresh eyes, compare notes and put together a joint piece? I readily agreed, and thus set the course for a singularly happy association.

Despite a gap of fifty years between us, Victoria and I found we had the same eye for what makes a good news story at home or abroad, the same ear for a joke. Furthermore we could put together a joint piece on the screen expeditiously and harmoniously. On the office computers or on the road using our laptops, we played a duet. Victoria handled the lighter passages. On the more ponderous stuff, I moved in. We shared the news reporting. I persuaded myself that I was helping a promising young reporter to find her way to the stars. It would be nearer the mark to say that Victoria was helping me not to become a geriatric bore. Later on she injected ideas into my Monday column, which meant that it was not addressed exclusively to my own generation. When in 1996 I received the James Cameron Award for journalism, I was glad to be able to extend my gratitude to her publicly. Victoria Combe, I said in acknowledging the award, had made me look a better reporter than I really am.

On this initial venture, we quickly agreed on the best way of going about it. We decided to pick half a dozen constituencies near London and spend a day in each of them talking to people on the street, reckoning that would throw light on the prevailing mood, as indeed it did. We chose five true-blue constituencies – Eltham, Orpington, Chelmsford, Petersfield and Worthing. We then spent several days in a snowy February feeling the political pulse. It was not an exercise I would have dreamed of undertaking alone. At every Tory headquarters, we talked to the local MP or the chairman of his association or the agent. For the rest, we worked on the streets, round shopping centres, in newsagents' shops – anywhere where we could induce people to stop for a few minutes and talk. This sort of work has much in common with door-to-door canvassing in election campaigns. You start the day nervously, expecting on every doorstep to be rebuffed. The limbs seem stiff, the tongue dry. You long for the lunch break. After a while these inhibitions wear off. It also helps, as I had discovered during eight election campaigns on my own behalf, to work with an attractive companion.

It was a strange experience. I had spent twenty-five earlier years of my life in politics. Now, twenty years after leaving them, I was listening to what people thought about the present-day political scene, which was often uncomplimentary. 'This was your life,' I thought ruefully. Victoria, who was then twenty-seven and had been living in Bangkok for three years, held views of her own. Coming from a region where people had a fight on their hands to win any kind of democracy, she was immediately struck by the indifference shown by so many in this country towards our own system of parliamentary democracy. She thought we had become spoiled. It suggested the opening line of the joint piece we ultimately wrote: 'After a week's travel through the Tory heartlands of southern England, we found democracy under a blanket of snow.'

Though starting from different viewpoints, we found that we reached roughly the same conclusions. I was familiar with the sort of public apathy you find at by-elections, but the indifference we had encountered ran deeper. We noted the number of young people we met whose eyes glazed over when we asked them what they expected from government. Many laughed at the question, and made it clear they had no intention of voting. Victoria contrasted these attitudes with some of the young Thais who cared passionately for their right to democracy. Two years earlier she had reported a demonstration in defence of this right in which many were shot by soldiers in the streets of Bangkok.

The attitudes we struck also set me thinking about our own profession of journalism. You cannot be as long as I have been in journalism – which at the time of writing is sixty-six years – without witnessing changes; and, as you grow older, they will often appear to be changes for the worse. The most noteworthy change in my time has been in the social standing of journalists to politicians. Before the war proprietors and editors were captains of their ship and pretty well everyone else was in the ranks. Almost all reporters in the broadsheets wrote anonymously.

These days, proprietors and editors are still in charge, but the forces they command are stronger and more independent. Journalism has risen in power, attracting to newspapers, to radio and to television countless young men and women of talent, some with very good university degrees. In many respects, it has become a more attractive profession than politics; and it increasingly attracts able young men and women who might otherwise feel drawn to politics. It is often better paid. Above all, it offers the appearance of power to journalists who write under their own name and are granted freedom to write much as they please.

Thus, in my judgement, a new rivalry has arisen between the journalist and the politician. When I became a lobby correspondent in 1937, I knew my place. It was to report what the politicians did or were about to do. Comment on what they did was confined mainly to the leader writers. Radio was primitive. There was no television. Politicians led a relatively carefree life. Nobody investigated their private failings. Nobody called them at 7 a.m. demanding they explain on the telephone to *Today* listeners why they had said something silly in the House of Commons. Cartoonists like Low and Strube had fun with them. Proprietors occasionally thundered. But the sort of razor-slashing in which some columnists today are encouraged to indulge was absent. In short, the ruling class enjoyed a lot more respect than they get from their equals in today's news media.

I am persuaded that this habit of disparaging politicians is having certain consequences. Persistent disparagement of some members of the Royal Family has begun to put a question-mark over the future of the monarchy. Perpetual disparagement of politicians may well lead people to question our system of parliamentary democracy.

I have lived on both sides of the fence. I have been in a Cabinet under fire from the news media. As the editor of a national newspaper I have done some firing of my own. The late Iain Macleod once sagely observed that relations between the politician and the press should be *abrasive*. It is a good word. When you find them in each other's pockets, the chances are that democracy does not exist. Tension between press and politician is one of democracy's safeguards. But, in a society which has become far more equal than it was, the press should not be too contemptuous of our rulers. We no longer have the hierarchical society into which I was born. We are socially on more level ground. The authority of the politician is more open to challenge than it was. If the public are persuaded that their politicians are a poor lot, then we shall run into difficulties.

Some of my friends in the news media will shake their heads. Politicians have lost standing through their own folly and misbehaviour, they will say. In fact during our political tour, Victoria and I found that petty scandals count for less in the public mind than we suppose. Self-confessed adultery did not stand in the way of Alan Clark when he sought and won the confidence of the South Kensington and Chelsea Conservatives. I doubt very much if the morals of politicians have changed much over the years. But, in the furiously competitive world of the British national press, parliamentary scandals nourish circulations, especially on Sundays.

Our political tour had other consequences. The *Daily Telegraph* liked the story and gave it a good show. On the strength of this, we decided to repeat the experiment and look at attitudes to Europe both sides of the Channel. We chose the cities of Norwich and Rouen, which were twinned. Norwich went well and produced a small joke that brought a bigger mail-bag to my column than ever before or since. As we left one office, somebody considerately asked Victoria, 'Would you care to visit the facilities?' There must be a prettier way of putting it than that, I said later, and invited readers of my column for ideas, offering two bottles of champagne to the winner. The contest attracted 400 entries and the winner produced a forgotten phrase found in an Oxford English Dictionary: 'Would you care to pluck a rose?' I then received letters of protest from people saying it was open to misunderstanding, and a second winner came in with: 'If anyone needs to spend a penny, that is the door.'

Rouen turned out to be a stiffer test of Victoria's resourcefulness. I forgot to bring my passport to Gatwick, but anticipated no serious difficulty. We rang Rouen, where staff declared that without it I would be *persona non grata*. I proffered my House of Lords pass. It was dismissed as useless. We'll go to Paris, Victoria said, and we amended our travel arrangements. When the Post Office opened, she steered me through the humiliating process of acquiring a temporary passport. There was one of those terrible cabins, where the photograph you take of yourself suggests you have just been disinterred. This particular cabin had a wonky stool. Name? asked the clerk. 'Lord Deedes,' I said. 'Mr Lord William Deeds,' he wrote, omitting the last 'e'. More by luck than judgement we eventually reached Rouen in time for all our appointments.

In Rouen's Notre Dame Cathedral, I found cause to reflect on another chapter in my past. Six weeks before D-Day in 1944, Allied forces had set out to destroy Rouen's bridges over the Seine. That must have sounded very good news to some of us who were going to take part in the invasion; but they missed the bridges and hit the cathedral. On the morning of 19 April 1944, the twelfth-century nave was full of broken glass and rubble. 'There is this story,' the chairman of a company in Rouen told us both drily. 'On the morning after the raid, people were asking each other, "How did you survive the bombardment?" The reply was, "We went on the bridges . . ."'

Our expedition compelled me to think more deeply about Europe, and what originally lay behind the idea of a united Europe. We have become so aggravated by the bureaucrats who have taken charge in Brussels and so obsessed about the political consequences that we tend to overlook what was in Churchill's mind when, soon after the end of the Second World War, he raised the cry, 'Let Europe unite!'

Churchill was permanently affected by the fearful human waste of the First World War. He saw much of his own generation perish. He knew the extent of our losses. He dreaded it happening again in the Second World War, for if it did he doubted that we could survive as a nation. With his vast experience, as I have observed earlier, he saw ahead more clearly than anyone else. Who saw more clearly than he did the post-war future with Stalin's Soviet Union? His speech in America about the Iron Curtain, which drew criticism from some quarters at the time for being bellicose, was proved right by events.

So, during this European expedition, I remained – and still remain – respectful of his judgements. We are fifty years on since his pronouncement about Europe. The Soviet Union has cracked up, but human nature – or rather man's nature – has changed very little. I am not persuaded that men have turned away from war. I have seen too much of it in the world. The Cold War, the nuclear bomb, the prospect of total war between the superpowers concentrated minds wonderfully for a while; but not, I think, finally. Working on another story with Victoria in the early summer of 1995 brought that home to me. During the VE-Day anniversary week-end, we went over to France to look at some of the war cemeteries in Normandy. I looked at the graves of soldiers I had fought alongside in 1944. 'Never again,' I said on behalf of my own generation. 'There are still a lot of young men', Victoria replied unexpectedly, 'who long for the glory of war. It is the only way they feel they can truly prove themselves.' I recorded this in my column. Some readers wrote more in sorrow than anger. One or two young men declared that she was right.

Through all this we became well acquainted with each other's thinking. So when Victoria put a message on my screen,

'What about Sarajevo next?', in the summer of 1995, I gave it serious thought. I called my friends at CARE. It might be possible, they said. We obtained the support of the *Sunday Telegraph*, who said they would welcome an upbeat feature, dwelling on heroism rather than horrors. With that in mind, our visit was well timed because a massacre outside a market in Sarajevo had given NATO the long-awaited pretext for silencing Serb guns and mortars around the besieged city. As we arrived, under the guidance of CARE International (Canada), life was beginning to run through its veins again.

We listened to tales of human pain, endurance and bravery. We learned about children who had been traumatized by four years of war. We heard what life had been like in the blocks of high-rise apartments which run down what was called Snipers' Alley. What caught our imagination was the way in which the women of the city had made their contribution. They turned out looking their best. That was their gift to morale. They felt it was a way to unnerve the enemy.

It would, we reckoned, take many children a long time to recover from their ordeal. Brenda Cupper, CARE Canada's country director in former Yugoslavia, told us this story. There was a thirteen-year-old girl whom Cupper encountered while she was sorting out a new water point in the city. Every day this child went to get water for her family at a point so dangerous that all the aid workers avoided it. She went because she was fleetest of foot, and she went at night because of the snipers. 'But now', she told Brenda Cupper, 'the snipers have got infra-red sights on their rifles, so they can see me in the dark and I am scared.' 'You don't have to go there any more,' said Brenda, 'we have installed a new and safer water point.' The girl fell on her knees and embraced Cupper's legs.

One morning Victoria and I walked from our hotel to the bridge in Sarajevo where, on 28 June 1914, the Archduke Franz Ferdinand, heir to the Austro-Hungarian throne, was assassinated by a nineteen-year-old student, thus starting the landslide to war. They had removed a plaque marking this episode because the assassin, Gavrilo Princip, was also a Serb. I looked at the shattered buildings around us. 'Man's inhumanity to man still prevails,' I said.

They gave our joint piece a full page in the *Sunday Telegraph*. We both had reason to draw peculiar satisfaction from this because while we were out of the country, my successor as editor of the *Daily Telegraph*, Max Hastings, left the newspaper, thus confronting all of us with a large question-mark over our future. On return to the CARE main office from a visit to UNICEF (The UN Children's Fund), a cryptic note from London awaited us. 'Max has resigned. Gone to the *Evening Standard*.' Later that evening my son Jeremy, who became temporarily the editor, telephoned to explain what he thought was happening. 'The situation remains foggy,' I reported to Victoria. We decided to put the matter out of our minds and concentrate on the story in hand.

I had thoroughly enjoyed my years under Max and regretted his going. We never had a cross word. On hearing the names mentioned as candidates to succeed Max, I reckoned Sarajevo could well be the last story Victoria or I wrote for the Telegraph Group. These fears proved groundless with the appointment of Charles Moore as the new editor. He had joined the newspaper while I was editor. He wrote in generous terms and asked me to carry on, so I carried on. I began to feel that I qualified for a place in the *Carry On* farce series. Victoria was promoted to church affairs correspondent.

When not expressing incredulity at my persistent attach-ment to Canary Wharf, kind people sometimes ask me what contribution I make to the House of Lords. The answer to that is, virtually none. It is not possible at my time of life to combine daily work on a national newspaper with the legislative duties of a peer. I always open my Whip, which arrives by Friday morning's post and scan it for days on which the Conservatives will be desperate without me. If the Whips call me with an SOS,

I will turn up. A friendly Labour peer observed to me in 1995, 'We get quite excited when we see you here. We know the Tories are in trouble.'

I have retained one strong political interest which represents my last crusade. I am at war with anti-personnel mines in the world and everyone who promotes them. I started this campaign some three years ago at the suggestion of Brigadier Paddy Blagden, who was then our man on mines at the United Nations in New York. Early in 1994, just before Victoria and I embarked on our political round, I went over to see him, and was appalled by what he told me.

The more I examined the subject, the more I felt impelled to do something about this plague of mines in the world. I had seen enough of the Third World with CARE to know how grievously these mines impeded recovery after wars in Asia and Africa. They laid waste to life and limb and land among the poorest people in the world. They made resettlement of millions of refugees hazardous. Mines victims die singly in far-off countries of which we know little. Their fate is never reported. The world, with many other preoccupations, remains uneasy but insufficiently roused to influence governments.

I got in touch with an old parliamentary colleague, the late Lieutenant-Colonel Colin Mitchell, 'Mad Mitch' of the Argyll and Sutherland Highlanders. He had founded a charity called the Halo Trust, which he ran more or less single-handed from his flat in Dolphin Square. Halo then comprised a small corps of trusted army friends who made it their job to set up shop in the minefields of countries like Mozambique, Afghanistan, Cambodia and Angola. There, on military lines, they recruited and trained men of the local population to set about mine clearance.

Colin Mitchell suggested I went to Cambodia, where I travelled round the country with one of his senior colleagues, Matthew Middlemiss. Middlemiss was relatively young and very fit. I was neither. A week of travel on bad roads, rough living, watching surgeons at work on the mines victims left me feeling whacked. On the plane returning to London I was violently sick. But I returned from the expedition convinced that the a/p mine transgresses a fundamental principle of war: no weapon should be used that causes human suffering out of all proportion to its military value. And no civilized nation should traffic in such weapons.

To further my campaign I went to Angola in March 1996 with Clare Crawford of the Mines Advisory Group. As we arrived at the airport in Luena on the west side of the country to meet our MAG hosts, a refugee, scavenging for wood on the edge of the airport, trod on a mine. We took him to the local hospital. Next day, Clare and I visited him. We reckoned he was in the closing stages of life. A homeless refugee in great pain, parted from family, without a leg and without hope – what did the future hold for him?

For almost a week, Clare and I shared a small mess with half a dozen British ex-soldiers in MAG who were working in the district. Their discipline on the minefields was exemplary. In a thoroughly dangerous area, they and the local workers had suffered no casualties over a two-year period. Clare and I flew back from Luena to Luanda in an unheated freight plane. It had three seats. Beside us sat a sister of some holy order. 'I am certain', I murmured to Clare, as we rattled off, 'that He will preserve her – and so us.' She did her best to look cheered.

One Sunday afternoon in January 1997, the office called me at home. 'Diana, Princess of Wales is going with the Red Cross to look at mines in Angola. Would you like to write something?' I suggested to Charles Moore that I accompany her. Reporters and photographers who report the movements of the Royal Family, the so-called 'royal pack', joined the expedition. Suddenly, mines became front-page news and pictures. As if this was not enough, a junior member of the Government, Lord Howe, over lunch with political correspondents of *The Times* and the *Daily Telegraph*, complained that Diana's mission was untimely and described her as a 'loose cannon'. Late that evening the office called me in Luanda to say that this story was running. Had I anything to add? Had I not? The mission was well handled by the Princess. It would be followed by others, she promised. Angola was not to be seen as a one-off. But where next? In Cambodia there was a risk of being kidnapped, in Afghanistan Taliban was shelling Kabul. So Bosnia, I suggested, might be her best bet, and left her to think it over.

In April Rae McGrath of the Mines Advisory Group invited her to speak at a one-day international conference on landmines at the Royal Geographical Society in London in June. The idea coincided with her own thinking at the time. After the visual impact of her visit to Angola, a speaking engagement would seem the next appropriate step. What did I think? I urged her to go ahead and lent a hand with the speech.

The line she took was uncontroversial. Millions of mines would remain in the earth and would continue to kill or cripple thousands of people, even if the international community, under Canada's leadership, agreed to a global ban. The immediate challenge was to reduce this loss of life and limb and land. A few days later she attended a dinner for the American Red Cross in Washington and delivered a similar message.

She had decided on Bosnia, she told me, and would go some time in the first fortnight in August. I agreed to keep it open, and on Friday, 4 August we flew from London to Sarajevo in a private six-seater jet. Diana was accompanied by her butler and faithful friend, Paul Burrell. Jerry White of Washington, himself a landmine victim and joint leader of Landmine Survivors Network which had helped to arrange the tour, made up the party.

As Victoria Combe and I had discovered in the autumn of 1995, if you are going to concern yourself with the consequences of man's inhumanity to man, Sarajevo is the place to go. On the first day we had no time to stop there because of engagements in Tuzla which was a three-hour drive away. So we drove straight through the city, past its huge cemeteries, down the well-named Snipers' Alley, through streets of shattered offices and factories and homes. Mostly we sat in silence, as Diana looked around at these scenes of desolation, saying little, betraying no emotion.

From Sarajevo we travelled along the winding road to Tuzla and there began a series of meetings with landmine survivors. Sensibly, Diana had stipulated that at least thirty minutes should be set aside for each interview. People who have experienced tragedy in their lives need time in which to tell their tale.

'This was a bitter war,' I said to her at one point, 'and so many people are longing to find someone who will listen while they express their inner feelings about it – and they have found you.' Sad smile, no response. Part of her gift in bringing comfort to the bereaved or the afflicted lay in this acute sense of when silence is best. She was not voluble with expressions of sympathy, quite the reverse. At some point during the outpouring of grief she would stretch out and touch the person on the hand or the face.

Our voyage was not all grief. We shared small jokes as we travelled along. She had the engaging trick of approaching me with one hand behind her back. 'Have a gin and tonic?' she would say, watch my face light up in anticipation and then hand over a small bottle of water. I spent much of our time on the road scribbling copy for the *Daily Telegraph* and the *Sunday Telegraph*. At regular intervals I apologized for this graceless behaviour. Her response was to offer me use of the satellite telephone which accompanied us. The Special Branch men who travelled in our small convoy knew how to set it up, and it spared me the nightmare of seeking unreliable telephones in remote parts of Bosnia.

I found it hard not to be overwhelmed by some of our encounters. There was a man who had lost both his feet on a mine. He had a long tale to tell, and was insistent that Diana should see the nature of his injuries. There were two sisters who had been caught on a minefield. One of them had almost bled to death. We learned every detail. Diana never flinched. I came to the conclusion that when it comes to grisly detail, women are altogether more stoical than men.

At the end of a long Saturday, we discussed which of six or eight interviews had moved us most. We had met a young Muslim widow, whose husband had stepped on a mine earlier that year while fishing, his favourite pastime. The Princess sat on a sofa between her and the man's mother, who spoke of her son's last moments, 'before he died, smiling'. The widow said quietly, 'We had such a happy married life together. He was such a good person, an honest man, and he was only twenty-nine.' The mother went on to say that in a recent dream her son had returned to her and declared that he was happy where he was. 'That might well be,' said Diana quietly. Then she took both their hands, without saying a word. Tears flowed from the two women. Our interpreter was not needed. Diana had her own way of breaking through the language barrier.

We visited a girl of fifteen who had recently lost her leg on a mine. As we entered the house, poor and ill-kept, Diana saw on a rough bed the girl's younger brother, a victim of cerebral palsy. She stooped over the bed and caught the child in her arms, and for a moment or two his limbs and features relaxed. 'Where is the mother?' she asked. Nobody was sure. It seemed that for much of the time the sick child was dependent on the young mine victim.

There were some moving pictures taken of Diana during this expedition to Bosnia and they raise the question that will never be resolved to everyone's satisfaction. Did reporters and photographers exploit her, or did she sometimes make use of them? At the time of her engagement to the Prince of Wales, Diana found the close attentions of photographers a trial. The Queen saw some of us who were then editors and asked us to be more considerate. Later, after the birth of William and Harry, Diana's worries about photographers shifted from herself to her sons. At one point, we discussed it over lunch at Kensington Palace without reaching any useful conclusion.

Of course, the photographers were entitled to argue that some of their work greatly enhanced her public appeal. Much of the world which mourned her death had never met her. Their impression of her style and beauty had been drawn from countless photographs. Most of the memories we have of her come from these, so unquestionably the photographers are entitled to claim that they had a place in her life. They reflected this when, after the marriage failed, she entered a trough of despair. They also reflected, no less vividly, that last summer when I have every reason to believe she emerged from that trough, had found her true self again, saw a useful humanitarian role for herself with landmines, and was enjoying life to the full. Some of the best pictures of her life were taken then.

But of course there was another side to all this and I caught a glimpse of it in Bosnia. Photographers, film crews and reporters in a pack, competing fiercely with each other over a single individual, are intimidating. The Princess of Wales was by no means alone in feeling this; scores of celebrities – and scapegoats – tell the same tale, but she was made to feel it more intensely than anyone else. She also knew that some would be happy to catch her – or one of her sons – at a disadvantage, looking angry or shedding tears, and that added to the tension. It was an instructive experience to move alongside her in Bosnia, because when we encountered relatively small packs of the media, one got a sense of these innermost fears.

Mission accomplished, we returned to London cheerfully in the private jet on the evening of Sunday, 10 August. 'Have a glass of champagne?' she said. With the water joke in mind, I responded cautiously, but this time a cork popped. We agreed to keep in touch about a planned visit to Oslo early in September.

Around 3 a.m. on the morning of Sunday, 31 August, the BBC called me at home. There had been a serious accident in Paris, they explained. Dodi Fayed was dead. The Princess of Wales had been injured. They were sending a car to my home in Kent. As we drew close to the Television Centre, they called my driver. How near to the Centre were we? Did I know that Diana was dead? Once inside, I found Martyn Lewis and Jenny Bond, the BBC's Court correspondent whom I had come to know on Diana's trip to Angola. Both seemed close to tears. I made a third in that category, but we stumbled through a very early programme. Back at the *Daily Telegraph* office by 8 a.m., I arrived simultaneously with Charles Moore, the editor. He offered as much space as I could fill on our leader page. It was not difficult to write and it came to 3,000 words which they headed, 'Princess of Sorrows'.

A week later I reported her funeral in Westminster Abbey. It called for another 3,000 words, much harder to write. Putting together that beautiful funeral service amid so many conflicting emotions and wishes struck me as a modern miracle. It so faithfully reflected the many sides of Diana, Princess of Wales. For it was, as I wrote later in the introduction to a book about her produced by the *Daily Telegraph*, a life of extraordinary contrasts. 'There were the troughs of despair. There were also peaks of delight. There were times when she appeared publicly to be inflicting wounds on herself. There were moments when she seemed sublime.'

But the Dean of Westminster, the Very Reverend Dr Wesley Carr, came nearest the mark in the Bidding Prayer he read at her funeral on 6 September 1997. 'In her life, Diana profoundly influenced this nation and the world. Although a princess, she was someone for whom, from afar, we dared to feel affection, and by whom we were all intrigued . . .' 'Intrigued!' That is the word, there was the magic.

*

I have been lucky in my life, which has run through the two world wars. Lucky in 1931 to enter journalism and, more or less by accident and with no qualifications at all, to be given a chance on a national newspaper. Lucky to be chosen to contest the only parliamentary seat which, for family reasons, attracted me; luckier still to have a boss in the Viscount Camrose who supported me. Lucky in my subsequent political career. Lucky to be welcomed back by the *Daily Telegraph*, to be appointed its editor for twelve years and then invited by my successor, Max Hastings, to stay on, take a look at the world and write about it.

Luckiest of all to be guided towards a good regiment in 1939 and to come through that war unscathed, as so many of my friends did not. I thought about that phase of my life when, late in May 2004, I spent a few days in Normandy with the *Daily Telegraph* photographer Abby Trayler-Smith. Starting from Caen, we went the whole length of what had been the D-Day invasion front sixty years earlier, then travelled inland and saw villages on the perimeter of the Normandy bridgehead through which the Allied armies had broken out in July 1944. On our way round, we visited the war cemeteries.

I had revisited Normandy before, but less thoroughly and without the feelings that ran through me this time. Perhaps age had something to do with it. What a feat of arms that D-Day operation had been, I reflected, first to regain a foothold on Europe's coast, which Germany had spent four years in fortifying; and then to put its formidable army to flight. And at what cost, I further reflected, when I saw for the first time the vast American cemetery above Omaha beach where almost 10,000 Americans have their graves.

It was close to high summer, as it had been when we fought our way through the orchards, high hedges and sunken lanes of Normandy sixty years before. The countryside, all traces of battle healed, was in full flower. Lilac, wisteria, red and white chestnut were in bloom. Villages in the bridgehead, blown to bits in 1944, had been rebuilt. There are not many old houses to be seen in that region of France. We took a look at Tessel Wood, dark and deep, where our battalion had experienced an early encounter with German Tiger tanks, and the tiny hamlet of Rauray nearby, round which there had been a furious battle. I felt as we do when we wake from a bad dream and try to make sense of it.

Then I sat with Abby by a pond in the village of Livry, where there had also been hard fighting, watched two swans and some ducks paddling serenely in the sunshine and thought back to long ago. For all of us who took part, it had been the big test of our lives. Nothing to come would match it. What an honour it had been to lead men of a rifle company along that line of advance to Germany. Then, thinking of the riflemen who fell and lay in their flower-decked graves nearby and beyond, I felt sad to think that I had not led them better. 'No more cemeteries today, Abby,' I said as we went back to the car.

Surviving such an experience leaves a sense of obligation. So in the closing years, I have felt that one should try to make some sort of return. I am glad to have lent a light hand to the work of aid agencies trying to save life in the world, like CARE and Plan, Save the Children (who got me into Darfur in the summer of 2004) the African Medical and Research Foundation (Flying Doctor) and the United Nations Children's Fund. It was right too, I felt, to support the efforts of bodies like the Mines Advisory Group and Landmine Action, who work to rid the world of weapons that lie in wait to kill or cripple innocent victims. And I feel thankful to my employers, the *Daily Telegraph*, for encouraging me to do it all in return for scraps of copy.

We go this way only once, and there seems so little time in which to explore the world and its wonders, to find out more about the human tragedy – or, as I more often find it, the human comedy – of which we are part. 'Never forget,' the

Dear Bill

Austrian poet Rilke said to his wife as he lay dying, 'life is magnificent,' and that is right. I believe there is a future life, but I do not let that discourage me from trying to get the most out of this one.

Index

Index

Index

Index

Index

Index

Index

Index

Index

Index

Index

Index

Index

Index

Index

Index

University House, 11
Utley, Peter, 263–5, 332

VALA (Viewers' and Listeners'
  Association), 229
Vassall, John, 159–60, 164, 174
Vietnam, 411–12
Vietnam War, 231, 359–60, 411

Wadley, Veronica, 327, 362
Wakefield of Hythe, Lord, 3
Walker, Sir Harold (Hooky), 343
Walker, Mark Chapman, 204
Wall, Lieutenant-General Peter,
  380
Wall Street crash (1929), 17, 94
Wampach, Eva, 9
Wapping, 324–5
Ward, Barrington, 55, 61
Ward, Ian, 312
Ward, Stephen, 164–5, 168, 169,
  172, 173–4
Washington Post, 300
Watson, Arthur, 46, 66, 87, 94,
  262
Waugh, Auberon, 36, 147, 283–4
Waugh, Evelyn
  in Abyssinia, 32, 34, 35, 367–8,
    407–8
  Black Mischief, 32, 35
  and *Daily Mail*, 31–2, 35–6
  Scoop, 31, 36, 330
Waugh in Abyssinia, 407
Wavertree by-election (1934),
  22–4
Wayne, Sir Edward, 234
Weald of Kent Society, 141
Weidenfeld, Lord, 285, 286
Weigand, Karl von, 32

Welch, Colin, 254, 258, 263
Welensky, Sir Roy, 370
Wells, John, 278
West Toxteth by-election, 26–7
Whickman, Leslie, 138
White, Sandra, 282
White, Sir Thomas, 27
Whitehall Newsletter, 63
Whitehead, Edgar, 370
Whitehouse, Mary, 228–30
Whitelaw, Willie
  and golf, 275
  and Michael Fagan incident,
    274–5
  and Northern Ireland, 241, 246,
    247, 248, 251–2
Whittam Smith, Andreas, 320–2
Whyne, Cari, 354
Wigg, Colonel, 164, 165
Willans, Major-General Harry, 69
Williams, Shirley, 281
Williams, Tam, 67
Wilson, Harold, 194, 195, 214,
  377, 378
Winn, Anthony, 61
Winterton, Earl, 366
Women's Advisory Committee on
  Europe, 155–6
Woodfield, Philip, 151, 152, 160
Wootton, Lady, 234
Worsley, Marcus, 231
Worsthorne, Peregrine, 319, 323,
  324
Wortham, Hugo, 91–2, 207
Wyndham Goldie, Grace, 126, 159

Zambia, 353–5, 355–6
Zimbabwe, 353, 356–8 *see also*
  Rhodesia

Visit **www.panmacmillan.com** to read more about all our books and to buy them. You will also find features, author interviews and news of any author events, and you can sign up for e-newsletters so that you're always first to hear about our new releases.

www.panmacmillan.com

GIFT SELECTOR
YOUR ACCOUNT
WISH LIST
WAITING LIST

HOME | ABOUT US | IMPRINTS | TRADE/MEDIA | CONTACT US | ADVANCED SEARCH | SEARCH | GO

BOOK CATEGORIES | WHAT'S NEW | AUTHORS/ILLUSTRATORS | BESTSELLERS | READING GROUPS

Coming Soon...

Reading Groups

Competitions
Feeling Lucky?

Extracts
Sneak Previews

Interviews

Events
Meet Our Stars

Reviews
What The Critics Say

News & Awards

Editor's Choice
What We're Reading